32.50

THE ECONOMIC THEORY OF MODERN SOCIETY

MICHIO MORISHIMA
Professor of Economics at the
London School of Economics and Political Science

The economic theory of modern society

TRANSLATED BY D.W. ANTHONY

CAMBRIDGE UNIVERSITY PRESS
CAMBRIDGE
LONDON · NEW YORK · MELBOURNE

Published by the Syndics of the Cambridge University Press
The Pitt Building, Trumpington Street, Cambridge CB2 1RP
Bentley House, 200 Euston Road, London NW1 2DB
32 East 57th Street, New York, NY 10022, YSA
296 Beaconsfield Parade, Middle Park, Melbourne 3206, Australia

First published 1976

Typeset by EWC Wilkins Ltd., London and Northampton
Printed in Great Britain at the University Printing House, Cambridge
(Euan Phillips, University Printer)

Library of Congress Cataloguing in Publication Data

Morishima, Michio, 1923–

The economic theory of modern society.

Translation of Kindai shakai no keizai riron.

Includes bibliographical references and index.

1. Microeconomics. I. Title.
HB180.J3M6713   330   75–39375
ISBN 0 521 21088 7 hard covers
ISBN 0 521 29168 2 paperback

CONTENTS

(v)

PREFACE TO THE ENGLISH EDITION

This is a translation of my book entitled *Kindai Shakai no Keizai Riron* which was published in 1973 by Sobunsha, Tokyo.

Mathematical economic theory has recently become more and more abstract, transparent and sterile. The main motivation behind the book is to paint present economic theory colourfully; the book contains my tentative, personal answer to the problem of optimum use of mathematics in economics.

In this edition a labour saving technique has been used in order to minimise production costs. Notes which appeared at the foot of each page in the Japanese edition have now been gathered at the end of the book. I must encourage the reader to make the effort of going back and forth between the text and the notes. I hope this will be made easier by the fact that I have distinguished the numbering for important notes by a starred indicator number, e.g.$^{6+}$.

It is my great pleasure to have had Dr D. Anthony of Sheffield University as my translator. The book covers history, sociology and mathematics as well as economics; he is one of the very few scholars who are familiar with Japanese terminology over such diverse areas.

March, 1976

Michio Morishima

PREFACE

In the normal textbook on economic principles or economic theory, the ecology of firms and households is explained, and the structure and movement of societies is analysed on the assumption of an 'ideal' form of capitalism. However, actual capitalist societies are not cast in the 'ideal' mould, and the various capitalist countries form only one part of the world. We have already reached the stage where, if we ignore or neglect non-capitalist elements and influences, we shall fall into the trap not only of being unable to understand many important phenomena in real societies, but also of viewing the world inflexibly from a fixed angle.

However, logically there are many features in common between non-capitalist and capitalist economies, because both are modern economic systems. Furthermore, even though actual capitalist economies, such as Japan for example, depart from the 'ideal' pattern, 'aberrations' are not without rules; even in the 'aberration' there is the logic of the 'aberration'. In this book my object will be to try to make clear the economic logic of modern societies, which is not confined to the 'ideal' capitalist economy but applies also to the socialist economy. In addition I shall try to provide a convincing analysis of the peculiar course of economic development followed by the Japanese economy since the Meiji revolution. Consequently, in a broad sense this book probably belongs in the domain of the theory of comparative systems, but it is rather more theoretical and analytical than the average research conducted in that area. At the same time it must be pointed out that it is incomplete in the sense that its horizon is a short-term one, and may turn out to be no more than the first volume of a more bulky work.

The book is based on lectures I gave to the Part I economics students of Osaka University in 1967—8. At that time the radical student movement was not particularly active, and Osaka University

(ix)

was perfectly peaceful. Nevertheless, there had been no change in those aspects of life in the Part I course with which the students had been dissatisfied. My lectures were given at the request of Professor S. Kawaguchi, the then convener of the course. Their subject was left to my own discretion; they were separate from the normal introductory economics course, and they were given in order to arouse in the students an interest in economic theory. The content of the lectures and the technique of analysis were too difficult for first year students, but I believe that I was successful in stirring their interest. Consequently, despite the fact that this book is most suitable for third year, fourth year, and even more advanced students of economics, I feel that first year students too can read it with interest, although a certain amount of extra effort will be required of them. However, since chapter 4, Changes in plan, is somewhat difficult, I recommend that first year students and others too defer reading it until later. Further, there may be those who feel that the mathematics used in the book is beyond high school (sixth form) level. I should like these people to read on, without pause, even though they may come across places where the mathematical equations used are difficult for them to understand. I believe that the reader will certainly not lose sight of the economic logic, even though he may skip over some of the mathematical equations.

Finally, the book is based on my final lectures in Japan, but the greater part of it was written since my coming to England. As a result, I have missed much Japanese material, and it is especially unfortunate that I have been unable to use adequately the literature on the history of the development of Japanese capitalism. In order to make good this ommission, I have attempted to have discussions with the many Japanese economists who have visited here. At all events, my view of Japan is a singular one, and even if it is imperfect I present it to the reader in frank form in the belief that it is better submitted to criticism.

January, 1973   M.M.

The modern national economy

A. As an 'ideal' type

From the point of view of economics, of what kind is the modern society in which we live? What are the economic laws which control the modern national economy? These are the sorts of basic question which I should like to consider in this book. Even though we refer sweepingly to 'the modern state', there are in fact a great variety of different types of modern state. For example, Japan, the United States, the United Kingdom, Sweden, the Soviet Union, Yugoslavia and others, are all properly called 'modern states'. However, in a more detailed classification they would be called capitalist countries, modified capitalist countries, welfare states, socialist countries, etc. Furthermore, even among capitalist states of the same type—for example, Britain and Japan — there are considerable differences in sociological characteristics. Although we refer to 'modern societies', there are many varieties of these, and modern history is largely the history of competition amongst them. So-called orthodox economics normally assumes a perfect capitalist state, and examines how the economy works under these purely abstract conditions in order to obtain its laws of movement. However, while in any capitalist country there operate laws which are peculiar to capitalism, since such a country is also a 'modern state', it is also bound by more general laws whose validity is not restricted to capitalist countries. As Mishan has pointed out, for example, in the problem of environmental pollution there are factors which are inherent in the nature of capitalist systems; but there are also those which are inherent in the nature of modern technology.[1] Again, even between capitalist countries which are very similar in a broad sense, where sociological characteristics differ, an economic issue which poses a problem in one country may not pose a problem to the same extent in another. For example, up to the present time disguised unemployment, excessive wage differences between firms, and wage differences based on sex have continued to be a chronic complaint of the Japanese economy. By contrast, the reason why the United Kingdom has, for some time, more or less solved the problems of disguised unemployment and excessive inter-firm wage differences, while the problems of wage differences based on sex remains unsolved, can be taken as deriving from the different sociological characteristics of the two countries.[2] For this reason it is both extremely important and theoretically interesting not to look at the economy of a particular country merely as an example of the 'ideal' type of capitalist or socialist economy but, instead, to look at it in more general terms as an example of a modern economy; or alternatively, in more specific terms as a particular, individual capitalist or socialist economy.[3+] In this book I shall, as a rule, analyse capitalist economies and socialist economies in their ideal states. However, I intend frequently to regard them as two subdivisions of the modern national economy, and to consider them on a more universal level; and occasionally I intend to be more specific and to discuss them at a more individual level (as, for example, when I discuss Japan as a type of capitalist economy).

Let us begin with a general conceptual prescription of the modern national economy. It goes without saying that, in whatever kind of society, while that society lasts, it will continue to be peopled, and a certain order will be maintained between its members. Furthermore, for that society to persist, it must have a material base. That is, it must possess wealth in order to continue to exist; and in order to continue in the future it must repeatedly reproduce this wealth. The wealth which is produced has to be distributed among the members of the society, but if the laws which govern the distribution do not satisfy certain kinds of conditions, that society will, in due course, disintegrate.

If we accept that these facts are true of societies in general, then modern society, too, can be defined in these terms. What sorts of members make up a modern society, or a modern national economy; in what way is order maintained; how is its wealth produced, and how is it distributed? If we consider these questions, we shall understand the sort of society we are dealing with.

Let us start by considering the problem of maintaining order. In the modern national economy, order is maintained by the state. Over the inhabitants within its own territory, the state possesses the authority to put into operation physical means of coercion (conscription, imprisonment, powers of taxation, executive power, compulsory declaration of bankruptcy, etc.). Now in premodern societies, bodies able to exercise physical coercion were not confined to the state. For example, the medieval guilds possessed the right to police and to administer justice to guild members. Again, before the modern state with its centralised powers was perfectly formed, warlike factions and bandits existed, and the inhabitants were subjected to two or three sources of coercion besides the central government. Where several groups with powers of coercion exist in this way within the same territory, the term 'modern state' is inapplicable. In modern societies, the state is the one body able to exercise physical coercion, and the various means of compulsion are monopolised by the state. National integration, which is a feature of modern history, is the centralisation of the physical means of coercion. In other words, this unique body the 'modern state', which possesses the physical means of coercion and whose power is centralised, has been formed as a result of the relinquishing of all physical powers of coercion (however partial or imperfect), which were formerly in the hands of other kinds of bodies (such as the free city, the manor and various others), and their handing over to the central government.

According to Schumpeter, the state is merely the product of clashes and compromise between feudal lords and bourgeoisie, and therefore in the analysis of feudal or socialist societies, the concept of the state does not play an important role. That is to say, he held that 'the state should not be allowed to intrude into discussions of either feudal or socialist society, neither of which did or would display that dividing line between the private and the public sphere from which the better part of its meaning flows'.[4] In addition, he also said that it would be possible to abolish taxation along with the state, by which he meant his bourgeois state. 'For, as a matter of common sense, it would clearly be absurd for the central board to pay out incomes first and, after having done so, to run after the recipients in order to recover part of them.'[5] However, even in a society where private ownership of the means of production is denied, in the case where

individuals are allowed to make independent decisions over the
purchase of consumption goods, and where the government (or
the central planning authority) exercises its own right of decision
over the distribution of resources, public and private spheres
exist independently. The important thing is not whether the
right of private ownership is recognised or not, but whether or not
the right of independent decision making is accorded to individuals
and enterprises. Apart from extreme state-regulated economies
where freedom of consumer choice is denied, in all other socialist
societies there always exists a sector on which the will of the state
does not directly impinge; and for that reason, not just in law but
from the economic point of view too, the private individual and
the state are opposed, but coexist. (The socialist society of
Schumpeter's blueprint is also a society of this type.) Now the
state has a budget with which to put its decisions into effect, and
even in socialist societies a part of the state budget is derived from
taxation. However, as Schumpeter pointed out, in socialist
societies the proportion of the state budget made up out of direct
taxation is very samll. (For example, in the Soviet Union it is
usually less than 8% of average total revenue. However, when
'the deduction from profit' is added, which corresponds to a
profits tax in a capitalist society, the proportion becomes quite
significant.)[6]

Furthermore, in the modern state, a fundamental principle is
that the police and the army render service not to any particular
individual, but impartially for the sake of the public good and
society as a whole. As Max Weber said, in modern bureaucracies
there is 'the dominance of a spirit of formalistic impersonality:
"sine ira et studio", without hatred or passion, and hence without
affection or enthusiasm. The dominant norms are concepts of
straightforward duty without regard to personal considerations.
Everyone is subject to formal equality of treatment; that is,
everyone is in the same empirical situation. This is the spirit in
which the ideal official conducts his office.'[7] In prewar Japan, the
military were regarded as the forces of the emperor; but if the
word 'emperor', as used in this sentence, is interpreted correctly,
it means an emperor who could not be regarded as an individual,
but was an impersonal organ of the state (in postwar terminology,
the emperor as the symbol of the country of Japan). By 'impersonal' is meant here 'compliant with fixed rules decided on by the

legislature'. In this way, in a modern state the maintenance of order through the activities of the administrative bureaucracy, the police and the army (which activities are in accordance with rules decided upon formally and with due procedure), is conducted legally and solely by the hand of the state.

Within the various government offices, the police and the army, order is maintained by means of a universal civil service system and, except for the occasions when they are officially requested to give their opinion on a particular matter, lower-ranking officials have to obey their seniors. The justification for imposing the will of the higher-ranking official on one of lower rank, is based on its legitimacy. For that reason, the obeying of the higher-ranking official by his junior is not obedience to an individual, but compliance in conformity with established rules. Consequently, if the route by which an order descends is wrong, the higher-ranking official need not be obeyed, despite his higher rank. In order that the will of those who issue commands be executed quickly and surely, it is necessary that lower-ranking officials act in accordance with discipline; that is to say, they must act according to the will of their superiors impersonally and with despatch. A civil service system which imposes on its members such rules of disciplined conduct, and demands strict observance of the commanding/ obeying relationship, is very effective as an organisation by means of which a large group can put its will efficiently into practice. Consequently, this sort of structure is not confined to modern government administrations or modern armies, but is also a conspicuous feature in modern enterprises (both public and private). The system of management in the business firm is not democratic but bureaucratic, and is thus legalistic, civil-service-like and disciplined.

Next, let us consider how wealth is created in a modern national economy. It is possible, in Robinson Crusoe fashion, to produce goods with scarcely any collaboration with anyone else. However, in modern societies this form of production is an extreme exception, people normally forming groups and engaging in productive activity in group form.[8+] Among these groups there is private enterprise (for example the sole-trader, the Limited Company, etc.), and government enterprise (for example ministry-run enterprises in socialist states). There is also a type which is intermediate between private and public spheres, like the Japanese public corporation, the industrial co-operative, the Chinese collective enetrprise, etc. Thus, whether or not an enterprise is a 'modern enterprise' has nothing to do with the question of whether it is publicly or privately managed. Modernity, from the point of view of the maintenance of order, means the taking of various powers into state hands; but, from the production point of view, it does not necessarily signify the taking of enterprise into state hands.

The large-scale nature of operations in the modern enterprise necessitates an organisational and technical background which enables large-scale production to be profitable; but more fundamentally, it is founded on the existence of a large-scale, free market for labour. Both Marx and Weber insisted on this point. Marx discusses its relationship to capitalism in the following way: 'The private property of the labourer in his means of production is the foundation of petty industry', which prospers 'only where the labourer is the private owner of his own means of labour set in action by himself: the peasant of the land which he cultivates, the artizan of the tool which he handles as a virtuoso. This mode of production presupposes parcelling of the soil, and scattering of the other means of production.' If it reaches a specified high degree, 'From that moment new forces and new passions spring up in the bosom of society; but the old social organisation fetters them and keeps them down. It must be annihilated; it is annihilated. Its annihilation, the transformation of the individualised and scattered means of production into socially concentrated ones, of the pigmy property of the many into the huge property of the few' occurs. Thus the members of society are divided into a class which owns the means of production, and a class which owns only its own labour, and 'labour-power can appear upon the market as a commodity only if, and so far as, its possessor, the individual whose labour-power it is, offers it for sale, or sells it, as a commodity. In order that he may be able to do this, he must have it at his disposal, must be the untrammelled owner of his capacity for labour, i.e. of his person.' The free labourer is 'free in the double sense, that as a free man he can dispose of his labour-power as his own commodity, and that on the other hand he has no other commodity for sale, is short of everything necessary for the realisation of his labour-power'. 'If the owner of labour-power works today, tomorrow he must again be able to repeat the same conditions as regards health and strength. His means of subsistence must therefore be sufficient to maintain him in his normal state as a labouring individual.' In this fashion, a base is established by a small number of capitalists who own large quantities of the means of production, using large numbers of free labourers for the genesis of large-scale enterprises which produce the large quantities of the means of subsistence which are demanded by the labourers. That is, we can say that capital 'can spring into life, only when the owner of the means of production and subsistence meets in the market with the free labourer selling his labour-power'. Therefore we can consider that in a socialist economy too, large-scale production does not lose its social basis, since, even if the circumstances described above develop into a socialist society, and even if the further socialisation of labour, i.e. a further transformation of the land and other means of production into socially controlled, common means of production, occurs, the situation is not altered.[9+]

The production which takes place in these large-scale enterprises is accomplished with the use of modern productive techniques. The different forms of modern technology cause labour to be divided between various operations, but each of these has the common characteristic of equipping the labour force with machinery. Mechanisation is especially important in industries where large-scale production is necessary, and as a result of it the efficiency of production is extremely high. Thus, leaving aside very exceptional cases, in industry in general workers engage in production in groups and with the use of machinery. When work comes to be done with machines, the worker has to adapt the rhythm of his work to the movement of the machines, and is not allowed his own choice of movement. Thus, finally, it becomes the characteristic or nature of the workers to work as does a machine.[10+] Moreover, where division of labour in production occurs, the worker becomes a specialist at one particular operation in the productive process, having to carry out a simplified task over and over again, and is no longer responsible for the making of a product from beginning to end. For him, or for her, there is no joy of completion. In this sense the modern worker is no longer a craftsman; he is no more than a machine who commutes to work.[11+]

These considerations apply equally to the capitalist country, the welfare state and the socialist country. In the United States, in

the Soviet Union and in all modern countries, the worker is
compelled to lead a completely inhuman working existence, having
to work alongside machines all day, having to work according to
the laws of machines, and having been transformed into a human
machine, only one part of a large organisation. Furthermore,
specialisation and co-operation in industry require of the
labourer work which admits of regulation. That is to say, each
worker is a cog in the total working mechanism, and each has to
function so as to maximise the efficiency of the whole through
his mutual interconnection with the other cogs. As we saw earlier,
there is an extremely impersonal internal order in modern bureaucracies, police forces and armies; and similarly, in the workplace,
modern labour is organised completely impersonally. Workers are
subject to a discipline no longer different in its nature from that
of the civil service or the army, although it has been created by a
contract concluded in the labour market by formally "equal"
parties through the "voluntary" acceptance of the terms offered
by the "employer".[12] In modern enterprises, the processes of
subordinating the worker to the machine, and of making the
worker a part of the mechanism for having orders obeyed, are
mutually reinforcing and develop together. In this way the total
development of modern high capitalism corresponds with the
progress of the bureaucratisation of economic management. In the
modern state the role of the bureaucratic structure of control is
everywhere increasing.[13]

In order to maintain and improve our standard of living, we
have to produce various kinds of goods. To do this many inputs
of goods and labour are necessary. Whilst this input—output
activity can take place without any particular aim, unconsciously
and unplanned, it can, alternatively, be performed with the utmost
sagacity, purposefully, rationally, calculatedly and minutely
planned and with the precision of a clock. Of course, various
intermediate states are possible between these two extremes.
However, the ideal modern enterprise, be it privately or publicly
run, will adopt the most economic form of operation from the
variety of forms which are possible. That is to say, it will form a
clear objective, calculate the most efficient way of achieving that
objective, and conduct its input—output activity on the basis of
that calculation. In addition, after the plan is executed the
operation is recorded quantitatively. That is, the operation is made

objective, and its details are preserved so as to make an audit possible.[14+] Thus it is always possible for the manager of the modern enterprise to be confronted by criticism from outsiders, so that he can no longer be an absolute monarch. However, in order that this criticism may be objective, the aims of the enterprise, the sacrifices needed to achieve these aims, and the method of appraising its results must be defined objectively. When the aims and sacrifices are determined in relation to only one kind of good, then no particularly troublesome problem arises. However, they are usually related to a number of goods, and how to evaluate each good in terms of a common measure becomes an important problem.

Usually each individual good is evaluated in terms of its price, but the method of determining price is not uniform, and can be different for every good. The most typical method (although it does not necessarily follow that it is the most widely used) is one where the price is determined by competition between buyer and seller so as to equate supply and demand. In addition, there is the case where price is decided after having multiplied unit costs by a standard rate of profit (the mark-up method), and the case where price is fixed unilaterally by the state or the monopoly enterprise. Normally, prices perform more than the function of being a simple valuing-rate for accounting; it is necessary that goods be actually exchanged at that rate in the market. However, goods which contribute to the processes of production and are present in the factory, but which do not emerge onto the market, such as work in progress and intermediate products, do not have a price which is a rate of exchange. But even for this sort of good, an accounting price is necessary for the purpose of valuation. These prices are called shadow prices and with intermediate products they are normally based on the costs incurred in their production (including interest).

Now, whatever method is used, if all goods are given prices (including shadow prices), both private enterprises and state enterprises can measure their own results by means of them. In other words, if both the goods used as inputs and the goods which are produced are valued at their respective prices, then the total value of output, the total value of inputs and the difference between them (profit, or surplus) can be measured by a common unit, such as the yen or the dollar. Thus the aims, the sacrifices, the efficiency, etc. of the enterprise, are defined in the form of totals measured in this way, or by their respective proportions. As is well known, private enterprises in capitalist countries seek to maximise profits or profit rates, and in certain kinds of socialist countries the norm for each enterprise is often given by net or gross value of output, or by their respective growth rates.

However, we do not necessarily have to use prices as a valuing-rate when reducing various kinds of goods to a common unit. Indeed, although in capitalist economies prices are generally used as a measure of value, in welfare and socialist states this is not necessarily the case. In these states the economic ministry or central planning authority draws up an order of preference among the various possible combinations of products, based on its own policy judgements. The central planning authority will probably also consider effects which cannot be calculated by means of prices (car exhaust fumes, jet noise, national prestige enhanced by giant aircraft carriers), and decide on their preference ranking. Consequently, there is absolutely no reason why the preference ranking given to goods as a result of the policy judgement of the planning authority should necessarily correspond to their values calculated according to prices.

The future behaviour of the various economic units will be determined by one or other of the decision making bodies, but it is not necessary that the decision making body be the central planning authority of a country or the board of directors of an enterprise. The complete centralisation formula, whereby the central planning authority constructs a centralised, comprehensive plan and then instructs each enterprise to carry out its part; and the complete decentralisation formula, whereby the microplan formulated individually by each enterprise is regulated only indirectly through the price mechanism, without direct or conscious mutual adjustment, are both extreme cases. Between them there are a variety of intermediate formulae. For example, there is the planning authority Gosplan, which is divided into the central Gosplan and the regional Gosplans. The former decides on the broad overall plan and those for the important, directly controlled enterprises, while the latter are left to draw up detailed estimates for each region. On the other hand, there is the case where a number of competitive or co-operating enterprises draw up plans by collusion or agreement (the trust, the cartel, the Konzern, the industrial co-operative, etc.). Usually the relationship between the planning body and the executive bodies is one-way, directives passing from the former to the latter. However, this is not inevitably the case. There is the 'two-way' formula of the Soviet Union for example, whereby the various enterprises draw up the original plans along the lines of the basic policy announced by the party or the government. These they send to Gosplan. Gosplan then integrates and adjusts these original plans, and has them carried out by the enterprises as amended.[15+]

We saw above, the modern enterprise is operated rationally in a way which renders it capable of inspection, and uses modern techniques. When the aims and sacrifices are multidimensional, a process of evaluation is necessary, in order to reduce the number of dimensions and make the formulation of the plan easier. However, the evaluation method is not necessarily restricted to the use of prices, and neither is the decision-making method limited to either the completely centralised or the completely decentralised formula. Thus, various kinds of enterprise can exist within the framework of 'modernity', and their differing forms of behaviour can all be explained consistently with the logic of objective rationality. Of course, in the case of the centrally-planned economy where the firm has to follow implicitly the instructions of a higher authority, as long as the plan formulated by the central planning authority does not contain mistakes, then the behaviour of each firm will accord with the criteria of objective rationality. But it also goes without saying that when the planning authority uses an incorrect index as a measure of its success in achieving its objectives, irrespective of whether it is centralised or decentralised, a state of affairs will occur which is not what was intended. For example, if an enterprise producing a variety of products measures the achievement of its objective in the plan by total value of output, it will try to produce only high cost, high price goods, and it will be impossible to make it economise in the use of raw materials. Again, when the object of economic policy is to maximise the gross national product or its growth rate, or to minimise unemployment, environmental pollution will go unchecked. Furthermore, there is the important problem of how to fit intermediate products into the target index. For example, where the strict definition is operated that aeroplanes without engines are not counted as aeroplanes, and an order is made to increase the output of aeroplanes, then enterprises will neglect the supply of new work-in-progress, and be intent only upon converting existing work-in-progress into finished aeroplanes. However, where engineless aeroplanes are defined as being a certain percentage equivalent of completed planes, and this percentage is made unduly high, a situation will arise where enterprises produce only engineless aeroplanes.[16] Thus, when the measure used to gauge success in achieving the planning objective is incorrectly chosen, society will inevitably be induced to proceed in a mistaken direction.

Next, let us consider the individuals who make up an economy. People have many and varied wants (to eat, to amuse themselves, to read books and so on). Until man has reached a fairly high level of attainment, the systemisation of these wants and the ordering of preferences within the possibilities permitted to the individual (that is, deciding clearly on an order of preferences so that from amongst the various possible states one is designated the most desirable, another the next most desirable, and so on), is not possible. Where this high level has not been reached, man's behaviour will be determined entirely according to custom or impulse. In the former case a person's behaviour always fits a fixed pattern which is decided by custom. Even where it is possible for him to follow a course whose outcome would clearly be more favourable than that given by custom-dictated behaviour, being unaware of it, he will behave as he himself did in the past, and as other people are doing at present. On the other hand, in the latter case, a person's conduct is subject to no rule whatsoever; from the various possibilities confronting him he simply adopts randomly whichever enters his head. These are two extreme cases, but they have this in common: there is no surveying of the totality of possibilities facing a person; there is no comparative consideration taken of them.

People who are unable to order their wants and to exercise self-control will probably belong either to the type which is ruled by blind obedience to custom, or to the type governed by impulse. They are unable to behave with objective rationality. However, educational systems have been established, and as a result modern man is educated, at least up to the point where he can arrange his wants in his own preference order. When people are able to order their wants, what has to be done in order to be best able to satisfy those wants becomes clear. A person's behaviour may

change in the face of each change in circumstance, but the conclusion to be drawn from this is not that he is arbitrarily changing
his mind, but that he is adapting his behaviour to changing circumstances in order to carry through the principle of maximum satisfaction of wants. Therefore it can be seen that the same objective
rationality which applies to modern enterprises is also applicable
to modern man.[17]

Thus, modern man can be regarded as a being with a systematic
will which conforms with rational rules. However, one fact which
we ought to note at this point is that modern man behaves with
objective rationality *under given circumstances and conditions.*
Leaving aside the various forms of government and regional
taxation, there are cases when restraints are imposed other than by
the usual budget contraints. As many nations will have experienced
in wartime, and some planned economies discover even in peace-
time, when there is a shortage of consumer goods, a controlled
supply system, a coupon rationing system, or some other form of
control will be implemented. In this case, each individual will
choose that which he most desires from the various possibilities
which satisfy all these constraints. However, consider the case
where one of the conditions is nonsensical, being excessively
restrictive in the sense that the whole group (or a subgroup) of the
members of the society finds that, by disregarding the condition
within the group but satisfying it as a group, none of the members
is worse off than if each obeyed it, and, in fact, some are better
off. Then a number of individuals will form a group so as to obey
the condition as a group but to abolish it internally. In this way a
black market will be formed. In both the normal and the black
market, goods are distributed among the transactors not by
command or by violence, but by buying and selling and mutual
consent. And the following preconditions are necessary for trade
to take place smoothly: that there be no irrational restraints
imposed by social status; that a well-organised market in commodities come into existence; that a transportation network and a
banking system be sufficiently established, and that a uniform
currency, officially recognised by the state, circulate.

As already repeatedly stated, there are many varieties possible
within the genus 'modern state'. These can range from classical
capitalism with its insistence on total non-intervention, to the
conception of the totally administered economy: without money,

without markets, without cost accountancy and without traded
goods, completely planned, and with the national economy almost
capable of being treated as a giant family. When one considers all
the different hues and shades, they appear virtually numberless.
Needless to say, those with a form near that of the administered
economy require for their operation a large number of highly
trained economic bureaucrats. This is because it is impossible to
pursue a plan on a national economic scale without them. By
contrast, economies which make free exchange their basis cannot
do without modern free markets (or at least markets which have
developed to the point where prices can be decided competitively).
In order to build up such an economy, transport mechanisms,
currency systems and education systems are set up, and freedom
of labour is established.[18+] When these preconditions are met, a
modern economy can be built based on them. At that point, the
bill of fare presented to us is by no means a poor one. There is the
possibility of choice both in the method of formulating the
production plan, and in the formula for distribution. On the plan-
formulating side, there is on the extreme right the completely
decentralised system, whereby each firm formulates its own
production plan. On the extreme left there is the perfectly
centralised system whereby the central planning authority
decides on the production plan for the whole of the national
economy. On the distribution side, we have at one extreme a
complete non-intervention system, where private ownership of all
the means of production, land, labour and capital is recognised.
At the other, we have the administered economy where the means
of production are owned by the state, and not only is no person
allowed to earn rent from land or profits, but even freedom of
employment is denied or limited. There are various configurations
between these extremes, and the situation at the present time is
that all countries choose intermediate states some way to the
right or to the left.

Among these intermediate states we have the case where
complete decentralisation, with production planning based on the
individual enterprise, is hampered by the presence of trusts,
cartels, etc. We also have the case where complete centralisation
takes place within certain industries (for example, state control of
heavy industry during wartime). The right of private ownership of
the means of production is also partly denied and checked, but the

degree of denial can differ between industries (for example Japan's
tobacco industry and her sake industry; England's railways and her
road haulage industry), and between firms (for example Japan's
national railways and her private railways, Soviet Russia's
sovkhoz and *kolkhoz*, Communist China's peoples' communes
and co-operatives).

Thus actual economies are mixed economies, from the point of
view of both production and distribution. Distribution conditions
will differ in accordance with the degree of mixing, but whatever
the degree, a common feature is that uniform wages develop in
all modern economies. The difference in rewards based on
difference in social status found under the feudal system has
disappeared in modern society. In an ideal modern society,
abstracting from differences in intensity and in varieties of labour,
and calculating in terms of homogeneous labour, it can be seen
that all workers will receive equal rewards irrespective of the
industry or enterprise in which they are engaged. In the free
economy, what guarantees this is the existence of a free market
for labour. In the managed economy it is guaranteed by the wage
system consciously calculated by the planning authorities. It is
true that the situation exists where the wage system fixed by the
state depends heavily not only on the quantity of labour and the
type of work, but also on the status of the worker and his length
of service. It is also possible that a shortage in the supply of
certain kinds of labourer will make the wages of these workers
relatively high. However, where a free market for labour exists,
this kind of phenomenon is wholly transitional, and, on the
premise that there is a potential free market for labour, even in a
managed economy it is not possible for the planning authority to
fix upon a wage system which incorporates extreme differentials.

B. Japan as an example

I have explained what a modern national economy is,
but in fact the character and structure of such economies are not
restricted to the types mentioned. We obtained the ideal types
of the modern national economy by a process of simplifying and
purifying reality, and we must not think of them as reality itself.
The modern national economies which appear within the confines
of economic theory (capitalist economies, socialist economies and
the rest) certainly do not really exist in that perfect form, in the

same way as the triangles of geometry (right-angled triangles, equilateral triangles and the rest) do not exist. They are the sort of idealised, pure concepts which, having been conceptualised by abstraction, and having had their various laws obtained, are very instructive for the understanding of reality. As Poincaré says of the objectives and uses of mathematical physics, 'they do not stop merely at making the calculation of certain constants, or the integration of certain equations in the differential calculus easy for physicists. Rather they cause us to recognise the hidden harmony of things and to observe them from a different stand-point.'[19] In exactly the same way, analysis in terms of the ideal-type concept gives us a fixed point of view for the cognition of reality, and is useful for enriching our understanding of reality. However, since these laws certainly do not appear in their pure form in the real world, we must, at the same time, maintain a strong interest in knowing in what direction and how far away the ideal type of the modern national economy is from the real modern national economy.

The actual modern national economy, as an historical fact, contains many non-modern elements. For example, the USA is indisputably the most modern of states. Its population is made up of several races. Formally, freedom of choice of occupation is guaranteed, to the black population as well as to the white. However, there is in reality the problem that job opportunities for black Americans are clearly fewer than for white Americans. Not only are black citizens excluded from high-grade employment, but even where they perform the same simple tasks as white citizens (dish-washing, for example), they often have to be content with a wage lower than that paid to whites. Not only that, but the black citizen is the last to feel the benefits of prosperous times, and the first to feel the effects of bad times. As a result, striking differences arise between the wages of black people and white people, those of black citizens being about half those of white citizens. Again, the majority of agricultural labourers in America are migrant workers.[20] As a result, there exists, as in Japan, a marked difference between agricultural and industrial wages (agricultural wages are less than half industrial wages). In America this difference in wages has causes altogether different from those in Japan, originating as it does in the multi-racial character of American society; it is a phenomenon which can also be seen in the Republic of South Africa, Malaysia and other former colonial states.

As with the United States, the special characteristics of the Japanese economy depend strongly on the historical circumstances surrounding Japan at the time when her modern state emerged. This is true in two senses. As we saw previously, there are various types of modern national economy, and the actual economy of every country takes on one of these forms. However, this form is not freely chosen from the various types which exist. The constraints imposed by historical circumstance result in the choice of a specific type being made. Consequently, in accordance with the differences in the circumstances of their coming into being, even similar capitalist economies are very different in their detailed characters. Secondly, each and every economy differs from the ideal type and includes 'impure' elements. The kinds of non-modern elements included in a specific modern economy depend on the circumstances of its historical emergence. As a result, in certain economies certain kinds of non-modern characteristics are chronic, while in others different kinds of non-modern characteristics persist for long periods. For that reason, the phenomena which appear in the various economies do not deviate randomly from the pure laws, but with a particular bias in each economy. Adopting this viewpoint, I shall try below to explain a few of the important characteristics of the Japanese economy which relate to the Meiji Revolution (1867—8), from which modern Japan originated.

During the Edo period (1603—1867) methods of transportation were widely developed, and while the country-wide market for goods was small it had been established in outline. The currency and financial system too were remarkably well developed, although the stage where there was a standard of value accepted throughout the country had not been reached. One part of the commercial economy developed as an economy dealing with the goods traded by feudal landlords. On the other hand, however, agriculture too became commercialised, hand-producers developed, large merchants appeared and the feudal nobility and the warriors came under the financial dominance of the money changers, money lenders and bill brokers of the money industry. The economic base of the feudal system had come to be threatened. In this process of breakdown of the feudal economy those who were dealt the most serious economic blows were the lower order samurai, almost all of whom were compelled to find auxiliary employment.

At this critical stage, confronted with the arrival of Commodore Perry's ships, the Tokugawa government had to face up to Japan's hopeless military, scientific and economic backwardness, which had accumulated over the two hundred years of the period of isolation. In order to cope with the demands of the foreign powers to open Japan up to foreign trade, and to deal with the emergency conditions which accompanied these demands, the government tried to institute the absolutist policy known as Fukoku Kyōhei (a rich country with a strong army). However, the contradictions in the feudal structure were, by that time, being experienced by the peasants and the lower order samurai, and opposition to the government was becoming stronger. The lower level of the warrior class, in particular, who were the intelligentsia of that time, knew (consciously or unconsciously) that under the feudal system it was impossible to overcome this danger and that while the shogunate remained to be overthrown, national unity remained unenforced, and a clean sweep of the entire old order was not made, they could not protect Japan against the imperialist agression of the advanced countries. However, the great merchants who were growing rapidly in power, and who might have been expected to form the central power in the forthcoming new era, clearly did not grasp the new situation as well as the lower order samurai. Seduced by quick profits, they supported the leaders of the feudal regime, and played the part of a mere reactionary force. Again, the peasants opposed the feudal powers by means of riots and destruction. However, although these uprisings were violent and shocking, they were unorganised and sporadic and did not have the overthrow of the feudal system as a clear and conscious objective. It is true that the lower order samurai, who were most aware of the approach of the revolution, had not prepared a definite blueprint for the society they intended to build after the revolution. It is also true that they risked making many mistakes during the course of the revolution. But, using the slogans 'Expel the barbarians' and 'Revere the Emperor',[21+] they vigorously opposed the reactionary programme of strengthening and reconstructing the absolutist feudal system, which the higher order warriors supported. One can say that the

Meiji Revolution thus produced was a revolution on behalf of
national unity, without the proletariat and even without any
important help from the bourgoisie and the peasant, conducted
almost alone by the intelligentsia.

This characteristic of the Meiji Revolution naturally prescribed
the character of the new regime to be built thereafter. Since the
major influence in the revolution was the intelligentsia and not the
bourgeoisie, under the Meiji regime those whose status was predominant were the intelligentsia and not the bourgeoisie. Consequently, the modern state which they attempted to build was
very different from those modern Western states which came into
being as a result of bourgeois revolutions. However, since the
models they were able to use were almost all those of bourgeois
states, the Meiji system did not entirely avoid the influence of
bourgeois elements. But the state which the predominant class in
the Meiji era tried to build was certainly not a bourgeois dominated one. It was one in which intellectuals who were bureaucrats,
officers, scholars, etc. were to predominate.

The new government reformed government organisation at
the very onset, and set up a modern bureaucratic structure centring on ex-samurai of the Satsuma and Chōshū clan. In Meiji Five
(1872), they set up a modern conscript army. Furthermore, in the
same year they proclaimed the 'educational system', and started
to establish a modern school-system. That is to say they divided
the country into roughly fifty thousand primary school catchment
areas, having a population of six hundred people on average, and
looked forward to the setting up of a national, compulsory
education system with one primary school for every catchment
area. The schools they started were non-selective, with no distinction made according to status, creed or sex.[22†] These facts clearly
reveal that the object was to set up a modern state. The new
government also directed its attention towards higher education.
In the first year of Meiji (1868) the higher educational organisations of the Tokugawa government were resuscitated as new
government schools, and in the following year combined into a
university. Thereafter, the government turned its attention to the
setting up of national and private organs of higher education, and
continued to dispatch a large number of students overseas. In
1887 the Imperial University Law and the Middle School Law
were enacted; the first clause of the Imperial University Law

declared that the Imperial Universities were the highest educational organs of the state, with their objective being 'to teach science and art and to study their principles, in accordance with the needs of the state'. This clause, especially, made it clear that education was to be subordinated to the supreme objective — the building of a modern state.[23+]

The Meiji regime, supported by this kind of bureaucratic, military and educational system, was, to put it in extreme form, a classless society — at least a society whose class structure was very different from what we see in most Western countries. The most fortunate thing that could happen to an individual under the Meiji system was, not to be born the child of a rich father, but rather to be born with a good intellect. Although intelligence was not highly esteemed by the people, it was nevertheless very desirable, and exploitation by the most intelligent of those of lesser intellect was continual and excessive. Since the development of modern industry was a key point in the programme for building a modern state, how to treat and how to foster a bourgeois class was an important question. It could not be claimed that the Meiji government had a fixed, long-range policy on this matter, but ultimately their way of proceeding proved to be ingenious. At first they managed a great many mines and model factories as state enterprises; but with the coming of state financial stringency, they sold them off into private hands. These sales of government enterprises were made to the so-called businessmen with political connections, and provided the basis for the later development of *zaibatsu*.[24+] It is certainly not surprising that the bourgeois class in Japan, with such origins, became traditionally subservient to the intelligentsia of the bureaucracy.

It was an age when the saying 'If he is a university graduate, I'll marry my daughter to him' was literally true. Intellectual training was made too much of, and the intelligentsia banded together. Students of the major universities formed 'graduate cliques' (Gakubatsu) and started to infiltrate the *zaibatsu*. However, this does not mean that no-one was dissatisfied with the system. When they realised that the promise of a democratic system made by the Meiji government in the Charter Oath was no more than empty words, and that the major objective was the establishment of a modern state run by the intelligentsia, the disappointed landowners, farmers and ordinary former samurai started the 'Freedom and Peoples' Rights Movement'. Ostensibly this movement seems to have been successful in achieving the opening of a parliament, but in effect the leadership was held by the intelligentsia and political parties were for a long time held in contempt by the people. This is also clear from the fact that both the great politicans Itō Hirobumi and Yoshida Shigeru, who represent respectively pre- and postwar Japan, strongly disliked political parties, and from the fact that most Japanese political parties are disguised parties of the intelligentsia of the bureaucracy. The second source of opposition came from the so-called Taishō democracy movement, which centred on the scholars and students of that period (1912—25) who held liberal or socialist ideas. However, this opposition from the intelligentsia itself was unable to change the basic character of modern Japan.

According to the normal Marxist scheme, the intelligentsia is divided into two groups. The first belongs to the bourgeoisie, and the second the proletariat. In Japan the intelligentsia is also divided into two: the first group assumed the real power and dominated the bourgeoisie; the second organised the proletariat and attempted to counterattack. However, there were several periods during which national feeling ran against the intelligentsia of the military and the bureaucracy. One was during the so-called Rokumeikan era,[25+] when they attempted to produce an aristocracy and a bourgeoisie; the next was when those among them who came from the Satsuma and Chōshu clans came to predominate, and it seemed as if it was to become almost a government of these two clans. However, by luck and ingenuity they came victorious through several wars, and the Japanese-style, modern control structure which they established went from strength to strength. As the saying 'Japanese spirit with Western technique' (Wakon Yōsai) illustrates, modern Japan imported a capitalist system, but purely as a technique for modern management. The intelligentsia of the military and the bureaucracy did not allow the bourgeois spirit to dominate the control structure. Consequently, the bourgeois were consistently seen as villains right through the period, by people in general. Thus it was very easy for the intelligentsia of the military and the bureaucracy to control the bourgeoisie in a society structured so that their development was impossible without the protection of the intelligentsia. In this way, they subdued the bourgeoisie and turned towards the continent determined upon a course of imperialistic aggression. Finally they went as far as to link up with Hitler, and if one recollects that Japanese capitalism had many points of similarity with German national socialism, one could even say that this tragic international marriage into which modern Japan finally entered was inevitable.

The Meiji system of government outlined above went on smoothly reproducing itself until it finally met the catastrophe of the Shōwa period. The military was high in morale; the bureaucracy was able. The universities brilliantly fulfilled their role of supplying the intelligentsia. Moreover, although the intelligentsia had had a dangerous period when they had been temporarily governed by cliques based on clan origin, generally speaking they were selected 'fairly' and the able man could become a member irrespective of social position or wealth.[26+] However, personal and family status was not entirely absent, nor could it be rendered invalid without cost. In order to neutralise a poison, another poison is needed. In Japan the 'graduate clique' (Gakubatsu) was this kind of second poison. As a result of the monopolising of government circles, monopoly of capital and higher education by a few large groups of this kind, collusion and co-operation were made easy in many fields and many industries, simply by turning the pages of the lists of alumni. As a result those twin pillars of the bourgeois state, the competitive philosophy and liberalism, were never erected in Japan, and the trend to totalitarianism, traditionally strong in Japan from ancient times, increased.[27+]

As we saw above, the prime object of the Meiji government was the building of a modern nation-state, and for that purpose the following two basic policies were available. The first was a formula for the uniform modernisation of the whole of Japan (called for convenience the 'balanced modernisation' policy). The second was the formula whereby a kernel within Japan would be completely modernised, and this kernel then expanded (called for convenience the 'expansion-of-the-core' policy). The Meiji government wisely employed the latter. As a policy for modernisation it is much more effective than the former. That is to say, the expansion-of-the-core policy is one whereby within the territory of Japan, a new country — 'modern Japan' — is built alongside the traditional or 'premodern' Japan. Since they share the same territory, and since one Japan exploits and erodes the other, as the theory of imperialism says, it is clear that modern Japan, the exploiter, will steadily grow and develop. Moreover, since there is no physical distance between the colony and the motherland, as there is with normal imperialist growth, the motherland can expect remarkably rapid growth.[28+]

In this way, from the Meiji period onwards a dual structure was imparted to Japan; this expansion-of-the-core policy was supported not only by the citizens of 'modern Japan', but also by those of 'premodern Japan'. Factors in this support were firstly the patriotic sentiment felt for the 'whole' of Japan by the citizens of 'premodern Japan', and secondly the freedom of migration between the two countries, which easily enabled anyone to become a citizen of the 'modern Japan', provided only that he was well educated.[29+]

'Modern Japan' discriminated heavily against 'premodern Japan'. Between industry and agriculture, modern industry and premodern industry, large enterprises and small and medium-scale enterprises, wage differentials persisted to an extent which is only normally to be seen between different countries. Since the government was extremely discriminatory in its economic policies, those industries which were near to the government in the input—output chains of industries were clearly distinguished from those which were not. Moreover, these distinctions were not of a transient character but persisted over a long period, so that it was practically impossible to break them down through pure, economic competition.

However, in awarding the right of citizenship of 'modern Japan' the government maintained its 'fair' competitive principle. Indeed, after the lifetime employment system came to predominate, the once acquired right of citizenship was rarely lost in a lifetime; but cruelly, the children of the citizens of 'modern Japan' could lose it very easily. Since the acquisition of the right to citizenship of 'modern Japan' mainly depended on a child's school record, it was not at all unusual for a family with a child of poor intellectual capabilities to be ruined within a generation. On the other hand, an intelligent child could very easily become a citizen of 'modern Japan', however poor the family in which he was born. We must admire the extreme stoicism of the ruling class which has maintained this competitive intellectualism over such a long period.[30+]

I do not deny that the Japanese economy from the Meiji Revolution onwards was, broadly speaking, capitalist. However, as we have seen, by reason of the historical circumstances of its coming into being, capitalism did not occur in Japan in its pure, 'ideal' form; instead it appeared in a very singular form, mixed with various other non-capitalistic elements. Although we cannot say that the socio-economic structure which came about after the Meiji Revolution was historically inevitable, nevertheless, it was historically very natural, and the successes and failures of the Japanese economy stemmed fatefully from that structure. The most conspicuous success was rapid economic growth, while there is probably no-one who would deny that the most conspicuous failure was the difference in the level of welfare and the level of wages between 'modern' and 'premodern' Japan, and the chronic disguised unemployment in the latter.

By the same token, no other country is purely socialist or capitalist. In the broad spectrum formed by the modern national economy, each country is no more than a point in the spectrum represented by capitalism and socialism. Even if it belongs to the band of colour called capitalism, it will contain socialist and other elements, and thus, as a consequence of the different mixture of these other elements, it will have its own peculiar structure and features.

Each structure will have its corresponding inevitable successes and failures. For that reason, choosing a social and economic structure is, in the macro-sense, the same thing as choosing one's fate. It would be difficult to deny that the choice is limited by strict historical constraints; but even so there remains room for choice, and in fact choices are made. In almost all cases the choice is made gradually. In some special cases it is made by revolution.

C. An outline of the book

How does one analyse a modern national economy? In economic science there are, traditionally, two ways. The first is the theoretical, or geometric, method; the second is the empirical, or historical, method. As you will soon understand, the term 'geometric' as I employ it here does not imply the use of diagrams, and the term 'historical' does not necessarily imply ferreting around amongst ancient documents. The meaning of 'empirical' and 'historical' that I have in mind is that when an actual economy is examined (be it partly capitalist, partly socialist or partly premodern), it is observed as it is, without imposing on it any special abstractions, and the phenomena which it experienced in the past, as well as those which it is experiencing now are, as far as possible, faithfully described. This method has the virtue of doing little harm to the reality and the historicality (referring to the fact of its having occurred) of the object (phenomenon), while at the same time it enables us to discover laws, by observing that in similar circumstances, similar phenomena will repeat themselves. (For example, the various waves of of the business cycle were discovered in this way.) However, the laws so obtained are no more than empirical laws, and the weakness of the method is that it leaves the investigation of the causal relationships between phenomena incomplete. In order to reveal the causal relationship, it is necessary to observe what happens when one factor is made to change while all others are held constant (*ceteris paribus*); but to be able to make this kind of observation of phenomena in practice, one must be able to conduct a controlled experiment. Thus, in the field of natural science, empirical methods of investigation and establishment of the laws of cause and effect are compatible. However, in the social sciences, where it is not possible to conduct experiments, the use of empirical methods implies that one is put at a decisive disadvantage in learning about the laws of cause and effect.

In contrast to this, the theoretical method is geometrically constituted. That is, by making abstractions from real economies we postulate the existence of idealised relationships and entities as axioms. Then, using this axiomatic system, we deduce by means of speculative experimentation and deductive logic what sort of phenomena will arise. This is exactly similar methodologically to the way in which geometry deduces theorems from axioms. Through this axiomatic method, the logical relationships between the phenomena caused are made clear and distinct. However, its disadvantage is that the phenomena which appear within the axiomatic system are very different from those which are continuously appearing in the real world.

Thus we have to face up to the choice between clarity of cause and effect, or logical clarity, and reality. Most would choose one of the two, according to their own preferences, taking their own comparative advantages into account, and the majority of people would give ambivalent answers to the problem of choosing. But economics as a whole would be wrong to restrict itself exclusively to either of the extremes since both methods have inherent advantages as well as shortcomings which cannot be avoided. The weaknesses of the axiomatic method (the unreality of the laws which are thus obtained) can be partially avoided through the gradual-approach-to-reality method which successively adds elements of reality to the ideal relationships postulated as axioms. Even so, unless one closes one's eyes completely to a degree of unreality, it is not possible to rely entirely on this method. In the social sciences, where the conducting of experiments is impossible, the two opposed methods, the historical and the logical, must coexist as supplements one for the other. Filling in with description the gaps which are incapable of logical solution is an impure method. However, the fate of social science is that methodologically it must inevitably be a two-horse carriage.

Thus, while I acknowledge the importance of the knowledge we can obtain from historical inquiry, in this book I will indulge only in axiomatic analysis. We shall consider the following kind of economy, made up of many enterprises and households. With given technology, the entrepreneur is given the responsibility and the freedom to decide on the most efficient production plan. In a capitalist economy he bears this responsibility in relation to the shareholder; in the socialist economy in relation to the state or the people. The raw materials necessary for enterprise are either allocated by the central planning authority or can be bought on the market by paying a price for them. When the allocation is stringent, feasible production plans are severely limited, and there is little scope for the head of the enterprise to show his ability. However, so long as there is the choice of at least two plans available to him, he is likely to choose the more efficient. As productive techniques are mostly common to capitalism and socialism, if the given conditions (the prices of producer's goods and products, the quantity of capital which can be used, the quantities of allocated raw materials, etc.) are the same, the rational form of the enterprise is much the same under capitalism or socialism. But needless to say, the distribution of the surplus acquired from this rational productive activity differs greatly according to whether it takes place in a society where the means of production are privately owned, or one where they are not.

In a capitalist society, the surplus is distributed among the capitalists; in a socialist society it is distributed amongst all those who participated in its production (workers and managers) after the capital charge has been repaid on the capital loaned by the state. But even in a capitalist society there is no reason why the surplus should not be distributed amongst the workers too; and in a socialist society, it may be that a part of the surplus ought to be paid to the state as a charge supplementary to that specified. In fact if the reason why the surplus arose was that wages were too low, then it ought properly to be paid out in bonuses to the workers; or if it was because the charges on capital fixed by the state were inappropriately low, then it ought to be distributed to the state. Up till now the problem of what distribution (of the surplus) is a rational one has hardly been analysed. However, if rational distribution rates are calculated in the way which will be shown in chapter 3, and if it is assumed that the surplus is distributed to all the factors which participated in production according to these rates, then the distance between capitalism and socialism will probably be seen to decrease even further.

Next we turn to the household. The consumption plan of the household is decided in some instances by custom, in others by impulse. However, it is assumed here that the household too, under the given circumstances, will form the most rational consumption plan. Circumstances can be quite markedly different according to the economy and the age. In Japan, rice rationing is certainly not a thing of the far distant past, and there are probably many people who remember the points rationing system for clothing. Again, it is possible to have countries where medical care is totally, partly, or not at all socialised. For reasons of space I shall have to abandon any attempt to analyse the individual's rational response to the given environment in each of the many possible cases. But one thing that can probably be said with more certainty than in the case of the enterprise is that, although households may belong to different economies, they will exhibit virtually the same responses in identical circumstances. In this book we shall analyse the conduct of the household under a completely free economic system and its conduct in an economy where a points rationing system is operated, as representative cases of consumer activity in differing circumstances.

In a commodity production economy, the demand for factors by enterprises and the demand for consumer goods by households, respectively, must be balanced in the market by the supply of factors from households and the supply of commodities by firms.

It is possible for private ownership of either all or some of the factors of production to be forbidden and for them to be alloted to enterprises by the state; but apart from the cases of the completely managed economy or the completely controlled economy, some degree of free demand must be permitted with respect to consumer goods. However, freely determined demand will not necessarily be equal to planned or freely determined supply. Demand depends on price; supply depends on prices or the physical quantities of allocated factors of production, and so, as long as prices or the allocation of factors do not change, equilibrium between demand and supply will not be established. Together with unsatisfied demand for some goods, there will arise a supply of other goods for which there are no buyers.

Thus, how to regulate prices and how to allocate factors is an exceedingly important problem, not only in capitalist economies, but also in various types of socialist economies. Normally, comparative research into capitalism and socialism is conducted from the point of view of determining how widely private ownership is recognised, what industries are nationalised, and, as a consequence, what differences emerge in the distribution of wealth and income. However, in this book I want to analyse the national economy from a different viewpoint. I want to examine how the price mechanism functions, and whether and what sort of equilibrium is established as a result. Again, where the equilibrium which is established is unsatisfactory (for example, an imperfect employment equilibrium which brings with it unemployment or disguised unemployment), I want to examine what is required to bring about a more satisfactory equilibrium.

In the case where the supply of factors is restricted by rationing etc., the enterprise cannot expand its scale of output beyond a given limit. For that reason, when prices are given, the enterprise will not only choose its production technique in response to this limit, but the absolute level of the volume of production will also be determined by it. In contrast, in the case where the state flexibly changes the allocation of factors; or where the enterprise can purchase on the market factors which are in short supply, prices determine only the technique employed and the enterprise can expand the quantity of its output. So then, how are prices and quantities regulated?

There are two contrasting methods of regulating prices and quantities. First, there is the method found in classical, perfectly competitive economics, where prices are adjusted according to excess demand and quantitites according to excess profits. That is, where the demand for a good exceeds its supply, its price is raised, and vice versa. When excess profits obtained from the production of a good are positive, the output of that good will be expanded (or contracted where the reverse holds). In contrast to this, according to the second method it is prices which are adjusted according to excess profits, and quantities which are regulated according to excess demand. That is, the factors of production needed to produce one unit of a commodity are valued at given prices, and to the cost so calculated is added an allowance for profit at the normal rate. Now if this value is less than the price of the good (that is, if excess profits exist), since the price of the good has been fixed too high, the firm or the central planning authority will refix the price of that good at a lower level. In the opposite case they will give it a higher value. Where prices are determined according to this full-cost rule (or mark-up system), they do not directly perform the function of bringing demand and supply into equilibrium. The quantity of goods produced by each enterprise will exceed the demand for them; or alternatively output will fail to meet the demand. Where an excess supply of a good arises, the enterprise will reduce its supply either automatically or at the command of the central planning authority. Conversely, where an excess demand arises, either the enterprise will spontaneously increase the scale of its output, or the central planning authority will change its allocation so as to make possible an increase in output.

These two adjustment formulae are possible in both the capitalist and the socialist economy. In capitalist economies, the first method was mainly to be found in the period when classical, perfect competition actually existed; but when such competition ceased to exist and oligopoly became the commonest state of affairs, the second method came to predominate. In socialist economies too, in the kind of competitive socialism that Lange advocated, it is assumed that adjustment is conducted according to the first method.[31] Where the plan is formulated using Leontief input—output tables, adjustments to the plan may be made according to the second method. Consequently, it is extremely important from the point of view of the theory of comparative systems to compare and contrast these two adjustment mechanisms.

Leaving aside differences in the distributional aspects, the capitalist economy regulated according to the second method shows a far greater similarity in its pattern of movement to the socialist economy managed according to the same method than it does to the capitalist economy using the market mechanism of the first method. Conversely, the capitalist economy which adjusts through the first method is likely more closely to resemble the socialist economy which is similarly regulated.

As already stated, capitalism made necessary the formation of a 'free labour market'. However, the constitution of this market for labour changed remarkably as capitalism developed. On the one hand trade unions were formed and the supply of labour was regulated, while on the other hand workers came to be less affected by unemployment with the setting up of social security systems and unemployment insurance. Consequently, a free market for labour — in the sense that with an excess demand for labour wages would rise, whereas with an excess supply they would fall — disappeared. Wages came to be inflexible in the downward direction. As a result, once money wage rates are set at an excessively high level (so long as inflation does not occur and the value of money does not fall), the excess supply of labour that has its cause in excessively high wages will not be removed.

Thus the tendency to chronic unemployment was born in capitalist societies, which, as everyone knows, finally brought about the great depression of the 1930s. However, it is possible for the same thing to occur in a socialist state too, in a disguised form. For the moment let us think of a socialist economy where every worker is allocated to his respective enterprise, and the state requires that all be continuously employed in these enterprises. Naturally there can be no unemployment in such an economy. The level of production is fixed so as to supply the consumption demands of workers, military procurements by the state and investment demand, etc.; but, although one can say that the consumption of the workers is fixed at the full employment level, where demand by the state is not great, the level of production is not necessarily large. Therefore the quantity of labour necessary to conduct productive activities at the equilibrium level can be below the full employment level. Even in this situation, since the enterprise must employ all the workers who have been allocated to it, each worker will go everyday to the enterprise. However, once there, since there is not enough work to go round, no worker will do a full day's work. That is, disguised unemployment will arise. Thus, overt unemployment in capitalist societies and disguised unemployment in socialist societies will both be based on the fact that wages have not taken on an appropriate value in relation to demand by the state and other exogenous demands. For this reason it is necessary either to alter wages or to raise demand by the state, in order to get rid of both overt and disguised unemployment. It is therefore inevitable that in both capitalist and socialist countries the government will tend to become bigger as labour-saving techniques of production become more predominant. Where disguised unemployment arises in a socialist economy as a result of a deficiency of effective demand, the enterprise will of course sustain a loss; in the final analysis the state will have to bear this loss.

In capitalist economies disguised unemployment does not arise for this reason, but it can arise from another cause. For instance, as in the case of Japan, where the economy is made up of two parts, the 'modern' and the 'premodern', and the latter part consists of a large number of family farms and family enterprises, those workers who are excluded from the 'modern' sector have to survive by sharing out the poor returns of the 'premodern' sector. Thus disguised or latent unemployment, which gives rise to large wage differences, is concentrated in industries such as building and furniture, which are made up of very small-scale, family enterprises, and in agriculture and the retail sector. Thus, the question of why latent unemployment is chronic in Japan has to be answered in the light of her special socio-economic structure, as has already been pointed out.

The above is a resumé of the problems to be considered in this book. In what follows here I want to make clear its limitations by listing the problems which will not be dealt with. Firstly, the actual national economy made up of firms and households is not frozen or rigid, but is open to influences from many directions. It is open to other countries, to the future, and to political and other essentially non-economic factors. However, in this book I shall completely disregard foreign trade; also I shall restrict to a minimum my analysis of all those economic activities, such as investment or capital accumulation, which we conduct for the sake of the future. I shall deal in a reasonable amount of detail with government influence on the economy, that is with the problems of public finance policy. However, the analysis will always be confined to the effect of government expenditure on the level of output, employment and prices in the various industries; how the supply of public goods by the government effects the levels of productive activity and welfare is a question which will not be discussed at all. Again, I shall analyse the demand for money by households, but this is done for no other reason than to suggest a direction in which traditional non-monetary consumer theory might be extended. Otherwise this book is consistently concerned with the real economy. There is no scope for dealing with monetary policy; nor is the problem of uncertainty discussed. Finally, it is assumed that there are constant returns to scale with each productive technology. For this reason, increasing returns which stem from indivisibility in the producing unit and the tendency towards large-scale enterprise (and consequently oligopoly and monopoly) are not considered. It is also assumed that external economies and diseconomies (and thus environmental pollution of various sorts) do not exist. In short, the economics dealt with in this book is static, short period and non-monetary.

Since I have forgone consideration of many of the problems which are attracting the theoretical and practical attention of economists nowadays, the limitations referred to above are extremely significant. Nevertheless, I believe that in this book I am able to throw a certain amount of light on the fundamental laws which are obeyed by the various types of economy which belong to the broad category of the 'modern national economy'. In the broad sense this book can be seen as being about the theory of comparative systems; but the discussion is conducted entirely in static terms, and says nothing about the dynamic development of systems. According to the economic historians' theories of the stages of economic development, or Marxian Historical Materialism, the individual economies which belong to the category of 'modern national economies' are not in a static, synchronous relationship (as we have assumed), but are bound together in a fixed chronological relationship. It is the task of a dynamic theory of the development of systems to explain this chronological relationship. The theories of this kind expounded in the pioneering works of Marx and Schumpeter are certainly fascinating. However, I shall not be dealing with them in this book.

Part 1: Rationality at the microeconomic level

1 Techniques of production

A. The genealogy of production

From the political point of view, the modern state takes as its framework the separation of the legislative, judicial and administrative powers; from the economic point of view the separation of production and consumption is the basic principle. On Robinson Crusoe's island — and as is clearly seen even today in the small retail trade and in agriculture — production and consumption were originally bound up to the extent that they were impossible to separate. However, in the ideal modern society (or in the modern sector of an actual society), production and consumption are separate — in space, by constituent and in the accounting sense. In the four sections following, I shall analyse firms, which are mainly responsible for production in a modern society. However, in this section I am going to analyse the technical aspect of production in manufacturing industry.

To begin with, let us define production as the activity of combining raw materials and labour (and fuel, machinery, etc.) and transforming the raw materials into products. This process of transformation of raw materials into products is not necessarily a short one; indeed there are usually many processes to be undertaken (for example, the production of ready-to-wear clothes is divided into more than fifty processes). Thus, it is well known that, rather than have one worker responsible for all the processes, it is more efficient to have the materials on a conveyor belt and passed around among workers whose tasks are separate.

Adam Smith in his *Wealth of Nations* wrote as follows on this point, in the section on the division of labour:

> But in the way in which this business is now carried out, not only the whole work is a peculiar trade, but it is

divided into a number of branches, of which the greater part are likewise peculiar trades. One man draws out the wire, another straightens it, a third cuts it, a fourth points it, a fifth grinds it at the top for receiving the head; to make the head requires three distinct operations; to put it on is a peculiar business, to whiten the pin is another; it is even a trade by itself to put them into the paper; and the important business of making a pin is, in this manner, divided into about eighteen distinct operations, which, in some manufactories, are all performed by distinct hands.[1]

Modern production techniques too, can be explained by following Smith's description. What Smith calls a 'distinct operation' is referred to as a 'process' in modern usage. During the first process the wire is straightened using a rolling machine; in the second process the straightened wire is passed through a cutting machine and cut into short lengths; in the third process these short lengths are transformed into sharpened wire by using a lathe. These transformations can be shown in chart form as follows:

Process 1:	Metal	(Raw Material)	Straightened wire
	Rolling Machine	(Machine)	(Intermediate
	Labour	(Labour)	Product)
Process 2:	Straightened wire	(Raw Material)	Short lengths of
	Cutting Machine	(Machine)	wire (Intermediate
	Labour	(Labour)	Product)
Process 3:	Short lengths of wire	(Raw Material)	Sharpened short
	Lathe	(Machine)	lengths of wire
	Labour	(Labour)	(Intermediate
			Product)

Thus at one end of the process the inputs of raw materials, machinery and labour are made, and at the other the outputs of intermediate (or finished) products emerge. The intermediate products of one stage are the inputs of the succeeding stage.

Now, as we have already seen the total operation is first divided vertically into a number of separate processes. Passing through these vertical processes, the raw materials gradually mature through higher stages of intermediate products into a form approaching the finished product. However, it is rare that the finished product can be arrived at along one of these vertical channels alone. As Smith observed, operations which have been organised into vertical channels take place simultaneously, and at certain stages the fruits of these several operations are combined. The combined result is then, at the next stage, united with the results of the chain of operations which have been taking place simultaneously in a separate vertical channel. It is usual finally to arrive at the finished product as a result of repeating this course of events several times over. (In Smith's example the shaft of the pin is being made, while at the same time the head is being formed elsewhere. Finally, the head is welded onto the shaft.)

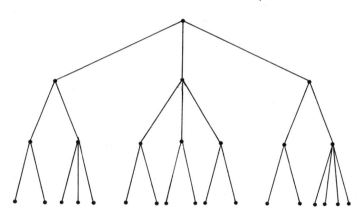

Fig. 1 *The genealogy of production*

When the whole system of operations is shown diagrammatically, it takes the form of a tree. Where operations are complicated, the form of the tree is similarly complicated; but, however complicated, they can be systematised in the same way into the shape of a tree. I shall call this systematic representation the 'genealogy of production'.[2]

B. The production function

Despite the fact that Adam Smith had already clearly pointed in that direction, it is only very recently that economists have started to analyse techniques of production by using a genealogy. Previously, most economists (especially neoclassical economists) used the production function to analyse the technical side of production, instead of the production genealogy.

In the production function the fact that processes are connected vertically, or they are operated in parallel with each other, is completely ignored; the original inputs of raw materials (metal), the various kinds of machines used during the operation (rolling machines, cutting machines and lathes), and the labour used, are related directly to the final product (the pin). In the production of commodities generally, raw materials, machinery and labour (and land) are necessary. Furthermore, in order to increase the output of commodities, the volume of raw materials has to be increased, and either the number of machines has also to be increased, or existing machines must be made to operate at a higher intensity. It is the same with labour. Consequently, the volume of production can be thought of as a function of the volume of the inputs, machinery, labour and raw materials. If the volume of production (output) is shown by Y, and the volume of the inputs of machinery, labour and raw materials by K, L, M respectively, then the production function can be written

$$Y = F(K, L, M). \tag{1}$$

Thus, the technical relationship between inputs and outputs can be shown in a production genealogy, or they can be analysed by using the concept of the production function. What then is the relationship between these two ways of tackling the problem? Is the difference between them merely on the surface, so that in fact they ought to be regarded as the same thing? Or can one be deduced from the other while the converse does not hold; and, if so, by what process is the deduction made? These are the questions that may arise.

They are questions which are by no means difficult to answer. First, if we consider Smith's pin-production from the standpoint of the production function, the number of pins produced, Y, is treated as a function of the volume of metal M, the total operating time of the rolling machine, K_1, the total operating time of the cutting machine K_2, the total operating time of the lathe K_3, etc., and the volume of labour L.[3] However, where the same amount of metal is used, but the whole is cut into shafts alone (where the machinery which punches out the pinheads is idle), headless pins alone are produced, and the Y which is sold is zero. On the other hand, where all the metal is used to make only pinheads (in which case all the machinery associated with the making of shafts remains idle), then again Y equals zero. Between these two extremes, there must be a distribution of metal between the shaft-making section and the head-making section which maximises the total production of pins Y. If the distribution is bad, Y takes on a value below its maximum, and, as we saw above, in the extreme case it can fall to zero. In the same way, where mistakes are made in the disposition of labour, or the arrangement of machinery is inappropriate, Y will not reach its maximum value.

Thus, to the same $K_1, K_2, \ldots, L, M$, there may correspond different values of Y from zero to the maximum value. Of these, the production function concerns itself with the relationship between K, L and M and the maximum value of Y (Y's frontier). Consequently, (1) should correctly be written:

$$\max Y = F(K, L, M).$$

Thus the production function ought not to be seen as a simple description of a technical relationship; it can be thought of as a concept in economics only on the presumption that some sort of consideration has been given to the problem of efficient management. Only when the will towards efficiency operates on techniques can the input—output relationship be located on the frontier stipulated by the production function. The genealogical chart, which is a pure description of production techniques, is a 'given' to economists. However, the production function, which presupposes that techniques are used efficiently, is not a 'given'; it is rather a construction within economics for whose existence the economist has to take responsibility. Thus the production genealogy is a more basic concept, and from it the production function can be deduced. The converse is not possible.

C. Links between production processes

Thus, in contrast to the production genealogy, which is a purely technical description of the methods of production, the production function presupposes the existence of a form of efficient management. To put it in another way, this means that where production is not being conducted efficiently, the existence of a production function must not be presumed. If, as all neoclassical economists do, we begin our analysis not from the production genealogy but from the production function, then efficiency is presupposed, and this produces the mistake of looking at the reality of economics in an inappropriately optimistic fashion. I shall return to this point in detail later. Here, I shall consider how the production processes which are arranged in the form of a genealogy might be synthesised into the production function.

From the point of view of the production genealogy, the total production operation is divided into a number of processes, and each process can be seen as a procedure whereby such inputs as raw materials, machinery and labour are transformed into outputs, in the form of intermediate or finished products. A record is then made of all the goods which appear at least once, either as inputs or outputs, in any of the processes; and where a process is operated in certain units (I will explain how to fix on the unit later), how much of each good is necessary and how much of each good is produced is entered in the record. In recording, inputs are given a minus value, and outputs a plus value. Each good will appear in some process or other either as an input or an output; but since in a specific process, a certain good many appear neither as an input nor an output, it is possible to have many goods with a space left against them in the column or a nought entered. If the first and second processes in the manufacture of pins are recorded in this form, the result is as follows:

Goods	First Process	Second Process
Metal	− 10 kg	0
Straightened wire	+ 1 km	− 1.5 km
Short lengths of wire	0	+ 30,000
Rolling Machines	− 1 machine-hour	0
Cutting Machines	0	− 1 machine-hour
Lathes	0	0
Labour	− 1 man-hour	− 4 man-hours

Smith's eighteen processes in the manufacture of a pin can all be shown in the same way. The finished product, which is the pin, is only produced in the final process, and since it is neither produced nor used as an input in the other processes, in the row which contains the good 'pin', a nought must be entered in each process up to the eighteenth, when for the first time a positive value appears.

Process 1 and process 2 are each standardised so that one unit of operation of these processes uses one rolling machine, or one cutting machine, for one hour. Where the first process has to run in two units, the rolling machine is operated for two machine-hours (either by running two rolling machines in parallel for one hour, or one machine for two hours), and the other inputs are twenty kilogrammes of metal and two man-hours of labour. The output is two kilometres of straightened wire. The same is true for process 2 and other processes. Hereafter, where the intensity of operation is increased, we shall assume that the relationship whereby the quantities of inputs and outputs increase in direct proportion does not only hold where the intensity of operation increases by multiples which are natural numbers, such as two or three, for example; it will also hold whatever positive real number is the multiplier. Since ½ pin or $\sqrt{2}$ pin is meaningless, the unreality of this assumption is clear. However, by admitting it, the mathematics will be greatly simplified. The reader will later recognise how profitable this trade-off between simplicity and reality proves to be.

Once we make this assumption, it is possible to standardise each process not just for machinery, but also in terms of raw materials, labour and products. For example, if we divide the figures in process 1 by 10, we obtain the coefficients of production of process 1 with the input 1 kilogramme of metal raw material as the base (standardisation with raw materials as yardsticks). If we divide the figures in process 2 by 30,000 we have the coefficients of process 2, on the basis of the conditions under which 1 short length of wire is produced (standardisation with the product as yardstick). In the same way, by dividing the figures of process 2 by 4, we can standardise it by means of labour.

Thus, for all processes we can standardise by means of whatever good we choose as a measure, as long as that good is related to that process; in other words, as long as there is no 0 entered in the column against that good. Furthermore, the fact that processes can be operated at a rate which may take on the value not only of any natural number but of any sort of fractional number (the multiplicability and divisibility of processes), means that production activity is a continuum. When processes are divisible, operation of a given process at x units will give rise to x times the inputs and outputs of the standard condition. For example, the operation of process 1 at x units will yield x kilometres of straight wire with inputs of $10x$ kilogrammes of metal raw material, x rolling-machine-hours and x man-hours of labour. In this case the scale of production is shown by scalar x, and even though the scale of production were to expand, since the input and output per scale are the same as under the standard conditions, there are constant returns to scale. Thus, the divisibility of processes means that there is constancy of returns in relation to scale, and it is by reason of this very constancy that standardisation comes to have a meaning. Where there are not constant returns to scale — where advantages or disadvantages accrue as the size of the output increases — the standardisation of processes is meaningless.

Let us formulate what we have been considering above in more abstract terms. We shall assume that there are n types of goods associated with the production of a certain commodity and that the total manufacturing process of that good is divided into m individual processes. In each process the appropriate standardisation is undertaken. Under the standardised conditions we write b_{1i} for the quantity of the 1st good produced by the ith process, and b_{2i} for the quantity of the 2nd good produced by the same process. Similarly for the quantity of the nth good, which is shown by b_{ni}. In order to deal symmetrically with inputs and outputs, we give a positive value to the coefficient of b of the good (final good or intermediate good) produced by the ith process, and a minus value to b for the goods which are inputs.

b is 0 in the case of goods which are unrelated to the ith process. In order to make the distinction still clearer, where the good j is an input we write $b_{ji} = - a_{ji}$, a_{ji} being called an input coefficient; where it is an output, b_{ji} is called an output coefficient. Before distinguishing a_{ji} and b_{ji}, a general b_{ji}, which can take on a positive or a negative value, is designated as a technical coefficient. Using these symbols, the m individual processes can be expressed abstractly as shown in table 1.1.

Table 1.1.

	Process 1	2	3		m
1	b_{11}	b_{12}	b_{13}	$\cdots$	b_{1m}
2	b_{21}	b_{22}	b_{23}	$\cdots$	b_{2m}
Good 3	b_{31}	b_{32}	b_{33}	$\cdots$	b_{3m}
.	.	.	.	$\cdots$	.
.	.	.	.	$\cdots$	.
.	.	.	.	$\cdots$	.
n	b_{n1}	b_{n2}	b_{n3}	$\cdots$	b_{nm}

This table includes all the necessary standard processes in the production of a specific commodity (for example, a pin), and shows plainly the processes through which that good passes during its manufacture. However, this sort of table only shows the processes used in the production of a commodity; it does not show the intensity of operation of each process, or the proportions in which they are linked. Putting it in terms of process 1 or process 2, only their standard states are revealed in the above table; the table tells us nothing about the rate at which they actually operate. However, let us assume that they are each being operated at one unit. Only 1 kilometre of straight wire is produced from process 1, but since process 2 requires 1.5 kilometres of straight wire, it is not possible to link the processes at one unit each. Two-thirds of a unit of process 2 has to be linked to the one unit of process 1. It is at this point that the problem of the rate at which to link each process arises for the enterprise.

Now let us show the rate of operation of the ith process by x_i. Operating at x_i units, $-b_{ji} x_i$ is the input of good j (if good j is an input of the ith process), and $b_{ki} x_i$ is the output of good k (if good k is an output of the ith process). The total quantity of inputs of good j where each process is operated respectively at rates $x_1, x_2, \ldots, x_m$ is

$$-b_j = -b_{j1}x_1 - b_{j2}x_2 - \ldots - b_{jm}x_m$$

The total output quantity of good k is

$$b_k = b_{k1}x_1 + b_{k2}x_2 + \ldots + b_{km}x_m.$$

However, although there are goods which appear in all processes as only either an input or an output, there are also goods (such as intermediate products) which appear in some processes as inputs and in others as outputs. Since the technical coefficient is given by a plus in the case of outputs, and a minus in the case of inputs, b_j or b_k shows the net value of output when inputs are subtracted from outputs.

We can group goods from 1 to n into the following five kinds: machinery (including land), labour, raw materials, intermediate products and finished products. Let us place goods in the following order: good 1 to good $l - 1$ machinery; good l labour; good $l + 1$ raw materials; good $l + 2$ to good $n - 1$ intermediate products; and good n finished products. Then $-b_1, -b_2, \ldots$ must not exceed the enterprise's capacities $K_1, K_2, \ldots ; -b_l$ must not exceed the amount of labour which the enterprise employs; and $-b_{l+1}$ must not exceed the amount of raw materials, M, which are given to the enterprise. (We assume, for the sake of simplicity, that the enterprise uses a single kind of raw material as well as a single kind of labour.) Since the enterprise has to furnish its own needs for intermediate products out of production, the net quantity of outputs $b_{l+2}, \ldots, b_{n-1}$ must all be non-negative. If this is not so, a need will arise for goods over and above those produced, and operations will stagnate for want of intermediate products. The b_n, or Y in our previous notation, will be the quantity of final output obtained.

For that reason, the following conditions have to be satisfied for it to be feasible to operate each process at the rate of $x_1, x_2, \ldots, x_m$:

$$\left.\begin{aligned}
b_{11}x_1 + b_{12}x_2 + \cdots + b_{1m}x_m &\geq -K_1, \\
b_{21}x_1 + b_{22}x_2 + \cdots + b_{2m}x_m &\geq -K_2, \\
\cdots\cdots\cdots\cdots\cdots\cdots\cdots\cdots\cdots \\
b_{l1}x_1 + b_{l2}x_2 + \cdots + b_{lm}x_m &\geq -L, \\
b_{l+11}x_1 + b_{l+12}x_2 + \cdots + b_{l+1m}x_m &\geq -M, \\
b_{l+21}x_1 + b_{l+22}x_2 + \cdots + b_{l+2m}x_m &\geq 0, \\
\cdots\cdots\cdots\cdots\cdots\cdots\cdots\cdots\cdots \\
b_{n-11}x_1 + b_{n-12}x_2 + \cdots + b_{n-1m}x_m &\geq 0,
\end{aligned}\right\} \quad (2)$$

$$b_{n1}x_1 + b_{n2}x_2 + \cdots + b_{nm}x_m = Y. \quad (3)$$

In order for production to be carried out, these conditions for feasibility have to be satisfied. Where processes are linked in such a way that even one of these conditions is not fulfilled, production activity will come to a halt at some stage, through an insufficiency of machinery, of labour, of raw materials, or of intermediate products.

Under the conditions formulated above, the values of $K_1, K_2, \ldots, L, M$ are data to the firm when it makes its production plan, but xs are not. They are determined by the firm. If there is only one set of $x_1, x_2, \ldots, x_m$ which satisfies the above conditions as formulated, the firm's decision is self evident. However, where multiple sets of x alike satisfy the above conditions, there remains to the firm some freedom to adjust productive activity, since it may choose any one from among these sets, as long as it disregards efficiency of production. In fact, in the case of the manufacture of pins, where process 1 is operated at one unit, process 2 can be operated at 2/3 unit. If the intermediate product 'straight wire' is allowed to remain unused, the firm can operate process 2 at any rate, as long as it is less than 2/3 unit. Where production efficiency is ignored the enterprise can even choose not to operate process 2 at all. However, this flexibility in production plans exists only where there is disregard for production efficiency; as we shall see below, where production has to be conducted efficiently, each process has to be combined at a fixed rate.

It goes without saying that from amongst the various possible combinations of x, the firm will choose a combination $(x_1^0, x_2^0, \ldots, x_m^0)$ so as to maximise the quantity of output Y. Where processes operate at rates $x_1^0, x_2^0, \ldots, x_m^0$ they will be interlinked with the minimum waste and the maximum efficiency. There is a fixed corresponding value for max Y where values for $K_1, K_2, \ldots, L, M$ are given; with different values a different value for max Y is obtained. This relationship of correspondence between max Y and K, L, M (that is to say, the relationship between, on the one hand, the volume of output where each process is combined most efficiently, and on the other, machine capacity, labour employed and the volume of raw materials used) is clearly the relationship we attempt to express in the production function, and we can write it generally in the form of equation (1).

However, we must not forget that the processes included in table 1 are only those which are indispensable for the production of the finished product in question. In order to produce a finished product various intermediate products have to be produced, but there is only one process available for each of these (alternative, substitutable processes do not exist). Consequently, since each is unique, each process is indispensable. In this case, instead of linking processes by proceeding from process 1 towards the final process where the finished product is produced, it is also possible to proceed in the reverse direction, moving from the final process towards process 1. That is to say, we determine the intensity at which each process is to be operated in order to produce one unit of the final product, by calculating back. We thus decide how many units of intermediate products are necessary directly to produce one unit of the finished product; and in order to produce that number of intermediate products, how many units of other intermediate products are needed. There are many processes and, at first sight, it would seem possible to regulate the rate of operation of each of them independently. However, as long as processes are to be linked efficiently, the method of linking them is determined; and consequently, since processes are always bound together in the same ratios, it is the same as if the final product were produced by one process only. Where $K_1, K_2, \ldots, L, M$ change, the size of max Y changes, and the absolute level of $x_1^0, x_2^0, \ldots, x_m^0$ also changes. However, their mutual relationships do not change. If we make $\bar{x}_1, \bar{x}_2, \ldots, \bar{x}_m$ the values for x where 1 unit of Y is produced and write:

$$b_{j1}\bar{x}_1 + b_{j2}\bar{x}_2 + \cdots + b_{jm}\bar{x}_m = \bar{b}_j,$$

$-K_1/\bar{b}_1$ expresses the ceiling placed on the volume of output by the limits of machine 1 (where other machines, labour and raw materials are given without limit). In the same way, for example, $-L/\bar{b}_1$ expresses the ceiling to the volume of output deriving from the limits to the quantity of labour (where there is no limit to machinery and raw materials). The volume of output is determined by the lowest of these various ceilings. That is to say:

$$\max Y = \min\left[\frac{-K_1}{\bar{b}_1}, \frac{-K_2}{\bar{b}_2}, \ldots, \frac{-L}{\bar{b}_l}, \frac{-M}{\bar{b}_{l+1}}\right].$$

Where the production function of (1) takes this special form, we refer to it as being 'limitational'.[4] Thus, as is clear from the above, where there is no process which can be substituted and all processes are indispensable, whatever the number of processes the production function derived from them must be limitational.

D. Alternative production techniques

The most basic case is where, as above, there is only one method of producing a good; but it is, at the same time, the exceptional case. Normally, there are various different methods of producing the same good, and the enterprise is confronted with the problem of the 'choice of techniques'. For example, in the case of pin production, there are a variety of methods of welding the head of the pin onto the shaft in the final process, even though there may be no choice in all other processes.

Where there are a number of production techniques (or production methods), every technique is divided into several processes, and the genealogies of processes can be shown in the form of a single table — like table 1.1 — for each productive technique, by using the technical coefficients. If we call these tables the blueprints for each respective production technique, we shall have blueprints to the same number as the given techniques, and from these we can obtain a book of blueprints or a catalogue of techniques.

Figuratively speaking, the problem of choice of techniques is the problem of which page to choose in this catalogue of blueprints. As we shall see later, the enterprise's response to this problem is not necessarily always the same. In accordance with changing circumstances, it is perfectly possible for an enterprise which up till now has been using the blueprint on page 5, to turn to the one on page 13. However, it is possible at the same time to have techniques which will never be used, no matter how circumstances change. If this is so, it is inefficient to have this sort of technique retained in the catalogue, and the publication of a convenient, shortened edition of the catalogue of techniques which does not include them is desirable.

The production function is not the catalogue of techniques itself; it is the abridged edition of it, made concise by introducing considerations of efficiency. How in fact is it edited?[5] Here let us first examine (by means of the procedure explained in the previous section) what max Y can be obtained for each technique, with given machine capacities, $K_1, K_2, \ldots$, volume of labour, L, and raw materials, M. A given technique will yield a certain size of max Y, while another technique may give a larger (or smaller) max Y. In one corner of the blueprint of the technique which gives the maximum value for max Y, we record the values of $K_1, K_2, \ldots, L$, M considered as given, and the size of max Y observed. Since there may be several techniques which will give the maximum value for max Y, such a record will be entered on a number of blueprints.

We do the same thing in relation to all other sets of $K_1, K_2, \ldots,$ L, M. As a result, there will be techniques which give the highest value for max Y for several sets of $K_1, K_2, \ldots, L, M$, and there will be some techniques which do not give the highest value for max Y for any sets. Since it is pointless preserving the blueprints of the latter, they ought to be deleted from the concise edition. Thus, in a corner of each of the pages of this edition there will be a record of the sort of circumstances in which that technique can be recommended, and also of the maximum upper limit to the output that can be expected at that time. This information will be even more useful if it is rearranged lexicographically so as to be more easily scanned. In other words, first we rearrange the blueprints in sequence according to the value of K_1 which is recorded in the corner of each blueprint. Next we arrange those blueprints which have the same value for K_1 in sequence according to the value of K_2, and so on successively, finally arranging them in sequence according to the value of M. As many copies of each blueprint are made as there are sets of $K_1, K_2, \ldots, L, M$ written in the corner of the blueprint, and each is inserted in its place in the appropriate section in the dictionary. The dictionary of techniques for a particular product which has been edited in this way is entitled 'the production function for that good'. It is an indispensable reference book for the office of the chairman of the company and for that of the technical manager, and it gives the frontier for the production of that good.

E. The aggregate production function

After pointing out that the various processes in the manufacture of pins are arranged in genealogical form, Smith observed that the same sort of division of labour can be seen between industries on a nation-wide basis; that is, he observed that in order to produce the nation's final products (or the gross national product) industries are mutually connected in a genealogical formation, or like the mesh of a net.

> The woollen coat, for example, which covers the day labourer, as coarse and rough as it may appear, is the produce of the joint labour of a great multitude of workmen. The shepherd, the sorter of the wool, the wool-comber or carder, the dyer, the scribbler, the spinner, the weaver, the fuller, the dresser, with many others, must all join their different arts in order to complete even this homely production. How many merchants and carriers, besides, must have been employed in transporting the materials from some part of those workmen to others who often live in a very distant part of the country! How many merchants and carriers, besides, how many ship-builders, sailors, sail-makers, rope-makers, must have been employed in order to bring together the different drugs made use of by the dyer, which often

come from the remotest corners of the world! What a
variety of labour, too, is necessary in order to produce
the tools of the meanest of those workmen. To say
nothing of such complicated machines as the ship of the
sailor, the mill of the fuller, or even the loom of the
weaver, let us consider only what a variety of labour is
requisite in order to form that very simple machine, the
shears with which the shepherd clips the wool. The miner,
the builder of the furnace for smelting the ore, the
seller of the timber, the burner of the charcoal to be
made use of in the smelting-house, the brick-maker, the
brick-layer, the workmen who attend the furnace, the
mill-wright, the forger, the smith, must all of them join
their different arts in order to produce them.[6]

Thus we arrive at the following understanding: that the goods
which form the necessities of life can be produced only after passing through an incalculable number of processes. Pins and needles
are necessary, as well as cloth and thread, in order to produce the
clothes we wear, and 18 processes have to be gone through before
the pin is completed. It is apparent that many processes are necessary in order to make the cloth and the thread. The work which
produces the loom that is used to make the cloth is also divided
into many processes. If we standardise each of these respective
processes and arrange them, we can derive a single huge chart
which we can call the blueprint of national production. It is made
up by laying the blueprints for the manufacture of pins alongside
those for the manufacture of cloth, and alongside those the blueprints for making looms; and so on. The result will probably be
long enough to stretch around the earth, but let us imagine that it
is possible, if we put it on ultra-small micro-film, to reduce it to
the size of a single page in a book. There were a number of blueprints for the making of a pin, and so, too, in the case of other
goods there will be a number of blueprints, and not simply one for
each respective good. (The number will differ for each good.) Since
the blueprint of national production is a combination of blueprints
for the production of each commodity, there are as many blueprints
of national production as the total number of possible combinations.
Since the number of goods is incalculably large, and since there is
a large number of production methods available to produce each of

them, the total number of combinations will be enormous. Consequently, a very large repository will be necessary even to store one volume of the micro-film edition of the book of blueprints which contains all the national production methods. Confronted with this huge book of blueprints it would not be very surprising if someone were to try and edit it so as to produce a pocket edition: that is to say, a 'national production function' or an 'aggregate production function'. However, as opposed to the case of pin manufacturing, there is, in the case of national output, not just one but an incalculable number of types of product. Moreover, the number of types of different machines used is incalculably great. Thus the convenient edition will probably not prove all that useful, unless we find a way of getting rid of troubles arising from this diversity.

Accordingly, by producing an index representing the many kinds of products and one representing the many kinds of machinery, the neoclassical economists (and Keynes too) at one stroke produced a transistorised aggregate production function. That is, they produced the edited, two variable aggregate production function:

$$\max Y = F(K, L),$$

or the three variable:

$$\max Y = F(K, L, M).$$

In these, Y is an index of output, where the quantity of each good is weighted by its respective price ratio. K is aggregate capacity, where the capacity of each machine has been weighted by its respective price ratio; and L and M are the aggregate quantities of labour and raw materials respectively, having been rendered into index form in the same fashion. In the two-variable edition, either raw materials can be regarded as intermediate products in the national product, or they are absorbed in K as working capital. (Raw materials can be seen as machinery which has been destroyed after having been used once in production.)

However, we have naturally lost a great deal by this neoclassical transistorising. The production function was a guide book to techniques which fulfilled the purpose of showing which technique was the most efficient under different circumstances. However, its usefulness as a guide book was severely limited by weighting the quantity of output of each good, the extent to which each machine is used and the amount of each kind of labour employed by their respective price ratios and totalling them up, though we can say that this was unavoidable in order to frame indices for the pocket edition. That is to say, as we shall see later, where a certain price system comes into being, firms arrange production so as to maximise profits under that price system. Thus by adding up the volume of output actually produced, and the volume of machinery input and the volume of labour input actually used in production (weighted by the price ratios used when framing the aggregate production function), we can derive the correct index values for the aggregate volume of output, and for the aggregate capital and the aggregate labour employed. If the true values of these are (more or less) the same as those calculated as the maximum point of profit by the use of the aggregate production function, there is no particular problem in using this aggregate production function in the analysis. But if this is not the case, using such an aggregate production function becomes a source of analytical error.[7] In general, and apart from cases of extremely peculiar genealogies of production, we ought to think of this error as being large so long as actual price ratios are different from those used in framing the indices.[8+] However, actual price ratios vary with circumstances, while the aggregate production function was constructed on the assumption of fixed price ratios. Unless the aggregate production function is revised as soon as actual prices become significantly different from those used as weights for the indices, the error referred to above will not remain within permissible limits. That is, it has to be said that the usefulness of the aggregate production function is extremely limited unless this huge task of revising it is often undertaken.

Even if we shut our eyes to the error which arises because actual price ratios differ from those used as the weights of the indices, a problem still remains. Let us consider situation A, where we have large numbers of machine 1 but very few of machine 2, and situation B, where the opposite is the case. We assume that there is no difference between A and B in the number of other machines available, or the given quantities of labour and raw materials. Even where the circumstances relating to the possession of machinery differ in this way, in index terms it is perfectly possible to arrive at a state of affairs where the size of K is the same for A and B. Consequently, A and B are two states where there is no difference in K, L and M; but clearly in A a great deal of the good which uses machine 1 will be produced and very little of the good which uses machine 2. The opposite state of affairs will arise in B. By making these outputs into indices, we can derive the Y in situation A and that in situation B; but, apart from the case where the genealogy of production for each good fulfils exceedingly exceptional conditons, there is no proof that these two Ys will be equal. Even if K, L and M as indices are the same in the two situations, Y as an index does not necessarily take on the same value. This fact disproves the existence of the aggregate production function as a single-valued function.

However, the aggregate production function as a single-valued function is admissible where the following conditions are satisfied. Suppose there exists an infinitely great number of combinations of capital goods which produce the same value for their index K. Then there exists a corresponding infinitely great number of values for Y; but if capital goods are always provided in that composition which gives the maximum value for Y, then the relationship between Y and K, L and M is as revealed by the neoclassical aggregate production function. However, actual combinations of capital goods are not limited to this one kind. The neoclassicals thus defended the single-valued nature of their aggregate production function by ascribing magical properties to societies, considering that capital would always be given by that kind of special combination.

If we assume that society does posses this kind of magic, it must be the task of the economist to make clear through what sort of arrangement it is furnished with it. (As is well known, Smith made it one of his personal missions to investigate the mechanism of the 'invisible hand'.) But, confronted with this task, the measures taken by the neoclassicals were quite the opposite. That is to say, instead of investigating whether their assumption was appropriate to real societies and economies, they justified the assumption by re-creating reality so as to satisfy it. They assumed that all capital goods are made of putty. They assumed that if the given combination of capital goods does not give the maximum value for Y, it will be remodelled so as to produce such a combination — instantly and, moreover, costlessly (the so-called malleability of capital). However, to admit an aggregate production function with regard to this fabrication-as-substitute-for-reality, and then, with it as a basis, to construct precise theories (marginal productivity theory, the theory of technical progress, the theory of stable growth, etc.) is like trying to build a tower on a large ant-hill.

Many of the neoclassical fallacies originate in the constructing of indices by lumping together many machines into the one composite capital good, K, many different kinds of workers into the one composite labour, L, and many products into the one composite product, Y.[9+] Without this aggregation we may compute the quantity of output and of inputs of each good separately; then we may derive a multi-dimensional national aggregate production function

$$\max Y_1 = F(K_1, K_2, \ldots, L_1, L_2, \ldots, M_1, M_2, \ldots, Y_2, Y_3, \ldots)$$

which gives the maximum upper limit to the amount of Y_1 that can be produced, on condition that the amount of use made of each machine does not exceed $K_1, K_2, \ldots$, the amounts of labour used do not exceed $L_1, L_2, \ldots$, the amounts of raw materials used do not exceed $M_1, M_2. \ldots$, and that at least the quantities of output $Y_2, Y_3, \ldots$ of good 2 and those thereafter are produced.[10]

Clearly, this kind of production function avoids to some extent the errors which accompany the use of indices. But it overvalues max Y_1, to a greater or lesser degree. The reason for this is that once machinery has been set up in a factory, it will not be moved to another factory without some compelling reason. Consequently, machines will not move to supply each other's needs, even where one factory has a deficiency in K_1 and another a surplus. Even though the nation's holdings of K_1 are unchanged, the volume of Y_1 will vary according to whether it is distributed efficiently between factories. Thus, as in the case where we assumed a national aggregate production function in a few dimensions, so in the case of the multi-dimensional national aggregate production function: we either have to assume that the nation possesses some magical property which ensures an efficient distribution of capital goods; or we have to make the unrealistic assumption that the prompt and costless movement of capital goods between factories is possible; or else the production genealogy needed to produce every good has to be extremely exceptional.

This realisation leads to the conclusion that we must not simply add together even the same types of capital goods. Immobile goods have to be treated as separate goods if they are in different places. For this reason, the dimensions of the aggregate production function appear to become greater and greater as we consider the immobility of capital goods. As a result, a repository of roughly the same size as was needed for the complete version of the book of blueprints will be needed to hold one volume of the aggregate production

function. The benefits of producing an edited, abridged version of
the book of blueprints are thus not large. We have to conclude
that it is not possible to so condense it as to produce an easily
handled version.

It took a long time for economists to arrive at this conclusion,
but practical men realised it early on, either by intuition or through
experience. In capitalist countries, heads of companies and technical managers knew that their technical knowledge was complete
with regard only to the industry to which their company belonged,
and that they knew only a small part of — or had an unclear view
of the whole of — the techniques of related industries. In socialist
countries the view was generally held that there would be a central
library built to contain the complete, or the concise, version of the
book of blueprints, and that production would be decided by the
central authorities. Indeed, plans were drawn up along these lines;
but since the plan often did not accord with actual circumstances,
and experience demonstrated that it was not an optimum plan,
plans are now formed in more or less decentralised fashion, even in
socialist states.

Thus the central library of techniques is unnecessary if the
right of independent decision making by each respective plant is
recognised. It will suffice if information relating to techniques is
divided between a large number of small branch libraries and kept
in them. However, in this case each production plant forms its own
production plan without knowledge of the whole corpus of
techniques, and without correct, detailed knowledge of the contents of the plans of other production plants. As the early socialists
pointed out when criticising capitalist society, in a decentralised
polycratic society there is always the danger of anarchy. If there
is no smooth flow of information between the many productive
plants, or if some plants do not regulate their own conduct in response to the information received, anarchy will cause the destruction of society in all nations. For the sake of their own reproduction
— that is for their own continuance and development — all societies
have to instal mechanisms to ensure the flow of information. Moreover, they have to ensure that appropriate information flows along
the information pipelines (that is to say, the sort of information
which will cause the production plant voluntarily to revise its
opinions, and ultimately to arrive at the correct decision). While
modern societies permit the decentralisation of decision making,

they must at the same time command each cell, through the agency of the nervous system, so as to ensure that the whole does not fall into disorder. Smith's 'invisible hand' does not exist for the defence of *laisser-faire*. We can say that one of the central questions for economics in a modern society is to find out what information mechanism is most effective, that is, best suited to minimise the danger of society's being led in the wrong direction.

2

The choice of techniques

A. Parallel use of several techniques

Private enterprise systems, which came into being against a variety of different historical backgrounds, have certain advantages in the formulating of production plans. These have recently also come to be highly regarded in socialist countries, where, on principle, uniform decision making is conducted at the centre and on the scale of the entire national economy. This is because it has come to be understood that rationalisation of the component parts of the economy, which is necessary for rationalisation of the whole, is very difficult to realise in the centrally planned economy. In this chapter we shall turn from consideration of the aggregate production function to the problem of the choice of production techniques for the individual firm; and we shall analyse the conduct of the firm in the light of the circumstances in which it is situated.

This question has already been discussed to a certain extent in the previous chapter, when we talked about the construction of the production function from the production genealogy of the single firm. However, the solution given there was insufficient. We took the numbers of each machine $K_1, K_2, \ldots$, the quantity of labour L and of raw materials M given to each firm as fixed, and under these quantitative limitations to factors of production, we considered which would be the most efficient technique to choose from among those the firm could employ. The answer given to the problem was that the one chosen would be the one which would enable the firm to get onto its production frontier with its given quantities of $K_1, K_2, \ldots, L$, and M (this could easily be found by drawing up the production function of the firm). That is to say, in the preceding chapter we explained the decision of the firm in a situation where the sizes of $K_1, K_2, \ldots, L$ and M were specified.

However, these are not necessarily the circumstances which

confront the firm. It is true that if we take a short time period, the number of machines a firm can make use of is probably fixed. But by paying appropriate wages and prices, exactly those amounts of labour and raw materials which are needed can be acquired (where a well organised market for those factors exists). In that case, it is not possible to specify the quantities of labour and raw materials. Many pages of the *Production Function* — the abridged edition of the book of blueprints of production techniques — remain eligible; the head of the firm has to pass judgement on which of them to choose. However, we have not yet dealt with the problem of what rules he follows in making this decision.

One of the subjects of this chapter is the establishing of rules for the formation of the firm's production plan where it is possible to purchase some of its producer goods on the market. In relation to that problem, two concepts play an important role: feasibility and efficiency. In view of their importance, I shall return to an explanation of them below; but first, I should like to add a few comments on one point which was made insufficiently clear in the preceding chapter.

Where there are a number of techniques for producing a good, it is not necessarily the case that exactly the same types of machinery, labour and raw materials as were used when one technique was employed, will be needed when another technique is used; not just machinery, but even raw materials can change. Where factors differ with different techniques in this way, since the catalogue of factors is not consistent through all techniques and inconveniences arise from the point of view of analysis, it is necessary to make one large, comprehensive catalogue by combining each individual catalogue. This will contain all factors, in whichever technique they appear. For example, where technique 1 uses machines K_1, $K_2, \ldots, K_h$ and technique 2 uses machine K_{h+1} instead of K_h, we make a comprehensive catalogue which includes $K_1, K_2, \ldots, K_h$, K_{h+1}. In the processes of technique 1, we think of all the technical coefficients relating to machine K_{h+1} as being 0, and in the processes of technique 2 we think of all those technical coefficients relating to machine K_h as 0. Here we write the table of technical coefficients for technique 1 (see table 1) shown in the comprehensive catalogue as

$$
B_1 = \begin{bmatrix} b_{11} & b_{12} \cdots b_{1m} \\ b_{21} & b_{22} \cdots b_{2m} \\ \cdot & \cdot & \cdot \\ \cdot & \cdot & \cdot \\ \cdot & \cdot & \cdot \\ b_{n1} & b_{n2} & b_{nm} \end{bmatrix}
$$

In the same way we write B_2, B_3, etc. to show the table of technical coefficients for techniques 2 and 3, and so on.[1] Since not only the technical coefficients but also the number of processes can change with each technique, the m of B_1 and the m of B_2 are not necessarily the same (Below we shall represent the m of B_1 by m_1 and the m of B_2 by m_2.) Thus the length of the tables of technical coefficients is fixed, but the width is not (this is because these tables of technical coefficients are constructed on the basis of the comprehensive catalogue of factors). As you will see below, the usefulness of the analysis derives from the uniformity in length; no inconvenience is produced if the width is not uniform. We shall make t the number of different techniques; B is the large table arrived at by placing the t technical coefficient tables (B_1, B_2, . . . , B_t) side by side, and linking them.

All these tables can be dealt with mathematically as matrices. B_1 is a matrix of n rows and m columns and B is a matrix of n rows and $(m_1 + m_2 + \ldots + m_t)$ columns. Next, we record the rate of operation of every process for each technique lengthways on a long tape, and call it the table of operation of techniques. For example, that for technique 1 is

$$
X_1 = \begin{bmatrix} x_1 \\ x_2 \\ \cdot \\ \cdot \\ \cdot \\ x_{m_1} \end{bmatrix}
$$

The same sort of tape is made for other techniques, and these are known as X_2, . . . , X_t. The length of the tape can be different for each technique; when all the tapes are joined together lengthways we have

$$X = \begin{bmatrix} X_1 \\ X_2 \\ \cdot \\ \cdot \\ \cdot \\ X_t \end{bmatrix}$$

All X_i or X can be treated mathematically as vectors.

In calculating the total quantity of inputs of each factor used by techniques and the total quantity of output produced, it is sufficient to multiply the technical coefficients by the rate of operation for each respective process and to add them for each good. This kind of calculation by summing of products can be easily shown in table form when matrices and vectors are used. That is, the quantity of inputs and outputs where processes of technique 1 are operated at a rate of X_1 is $B_1 X_1$.

However, for actual production the firm will choose a small number of techniques from the t techniques available; it will not necessarily choose one single technique only. It is perfectly possible for the firm to produce with technique 1 in factory 1, and in parallel, with technique 2 in factory 2. In this case, as an overall result of making use of techniques in parallel, we have the aggregate total of inputs and outputs of all techniques — that is to say:

$$B_1 X_1 + B_2 X_2 + \cdots + B_t X_t = BX.$$

The result of operating each technique at a rate X_i will be to produce the aggregate total BX for the inputs and outputs of all goods. If we designate this as Z, then Z is the vector of input and output quantities — the aggregate total of inputs and outputs for each good put lengthways onto a tape. Inputs are recorded as negative quantities, outputs as positive quantities. Intermediate products are entered by making the quantity of net output positive or zero.

So then, how does the firm formulate its production plan? This question has been dealt with in a great many books in relation to the firm in a capitalist economy, so I shall here consider it in relation to the firm in a particular type of socialist economy (for example, modern Soviet Russia). From the analysis the reader will see that the firm in the socialist economy and the firm in the capitalist economy behave in practically the same way.

In the socialist economy orders are issued by the central planning authority to each firm concerning its production activities. There are instances where the orders are precise, restricting the behaviour of the firm right down to the detailed level; but there are also cases where this is not so — where the orders are loosely framed. Here the central planning authority may simply set an upper or lower limit to a firm's (production) behaviour, and, as long as these conditions are fulfilled, the firm is free to make its own decisions. In the early stages of socialism firms were closely supervised by the state, but on reaching a higher stage of development, they have come to receive a good deal of freedom and independence.[2+] The central planning authority, or the state planning committee, allocates the supply of raw materials and labour to each enterprise and fixes a lower limit to its output. In the initial period the number of machines which each firm possesses is an historical datum. It usually happens that the state planning committee also fixes an upper limit to the number of new machines which can be installed and operated in production in each enterprise during the planning period. In the vector of input and output Z, a lower limit is indicated for both the quantity of inputs and the quantity of outputs. (I should like to emphasise that the quantity of inputs takes on a negative value. Defining an upper limit to the quantity of inputs expressed as a positive value is merely defining a lower limit to the quantity of inputs expressed as a negative value). Among these goods there are raw materials which can be bought freely on the market by paying a fixed charge (price); and there are instances where there are no limits on the amounts of machinery and labour used. In this case (expressed as a negative value) the lower limit to raw materials, labour and machine capacities is written as $-\infty$, and restrictions on them cease to exist. If we write the restriction vector as $\bar{Z}$, the central planning authority's orders require that production activity is conducted in the firm so that

$$BX \geqq \bar{Z} \qquad (1)$$

The firm in the capitalist economy, which at first sight appears to be totally unrestricted and to receive orders from no-one, is in fact restricted in the same way. Of course, if a firm wants raw materials or labour it can purchase them without limit, and it is given no production norm to fulfil. However, these firms too, in the short period, are subject to restrictions in relation to productive capacity (the number of machines, etc.) handed down from the past. That is, for the firm in the capitalist economy, in $\bar{Z}$ the lower limit on raw materials and labour is $-\infty$ and the lower limit to output is given by 0; but (expressed as a negative value) there is a negative lower limit to machine capacity. Thus for both the firm in a socialist economy and the firm in the capitalist economy, technical limitations can be expressed by an inequality of the same form: that is (1).

B. The feasibility and efficiency of the production plan

We explained above what conditions have to be fulfilled by an overall production plan where a variety of techniques are used together. They are usually known as feasibility conditons. We can discuss feasibility conditions at a variety of stages. Firstly, as we saw above, where a single technique is used, and where the net output of intermediate goods is negative, the production pipeline runs dry at an intermediate stage and it is impossible thereafter to produce as planned. However, in the case of the overall production plan, the pipeline will not run dry if there is a shortage of intermediate goods produced by one technique and required by that same technique, as long as there is a surplus of the same good produced by another technique, so that overall there is no deficiency. For that reason, feasibility ought not to be discussed in relation to each individual technique, but in relation to the total production plan which incorporates every technique.

Secondly, even where the net output of intermediate goods is not negative for the overall plan, if the amounts of machinery, raw materials and labour needed exceed those indicated by the central planning authority, the production plan cannot be fulfilled. (The same thing applies in the case of the firm in a capitalist economy, where a firm owns fewer machines than it needs to accomplish its production plan.) Furthermore, if the central planning authority imposes minimum output requirements on the enterprise, a production plan which only brings about output quantities of less than the norm should not be adopted. Thus the feasibility of a plan is prescribed by considering not just the technical aspects, but also the commands of higher organisations or the demands of society, as well as the historical background (the equipment inherited from the past). These various conditions, which the firm ought to consider when formulating its plan, are all reflected in the restriction

vector $\bar{Z}$. The value of components relating to the intermediate
goods of $\bar{Z}$ is given by 0: components relating to producer goods
(machinery, raw materials, labour) have a negative value and those
relating to outputs a positive value. Where it is possible to acquire
producer goods through the market without restriction, the corresponding components of $\bar{Z}$ are prescribed as $-\infty$ or a sufficiently
large negative value. Where the norm in relation to output is not
imposed, the components which express outputs in $\bar{Z}$ are prescribed
as 0 or a sufficiently small positive value. If a certain operating
plan X fulfils condition (1) for $\bar{Z}$ prescribed in this way, then we
say it is feasible. Since each component of vector X expresses the
operating rate for each process of each technique, each must have
a positive value or be zero. (A negative value would be meaningless.
That is, 'feasibility' requires that X should fulfil (1), and furthermore that it be a non-negative vector.)

The $\bar{Z}$ which is decided upon by the central planning authority is
not necessarily the result of its making a single, consistent, unified
decision. There are a variety of bureaux within the central planning
authority and the orders of each bureau are not necessarily compatible; often they are insufficiently well co-ordinated. As a result,
an enterprise which produces a variety of products receives instructions from many bureaux. The lower limit to the quantity of good
a to be produced is determined by planning office A, while that of
good b is fixed by planning office B. Moreover, the quantity of
labour or the wages fund is determined by planning office L, while
the number of machines to be used is fixed by planning office K.
The values of components in $\bar{Z}$ are fixed in this way by the various
offices, but since the maintenance of a close understanding between
offices over decisions is not easy, the various components of $\bar{Z}$ are
often inappropriately related. In the extreme case, it can happen
that it is impossible to produce the quantity of product a required
by planning office A with the size of wages fund allocated by
planning office L; and, moreover, that to produce the quantity of
a required by planning office A would necessitate operating machinery at full capacity, so that, as a result, none of the product b
ordered by planning office B is produced. Needless to say, in this
case the plan is impossible to operate, and either the head of the
enterprise has to resign, or he has to apply for a revision of the plan.

However, it is not usual for each bureau of the central planning
authority to issue its orders as a result of a unilateral decision,

completely ignoring the actual circumstances. The results of the previous year are taken as the basis for formulating the production plan for any given year. In addition, the returns relating to production capacity put in by enterprise heads are referred to; so that, apart from the exceptional case, we can assume that a $\bar{Z}$ under which production cannot be accomplished will not be ordered. Since enterprise heads fear that, if they report production capacity correctly, they will be set a very difficult norm to achieve, their returns are always under-estimates. Since supervisors too, have always preferred to tolerate under-reporting, rather than be called to account for having fixed norms which were too strict and designing a plan which was incapable of fulfilment, in most cases a not too strict $\bar{Z}$ will be given to firms.[3+] In a planned economy fulfilling the plan is the first requirement, and so heads of enterprises must choose an X which will satisfy planning condition (1).

Dealing in this way with the problem of the firm's choice of techniques implies limiting our examination to short-period planning. In long-term planning, consideration must be given not just to production in the current period, but also to production in the future. Consequently, thought has to be given to the problem of the quantity of intermediate products which needs to be prepared currently in order that finished products can be produced in the future. In addition, the problem of whether or not the firm has the capacity to develop new techniques becomes very important. In a capitalist economy, competition will urge firms on towards new and better techniques, while at the same time encouraging them to adopt various devices in order to conceal and monopolise these techniques. In a socialist economy it is true to say that, since there are no commercial secrets, it is possible for a new technique devised by one enterprise to be used forthwith by another enterprise. On the other hand the incentive to invent new techniques is lacking in the extreme. It is very difficult to include credit for developing new techniques in the index of plan achievement: moreover, this sort of development project is accompanied by risk, so that heads of enterprises are normally very conservative as regards technical innovation. In addition, where the period of responsibility of enterprise heads is short and their turnover-rate high, they will be prone to behave shortsightedly — thinking of their own period of tenure and neglecting long-term work to do with technical development. I have decided to restrict my analysis below to the short period only; hence I shall not look at investment and technical innovation; nor, consequently, shall I deal with the dynamic problems to do with risk-bearing and so on.[4]

Next, a concept which plays a very important role in analysing the formulation of production plans is that of efficiency. This, too, was explained in the previous chapter when I discussed the production function. However, it will be useful for the analysis below if I generalise to some extent what was said there. Efficiency first becomes a problem where a number of feasible plans exist. Let us assume that there are two feasible plans $X*$ and X^0. (* and 0 are added to indicate a specific X.) Where these specific plans are put into practice the respective results $Z* = BX*$ and $Z^0 = BX^0$ will be obtained. Since $X*$ and X^0 are feasible, the results ($Z*$ and Z^0) must have fulfilled the conditions of the orders: that is

$$Z* \geqq Z \quad \text{and} \quad Z^0 \geqq \bar{Z}.$$

Let us then compare the two production plans. We are, in fact, comparing two vectors $Z*$ and Z^0, but when doing so we shall use the following symbols of equality and inequality. (Vectors are, of course, compared through their respective components.) If, for each component z_i* of $Z*$, the corresponding component z_i^0 of Z^0 is the same, that is

$$z_i* = z_i^0, \quad i = 1, \ldots n,$$

then $Z*$ is the same as Z^0, and we write $Z* = Z^0$. Next, if each component z_i* is not smaller than z_i^0 (it may be equal to it), that is

$$z_i* \geqq z_i^0, \quad i = 1, \ldots n,$$

then we write $Z* \geqq Z^0$. This is an exceedingly general relationship which includes $Z* > Z$ (that is, where $z_i* > z_i^0$ for all the i's) and $Z* \geqslant Z^0$ (explained below); at the same time, it includes $Z* = Z^0$. However, since the need will often arise to consider circumstances where $Z* \geqq Z^0$ holds but $Z* = Z^0$ does not, it is useful to have a special symbol to show this relationship of inequality. In order to do so we shall use the expression $Z* \geqslant Z^0$ (that is the relationship where $z_i* \geqq z_i^0$ is established for all sets of components, but for at least one set $z_i* > z_i^0$). Thus the efficiency of a production plan is defined in such a way as to deny the relationship $\geqslant$.

Now when comparing two production plans $X*$ and X^0, if the relationship of inequality $Z* \geqslant Z^0$ is established between their respective results Z^* and Z^0, there will exist at least one component satisfying $z_i^* > z_i^0$. If that component is a producer good, z_i^* and z_i^0 both have negative values, and thus plan X^* is more economical than plan X^0, as far as those producer goods are concerned. Next, if that component is a final product or an intermediate product, plan X^* is more productive than plan X^0. Thus X^* is either more economical or more productive than X^0 (or both), and in this case we say that plan X^0 is not efficient. That is, by an efficient production plan X^0 is meant a plan in whose results the expression $Z^* \geqslant Z^0$ will never hold, no matter what other feasible production plan X^* we compare it with.[5+]

Where a production plan X^0 is inefficient, there exists another production plan X^* which brings about the result $Z^* \geqslant Z^0$. Since X^* is either more economical or more productive, enterprises will never adopt X^0. If circumstances are such as to make one consider using X^0, X^* is in every way preferable in those same circumstances. Thus an inefficient production plan will never be adopted. That is, feasibility and efficiency are two necessary conditions for the adoption of a plan.

However, these are not sufficient conditons for the choice of any given plan. When the central planning authority hands down extremely strict orders and there is only one feasible and efficient production plan, each enterprise has no alternative but to operate that plan; but along with the development of socialist economies, leaders have come to realise that it is unwise to issue such rigorous orders. As we saw above, in order to decide on a detailed plan for the whole economy in a centralised way, the central planning authority would have to construct a huge library of modern techniques, and calculate the production frontier of the entire nation in the minutest detail. Rather than turn its hand to this irksome task with its poor expectation of worthwhile results, the authorities will limit their own role to the fixing of lower limits in the production plan. They have come to believe that, provided these lower limits are exceeded, much better results will be obtained by entrusting everything else to the discretion of enterprise heads.

Let us think, for example, of a shoe firm. We assume that an order has come from the state planning committee to the effect that at least 500,000 pairs of men's shoes, 400,000 pairs of women's shoes and 300,000 pairs of children's shoes have to be

produced. At the same time the enterprise will probably receive
some kind of instruction concerning the use of machinery, raw
materials and labour. If the order is not too high in relation to the
capacity of the enterprise, then it can probably produce some
additional pairs of shoes over and above the target which it was
given. For example, either it can produce 500,000 pairs of men's
shoes as ordered, and 600,000 pairs of wormen's shoes together
with 500,000 pairs of children's shoes; or else it can produce the
quantities of women's and children's shoes that were required,
while producing 800,000 pairs of men's shoes. That is, various
possibilities are open to the head of the enterprise, and he has the
freedom to choose from among them. In other words, where there
are a number of feasible and efficient production plans, freedom of
choice is permitted to the head of the enterprise.

Where there are a number of plans, it is necessary to rank them,
and there are a variety of ranking methods. For a long time in the
Soviet economy, enterprise results were judged by the quantity of
output. However, at a plenary session of the Central Committee of
the Communist Party in September 1965, it was decided that profits
would thereafter be taken as the index of an enterprise's perfor-
mance. Since fulfilling the plan is the first duty of Soviet heads of
enterprises, where there are two types of production operation,
one of which satisfies the planning requirements of (1) and one
which does not, they have to adopt the former — even though
profits from the latter may be greater. In this sense Soviet enterprises are non-profitmaking; but where there are various production
operations which all satisfy the planning requirements of (1), the
profit motive has come to operate effectively in the Soviet Union,
in the sense that the operation is chosen which brings the highest
profits. From 1965 onwards, a part of the profits has been paid
over to the managerial group and to employees as bonuses, and it
has been possible to use them for welfare funds and housing funds
on behalf of employees. Because of this, the earning of profits is
equally advantageous for enterprise heads and for employees.[6]

At the time of the change from the physical norm method of
planning to the profits method, there occurred in parallel — or
perhaps as a link in the process — two reforms. The first was that
the large number of planning indices which the higher planning
organs determine was drastically reduced. As was explained earlier,
the values of many of the components of the planning limitation

vector $\bar{Z}$ were determined independently by a large number of higher planning organs (or bureaux of the central planning authority). Since there was hardly any opportunity for mutual adjustment, the overall plan could often give firms mistaken instructions. For example, let us assume that the instructions given to a firm by the various higher planning organs are $\bar{z}_1^0$, $\bar{z}_2^0$ and $\bar{z}_3^0$. If $\bar{z}_3$ were then indicated not by $\bar{z}_3^0$ but by $\bar{z}_3'$, or if the planning of $\bar{z}_3$ were made completely free, the firm could carry out more efficient production satisfying the requirements $\bar{z}_1^0$, $\bar{z}_2^0$; but it is conceivably possible that because the supervisory planning organ of $\bar{z}_3$ has wrongly specified $\bar{z}_3$ at $\bar{z}_3^0$, the firm is placed in the embarrassing situation where it has to carry on inefficient production. In this sort of case the planning organ has made no more than a negative contribution, and hence making planning freer in this respect, and having the enterprise itself choose the optimum value for $\bar{z}_3$, will not only simplify the business of planning but will probably economise on resources. The freeing of $\bar{z}_i$ signifies making $\bar{z}_i$ into $-\infty$ in the case of producer goods, and into 0 in the case of final products.

Secondly, capital goods were formerly in free supply from the enterprise ministry, but now enterprises have to pay a rent for these goods. When operating according to the profits method, it becomes necessary to calculate costs, and capital costs are calculated via this rent. But as will be seen later, whether or not the profits method is used successfully depends on whether prices (including wages and rents on capital goods) are fixed rationally. For example, when rents on capital goods are fixed at an inappropriately low level, there is very little change from the era when these goods were in free supply. For this reason, the establishment of a rational price structure is a vital matter for the survival of planning via the profits method. Thus, in July 1967, the Soviet Union undertook a revision of the wholesale prices of manufactured commodities, with the intention of rationalising the price system.

Let us here represent the price of the jth good as p_j, and the prices vector, which is the horizontal tape on which prices are entered, as

$$P = (p_1, p_2 \ldots, p_n).$$

Where the jth good is machinery, then p_j is machine rentals, or the price of the capital services which the machines produce. Where the jth good is labour it represents wages. If the results Z of production plan X are measured by these prices, enterprise profits, which are the index of the results, are given by

$$PZ = \sum_{j=1}^{n} p_j z_j.$$

If we remember that in Z outputs are measured as positive values and inputs as negative values, it will be easily understood that PZ is the money value of output minus the money value of inputs — that is, enterprise profits.[7] Taking any process (for example, the ith process), let us define the price of that process by the profits obtained when it is operated at the rate of a single unit — that is by

$$q_i = \sum_{j=1}^{n} p_j b_{ji}.$$

Since $Z = BX$ and $PB = Q$,[8] we know that total profits PZ are always equal to

$$QX = \Sigma q_i x_i. \tag{2}$$

In an economy operated according to the profits method, the object of the enterprise is the maximisation of (2). When attempting maximisation, the enterprise head is not free of all restrictions: since he has to follow the instructions $\bar{Z}$ of the central planning authority, what he can accomplish on his own initiative and at his own discretion is no more than the pursuit of a constrained maximum: maximising (2) subject to condition (1).

C. Profit maximisation
This is clearly a problem in linear programming. Here let us assume that at $X = X^*$, QX takes on a maximum subject to

$$Z = BX \geqq \bar{Z}.$$

Putting $Z^* = BX^*$, PZ takes on a maximum at Z^*, subject to the same condition. Now what special characteristics does such a maximum point have? Firstly, that X^* is a feasible point is self evident. It is also an efficient point: if X^* is not an efficient point, another feasible production plan X^0 will exist with corresponding Z^0,

$$Z^0 \geqq Z^*.$$

Since in this case the prices of all goods will take on positive values ($P > 0$) the state of affairs $PZ^0 > PZ^*$ will occur, which will contradict the fact that $PZ*$ (or $QX*$) is a maximum. (Since the above vector inequality would mean that, for at least one component, Z^0 is greater than $Z*$, and for the other components Z^0 is either greater than or equal to $Z*$, then the total profit evaluated in terms of the positive prices of these elements is clearly greater in the case of Z^0 than in the case of $Z*$.) It is impossible for $X*$, which produces maximum profits in this way, to be inefficient. That is, the enterprise will choose a point on the production function, because all efficient production plans are located on it.

Where there is only one set of efficient production plans, the point of maximum profits is of course found by the criterion of efficiency alone; where there are many such sets, the enterprise has to choose from among them. Therefore we have to ask by what criteria we can distinguish the efficient point which gives maximum profits from those which do not.

Here we take $Z*$ as a point which will maximise profits, and Z^0 as an efficient point which is different from $Z*$. The results of each will be evaluated using the price P, which is common to both. From the assumption of maximisation of profits at $Z*$, we have

$$PZ^0 \leqq PZ*. \tag{3}$$

This inequality shows that all efficient points must exist either below the price plane which passes through $Z*$ or on it. Consider now a set of Z such that

$$PZ = PZ*.$$

This gives us a plane which passes through $Z*$ with prices as its direction coefficients. If with this plane we bisect the commodity space, the upper half with $PZ > PZ*$ and the lower half with $PZ \leqq PZ*$, every kind of efficient point (if we assume one exists at all) must exist in the lower half of this space. There will never be an efficient point nor a feasible point in the upper half of the space.

Using this third conditon which a maximum point must fulfil (it is called a condition of separation), we can distinguish between an efficient point which will give maximum profits and one which will not. Taking Z^0 as any efficient point, let us consider the price plane $PZ = PZ^0$ which passes through it. If in the upper half of the space bisected by this plane there exists a feasible point, say Z', Z^0 does not give maximum profits, because it does not satisfy the condition of separation. We then consider the new price plane $PZ = PZ'$ which passes through Z' and examine once again whether there is a point where production is feasible, above that price plane. Thus, if a price plane of the sort which has above it no further feasible points can be produced by a given point $Z*$ where production is feasible, then that is the efficient production point which gives the maximum profits. All efficient production points exist either on this plane or below it. That is to say, when the space is bisected by a plane which has prices as its direction coefficients, and when we cause this dividing plane to move upwards in parallel to its original position, the point of maximum profits will be situated somewhere on the critical price plane which has just absorbed the last efficient point from the space above into the space below.

In order to put the above geometrical explanation into terms more appropriate to economics, economists have used the concepts of marginal productivity, and the marginal rate of substitution. Let us designate $Z*$ as a maximum point and Z^0 as another feasible point. If from $Z*$ and Z^0 (both of them vectors in n dimensions) we exclude two components (the jth component and the kth component), and make the rest equal,[9+] then we can derive

$$p_j z_j^0 + p_k z_k^0 \leqq p_j z_j^* + p_k z_k^*$$

from (3). From this

$$\frac{z_j^0 - z_j^*}{z_k^* - z_k^0} \leqq \frac{p_k}{p_j} \tag{4}$$

can be derived (provided that we make $z_k^* > z_k^0$).

Expression (4) implies the following three classical conditions. First, let j be a final product and k a producer good. Since z_k has a negative value, the fact that $z_k^* > z_k^0$ means that Z^0 uses more inputs of good k (in absolute values) than does $Z*$. That is, the left-hand side of (4) expresses marginal productivity in the sense that it shows what additional amount of good j ought to be produced from 1 more unit of input of good k; and (4) shows that for $Z*$ to be a maximum point it is necessary that the marginal productivity of producer good k should not exceed the price ratio of producer good k to final product j.

Next, let us assume that both the jth good and the kth good are producer goods. When the input of the kth good is increased (that is when $z_k^* > z_k^0$), it is possible to economise on the input of the jth good ($z_j^0 > z_j^*$). The left-hand side of (4) expresses this marginal rate of savings on inputs (or the marginal rate of substitution of k for j). (4) shows that where the marginal rate of substitution is greater than the price ratio, profits cannot be maximised.

Lastly, for an enterprise which produces a number of finished products (men's shoes and women's shoes), (4) has the following meaning. Let both the jth good and the kth good be finished products. In the case where the output of k is being reduced ($z_k^* > z_k^0$) and that of j increased ($z_j^0 > z_j^*$), the marginal rate of substitution between j and k (the left-hand side of (4)) will not exceed their price ratio at the point of maximum profits. If at a certain point the marginal rate of substitution were to exceed the price ratio, j ought to be substituted for k by producing more of the former or less of the latter (until finally the marginal rate of substitution ceases to exceed the price ratio).

These three, classical marginal conditons are all corollaries from the above separation theorem. Thus where the production frontier surface is differentiable at the maximum point, condition (4) becomes the conventional equation between the partial derivatives and the corresponding price ratios.

Thus all efficient points will be separated on one side of the price plane which passes through the profit maximisation point. Each of these points is independent of the price system P, and as long as techniques and the instructions from the central planning authority remain unchanged, they will retain an unchanged position in the commodity space. Moreover, when the price system is given, the direction of the separating plane is determined. Since the point of maximum profits exists on the separating plane which is in the furthermost limiting position (it having been moved parallel downwards from a high position and made to approach the set of efficient points), then if the slope of the separating plane (determined by prices) changes, the point of contact (tangency) between the separating plane and the set of efficient points — that is the position of the maximum point — will change. For that reason the maximum point is relative to the price system.

Where the point of maximum profit is a salient point, the maximum point can remain unchanged for small price changes. Where the price change exceeds a certain degree, or where the maximum point is not a salient point, the maximum point will change in correspondence with price changes.[10] This means that the price system has the power to lead the enterprise. The technique which the enterprise adopts depends chiefly on what prices are established. As we shall soon see, where a rational price system does not prevail, the enterprise will be led in a mistaken direction, and errors with respect to prices will produce errors on the production side. When the socialist economy becomes successful, and its scale becomes large so that direct supervision by the central authorities becomes impossible, the problem of markets and prices comes to assume paramount importance. It is not merely under capitalism that success makes reform unavoidable.

D. The mistake of worshipping gross output

The conduct of the firm thus pursuing profits in this most rational way is like that of the greyhound chasing an imitation hare. When the hare changes direction so does the dog, and when the direction of profits changes with a change in the price structure, so too will the direction in which the enterprise is running. In socialist economies this way of looking at the conduct of the enterprise was, until very recently, regarded as a capitalist way of thinking, and thus as criminal. However, as can be seen after a little consideration, measuring the results of the enterprise by the size of its profits has, of itself, nothing to do with the problem of capitalism or socialism. Socialism is different from capitalism not because profits are not made; nor yet because the way of making profits is fundamentally different from that of capitalism, from the point of view of both production and management techniques. It is true that the first duty of the head of the enterprise in the socialist economy is the completion of the plan and not the pursuit of profits. He differs from his counterpart in capitalist economies, in having to produce so as to fulfil conditions laid down by the plan, and in not being able to produce freely. The value of output has to exceed a lower limit of a certain number of roubles, and the commodity composition of output and the time within which output has to be delivered are also specified. However, as long as these conditions alone are fulfilled, the enterprise head is thereafter at liberty to create as much profit as he can, and to increase the size of his own or his employees' bonuses. We speak of the freedom of the head of the firm in the capitalist economy, but he also works under limitations imposed by his capital equipment and the scarcity of raw materials, etc. Hence the problems confronted by heads of enterprises or entrepreneurs in both kinds of economies —

especially in the short term — are certainly not different in kind; the question is one of a difference in the degrees of freedom permitted to each. Socialism differs basically from capitalism not in whether or not profits are allowed, but in the way is which the profits gained through the efforts of the head of the enterprise and his employees are distributed. As we shall see in the next chapter, the core of socialism is to be found in the denial of the capitalist method of distribution and, endorsed by a new philosophy, in the socialist way of distributing profits to all members of society who have contributed to production.

However, as regards this view, there may well be people who say that, since the 'profits controversy', the Soviet economy has become capitalistic, and has lost its old socialist spirit. The fact is that, until the profits method was introduced, maximisation of the volume of output was pursued in the Soviet Union, and heads of enterprises and employees were remunerated in proportion with the degree to which they fulfilled the gross output requirement. It is perfectly possible to run enterprises in this way according to objectives other than the earning of profits. This is not merely so in socialist economies; it is possible even in capitalist economies (as, for example, happened in wartime), to measure the results of production not through profits but by quantities produced, and to have enterprises pursue the maximisation of gross output. This is not at all difficult to achieve, especially for a limited period such as during a war. However, if we look at the basic principles of the 'gross output method' we can see that it is nothing other than a subspecies of the profits method; it is certainly not possible to assert that it is an entirely different kind of method. But in the long run the gross output method will run into trouble. This, as we shall see below, is because it is a deficient version of the profits method.

Even under the gross output method, the need to add up goods will arise, except in the unrealistic special case where there is only one kind of good. For example, where cars are produced there is the problem of how to add up fast and slow cars; where paper is produced, how to add thick and thin paper — and so on. Two methods of addition are available. The first is the method of calculation by physical quantities; the second is the price calculation method. For example, in order to calculate the total output of a factory which produces iron sheets of different thicknesses for roofing, calculation according to weight is a physical quantity method, while calculation according to the official prices is a price method. At first sight these two methods seem in principle to be of different kinds, but as we shall see below, the physical quantity method is only an inferior version of the price method. Many scholars in Western countries have familiarised us with concrete instances from socialist economies of the type whereby, for example, iron roof-sheeting output was first calculated according to weight, so that only thick, heavy sheeting had been produced and then — this having been stopped — the method of calculation was changed to one according to area, and only thin sheeting was produced.[11] This occurred as a natural result of placing value first only on the attribute 'weight', and next only on the attribute 'size', from among the various attributes of iron roof-sheeting. Since the price of a good is an overall index of value of all its various attributes, the method of calculation by physical quantities, using either weight or area, is the same as assuming an extremely peculiar price system to apply to each kind of roof-sheet. Where there is a change from the special price system at one extreme to the special price system at the other, naturally the response will provide material for amusement.

Even if gross output is measured according to price, as will be seen below, this gross-output method presupposes a very special price system, and so will provoke an absurd response from enterprises. That is, because raw material costs and capital costs will be totally ignored under the gross-output method, enterprises will behave in the same extreme fashion as they would under the profits method if raw material prices and rentals of capital goods were equal to zero. Since raw materials are recorded as being free in the enterprise's accounts, there is no incentive for it to economise on them; it will use high-priced raw materials as lavishly as possible and produce cars or lorries or whatever at as high a price as possible (consequently, they will also be unnecessarily heavy). Nor is that all; the enterprise will hoard and hold onto its fixed equipment and its raw materials as much as it can, and there will occur the so-called freezing of the 'production fund'. In order to avoid this state of affairs, raw materials will have to be allotted an official price, and a rental on capital will have to be levied so as to encourage enterprises to reduce costs, as well as encouraging them to increase output. If a price system is implemented such that increasing the value of output by one unit and reducing costs by one unit have the same significance, it is possible, by operating enterprises according to the profits method, to get them to exert themselves in both these directions at the same time.

Whether the profits method works successfully or not depends on whether or not a rational price system is established. Where the price system does not reflect scarcities, then goods which are needed will not be produced at all, even though superfluous goods are produced in larger and larger quantities; for example, all shoes produced will be for men if, in terms of the official price, it is more profitable to produce men's shoes than women's shoes. Thus, how to define rational prices which reflect scarcities, and how to arrive at these prices, is a question of life or death importance for a socialist economy.

3

The distribution of profits

A. Distribution and ideology

As we saw above, in capitalist economies, and in the
Soviet Union and many other socialist countries, enterprises devise
their production plans so as to maximise profits. This may seem
surprising at first glance, but on looking at the actual circumstances
we find there is no decisive difference between the two types of
economy on this point. The essential difference between the two
lies rather in the distribution of the profits, which are acquired in
accordance with the same principles. On this point, the philosophy
of socialism unmistakeably refuses to admit of the usual practice
of capitalism. In socialist societies it is a crime to distribute
profits in the capitalist fashion; and for exactly the same reason it
is an offence in capitalist societies to distribute profits in the socialist way. It is the supporting ideology of a society which determines its method of distribution. The two irreconcileable phil-
osophies demand that profits revert to entirely different factors of
production.

In a capitalist economy single private individuals, or groups of
private individuals, invest the savings they may make out of their
incomes in enterprises; with the capital funds so acquired, the
enterprise buys machinery, instals equipment for production and
so on. The entrepreneur produces goods with this machinery and
equipment, but he does not make a payment in consideration of
the services this machinery and equipment render in the production
process; he appropriates such a sum in respect only of raw materials,
fuel and so on. However, the repair and maintenance expenses for
machinery and equipment are calculated as costs. The figure which
remains when costs thus calculated are subtracted from the value of
output is profits. Behind the failure to regard the contribution to
output made by machinery and equipment as a part of costs, there

is the premise contained in the capitalistic view of profits; that is: 'Machinery and equipment give rise to profits, and since we have already remunerated the other productive factors, the persons who offer these other factors have no claim to a share of profits. It is therefore proper that the whole of profits revert to the remaining factors — machniery and equipment — and that they be distributed to capitalists in accordance with the amounts of money they invested in this machinery and equipment.'

As against this, in a socialist economy the enterprise is supplied with its machinery and equipment not by individuals, but by the state through one of its higher organs, the Enterprise Ministry. Sometimes this is done gratis, but there are also cases where the enterprise has to pay interest and rent for them. How then are profits — which are the surplus remaining after wage, raw material, fuel and power costs, machinery and equipment repair and maintenance costs, and interest and rents paid to the Enterprise Ministry are subtracted from the value of output — distributed? It is clearly in contradiction to the labour theory of value, which is (part of) the ideology of socialism, to regard these surpluses as the fruits of capital goods. Consequently, profits have to be made to revert to something other than capital goods. According to the philosophy of the labour theory of value, labour alone has the power to produce goods, and the value of output has to be imputed entirely to labour — either to living labour, which participates directly in the production of a good, or to 'dead' labour which participates indirectly in production through the medium of producer goods. Consequently, we would expect profits to be zero under socialist production where there is no exploitation. The fact that profits do nevertheless derive as a result of production must be because the heads of enterprises and their employees either put into production a special effort whose value is greater than their normal salaries, or have displayed some sort of originality. For that reason, the whole of profits ought to revert not to machinery and equipment, but to the workers who have made special efforts or the enterprise head whose supervisory capabilities have been outstanding, and they ought to be distributed among employees and officials as rewards.

It should be borne in mind that it was a long time before socialist economies came to be operated according to this view of profits. In the Soviet Union before the changeover to the so-called profits method, physical gross output was the main standard of plan achievement. The authorities also used cost reduction and the wages fund, etc. as indications of achievement, but in this system the level of physical output persistently took pride of place. At the September 1965 plenary session of the Committee of the Communist Party, Kosygin made a proposal to include the level of product sales as a subject of enterprises' plans, instead of the level of physical gross output. At the same time it was allowed that a part of profits be distributed to heads of enterprises and employees as bonuses.

Even before that, enterprise heads were allowed to keep back a part of profits as an enterprise 'fund' and they were allowed to use it for bonuses. However, the majority of enterprises did not have funds accumulated out of their own profits, and in those that had them their value was small. The greater part of bonuses and incentive payments did not come from profits, but was furnished out of the wages fund. Moreover, since the size of disbursements for bonuses depended mainly on how far it could produce in excess of its indicated gross output target, each enterprise hoped to be given as easy a production target as possible, and as large a wages fund as possible.[1]

As a result inducements towards efficient operations within the firm were very much lacking; but under the profits method the source of finance for bonuses was simplified, and a part of profits was transferred to the enterprise fund, to be used for paying out bonuses to employees. At the same time, in order to ensure that the production fund was used effectively, a reform was carried out which introduced a charge for the use of capital goods which had hitherto been supplied gratis.[2]

The fact that if there is no machinery production cannot take place, and the fact that a production plan which exceeds the capacities of the given equipment and machinery is not feasible, are not peculiar to capitalist economies, but are equally true for socialist economies. Furthermore, the fact that special endeavour and originality on the part of workers and entrepreneurs are the causes of increases in productivity is true in capitalist countries as well as in socialist countries. That is, the factors which prescribe the technical feasibility of a production plan are the same in both capitalist and socialist economies. Both types of economy comply with the same technical limitations. Consequently, if the same price system were to be established in both, we would expect the same techniques (processes) to produce the same profits; and if the quality and quantity of machines, and the quality and quantity of labour to be used were the same, we would expect the enterprise in a capitalist economy and that in a socialist economy to formulate the same production plan and produce the same results. However, each type of economy believes in a different social philosophy, and so each values differently the contribution of the factors which participate in production. As a result of this, profits in the two types of economy are distributed in different ways to different people.

Thus in actual societies, it is ideology which is the most fundamental factor in determining the distribution of profits, and, at first sight, there appears to be an irreconcileable difference between the capitalist and socialist methods of distribution. However, if we consider interposing a third principle between the two — what I shall call below the principle of rational distribution, which is a mathematical principle not dependent on any ideology — then bridging the gap between the two is not all that difficult. The fact that, as a result of rational distribution, a share of profits goes to both labour and capital, as well as to other productive factors, implies that these factors have been given a low price in relation to the price of output. For that reason, if we defined the price of labour, capital and other productive factors so as to include from the outset the profits which are later distributed as bonuses, then, as long as the enterprise carries on the same productive activity, we would expect profits to be zero. However, under these new factor prices, a different technique may appear to be advantageous, and so, by undertaking different productive activity, the enterprise may be able to make profits even under the new factor prices. If we assume this to be so, then these profits, too, have to be distributed rationally between productive factors. Factor prices will once again be revised so as to include bonuses beforehand. By repeatedly conducting this revising operation, equilibrium factor prices will eventually be derived (i.e., factor prices under which the maximum profits of the enterprise will be zero). When profits are zero, it makes no difference whether they go entirely to capitalists or to labour, or are divided between them, so that rational distribution accords perfectly with either capitalist distribution or socialist distribution.

However, since actual prices are not necessarily equilibrium prices, we cannot say that capitalist or socialist distribution is rational under real world prices. On the other hand, it is not possible for either system to diverge very widely from a rational distribution. As I shall explain in more detail later in this chapter, an irrational distribution of profits will not receive the support of the people who contribute to profit creation, and sooner or later the co-operation of dissatisfied elements will be lost. This tendency will increase along with the development of a faculty for criticism in the members of the society. We are able to say this more particularly about capitalist distribution, but it is clear that, in the case of socialist distribution also, there has to be prudence in not over-rewarding entrepreneurs and employees, and capital goods have to be used effectively. Thus both systems posses a tendency to move towards a just and rational distribution, and this fact in itself means that the distance between the two will narrow. We can say that, as with production, so with distribution too, there is a tendency for the principles of enterprise management under both systems to come to resemble each other more closely.

B. A rational imputation of value

On what principles of imputation is a rational distribution based? Before proceeding to an examination of this question, it will be convenient to summarise the analysis of the formulation of a rational production plan which we conducted in the previous chapter, since it is very closely related to the present problem.

In both the capitalist and the socialist economy, the enterprise has to produce within the limitations imposed by the number of machines it has (or the number it is allotted by the central planning authority or the Enterprise Ministry). These constraints were expressed in the last chapter by the restriction vector $\bar{Z}$. The quantity of producer goods and machine capacities permitted to the enterprise are entered as minus values in the appropriate places in $\bar{Z}$, and the lower limit to the outputs the enterprise has been ordered to produce are entered as plus values. Where the enterprise can purchase raw materials etc. from the market at the going price without restriction, then, since there are no constraints on the quantities of producer goods which can be used, we can think of the value of the limit on these goods in $\bar{Z}$ as being $-\infty$. Again, when the planning authorities assign no norm to the quantity of production, the value of the lower limit to this quantity in $\bar{Z}$ can be designated as 0. Next the list of technical coefficients of the techniques (or processes) which the firm can employ — the so-called 'catalogue of techniques' or 'book of blueprints' — is shown as B. In B output coefficients are shown with positive values and input coefficients with negative values. If we make X the rate of operation vector which expresses the intensities of operation of each process, then X has to satisfy the conditon

$$BX \geqq \bar{Z} \tag{1}$$

The price vector is shown by P. Goods with which the enterprise is associated are first final products, secondly intermediate products (hereafter, for simplicity, I shall ignore intermediate products), thirdly raw materials, fourthly machinery and fifthly labour. Prices for final products and raw materials are given, but there may be no prices for the services of certain kinds of machine and for certain kinds of labour. That is, there are two types of machine: those which the enterprise leases from the Enterprise Ministry or other sources, and those over which it already has proprietorial rights. It has to pay a rental for the first kind of machine, but it need pay no rental for second kind, however intensively it uses them. The rental is entered in the price vector P as the price of the services the machine produces, but the services of owned machines are valued in vector P as 0.[3+] There is also more than one kind of labour. Many kinds of labour, from the unskilled to the entrepreneurial, are listed in the catalogue of goods. A different rate of payment is made to each, but no price exists for an especially positive approach or special care shown by the labourer in the work process; nor does one exist for any particular initiative or powers of leadership exhibited by supervisors. However, it is clear that productivity will be different depending on whether or not this positiveness and care, special initiative, etc., is present. Moreover, since it is not possible to make use of these qualities without limit, they too, ought to be listed in the catalogue of goods. Thus the restricting conditions in equation (1) above ought to be regarded as including limiting conditons relating to these qualities. However, since they have no prices, the components in the vector P corresponding to them are 0.

If we value each process with this sort of price, we can derive each process's profits potential. That is, if we make

$$PB = Q$$

each component of vector Q will show the profits deriving when the appropriate process is operated at a rate of one unit. For that reason, the gross profits are QX when processes are operated at the intensities X, and by the most rational choice of techniques is meant the determining of the intensities of operations X so as to maximise QX under the conditions of (1). Let us call the rational operation vector so determined X^*.

As we saw above, the problem of the most rational choice of techniques is the problem of how to distribute the given $\bar{Z}$ between processes. It has a very close relationship with the (profits) imputation problem. That is, the imputation problem is: how to distribute profits Q among the components; and in the sense that the distribution problem consists of allocating a given $\bar{Z}$ between processes, or a given Q between factors of production, the two problems are formally of the same type. However, a price has already been paid in respect of raw materials, ordinary labour (including supervisory labour of the entrepreneur type), and the hire of machinery, among the factors of production. But since these prices are not necessarily fair prices, not only are profits distributed amongst such factors of production as owned machinery, the labour of employees who take especial care, the initiative of entrepreneurs, etc., which have not yet been remunerated, but an additional payment out of 'profits' should be made to those factors of production for which a price has already been paid, where that price was unjustly low. Here let v_j be the amount which a unit of factor of production j ought to receive as a share of profits and V the vector made by v_j. Generally, p_j is paid as a price to factor j; and a bonus v_j is also paid additionally out of profits. As already stated p_j is 0 in respect of certain factors of production, and, as we shall see later, v_j is 0 in respect of other kinds of factors.

What then is a 'rational' way of achieving the reversion of profits QX^* to factors of production? Firstly, where factors of production j receive profits at the rate of v_j per unit, the aggregate total of profits shared by all the factors of production of which the enterprise can make use is $- V\bar{Z}$. (Here a minus sign is used because we restore the quantity of factors of production entered with a minus value in $\bar{Z}$ to their original plus value.[4+]) Since the profits earned (QX^*) have to be distributed between the factors of production which contributed to their existence until they are totally exhausted, earned profits and distributed profits must be equal. That is, the following must hold:

$$QX^* = -V\bar{Z}. \tag{2}$$

Next, where the above relationship is established for total profits but not for those of each individual process, the profits earned by a single process will not all be imputed to the factors of production which were the inputs of that process — a part reverts to factors which were inputs in other processes. The result will be irrational, since some of the factor inputs in given processes will be rewarded at less than the value of their contribution, while others in other processes receive more than this value, so that there is an exploitation of some factors by others. For that reason, a relationship has to be established for each process whereby profits are imputed to the factors of production in that process without a residue. That is, the relationship ought to be established for all the i's whereby the profits q_i, which accrue from running process i at a rate of one unit, must not exceed the share of profits $-Vb_i$ (here b_i is the ith column of B, the matrix of technical coefficients) which the factor inputs of that process ought to receive. (If they do exceed it, then a part of q_i will revert not to the factor inputs of that process, but to factors which are inputs in other processes. This is irrational.) If we write this in terms of vectors and matrices, it implies that we must establish the inequality:

$$-VB \geqq Q. \tag{3}$$

We shall call an inputation which satisifes (2) and (3) a rational imputation. In conditions (2) and (3), which are necessary for this to be so, we regard B, Q and $\bar{Z}$ as already known. The problem is to find a vector V which satisfies these conditions. If such a vector exists, then profits will rationally be distributed at the rates v_j to factors of production j, without producing any residual. The v_j are called shadow prices. Shadow prices are not market prices, but merely prices which are internal to the enterprise; where these prices are established and profits distributed according to them, profits which are the fruits of production will revert justly to those who contributed to that production. Where they are not established and used, the profits from certain processes will not revert to the factors of production engaged in that process, but will irrationally revert to factors of production engaged in other processes.

C. The duality of rationality

Now what kind of laws do these rules of imputation imply for shadow prices to comply with? This problem is closely related to the so-called duality theorem of linear programming, which makes it clear that rationality in the enterprise's conduct over inputs and outputs (that is, problem 1: maximising QX under inequality (1)), and rationality in the assessment of the value of factors of production (that is, problem 2: determining shadow prices in accordance with rules (2) and (3)), are formally in a dual relationship. At first glance, while the first problem is a problem in linear programming, the second seems to be merely a problem of inequality which is not accompanied by maximisation or minimisation; so that there appears to be no formal duality whatsoever between them. However, on closer examination, there is a problem of minimisation hidden behind problem 2. Thus, once we are successful in stripping off this mask, it is not very difficult to answer the question: 'In accordance with what laws are shadow prices determined?'

First, since the components of vector X show the rates of operation of each process, they take on a positive value (or at worst, become zero); for that reason, the direction of the inequality sign will not change even if we multiply (3) by X. Similarly, since components of vector V express the shadow prices of the factors of production (these are positive or zero; they will not be negative), the direction of the inequality will not change, even if we multiply (1) by V. If we here let X^* be a special X so as to maximise QX under (1), then X^* will, of course, satisfy (1). Consequently, if we multiply (1) by V, then

$$VBX^* \geqq V\bar{Z}. \tag{4}$$

Next, if we multiply (3) by this special X^*, we will derive

$$- VBX^* \geqq QX^*. \tag{5}$$

From (4) and (5) we derive

$$QX^* \leqq - V\bar{Z}. \tag{6}$$

The left-hand side QX^* of this inequality is a fixed value, while the $-V\bar{Z}$ of the right-hand side depends on V (since V is an arbitrary, non-negative vector). For that reason, $-V\bar{Z}$ may be either large or small, but it cannot be made less than QX^*. That is, QX^* is the lower limit to the values that can be taken on by $-V\bar{Z}$.

However, conditon (2), which is the first requirement for a rational imputation of value, requires that $-V\bar{Z}$ has to take on this lower limit. Consequently, our problem with the imputation of value is the same as the linear programming problem of minimising $-V\bar{Z}$ under inequality (3). That is, in order to distribute rationally the profits derived from the maximising problem of making $\bar{Z}$ a restriction vector and QX an objective function between the components of restriction vector $\bar{Z}$, we must solve another linear programming problem (a minimising problem) of making Q the restriction vector and $-V\bar{Z}$ the objective function. Thus a shadow minimising problem is hidden behind a maximising problem. Unless this problem is clarified and solved in the glass-walled computing room, fairness and rationality in the distribution of profits will not be preserved. However, as I shall explain later, the minimisation problem involved in the imputing of values to the factors of prod-production in problem 2 is deliberately not solved rationally in either capitalist or socialist economies, both of which are plagued by ideological considerations (although problem 1, the maximising of profits, is solved rationally).

Now what relationship exists between the solution of the two problems — the maximising problem and the hidden minimising problem which ought to be its dual? That is, is it not possible to know how the one problem must be solved, on the premise that the other problem was solved in a particular way? Making clear the laws concerning the relationship of solutions is not only useful simply for deciding upon whether or not a given state of affairs is the solution to the problem; it can also be thought of as being extremely instructive when clarifying the nature of the rationality of which we are thinking when we refer to 'a rational imputation of profits'.

It is easy to derive information on the solution to one of the problems, by taking as a premise information on the solution to the other extremum problem with which it is paired. The solutions to the two problems are normally meshed together like gears by the two laws — or rules — which are called the 'rule of free goods' and the 'rule of profitability'. These two rules are certainly necessary in order that (6) be valid as an equality, as is required by (2); conversely, we know that a state of affairs which satisfies these two rules is certainly the solution to the problem.

These two rules are derived in the following way. In order to remove the inequality from (6), we must also remove it from (4) and (5),and make all these formulae into equalities. First, in order that (4) be valid as an equality, we must affix shadow prices of zero to factors of production j, of the sort where

$$\Sigma b_{ji}x_i^* > \bar{z}_j. \tag{7}$$

Secondly, in order that (5) be valid as an equality, we have to determine a shadow price system V so that, for processes with $x_i^* > 0$,

$$-\Sigma v_j b_{ji} = q_i. \tag{8}$$

For it would become impossible to have (4) in the form of an equality (as the left-hand side of (4) would certainly be larger than the right-hand side) if we had attached positive shadow prices v_i to factors of production j where (7) is true (since it is clear from (1) that other factors k, for which $\Sigma b_{ki}x_i^* < \bar{z}_k$, do not exist); in the same way, (5) would become an inequality if the inequality $-\Sigma v_j b_{ji} > q_i$, instead of equation (8), were valid for processes where $x_i^* > 0$, because from (3) there are no processes where $-\Sigma v_j b_{jh} < q_h$.

Thus in order to impute profits QX^* rationally and without residual to factors of production, shadow prices have to be determined so as to comply with the following two rules. (i) The shadow prices of goods of the sort whose supply exceeds their demand (goods of the kind for which inequality (7) is valid), are fixed at zero (the rule of free goods).[5+] That is, since there exists an excess of supply over demand, it is as if there were no restriction on the use of these factors; the enterprise regards them in the same way as it regards air — as free goods — and there is no need to pay positive shadow prices v_j for them. (That is, there is no need to allot profits to these factors.) For example, as with raw materials (and perhaps certain kinds of labour), since the $\bar{z}_j$ of those goods which the enterprise can purchase freely on the market in just the quantities it desires is $-\infty$, it will simply pay market prices p_j for these goods, and there is no necessity to pay an additional v_j from profits (v_j is 0). The paying of a positive v_j is limited to factors where the $\bar{z}_j$ permitted to the enterprise is being fully utilised — that is, factors where the left-hand side and the right-hand side of (7) are equal. (ii) The enterprise does not adopt those processes which are unprofitable according to cost calculations in terms of actual prices p_j and shadow prices v_j — those of the sort where the left-hand side of (8) is larger than the right-hand side (the rule of profitability). For that reason, processes which the firm is actually employing (processes of the sort where the rate of operation x_i^* is positive) will certainly be profitable processes (that is, only processes of the sort whereby the equality (8) is valid). A rational imputation of profits must comply with these two rules; and, since the converse is also true, we can decide whether or not actual capitalist or socialist imputation is irrational by examining whether they comply with these rules.

In the above explanation no special attention was paid to products. However, products were entered in the techniques matrix B and the restriction vector $\bar{Z}$ as positive items. Since in a capitalist economy there is no limit to the quantity of output, the relevant components in $\bar{Z}$ are 0; but since in the socialist economy norms are laid down to the effect that output quantities must be at least of a certain size, the relevant components of $\bar{Z}$ may take on positive values. Since, in relation to products, the left-hand side of (7) shows the gross quantity of output from processes, (7) is automatically satisfied in a capitalist economy as long as output quantities are positive (as $\bar{z}_j$ is 0). Thus the shadow prices of products are 0 by the rule of free goods. That is, there are no prices which are internal to the enterprise which ought to be added to market prices. However, in socialist economies there are norms, and so even if the gross quantity of output were positive, (7) would not necessarily be valid. When norms are set at low levels (7) will probably be established; but when they are set at high levels, enterprises can produce only the quantity of output which just meets the norm, and the inequality sign of (7) will be replaced by an equality sign. If (7) is valid we can derive $v_j = 0$ by the rule of free goods; but where (7) becomes an equality we cannot apply this rule and perhaps $v_j > 0$ will occur.

What will the fact that shadow prices for products are positive mean? First, it is clear that the occurrence of positive shadow prices for products originated in the assigning of high norms by the central planning authority. However, whether given levels of norms are high or low cannot be decided absolutely; they are all decided relative to the prices of products. If we had made the market price or the official price of a product not p_j but larger than $p_j + v_j$, the enterprise would have had a strong incentive to produce that good, and would probably have had no difficulty in meeting its given norm. That is, where the official price of a product is above $p_j + v_j$, (7) holds for the product; consequently the norm is not too high for the enterprise, and the shadow price is 0. The official price set at $p_j + v_j$ is the one at the cirtical point where the corresponding shadow price changes from zero to positive.

Actually, however, the official price is not given at $p_j + v_j$, but merely at p_j, and so the price is too low for the firm and the norm a difficult one. In these circumstances one thing the head of the enterprise can do is to proceed to the central planning authority and petition for a revision of prices. Another is to set his own internal prices (shadow prices) in such a way as to produce the same effect as if official prices had been revised.[6+] This is always possible.

Let us call the shadow price vector required here V^*, and let the first component of $\bar{Z}$ be for the product and all the rest for producer goods. (Where there are two or more kinds of product we can repeat the procedure given below.) We shall call V_1^* the vector in which all components of V^* but the first are substituted by 0; the vector where only the first component of V^* is substituted by 0 we shall call V_2^*. We decompose $\bar{Z}$ into $\bar{Z}_1$ and $\bar{Z}_2$ in the same way. ($\bar{Z}_1$ is the vector where all components of $\bar{Z}$ but the first are substituted by 0, and $\bar{Z}_2$ the vector where only the first component is substituted by 0.) Besides this, we decompose the production coefficient matrix B into B_1 and B_2 in the same way. By definition

$$Q = PB = PB_1 + PB_2 \tag{9}$$

When we multiply both sides of this expression by v_1^*/p_1 (v_1^* being the first component of V_1^*), and add it to $- V^*B \gtreqless Q$, we have, in view of the equation[7] $(v_1^*/p_1)PB_1 = V^*B_1$,

$$-\left(V^* - \frac{v_1^*}{p_1}P\right)B_2 \gtreqless \left(1 + \frac{v_1^*}{p_1}\right)Q. \tag{10}$$

In the same way, if we multiply the two sides of (9) by X^* and then by v_1^*/p_1, and add them to both sides of $QX^* = - V^*\bar{Z} = - V^*(B_1X^* + B_2X^*)$, we can derive

$$-\left(V^* - \frac{v_1^*}{p_1}P\right)B_2 X^* = \left(1 + \frac{v_1^*}{p_1}\right)QX^*. \tag{11}$$

Here, if we put

$$V^{**} = \frac{p_1}{v_1^* + p_1}\left(V^* - \frac{v_1^*}{p_1}P\right),$$

then from (10) and (11) we obtain

and

$$-V^{**}B_2 \geqq Q \tag{12}$$

$$QX^* = -V^{**}B_2 X^* \tag{13}$$

These will both give a rational distribution of profits to producer goods at the new shadow prices V^{**}. The new shadow prices for products are 0. The new shadow prices of producer goods whose old shadow prices were comparatively high (that is, $v_i^*/v_1^* > p_i/p_1$) are positive; the new shadow prices of producer goods whose old shadow prices were comparatively low (that is $v_i^*/v_1^* < p_i/p_1$) are negative. As a result of this adjustment in shadow prices, a rational distribution is possible. However, at this time the rule of free goods is not valid, because negative shadow prices exist. Consequently, for producer goods whose supply is in excess of their demand, we have to distinguish the quantity which has been used up in actual production from the existing quantity. Thus the condition for rational distribution (13) shows that it is that part of producer goods which is used in actual production which is relevant to the distribution of profits at the new shadow prices, and that the part which is not used is irrelevant to this distribution, even though it exists.[8+] If I were to comment further, it would be to point out that producer goods with negative shadow prices not only fail to receive a distribution from profits; they have to make a contribution to them. It is natural to think of this as being because the market prices of these sorts of producer goods are comparatively high ($v_i^*/v_1^* < p_i/p_1$). However, since the net income after this contribution has been subtracted from market prices is

$$p_i + v_i^{**} = (p_i + v_i^*)\frac{p_1}{(v_1^* + p_1)},$$

it will certainly not be negative.

When profits are distributed in this way through the new shadow prices, the rule of free goods will not be satisfied; but on the other hand the rule of profitability will. That is, there will be no process employed of the sort which will satisfy (12) by the strict inequality sign $>$. For, the components of X^* are positive or zero; and so, if such a process is employed, the impossible circumstances arise where the profits distributed are greater than those produced; (13) requires profits to be distributed without residue.

In the above we first solved problem 1, which was to maximise profits QX under (1); then we sought the solution to problem 2, which was how to decide on shadow prices, on the basis of our knowledge of the solution to problem 1. However, this is not the only method available. We can also, conversely, solve problem 2, and then proceed to solve problem 1 on the basis of our knowledge of that solution. That is, we now consider the problem of minimising $-V\bar{Z}$ under (3), and call the solution V^*. If we substitute V^* into (3) and multiply both sides by an arbitrary, non-negative vector X, we obtain

$$- V^*BX \geqq QX, \tag{14}$$

and if we multiply (1) by the non-negative vector V^*, we obtain

$$- V^*BX \leqq - V^*\bar{Z}. \tag{15}$$

We know from (14) and (15) that QX can never exceed $-V^*\bar{Z}$. For that reason, problem 1, which requires us to maximise QX, is equivalent to the problem of finding an X such that $-V^*\bar{Z} = QX$. At an X of this sort (which we call X^*), both (14) and (15) have to hold as equalities. For that reason, we know that processes such as i where

$$-\sum_j v_j^* b_{ij} > q_i,$$

will never be employed (that is $x_i^* = 0$), and that for goods which have been given positive shadow prices, v_j^*, the equation

$$-\sum_i b_{ji} x_i^* = - \bar{z}_j$$

must be valid. The former of these two rules gives us the rule of profitability; from the antithesis of the latter we obtain the rule of free goods which states that 'the shadow prices of free goods (factors of production whose demand falls short of their supply) are zero'.

D. The irrationality of ideology

In the previous section we demonstrated that a rational choice of techniques and a rational distribution of profits are in a dual relationship. This means that in the same way that a planning problem has to be solved mathematically in order to formulate a production plan which maximises profits, so, too, a mathematical programme is needed in order to distribute profits rationally. Mathematics is completely impartial on the problem of the rate at which to distribute profits between factors. While permitting, as a possibility, all factors of production to have positive shadow prices, it will solve the minimisation problem (or, which is the same thing, solve the inequality problem in compliance with the rule of free goods and the rule of profitability); and, as a result of the calculation, it will decide which factors really have positive shadow prices and which have shadow prices of 0. When calculating, all preconceptions will be eliminated, and until the computer produces the solution the possibility remains that all factors will share in profits.

In contrast to this, in actual capitalist or socialist economies, it is contrived on *a priori* grounds that certain factors of production will participate in the distribution of profits, whether or not they are in scarce supply. As I said at the beginning, the whole of profits in a socialist economy are looked upon as being the result of special endeavour or initiative on the part of the workers or heads of enterprise, and none is imputed to capital goods. However, this labour-theory-of-value ideology is only justified where all capital goods are free goods — a utopian stage which no socialist economy has yet attained. In all other cases, it is impossible to assert whether the shadow prices of capital goods are positive or zero, unless we actually solve the minimisation problem.

Of course, in capitalist economies profits are, as a rule, ascribed to capital; but since bonuses are paid to labour too, it would seem that it is possible for all factors of production to share in profits. However, if we look at the kind of distribution which takes place in the following special situation, the irrationality of capitalist distribution will at once be apparent. We shall consider an electronics firm where there is sufficient machinery and equipment, as well as raw materials and labour, but where a shortage of technicians causes a bottleneck. It is certainly possible for this sort of firm to earn profits; but in this case all capital goods, raw materials and labour are 'free goods', and only the services of technicians are scarce goods to the firm. For this reason, without the need for any calculation, it is clear that the mathematical solution to the problem of the rational imputation of profits is that they should all be imputed to technicians. However, the actual solution is likely not to be as calculated. Probably, the greater part of profits will be imputed to machinery — that is to the capitalists who own the machinery — and no more than a small part will be bestowed upon the technicians. This is the state of affairs even in the case where a mental calculation alone suffices; and so we are compelled to say that there is absolutely no guarantee, in other cases, that capitalistic distribution will meet the criteria for rationality.

In an actual distribution of profits on ideological grounds, one specific part of the factors of production is assigned a shadow price of 0 before the problem of imputation is solved mathematically and objectively. There is no (logical) basis for doing this; there may at best exist a particular ideological sympathy. Once this sort of forced assigning is done (that is, the fixing of shadow prices at values which differ from the mathematical solutions), even if for only some of the factors, the whole system of the distribution of profits will, as a result, be affected. Of course, in this case too, profits will be imputed to factors without a residue. That is

$$QX^* = -V\bar{Z}.$$

However, V has a value other than that of the mathematical solution, and hence the second condition for a rational imputation — that is (3) — is not valid for this V. For that reason, there must exist at least one process of the kind

$$-\Sigma v_j b_{ji} < q_i. \tag{16}$$

There are three possibilities in connection with these processes i. The first is where the firm employs these kinds of processes (that is $x_i^* > 0$), and at the same time also employs processes h, whereby

$$-\Sigma v_j b_{jh} > q_h. \tag{17}$$

The second is where the firm employs processes i of the sort described by (16), but does not employ processes h of the sort described by (17) (or else attempting to employ them, finds they do not exist). The third case is where processes i of the sort described by (16) do exist but are not employed ($x_i^* = 0$); the firm employs only processes where

$$-\Sigma v_j b_{jh} = q_h. \tag{18}$$

Of course in this case it does not matter if processes described by (17) exist. However, unless processes described by (16) are employed, those described by (17) must not be employed. This is because not employing processes described by (16), while employing those described by (17), would mean that the total of profits $-V\bar{Z}$ received by factors of production was larger than those QX^* which are produced. Such a distribution is therefore impossible.

In contrast to this, where the firm employs processes i, described by (16), it may or may not employ processes h, described by (17). First, where processes h are employed, as in the first of the above three possibilities, the total profits produced by processes i are not divided between these factors of production which were employed in processes i. Processes i give rise to further, surplus profits; on the other hand, the factors of production in processes h receive profits over and above those which they produced. But overall, produced profits have to be the same as received profits. This means that there is a transfer of profits from processes i to processes h. On the basis of this transfer, the factors working in processes h acquire profits greater than those they produce, while those working in processes i have to be content with less than they produce. Unless the factors of production are all owned by one person or are jointly owned by a multitude of people, the owners of factors will not tolerate this kind of irrationality in distribution for long. The owners of factors working in processes i, which receive a reward less than the profits they contributed, will demand that distribution be made fairly. If these demands are not satisfied, they will attempt to resist by lowering their own productivity.

Next, let us turn to the second case. Here the enterprise employs processes i, described by (16), but not processes h, described by (17). It is clear that if processes are employed which take forms other than that of (16), an equivalence between produced and received profits must be established for each individually. For this reason, surplus profits generated in processes i have to be imputed to factors of production which were not used in any process (that is, the unused part of factors of production which are free goods). Thus in the second case the rule of free goods will not be complied with. Even free goods will have a positive shadow price v_j, which will produce the irrational state of affairs where the unused part of exactly similar factors of production will receive the same share in profits as the part which was used. Here the kind of irrationality which arose in the first case, where a part of the profits of processes *i* accrued to processes *h*, will arise between processes *i* and unused factors. If the owner of the factors of production which worked in processes *i* and the owner of the unused factors of production is the same person, the loss from one pocket will be compensated for by a gain in the other, so that the irrationality will not come to the surface. Where they are not the same person, the owners of factors engaged in processes *i* will demand that the profits they produced should revert to themselves.

Finally, in the third case, where processes are evaluated according to ideologically determined shadow prices, there will exist processes *i*, described by (16); but since, in practice, these sorts of processes *i* will not be employed, there will be no profits deriving from them. Consequently, the irrationality of the kind seen in the first and second cases, where factors of production employed in processes *i* were exploited by other factors, will not arise. That is, in this case there exist processes of the three kinds (16), (17) and (18), but in practice, only processes of the type (18) are employed.[9] For that reason, factors employed in production share in profits according to their contribution, and there is no irrationality. However, in this case too, what appears as rational is only surface deep; it is clear that the firm is ready to employ processes (16) which enable it to allocate profits at shadow prices with positive surpluses, and so irrationality exists in disguised form.

This can be explained in the following way. Where the firm pursues the maximisation of profits with the $\bar{Z}$ given, let us suppose that the optimum rate of operation X^* satisfies the above conditions (namely, that the operating rates for processes (16) and (17) are 0, and those for processes (18) positive). In this case we may make a small change in the constraint vector from $\bar{Z}$ to Z' so that the optimum rates of operation for processes of the type (16) become positive. If, in spite of this change in $\bar{Z}$, we hold V fixed, the third case will easily change into the first or the second, and the overt irrationality mentioned above will arise. For that reason, when $\bar{Z}$ changes, V cannot remain fixed and will have to change; but even when the change in $\bar{Z}$ is very small, the change in V cannot be small. For strict inequalities of the type (16) must hold after any small change in V because they were fulfilled at the original V before the change. Thus, as long as the change in V remains very small, either case one or case two will arise after the very small change in $\bar{Z}$. Only in the third case is it possible for a V, other than the optimum solution which is calculated mathematically, to have a rational imputation (or for each individual process to satisfy the condition that profits revert without excess or shortfall to the factors of production participating in production). But even in this case, where the change in $\bar{Z}$ is very small, this V, and all the Vs which are adjacent to it, will bring about an irrational imputation. That is, the third case will come about when V takes on an extremely special value for a given $\bar{Z}$, and where a small change in $\bar{Z}$ takes place, a large change in V must take place, until it achieves another special value corresponding to the changed $\bar{Z}$ (this shows that the apparent rationality is an unstable one). Thus there exists no guarantee that the actual (real world) ideologically determined shadow price vector V will conform with this extremely special V, or with the mathematical solution V^*. Consequently, we must consider that the probability of conformity between them is exceedingly low. From this we must conclude that, be it a capitalist or be it a socialist economy, while an enterprise persists in an 'ideological' distribution of profits, there is little possibility that this distribution among factors of production will be a rational one. When an irrational distribution is enforced because of the intrusion of ideology the owners of those factors which do not receive a share in profits in accordance with their contribution will protest; their productivity will eventually decline, and the enterprise will not be able to obtain its scheduled profits. In order to encourage all factors not to lower their productivity, both capitalist and socialist economies must dispense with ideology and distribute profits in accordance with the optimum solution mathematically derived.

As we saw above, two kinds of prices are paid to factors of production; firstly prices p_j as costs and then, in addition, shadow prices v_j out of profits. For firms in a capitalist economy (ignoring depreciation charges), prices p_j are 0 for machinery, equipment etc. which the firm owns, and the total profits which are calculated as attributable to machinery and equipment are distributed proportionately to each capitalist in accordance with the sums invested. If we assume that the enterprise is able to purchase raw materials and fuel from the market, without limitation and at a specified price, no profits are imputed to them (the rule of free goods): for them $v_j = 0$. For many kinds of labour (including labour of the supervisory type such as firm managers), not only are market prices p_j paid, but bonuses at the rates v_j are paid out of profits. Among them, shadow prices cannot take on arbitrary values; they must take on optimal values determined mathematically. On the other hand market prices or official prices are allowed to take on any value. That is, for an arbitrary, given price system $P = (p_1, \ldots, p_n)$, the profits of each process $Q = (q_1, \ldots, q_m)$ are determined; the point of profit maximisation X^* and the shadow prices V^* are determined relative to Q and the production restriction vector $\bar{Z}$, as the solutions to a maximising and a minimising linear programming problem respectively. P is market prices in a capitalist economy; in a socialist economy it is official (government) prices. It is true that it may take on arbitrary values in the linear programming problem for determining the production plan; but where they are arbitrary prices which do not reflect the scarcities of goods, the production plan of the firm will be led in a direction which is unrelated to these scarcities through its reliance on these prices. When goods come to be produced with no regard for scarcities, even if each firm maximises its profits and even if the profits of each firm are distributed rationally, we cannot say that society as a whole is engaging in rational production. A single firm can formulate an efficient production plan with any arbitrary price system; but the price system must not be arbitrary from the point of view of society as a whole.

The analysis of this chapter ends with the above conclusion; but finally, by way of a precaution, there is something I should like to stress once again. As I said at the beginning, the profits of firms are not, in practice, distributed among factors of production in accordance with the rational principles of imputation outlined above. However, if distribution is to be rational, then distribution rates — that is, shadow prices of factors of production — ought not to be determined conventionally, according to the prejudices which constitute ideology; they ought to be determined objectively and mathematically as the solution to a mathematical programming problem. Thus it is important to understand that the mathematical programming problem of the determination of shadow prices is common to both capitalist and socialist economies. Consequently, as long as the trend of enterprises in both types of economy is towards a rational distribution of profits, it can be assumed that the differences and contradictions exhibited by the present-day 'ideological' methods of distribution in the two types of economy will gradually be harmonised and extinguished, so that a number of economies will approach a single, calculated system of distribution. The signs of this are already evident in some capitalist economies. In the postwar period Japan has established the tradition that a substantial part of profits is more or less regularly paid to workers as a bonus. Since 1964 the Dutch trade unions have been involved not only in the usual wage negotiations but also in bargaining for a capital-sharing payment which is paid to each worker in the form of non-transferable fixed interest obligations, until he finally receives his total accumulation in cash when he retires.[10]

The socialist counterparts of these are also evident in the Soviet Union. In 1965, as a result of the advocacy of the economists Nemchinov, Liberman, etc., 'use charges' began to be levied on the production funds of enterprises. In our terms these 'use charges' can be regarded as the official prices for the services of capital. The 'use charges' were introduced with the intention of placing the responsibility for the effective use of the production fund on the enterprise. However, as long as the levels of the 'use charges' fixed by the government do not coincide with values for p_i which would produce rational shadow prices of 0 for v_1, then they cannot completely fulfil the role intended for them. The reason is that, although the rational shadow prices for the services of capital v_i are positive (and consequently, although it is rational to allocate profits to the state in addition to the 'use charges' p_i), the fact that only 'use charges' are paid to the state and that the whole of profits are distributed among heads of enterprises and employees, means that the enterprise is using the services of capital at an unjustly low price, and that it will not use them carefully and economically. For that reason, unless the state collects additional 'use charges' at the rates v_i, it must and will adjust the official 'use charges' on each kind of capital service so that their rational shadow prices will be exactly 0 (probably by trial and error); and thereafter enterprises will distribute profits to their heads and employees in accordance with their respective rates of contribution. On the surface, this is a distribution which accords with the socialistic ideology of distribution and is at the same time rational. We may regard the introduction of these 'use charges' on the production fund as a sign that the socialist economy has begun to move in the direction of a rational distribution of profits. Of the two alternatives, ideology and rationality, the Soviet leaders have wisely chosen the latter.[11+]

4

Changes in plan

A. Relativity of the production plan

Before we turn to an analysis of consumer demand, there remains one aspect of the enterprise's conduct which we ought to analyse. If the prices of each good and each factor of production $p_1, p_2, \ldots, p_n$ are given, the profits $q_1, q_2, \ldots, q_m$ will be given for each process operated at a rate of one unit. Thus, if the upper limit to the quantity of factors of production and the lower limit to the quantity of outputs are given to the enterprise (we call these $\bar{z}_1, \bar{z}_2, \ldots, \bar{z}_n$; the quantity of outputs is measured with a positive value, the quantity of factors with a negative value), the enterprise will formulate its production plan so that the actual quantity of inputs will not exceed the given upper limit and the actual quantity of output will be above the lower limit norm. The rates of operation of each process $x_1, x_2, \ldots, x_m$ will be determined so as to maximise total profits $\Sigma q_i x_i$.

The value of x which will give maximum profits depends, on the one hand, on $Q = (q_1, \ldots, q_m)$, and on the other, on $\bar{Z} = (\bar{z}_1, \ldots, \bar{z}_n)'$.[1+] However, all the acquired profits QX^* are distributed to factors of production in proportion to their shadow prices $v_1, \ldots, v_n$ (X^* shows the rate-of-operation vector $(x_1^*, x_2^*, \ldots, x_m^*)'$ which maximises profits). That is, the total $- V\bar{Z}$ of the shares in profits of all factors is the same as the total profits QX^* which accrue. For that reason, shadow prices V must also depend on Q and $\bar{Z}$.

Thus the solution X^* of the maximising linear programming problem for the production plan, and its dual, which is the solution[2] to the minimising linear programming problem for the distribution of profits, are both relative to the weight vector of the objective function and the restriction vector of the constraining conditions of these problems. That being so, where Q is given in a different way (Q being the weight vector of the objective function in the maximising problem, and the restriction vector in the minimising problem), what values do the solutions X^* and V have? Again, where $-\overline{Z}$ is given in a different way ($-\overline{Z}$ being the restriction vector in the maximising problem, and the weight vector of the objective function in the minimising problem), what values do these solutions take on? These comparative statics questions in linear programming were first put forward by Samuelson (his conclusions were embodied in the famous inequality which is named after him). Thereafter, they were investigated more generally by Beckmann and Bailey.[3] The treatment below does not, essentially, go further than their analyses. However, I hope to develop the analysis along the same lines, and, finally, to link the discussion with the Stolper—Samuelson theorem and the Rybczynski theorem, which are so well known among scholars of international economics.

This kind of research is not simply interesting from the point of view of the theory of the firm; looked at also from the point of view of the economy as a whole, it is indispensably necessary for deriving important conclusions. That is, the profits vector Q is determined in accordance with an arbitrarily given price system P; but, as was stated in the previous chapter, where prices do not reflect the scarcities of goods, the economy will be led in a mistaken direction as a result of prices having these values. In order to lead the economy in the correct direction (that is, to achieve an optimum state), we must revise prices and give each constituent of the economy a proper impetus — the so-called parameter function of prices. In order to be able to revise prices skilfully, we must have the richest possible comparative statics information on the response of the constituents of the economy (particularly firms) when prices change. This is true for both capitalist and socialist economies.

B. The effect of a change in data: a special case

As we saw in the previous chapter, the rule of free goods and the rule of profitability are engaged together as the two great gears of a firm's rational behaviour. It is therefore extremely important to clarify this mechanism in order to understand the nature of 'rationality'. There is no other way to do this than to set the two gears in motion. That is, the structure of the gears will become plain if we compare a given Q or $\overline{Z}$, which takes on certain values in one engaged position, with those of different values in another engaged position. Since by its very nature this sort of analysis is mathematical or theoretical, the reader will have to suffer the painful task of following a fairly complicated theoretical thread. However, the mathematics used is certainly not difficult.

If, as we have up to now, we express the technical coefficients by b_{ji} and make B the matrix of technical coefficients, taking the pair of linear programming problems in question, the maximising problem can be formulated as

$$\text{to maximise } QX \text{ subject to } -BX \leqq -\bar{Z}; \qquad (1)$$

and the minimising problem as:

$$\text{to minimise } -V\bar{Z} \text{ subject to } -VB \geqq Q. \qquad (2)$$

As stated in chapter 3, the solutions to these problems comply with the rule of profitability and the rule of free goods. That is, let us denote the solution to problem (1) by $X^* = (x_1^*, \ldots, x_m^*)$ and the solution to (2) by $V^* = (v_1^* \ldots, v_m^*)$; if the firm adopted a process i with

$$-\Sigma v_j^* b_{ji} > q_i \qquad (3)$$

at V^* (i.e. a process i whose profits q_i are insufficient to be distributed to all factors of production at a rate of v_j^* — we call it an unprofitable process), then its profits would not be maximised. For that reason the equilibrium rates of operation x_i^* of these processes are 0. Next, if we call goods whose demand is less than their supply at the rate of operation X^* free goods, that is the kind of goods j for which

$$-\Sigma b_{ji} x_i^* < -\bar{z}_j, \qquad (4)$$

then profits are not imputed to free goods. Consequently, their shadow prices v_j^* are 0.

However, we must heed the fact that the converse of these rules does not hold. Even those processes whose profits q_i are just enough to be distributed to each factor of production at a rate v_j^* are not, in practice, necessarily employed; there are also cases where their x_i^* are 0. And even for factors of production whose demand exactly equals their supply, shadow prices are not necessarily positive — there are cases where they are 0. It will be useful at this point to divide goods and processes into the following three (or two) groups. First, among goods whose demand equals their supply, we call those goods with positive shadow prices non-free goods; goods for which the demand equals the supply, but whose shadow prices are 0, we call quasi-free goods; goods where the supply exceeds the demand, so that their shadow prices are 0, we call free goods. Where we make a broad division into only two groups, we can include quasi-free goods either with free goods or with non-free goods. The grouping we employ will differ with each case. This is because in certain cases quasi-free goods will show the same movements as free goods; while in others they will show the same sorts of movement as non-free goods. Next, among processes whose profits are used up in distributing them to factors at the rate v_j^*, those whose operating rates are positive we term porfitable processes; those whose operating rates are 0 we term quasi-unprofitable processes. The latter we can combine with the unprofitable processes described above (that is, processes where (3) is valid, so that their x_i^* are 0), to form a broad set of unprofitable processes. There are also occasions when we combine them with profitable processes to form a broad set of profitable processes.

Next we must note that division into sets in this manner is certainly not absolute; goods which were free goods in one case, and processes which were unprofitable, can, in another case, be non-free goods and profitable processes. For example, let us refer to the solutions to the problems (1) and (2), where Q has become $Q + \Delta Q$, by X^0 and V^0. Whether or not they are free goods is determined by whether or not the demand when X is X^0 is as great as the supply. (When we decided whether or not goods were free before the change in Q, we estimated demand at point X^* and compared it with supply.) In the same way, whether or not they are unprofitable is determined by whether the criterion by which we judge them is met at the equilibrium point V^0 after the change in Q. For that reason, it is not necessarily the case that, because goods were non-free goods before the change in Q, they will also be non-free goods after the change. We can also say the same of processes. We ought to regard quasi-free goods and quasi-unprofitable processes as easily changing into either non-free or free goods, or profitable or unprofitable processes. Thus, speaking generally, there are two possibilities: first, sets of goods and processes continue after the change as they were before the change; secondly, sets of goods and processes are different after the change as compared with before the change. Since the rules of comparative statics we derive

will differ in these two cases, I shall divide the discussion below
into two parts. I shall begin by analysing the case where sets of
goods and processes remain the same.

In our linear programming problem, the technical coefficients B,
the profit coefficients Q and the given quantities of factors $-\bar{Z}$ can
be regarded as data for the enterprise. These cannot be made to
alter by the behaviour of the enterprise itself, but can be thought
of as being able to change exogenously. We can think of three
cases of exogenous change. First, technical coefficients change
because of inventions, etc. Secondly, prices, and thus profit coefficients, change because of changes in market demand or supply, or
because of a decision made by the central planning authority.
Thirdly, as a result of the amalgamation of firms, natural calamities
and disasters, or a change in the allocation of factors by the authorities, the quantities of factors $-\bar{Z}$ which the enterprise can use may
change. In the following we shall consider first the case where Q
changes. When we look at the effects of a change in Q, quasi-unprofitable processes can be put in the same set as unprofitable processes,
and quasi-free goods can be put in the same set as non-free goods.
However, when we come to analyse the effects of changes in $\bar{Z}$,
quasi-unprofitable processes will be put into the same set as profitable processes, and quasi-free goods into the same set as free
goods.

Let us now renumber processes and goods in such a way that
profitable processes are in the left-hand side of the table of technical coefficients B, and non-free goods and quasi-free goods in the
upper rows. Thus we divide matrix B and write it as

$$B = \begin{bmatrix} B_1 & \vdots & B_3 \\ \hdashline B_2 & \vdots & B_4 \end{bmatrix}$$

Here B_1 contains the technical coefficients of profitable processes
with respect to non-free and quasi-free goods, and B_2 the technical
coefficients of the same processes with respect to free goods. In the
same way, we divide the operating rate vector X into the operating
rate vector of profitable processes X_1, and that of quasi-unprofitable
and unprofitable processes X_2. We also divide the vector of shadow
prices V into the vector of shadow prices of non-free goods and
quasi-free goods V_1, and that of free goods V_2. Both before and
after the change in Q, all the components of X_1 are positive, and

all the components of X_2 and V_2 are 0. The constraining conditions for maximisation (1) mean that they hold with equality for non-free and quasi-free goods, both before and after the change in Q; the constraining conditons for minimisation (2) mean that they hold with equality for profitable processes, again both before and after the change in Q. Therefore we can derive the following four simultaneous equations:

$$-B_1 X_1^* = -\bar{Z}_1, \qquad -B_1 X_1^0 = -\bar{Z}_1, \qquad (5)$$

$$-V_1^* B_1 = Q_1, \qquad -V_1^0 B_1 = Q_1 + \Delta Q_1. \qquad (6)$$

Here $\bar{Z}_1$ is the vector of the quantities of non-free and quasi-free goods available to the firm, Q_1 is the prechange vector of profits from profitable processes, and ΔQ_1 shows the change in that profits vector. The suffix $*$ expresses an optimum value before the change, the suffix ^{0}, an optimum value after the change.

Until now we have proceeded in our discussion, using technical coefficients which are defined per operating rate of one unit. If we here divide b_{ji} by q_i and write the result as a_{ji}, then the a_{ji} are the technical coefficients per single unit of profits. If we write the result of dividing each of the components of matrix B_1 by its respective corresponding q_i as A_1, and the result of dividing by $q_i + \Delta q_i$ as $A_1 + \Delta A_1$, then A_1 is the matrix of technical coefficients per unit profits before the change (for non-free and quasi-free goods produced by profitable processes), and $A_1 + \Delta A_1$ is the matrix of technical coefficients per unit profits after the change. Using these matrices, (6) may be written as

$$-V_1^* A_1 = E, \qquad -V_1^0 (A_1 + \Delta A_1) = E. \qquad (6')$$

Here E is a row vector consisting of unities in the same number as there are profitable processes. Geometrically, (6') shows that profitable processes standardised so as to give rise to profits of a single unit are located on planes of height 1 with direction coefficients V_1^* and V_1^0 respectively, before and after the change.

Let us now take two different processes. In the normal case they would be at two different points on one of the planes described above. But in some special case, if these processes are standardised so as to give rise to profits of a single unit, they may be at the same point on the same plane. For example, let us assume that before standardising in respect of profits, the technical coefficients of process 1 for quasi-free or non-free goods are a fixed multiple,

say α, of the technical coefficients of process 2; for free goods
there is no such relationship. In this case, if we do not standardise,
processes 1 and 2 are different; since the profits generated in process 1 are α times those generated in process 2, the technical
coefficients for quasi-free and non-free goods per unit profits are
the same for both processes. For that reason, if we standardise to
produce one unit of profits, the difference between the two processes disapppears in the space which ignores free goods, and both
come to be located at the identical point on the plane of height 1
with direction coefficients V_i^*. When a number of different processes
are at the same point after standardisation, we say that these processes are multiple; where this is not the case, we say they are
distinct. Processes which are each multiple are different processes
in the original n dimensional goods space which included free
goods; but in the space which excludes free goods, all these processes are, after standardisation, reduced to a single process.[4+]
Below we consider multiple processes to be a single process, and
assume that there exists a total of m_1 different profitable processes.

Some processes which are different in this sense may be dependent. That is, if an operation of a number, say h, of individual
processes at some given rates produces the same input—output
situation for all quasi-free and non-free goods as an operation of a
different k individual processes at some appropriate rates, then we
say that the $h + k$ processes are dependent processes.[5] We assume
below that from among m_1 processes, $\bar{m}_1$ are independent and the
remainder are dependent. Where profits have changed for only one
process, we can compare the number of independent processes $\bar{m}_1$
with the number of quasi-free and non-free goods n_1. Suppose now
that $\bar{m}_1$ is greater than n_1 (that is, it is at least $n_1 + 1$). If we standardise processes so that each of them produces a single unit of
profits, then before the change in profits these processes exist on
a plane (defined by the first equation of $(6')$); after the change,
they must exist on another plane (defined by the second equation
of $(6')$). These planes are both planes in n_1-dimensional space.
But $\bar{m}_1$ is at least as large as $n_1 + 1$, and since only the profits
from one process have changed, then at least the n_1 individual
points corresponding to the remaining processes do not move
when the change occurs. That is, the two different planes of n_1

dimensions must jointly possess at least n_1 independent points. This is clearly impossible. For that reason, the number of independent processes must either be the same as, or fewer than, the number of quasi-free and non-free goods.

Let us now rearrange the disposition of processes so that from among m_1 different profitable processes, 1 to $\bar{m}_1$ are independent and the rest dependent. We make $\bar{B}_1$ the matrix of technical coefficients (with respect to quasi-free and non-free goods) which is formed from the first $\bar{m}_1$ columns after the rearrangement. Since it is possible appropriately to reduce the operating rates of independent processes and increase those of dependent processes, while the converse is also possible, it is clear that a unique relationship cannot be established between the operating rates of independent processes and dependent ones. However, we can unambiguously ascertain the operating rates of independent processes when all dependent processes have been reduced to independent processes (that is, those particular operating rates $x_1, \ldots, x_{\bar{m}_1}$ of independent processes which are obtained when the operating rates of dependent processes are all put at 0). The reason for this is as follows. From (5) we have

$$-\bar{B}_1 \bar{X}_1^* = -\bar{Z}_1 \quad \text{and} \quad -\bar{B}_1 \bar{X}_1^0 = -\bar{Z}_1 \tag{5'}$$

where $\bar{X}_1^*$ is a vector of equilibrium operating rates before the change in profits, and $\bar{X}_1^0$ is the same sort of vector after the change —dependent processes have all been reduced to independent of processes. Assuming $\bar{X}_1^*$ is not equal to $\bar{X}_1^0$, and making $\bar{B}_{11}$ the block of $\bar{B}_1$ corresponding to processes with x_i^* larger than x_i^0, and $\bar{B}_{12}$ the block of $\bar{B}_1$ corresponding to processes with x_i^* smaller than x_i^0, then if corresponding to these blocks $\bar{X}_1^*$ and $\bar{X}_1^0$ are partitioned into $\bar{X}_{11}^*$, $\bar{X}_{12}^*$ and $\bar{X}_{11}^0$, $\bar{X}_{12}^0$ respectively, we obtain

$$-\bar{B}_{11}(\bar{X}_{11}^* - \bar{X}_{11}^0) = -\bar{B}_{12}(\bar{X}_{12}^0 - \bar{X}_{12}^*)$$

This equation shows that, where the processes of the first block are operating at rates $\bar{X}_{11}^* - \bar{X}_{11}^0$ and the processes of the second block at $\bar{X}_{12}^0 - \bar{X}_{12}^*$, there is no change in the inputs and outputs of quasi-free and non-free goods; consequently, these processes are not independent. This contradicts the fact that all processes which belong to $\bar{B}_1$ are mutually independent. The reason for this paralogism lies in the assumption that $\bar{X}_1^*$ is not equal to $\bar{X}_1^0$. Thus we know that the solution to (5') is unique — that is, even if profits change, $\bar{X}_1^*$ will not change.

As was made clear above, where the grouping of goods into free goods on the one hand and quasi-free and non-free goods on the other, and the grouping of processes into profitable processes on the one hand and quasi-unprofitable and unprofitable processes on the other, do not change, the operating rates of processes (after dependent processes have been reduced to independent processes[6]) will remain unchanged. (However, as we shall see later, the shadow price vector will probably change in accordance with the generalised Stolper–Samuelson rule). In the same way, in the case where the vector of factors of production permitted to the enterprise, $-\bar{Z}$, changes[7], we also have, instead of (5) and (6)

$$-B_I X_I^* = -\bar{Z}_I, \qquad -B_I X_I^1 = -\bar{Z}_I - \Delta \bar{Z}_I, \qquad (5'')$$

$$-V_I^* B_I = Q_I, \qquad -V_I^1 B_I = Q_I, \qquad (6'')$$

provided that no quasi-free or free goods become non-free goods (or the converse), and no profitable or quasi-unprofitable processes become unprofitable processes (or the converse). Here B_I represents the technical coefficients of profitable or quasi-unprofitable processes with respect to non-free goods, $-\bar{Z}_I$ the quantities of non-free goods which the firm is permitted to use, X_I^* the vector of equilibrium operating rates for profitable or quasi-unprofitable processes before $\bar{Z}_I$ changes, and V_I^* the vector of equilibrium shadow prices for non-free goods before $\bar{Z}_I$ changes. X_I^1 and V_I^1 are, respectively, the vector of equilibrium operating rates (for profitable and quasi-unprofitable processes only), and the vector of equilibrium shadow prices (for non-free goods only) after $\bar{Z}_I$ has changed.

A row of the matrix of technical coefficients B_I, for example the jth row, shows the input–output relationship of all the profitable and quasi-unprofitable processes with respect to the jth non-free goods (that is, when each process is operated at a rate of one unit, it shows in what processes and in what quantities the jth good is an input, and from what processes and in what quantities it is an output). There is this sort of relationship for each non-free good. If an appropriate weighted average of the input–output relationships of a number of non-free goods is identical with a similar weighted average of the input–output relationships of a number of other non-free goods, then we say that the input–output relationships of these non-free goods are dependent. Let the total number of non-free goods be n_2. There is no guarantee that the input–output relationship of these n_2 non-free goods are all independent; it is possible that the number of independent input—output relationships (that is, the number of independent rows of B_I) is less than n_2; Let the number of independent input—output relationships be $\bar{n}_2$; by the same reasoning that proved $\bar{m}_1 \leqq n_1$, we can prove that $\bar{n}_2 \leqq m_2$, where m_2 expresses the number of profitable and quasi-unprofitable processes. Thus we know that, where there is no alteration in the grouping of goods into free goods (including quasi-free goods) and non-free goods, and in the grouping of processes into profitable (including quasi-unprofitable) and unprofitable processes in spite of a change in the vector of factors of production permitted to the enterprise $-\bar{Z}$, the vector of shadow price of non-free goods V_I (provided that all goods which possess dependent input—output relationships have been reduced to goods which possess independent input—output relationships[8]) will not be influenced by the change in $-\bar{Z}$. (However, as we shall see later, the vector of operating rates X_i^* will change in accordance with the generalised Rybczynski rule.) Thus the responses of the vector of operating rates and the vector of shadow prices to a change in the vector of profits, and the responses of the vector of shadow prices and the vector of operating rates to a change in the vector of permitted quantities of the factors of production, are exactly symmetrical. And, as is well known, the Stolper—Samuelson rule and the Rybczynski rule are in a dual relationship. This duality is not only valid in the Stolper—Samuelson and Rybczynski case of two goods and two processes; it is also valid in the general case.

C. The standard case

I ought perhaps to deal with the Stolper—Samuelson and the Rybczynski theorems at this point. However, I have decided to postpone discussion of them until later, and to finish the analysis of the remaining case in this section. This is the case where what were free goods, before a change in the profits vector or the vector of the quantities of factors of production permitted to the firm, become non-free goods after the change (or the converse); and where profitable goods before such a change become unprofitable after it (and the converse).[9]

Until now, we have adopted a twofold division for goods and processes; that is, we included quasi-free goods in the free goods group or the non-free goods group, and quasi-unprofitable processes in the profitable or the unprofitable processes group as necessary. However, we shall return below to the original, threefold division for both goods and processes.

First, let us consider the case where Q, the profit per operating rate of processes, has changed. Noting that input coefficients are given by negative values, and putting

$$u_i = q_i + \Sigma v_j b_{ji},$$

then u_i is 0 when process i is profitable, 0 again when it is quasi-unprofitable, and negative when it is unprofitable. The first two cases, associated with the same value, 0, of u_i, differ in the values of operating rates x_i. In the profitable case x_i is positive, and in the quasi-unprofitable case x_i is 0. Before the change in profits v_j has the value of v_j^* (the corresponding u_i is u_i^*); after the change v_j has the value of v_j^0 (the corresponding u_i is u_i^0). By assumption, there is at least one process, say i, whose profitability differs before and after the change; there are six ways in which its profitability may change, shown in table 4.1.

Table 4.1

	Prechange		Postchange		$x_i^0 - x_i^*$
i	profitable:	$u_i^* = 0$	quasi-profitable:	$u_i^0 = 0$	−
ii	profitable:	$u_i^* = 0$	unprofitable:	$u_i^0 < 0$	−
iii	quasi-unprofitable:	$u_i^* = 0$	profitable:	$u_i^0 = 0$	+
iv	unprofitable:	$u_i^* < 0$	profitable:	$u_i^0 = 0$	+
v	quasi-unprofitable:	$u_i^* = 0$	unprofitable:	$u_i^0 < 0$	0
vi	unprofitable:	$u_i^* < 0$	quasi-unprofitable:	$u_i^0 = 0$	0

In case i, Δu_i, that is $u_i^0 - u_i^*$, is 0, and we know, from the profitability of the process before and after the change, that x_i^* is positive and x_i^0 is 0, so that Δx_i is negative. Similarly, in case ii $\Delta u_i < 0$, $\Delta x_i < 0$; in case iii $\Delta u_i = 0$, $\Delta x_i > 0$; in case iv $\Delta u_i > 0$, $\Delta x_i > 0$; in case v $\Delta u_i < 0$, $\Delta x_i = 0$; and in case vi $\Delta u_i > 0$, $\Delta x_i = 0$. From these, we see that in cases ii and iv, $\Delta u_i \Delta x_i > 0$ and in the other cases $\Delta u_i \Delta x_i = 0$. Thus it is impossible for the product of Δu_i and Δx_i to be negative.

When case i or ii occurs in process i, the operating rate of i will decline. Therefore, if there is no change in the operating rates of the other processes, some goods must turn out to be free. For that reason, if we assume free goods do not result, then either there must be other profitable processes whose operating rates increase, or there must be newly profitable processes among what were formerly quasi-unprofitable or unprofitable ones: case iii or iv will come about in this sort of process. In other words, this is a situation where case i or ii comes about in a certain process, and iii or iv in another process. In any event, if case i or ii occurs, unless free goods result, changes in the operating rate will not be confined to process i, but will spread to other processes too.[10]

Next, in case iii or iv the operating rate of i will increase, and unless the operating rate of another process (here called k) declines, an excess demand for some factor of production will occur. At this time, process k may continue to be profitable after the change, as it was before; but on the other hand it may not remain profitable after the change (becoming unprofitable or quasi-unprofitable), and the operating rate may fall at once to 0. In any event, a change in the operating rate of a process in case iii or iv will certainly affect the operating rate of at least one other process.

Finally, we have cases v and vi. According to the twofold classification of the profitability of processes (the profitable group on the one hand, and the unprofitable and quasi-unprofitable group on the other), these are changes within the second group and not movements from the first to the second group. Now, if the classification of goods — division into a free good group and a quasi-free or a non-free good group — does not change, we will arrive at the case dealt with in the previous section and no change will occur in the operating rates of any processes. Consequently, in cases v and vi, if a change has occurred in the operating rate of at least one process, it must have happened that either what were previously non-free goods have become free goods, or vice versa.[11]

As we saw above, free goods may become non-free goods, and vice versa, when a change in profits gives rise to a change in the profitability—unprofitability classification of processes. We can write

$$s_j = -\bar{z}_j + \Sigma b_{ji} x_i$$

for the excess supply of good j. When good j is a free good, s_j is positive; when good j is a quasi-free or non-free good, s_j is 0. The shadow price v_j of good j is 0 or positive according as it is a free or quasi-free good or a non-free good. Consequently, where a change in profits induces a change in the 'free–non-free' classification of good j, the shadow price of j may change from v_j^* to v_j^0 as shown in table 4.2.

Table 4.2

	Prechange		Postchange		$v_j^0 - v_j^*$
i'	non-free:	$s_j^* = 0$	quasi-free:	$s_j^0 = 0$	—
ii'	non-free:	$s_j^* = 0$	free:	$s_j^0 > 0$	—
iii'	quasi-free:	$s_j^* = 0$	non-free:	$s_j^0 = 0$	+
iv'	free:	$s_j^* > 0$	non-free:	$s_j^0 = 0$	+
v'	quasi-free:	$s_j^* = 0$	free:	$s_j^0 > 0$	0
vi'	free:	$s_j^* > 0$	quasi-free:	$s_j^0 = 0$	0

It is immediately clear from the table that: in case i' $\Delta s_j = 0$ but $\Delta v_j < 0$; in case ii' $\Delta s_j > 0$, $\Delta v_j < 0$; in case iii' $\Delta s_j = 0$, $\Delta v_j > 0$; in case iv' $\Delta s_j < 0$, $\Delta v_j > 0$; in case v' $\Delta s_j > 0$, $\Delta v_j = 0$; and in case vi' $\Delta s_j < 0$, $\Delta v_j = 0$. Thus $\Delta v_j \Delta s_j$ is negative in cases ii' and iv' and 0 otherwise; it never becomes positive.

We have already seen that each $\Delta u_i \Delta x_i$ is positive or 0, and now we find that each $\Delta v_j \Delta s_j$ is negative or 0. Thus

$$\Sigma \Delta u_i \Delta x_i \geqslant 0 \geqslant \Sigma \Delta v_j \Delta s_j. \tag{7}$$

But if there is a process which changes in the manner of case ii or iv, then the $\Delta u_i \Delta x_i$ of the process is positive; and so the sign in the first part of (7) will be strict inequality. If there is no process of this sort, the first sign will be equality. However, in this case the equality sign will drop out of the second equality/inequality sign. (We assume that before the change in the profits vector all goods are non-free or free goods, so that quasi-free goods do not exist.)

This is seen in the following way. We are considering cases i, iii, v or vi of table 4.1; but in cases v or vi, as we have already seen, either some non-free goods must at the same time turn into free goods, or else some free goods must turn into non-free goods (otherwise the free–non-free classification of goods will remain unchanged and we will return to the case dealt with in section B. Consequently, case ii' or iv' of table 4.2 comes about, so the sign in the second part of (7) becomes strict inequality. In case i, as we have already seen, either (a) non-free goods become free goods, or (b) case iii comes about in another process, or (c) case iv comes about in another process, or (d) the operating rate changes in another profitable process. Where (*a*) occurs, case ii' of table 4.2 comes about, and the second sign of (7) becomes strict inequality. Where (*c*) occurs, the first sign of (7) becomes strict inequality. Where (*b*) or (*d*) occurs while (*a*) and (*c*) do not, we know that processes related to (*b*) or (*d*) cannot be independent of process *i*. Therefore, when all dependent processes have been reduced to independent processes, this last situation cannot occur. Thus the remaining case is iii alone, and in this case, as we have already seen, either case i or ii will occur in another process, or else the operating rate will change in another, profitable process. Where it is case ii which occurs, the first sign of (7) will become strict inequality; where case i occurs, or a change takes place in the operating rates of other profitable processes, these other processes cannot be independent of process *i* (in which case iii holds). Consequently, where all dependent processes have been reduced to independent processes, such a case cannot occur. From the above we conclude that, where quasi-free goods do not exist before the change in the profits vector, at least one of the two equality/inequality signs of (7) must be strict inequality. (This is true as long as we reduce all dependent processes to independent processes.)

Since only the profits vector Q changes, while the matrix of technical coefficients B and the vector of the quantity of factors permitted to the firm $-\bar{Z}$ are preserved unchanged, we know that changes in the profitability u_i of process *i* are given by

$$\Delta u_i = \Delta q_i + \sum_j \Delta v_j b_{ji}$$

and changes in the excess supply s_j of factors of production *j* by

$$\Delta s_j = \Sigma b_{ji} \Delta x_i.$$

Therefore, substituting in (7) and subtracting $\Sigma\Sigma_{i\ .j}\Delta v_j b_{ji}\Delta x_i$ from both sides of the two inequalities of (7), we derive

$$\sum_i \Delta q_i \Delta x_i \geqslant - \sum_j \sum_i b_{ji} \Delta x_i \Delta v_j \geqslant 0. \qquad (7')$$

If we assume that, before the change in Q, goods were either non-free or free goods, then one of the equality/inequality signs of (7') is strict inequality, and we can immediately obtain Samuelson's strong inequality.[12+]

$$\Sigma \Delta q_i \Delta x_i > 0.$$

From this formula we know that, when the profits of process *i* alone have increased, while those of other processes have been held unchanged, the operating rate of process i has increased.

We can conduct the same sort of analysis when the vector of the quantities of factors of production permitted to the enterprise, $-\bar{Z}$, has changed. That is, we obtain the same inequality as (7); and, if no quasi-unprofitable processes exist before the change in $-\bar{Z}$, one of the two equality/inequality signs must be strict inequality. Now here

$$\Delta u_i = \Sigma \Delta v_j b_{ji}, \qquad \Delta s_j = -\Delta \bar{z}_j + \Sigma b_{ji} \Delta x_i,$$

so substituting in (7) we derive

$$0 \geqslant -\Sigma b_{ji} \Delta x_i \Delta v_j \geqslant -\Sigma \Delta \bar{z}_j \Delta v_j.$$

Since one of the equality/inequality signs of this formula must be strict inequality, we obtain

$$-\Sigma \Delta \bar{z}_j \Delta v_j < 0.$$

From this we obtain the rule that, where the permitted quantity of a factor of production j alone increases (that is, where $-\Delta \bar{z}_j > 0$), then the shadow price of that factor must decrease.[13]

D. 'Factor intensity' and 'factor importance'

Stolper and Samuelson have considered how the prices of factors of production will change in a two-commodity, two-factor economy when a commodity price changes.[14] In an economy producing clothing and foodstuffs using machinery and labour, let k_1 and l_1 be, respectively, the quantity of machinery and the quantity of labour necessary per unit output of clothing, and k_2 and l_2, respectively, the quantity of machinery and the quantity of labour necessary per unit output of foodstuffs. If we denote the price of clothing by p_1, the price of foodstuffs by p_2, the rent of machinery by q, and wages by w, we have

$$k_1 q + l_1 w = p_1, \tag{8}$$
$$k_2 q + l_2 w = p_2,$$

since sales prices are entirely imputed to factors of production. When p_1 or p_2 changes, q and w change. The rules governing the change are as follows. If clothing is more machine-intensive than foodstuffs, that is, if

$$k_1/l_1 > k_2/l_2, \tag{9}$$

the rise in price of clothing, which uses relatively more machinery, will cause a rise in the rent of machines greater than the rate of the price increase; it will also cause a fall in wages. For the same reason, the rise in the price of foodstuffs, which use relatively more labour, will cause a rise in wages greater than the rate of the price rise, and a fall in the rent of machines.

We can easily confirm these rules algebraically. Let us consider the case where the price of clothing increases. Since the price of foodstuffs is unchanged, where the rent of machines changes (we do not yet know whether it has risen or fallen), wages must have changed in the opposite direction. That is:

$$\Delta w = -\frac{k_2}{l_2}\Delta q$$

Consequently, the size of the change in total production costs, taking account of this change in w, is

$$l_1\left(\frac{k_1}{l_1} - \frac{k_2}{l_2}\right)\Delta q$$

Needless to say, this must be the same as the given change in the price of clothing Δp_1. At this point, if we taken into consideration the relationship of machine-intensity between clothing and foodstuffs, we can easily see that Δq has the same sign as Δp_1; that is, when the price of clothing increases, the rent of machines must increase (consequently, wages must fall). Considering the first equation of (8), we obtain

$$\frac{p_1}{q}\frac{\Delta q}{\Delta p_1} = \left(\frac{k_1}{l_1} + \frac{w}{q}\right)\bigg/\left(\frac{k_1}{l_1} - \frac{k_2}{l_2}\right)$$

The denominator of the right-hand side is of a positive value smaller than k_1/l_1, and the numerator is larger than k_1/l_1. From this we can tell at once that, if the price p_1 of clothing — which is the machinery-intensive product — increases, then the rent of machines q will increase with an elasticity greater than unity.

Recently, many scholars have attempted to extend the Stolper–Samuelson theorem, which was derived for a two-product, two-factor economy, to a more general case of n products and n factors.[15] The conclusion they come to is that when n is greater than 3 the Stolper–Samuelson theorem does not generally hold: that is, there is no definite relationship between industries'

factor-intensity and the direction of changes in factor prices. However, the reason that such a negative conclusion is reached is that
the definition of factor intensity in the n-good case is not appropriate for establishing the theorem. I shall suggest below a new
definition of factor-intensity, and I hope to show that on the
basis of that definition, the Stolper–Samuelson theorem is valid in
a weak form even for the n-good n-factor case.

At this point let us consider the relationship between our problem of the imputation of profits and the Stolper–Samuelson
theorem. As we have already seen, where the vector of profits Q
changes, the grouping of goods and processes, into free goods and
non-free goods and profitable and unprofitable processes, generally
changes. In the special case, where before and after a change in Q
quasi-free goods or non-free goods remain quasi-free or non-free
and profitable processes remain profitable, then the two sets of
simultaneous equations of (6) are valid respectively before and
after the change, as we saw in section B. Therefore,

$$- \Delta V_1 B_1 = \Delta Q_1, \tag{10}$$

where $\Delta V_1 = V_1^0 - V_1^*$; B_1 is the matrix of technical coefficients
in respect of quasi-free or non-free goods of profitable processes.
This is generally a rectangular matrix where it is not known
whether the number of rows or columns is greater. However, if we
here assume that all profitable processes are independent of each
other, then since, as we have already seen, the number of independent processes $\bar{m}_1$ will not exceed the number of quasi-free or
non-free goods n_1, there is no instance where the columns of B_1
will outnumber the rows. Further, the values of the coefficients in
B_1 may be positive or negative; but where the norm given to the
enterprise concerning its volume of output is not a high one and
it produces a quantity which is greater than that norm, products
do not enter the list of quasi-free or non-free goods. When, in
addition to this, we leave intermediate products out of
consideration, the technical coefficients which appear in B_1 are
all input coefficients, and thus the values of the elements of B_1 are
either negative or 0. If we write C for $-B_1$ then we can rewrite
(10) as $$\Delta V.C = \Delta Q, \tag{11}$$

where, for purposes of simplification, the subscripts 1 given to V
and Q are removed.

We can compare this equation with the equation derived from (8)

$$\Delta W.A = \Delta P, \tag{12}$$

where A is a matrix of two rows and two columns with row 1, (k_1, k_2), and row 2, (l_1, l_2); P is a row vector with components p_1, p_2, and W a row vector with components q, w. We see that C is a matrix made up of elements whose values are positive or zero — as is A. The point of difference is that while A is a square matrix, C is a rectangular matrix of n_1 rows and $\bar{m}_1$ columns. In a way (11) may be regarded as a generalisation of the Stolper—Samuelson equation (12). In particular, if we assume that $n_1 = \bar{m}_1$ in (11) (that is, we assume there are precisely as many factors of production of quasi-free and non-free goods as there are independent processes), C will also become a square matrix, and the extension of (12) into (11) will simply be a matter of expanding the number of factors and processes from 2 to n_1.

The above is the relationship between our imputation problem and the Stolper—Samuelson problem. In what follows I shall discuss the rules of change which can be discovered from (11) for V when Q changes, under the restrictive assumption that $n_1 = \bar{m}_1$ (Hereafter, for simplicity, I shall write n for the n_1 of $n_1 = \bar{m}_1$). In order to do this, we must first of all make clear how we define factor-intensity with n processes and n factors.

There are two possible ways of defining factor intensity. The first is a definition in terms of quantity (the q-definition); the second is in terms of price (the p-definition). Let us start with an extension of the former. If we write Y for $-\bar{Z}_1$, we can write equation (5), which is the dual of (6), as

$$CX = Y.$$

X is the vector of operating rates for profitable processes only — that is, the subvector denoted until now with the subscript 1 as X_1. Since there is no further fear of confusion, we simplify by leaving out all subscripts from now on. We can write the above matrix formula in the usual simultaneous equation form as

$$
\begin{aligned}
c_{11}x_1 + c_{12}x_2 + \ldots + c_{1n}x_n &= y_1 \\
c_{21}x_1 + c_{22}x_2 + \ldots + c_{2n}x_n &= y_2 \\
\vdots \qquad\qquad \vdots \qquad\qquad \vdots \qquad \vdots & \\
c_{n1}x_1 + c_{n2}x_2 + \ldots + c_{nn}x_n &= y_n
\end{aligned}
\tag{13}
$$

Needless, to say y_j shows the quantity of factors of production j permitted to the enterprise; below we shall call this quantity the supply of that factor.

Suppose x_1 increases by one unit. This implies an increase in demand not just for factor 1, but for factors $2, \ldots, n$. In order to balance the supply and demand for factors of production $2, \ldots, n$, we have to reduce some or all of the operating rates $x_2, \ldots, x_n$. This means that we economise on factor 1. If the direct increase in x_1 is greater than the above indirect economising on that factor, y_1 must increase. Since the more intensively process 1 uses factor 1 the larger is the increase in the demand for factor 1 through the increase in x_1, and the larger is Δy_1, the intensity of factor 1 in process 1 can be defined by the sign of $\Delta y_1/\Delta x_1$, given by the simultaneous equations

$$c_{11}\Delta x_1 + c_{12}\Delta x_2 + \ldots + c_{1n}\Delta x_n = \Delta y_1$$
$$c_{21}\Delta x_1 + c_{22}\Delta x_2 + \ldots + c_{2n}\Delta x_n = 0 \qquad (14)$$
$$\vdots \qquad \vdots \qquad \qquad \vdots \qquad \vdots$$
$$c_{n1}\Delta x_1 + c_{n2}\Delta x_2 + \ldots + c_{nn}\Delta x_n = 0$$

That is, if $\Delta y_1/\Delta x_1$ is positive, we say that process 1 uses factor 1 more intensively than do other processes.[16+]

However, there is one point of which we must take note. We saw before that when x_1 increased, all or some of $x_2, \ldots, x_n$ had to decrease; but where only some of $x_2, \ldots, x_n$ decrease and others increase, the overall effect, which is

$$c_{12}\frac{\Delta x_2}{\Delta x_1} + \ldots + c_{1n}\frac{\Delta x_n}{\Delta x_1} \qquad (15)$$

does not necessarily take on a negative value. Where it does have a negative value, and moreover $\Delta y_1/\Delta x_1$ has a positive value, the change from a negative to a positive value is caused by the demand c_{11} of process 1 for factor 1. Hence, we can say that process 1 uses factor 1 more intensively than do other processes. However, where the product sum (15) has a positive value, we cannot necessarily say that $\Delta y_1/\Delta x_1$ takes on a positive value because of the demand from process 1. (Even when c_{11} is 0, $\Delta y_1/\Delta x_1$ becomes positive.) Below we shall say that when $\Delta y_1/\Delta x_1$ is positive, process 1 makes intensive use of factor 1 in the 'broad' sense; when $\Delta y_1/\Delta x_1$ is positive and, moreover, (15) has a negative value, we say that process 1 makes more intensive use of factor 1 than do other processes in the 'specific' sense.

In the same way, we determine whether process 2 makes more intensive use of factor 1 than do processes 1, 3, . . . , n by the sign of $\Delta y_1/\Delta x_2$. Since it is possible that when Δx_1 is positive, some of $\Delta x_2, \ldots , \Delta x_n$ are positive, it is possible for both $\Delta y_1/\Delta x_1$ and $\Delta y_1/\Delta x_2$ to be positive. That is, there is what appears at first sight the paradoxical possibility that process 1 uses factor 1 more intensively than do the other processes 2, 3, . . . , n, while at the same time process 2 uses factor 1 more intensively than do the other processes 1, 3, . . . , n. No such possibility exists in the original two-factor, two-process system. However, in a system with 3 or more processes the result of the existence of processes from 3 onwards is that the factor intensity of process 1 is compared with those of the set of processes 2, 3, . . . , n and the factor intensity of process 2 with those of the set 1, 3, . . . , n; hence it should not be surprising that a paradox arises of the kind above, where we have what seems, at first sight, a contradictory state of affairs.

If we assume that process 1 uses factor 1 intensively, then factor 1 will, of course, play an important role when the process is operated. But process 1 may not only use factor 1 intensively; it may also, for example, use factor 2 intensively. In this case, we must compare them and discover which plays the more important role when the process is operating.

In order to make such a comparison, let us first look at how much the operating rate of process 1 increases when the permitted quantity of factor 1 is increased by Δy_1; we shall then see that it is Δx_1 which is given by (14). As against this, when we increase the permitted quantity of factor 2 by δy_2, the operating rate of process 1 increases by δx_1, which is determined by the following equations.

$$c_{11}\delta x_1 + c_{12}\delta x_2 + \ldots + c_{1n}\delta x_n = 0,$$
$$c_{21}\delta x_1 + c_{22}\delta x_2 + \ldots + c_{2n}\delta x_n = \delta y_2, \qquad (16)$$
$$\vdots \qquad \qquad \vdots \qquad \qquad \vdots \qquad \quad \vdots$$
$$c_{n1}\delta x_1 + c_{n2}\delta x_2 + \ldots + c_{nn}\delta x_n = 0.$$

Thus, when the quantity of factors of production which the enterprise can use increases, the operating rate of each process will change, and consequently the total of profits will change. But since profits Q per unit operating rate do not change, shadow prices, which are the rates which decide how we distribute profits to each factor, remain unchanged. (We must recollect here that we are dealing with the case where, despite the change in Y — that is $-\bar{Z}$ — the 'free—non-free' classification of goods and the profitability processes remain unchanged. As we saw in section B, in this case the change in $-\bar{Z}$ affects only X and not V.) Consequently, the change in profits due to a change in the permitted quantity of factor 1 by Δy_1 is $v_1^* \Delta y_1$; and where the permitted quantity of factor 2 changes by δy_2 the total change in profits is $v_2^* \delta y_2$. When comparing these two changes it is most natural that we should have Δy_1 and δy_2 of such a size that each will respectively cause an increase in profits of one unit. Thus

$$v_1^* \Delta y_1 \; = \; v_2^* \delta y_2 = 1.$$

Considering (14), (16) and the above formula, we obtain[17]

$$\Delta x_1 \; = \; \frac{D_{11}}{D} \Delta y_1 \; = \; \frac{D_{11}}{D} \frac{1}{v_1^*}, \tag{17}$$

and

$$\delta x_1 \; = \; \frac{D_{21}}{D} \delta y_2 \; = \; \frac{D_{21}}{D} \frac{1}{v_2^*}, \tag{17'}$$

where D is the determinant of matrix C, D_{11} is the cofactor of c_{11} in D and D_{21} the cofactor of c_{21} in D. If Δx_1 is greater than δx_1, we say that factor 1 is more important than factor 2 for increasing the operating rate of process 1 (or else more responsible for operating process 1). This is because in order to increase the operating rate of the process by adjusting the quantities of factors 1 and 2 permitted, while holding total profits constant, we have to increase the permitted quantity of factor 1 and decrease that of factor 2.

Parallel with the above quantity definition of factor-intensity we can define factor-intensity according to price movements (the p-definition). Here we make the shadow price of factor 1 increase by Δv_1. In order for the profits of processes $2, \ldots, n$ (per unit operating rate) to remain unchanged, some or all of the shadow prices of the factors $2, \ldots, n$ must decrease. Where $v_2, \ldots, v_n$ change, the change in profits (from process 1) per unit operating rate of process 1 is

$$c_{21} \frac{\Delta v_2}{\Delta v_1} + \ldots + c_{n1} \frac{\Delta v_n}{\Delta v_1}. \tag{18}$$

If the sum of the direct change in profits, c_{11}, due to the change in v_1 and the indirect change (18) is positive, we say that process 1 makes more intensive use of factor 1 than other factors 2, . . . , n in the 'broad' sense; if in the same case (18) has a negative values, we say that factor 1 is being used more intensively in the 'specific' sense. As can be easily seen, the 'broad' definition of factor-intensity is the same as the definition which states that $\Delta q_1/\Delta v_1$ given by the simultaneous equations

$$c_{11}\Delta v_1 + c_{21}\Delta v_2 + \ldots + c_{n1}\Delta v_n = \Delta q_1$$
$$c_{12}\Delta v_1 + c_{22}\Delta v_2 + \ldots + c_{n2}\Delta v_n = 0 \qquad (19)$$
$$\vdots \qquad\quad \vdots \qquad\qquad \vdots \qquad \vdots$$
$$c_{n2}\Delta v_1 + c_{2n}\Delta v_2 + \ldots + c_{nn}\Delta v_n = 0$$

has a positive value.

Thus we can define the factor-intensity of processes in two ways — from the quantity side and from the price side — and we know that these definitions are not different, but are in fact the same. Let us now prove this for the case where process 1 uses factor 1 more intensively than do processes 2, . . . , n. (Exactly the same proof applies in other cases — for example where process 2 uses factor 1 more intensively.) First, we multiply both sides of the first line of (14) — the simultaneous equations which gave us our quantity definition — by Δv_1, the second line by Δv_2, . . . , and the nth line by Δv_n and sum the whole; we then obtain

$$\Delta y_1 \Delta v_1 = \Sigma\Sigma c_{ji}\Delta x_i \Delta v_j$$

In the same way, when we multiply the first line of (19) — the simultaneous equations which gave us our price definition — by Δx_1, the second line by Δx_2, . . . , and the nth line by Δx_n and sum them, we can see that $\Delta q_1 \Delta x_1$ is the same as the right-hand side of the above equation. Therefore, $\Delta y_1 \Delta v_1$ is the same as $\Delta q_1 \Delta x_1$ and consequently

$$\Delta y_1/\Delta x_1 = \Delta q_1/\Delta v_1.$$

According to the quantity definition, when the left-hand side of the above equation is positive, we say that process 1 uses factor 1 more intensively than do other processes; according to the price definition, when the right-hand side is positive, we say that process 1 uses factor 1 more intensively than other factors. Thus the above equation shows that the two definitions are exactly the same.

In the same way, it can be proved that, if there is 'specific' factor intensiveness from the quantity point of view, so there is too from the price point of view. That is, the two definitions of factor intensiveness are the same not merely in the 'broad' sense, but also in the 'specific' sense. In fact, as can easily be seen

$$\Delta y_1 \Delta v_1 = c_{11} \Delta x_1 \Delta v_1 + (c_{12} \Delta x_2 + \ldots + c_{1n} \Delta x_n) \Delta v_1$$
$$= c_{11} \Delta v_1 \Delta x_1 + (c_{21} \Delta v_2 + \ldots + c_{n1} \Delta v_n) \Delta x_1 = \Delta q_1 \Delta x_1$$

and therefore we know immediately that

$$c_{12} \frac{\Delta x_2}{\Delta x_1} + \ldots + c_{1n} \frac{\Delta x_n}{\Delta x_1} = c_{21} \frac{\Delta v_2}{\Delta v_1} + \ldots + c_{n1} \frac{\Delta v_n}{\Delta v_1}.$$

It then follows that when (15) is negative, so also is (18). That is, if factor 1 is used intensively in process 1 in the 'specific' quantity sense, so too is it in the 'specific' price sense.

We asked earlier which factor is more important than others in the operating of process 1, and we defined factor 1 as being more responsbile for operating process 1 than factor 2 if (17) is larger than (17'). On the other hand, as we know from the first equation of (19), there is a change in the shadow prices $\Delta v_1, \ldots, \Delta v_n$ which comes about in parallel with the increase in the profits of process 1 (the profits of other processes remaining fixed). From (19) the elasticities of shadow prices in respect of an increase in profits are obtained as

$$\frac{\Delta v_1}{v_1^*} \bigg/ \frac{\Delta q_1}{q_1} = \frac{D_{11}}{D} \frac{q_1}{v_1^*}; \qquad \frac{\Delta v_2}{v_2^*} \bigg/ \frac{\Delta q_1}{q_1} = \frac{D_{21}}{D} \frac{q_1}{v_2^*}; \text{ etc.}$$

Considering (17) and (17') we are immediately able to say: if, for the operating of process 1, factor 1 plays a more important role than factor 2 (i.e. if it is more responsible, that is if (17) is greater than (17')), then when the profits q_1 of 1 unit of operation of process 1 increase, the shadow price of factor 1 will change (increase) more elastically than the shadow price of factor 2.

E. The Stolper–Samuelson and the Rybczynski theorems: an extension

Having completed these preliminaries, let us finally begin the task of generalising the Stolper–Samuelson theorem. We shall assumes here that factor 1 is used more intensively (in the 'specific' sense) by process 1 than by other processes $2, \ldots, n$. Where only q_1 has changed,

$$c_{11}\frac{\Delta v_1}{\Delta q_1} + c_{21}\frac{\Delta v_2}{\Delta q_2} + \ldots + c_{n1}\frac{\Delta v_n}{\Delta q_1} = 1$$

has to hold; but since factor 1 is used more intensively in the 'specific' sense, the sum of the terms of the left-hand side from the second term onwards is negative. Thus

$$c_{11}\frac{\Delta v_1}{\Delta q_1} > 1 \tag{20}$$

On the other hand, since

$$c_{11}v_1^* + c_{21}v_2^* + \ldots + c_{n2}v_n^* = q_1$$

held before the change in q_1, $c_{11}v_1^*$ is smaller than q_1. That is, c_{11} is smaller than q_1/v_1^*. Consequently, we can easily see from (20) that the elasticity of v_1 with respect to q_1 is greater than unity — the first proposition of Stolper–Samuelson.

This algebraic rule concerning elasticity holds with respect to all factors which process 1 uses more intensively in the 'specific' sense than do other processes. When there are a number of such factors, there exist a number of factor prices which change elastically. In this case, however, the responsibility of these factors for operating process 1 will generally differ. If we assume that factor 1 bears more responsibility for the operating of process 1 than do the other factors which are used intensively, then, as we have already seen, the elasticity of v_1 with respect to q_1 is greater than the elasticity of the shadow prices of other factors with respect to q_1 — the second proposition of Stolper–Samuelson. Consequently, assuming that there are some factors in each process which are used intensively in the 'specific' sense, we pick out from among them the one which is most responsible for operating the process. If we then assume that there is a one-to-one correspondence between factors picked out in this manner and processes (that is, a different factor is made to correspond to each different process), we can derive the following theorem.

The weak Stolper–Samuelson theorem   When the profits q_i of process i increase, the shadow price v_i of factor i which is the most responsible for the operating of process i rises with elasticity that is more than one; moreover, it is greater than the elasticity of the shadow price of any other factor that increases.

However, we must not forget that the assertions made by this theorem are weaker than those of the original Stolper–Samuelson theorem. That is, the original theorem concerning the two-process, two-factor (or two-good, two factor) system asserts that, when the profits q_1 of process 1 increase, a rise in the shadow price of factor 1 is accompanied by a fall in the shadow price of the remaining factor 2. In a two-process, two-factor system this truth is as self-evident as the observation that 'when the dog faces west the tail points east'. However, we cannot derive the same conclusion for a general, n-process, n-factor system, unless we make the extremely restrictive assumption that each process has only one factor which is used intensively in it. Thus when q_1 increases, there may be another factor among those remaining, besides factor 1, whose shadow price increases (and in certain cases with an elasticity of greater than unity).[18] However, being able to speak generally of a general system is only to say that, when q_1 increases, there is at least one factor of production whose shadow price increases, and at least one whose shadow price decreases. The shadow prices of the remaining factors may all fall, but it is also possible that a part or all of them may rise.

Thus the Stolper–Samuelson theorem may be valid in this weak form, but the reader must not forget that, even in this weakened form, it is premised upon fairly restrictive assumptions. The following are the two assumptions required for the weak theorem:

(a) that corresponding to whichever process we may take there exists at least one factor which it uses more intensively in the 'specific' sense (the q-definition) than do other processes;

(b) that it is not possible for a single factor of production to be that most responsible for the operating of two different processes (the one-to-one correspondence of the process and the most responsible factor).

It is true that every process possesses at least one factor of production which it uses more intensively than all other processes, but these are only factors which are used intensively in the 'broad' sense, and not necessarily factors which are used intensively in the 'specific' sense. Consequently (a) is not necessarily always fulfilled. Moreover it is perfectly possible for a factor which is most responsible for the running of one process to be most responsible for the running of another as well. Thus the one-to-one correspondence between process and factors asserted by (*b*) does not generally exist. Where the restrictive conditions (*a*) and (*b*) are removed, it is not possible algebraically to put forward more than the following theorem.

The Correct Stolper—Samuelson Theorem   In whatever process, there is at least one factor which is used more intensively (not necessarily intensively in the 'specific' sense) in that process than in any other. If we take from among these factors the factor which is most responsible for operating that process, its shadow price will increase with the greatest elasticity, though not necessarily with an elasticity greater than unity, when the profits of that process increase.

The content of this theorem is much slenderer than that of the weak Stolper—Samuelson theorem; but the truth Stolper and Samuelson sought to persuade us of, using their small-scale, two-process two-factor model, is probably this kind of 'reasonable' truth.

Next, it is also possible, in the same fashion as above, to generalise the Rybczynski theorem, which gives the rules governing the change in the operating rates of processes when there is a change in $-\overline{Z}$ or Y, the vector of the quantities of factors of production permitted to the enterprise.[19] Thus if we assume that:

(*a'*) in whatever process, there is at least one factor which is used more intensively in the 'specific' sense than any other factor (the *p*-definition); and that

(*b'*) there is only one factor of production whose shadow price will be influenced most strongly when there is a change in the profits which derive from 1 unit of operation of a specific process, and moreover, such a correspondence between processes and factors of production is one-to-one,

then we can derive the following theorem.

The weak Rybczynski theorem   If we assume that the shadow price of factor of production j is more strongly influenced by a change in the profits of process j than by changes in those of any other process,[20] an increase in the quantity y_j of the factor j

permitted to the enterprise gives rise to an increase in the operating rate of process j; furthermore the elasticity of this operating rate, which is greater than unity, is greater than the elasticity of any other process whose operating rate increases when y_j increases.

However, assumptions (a') and (b'), which are the premising conditions of this theorem, are strong assumptions. In the general case where these conditions are not fulfilled, no more than the following holds.

The correct Rybczynski theorem   For whatever factor of production j, there is at least one process where this factor is used more intensively (not necessarily in the 'specific' sense) than are other factors (the p-definition). If, from among such processes, we take the one whose change in profits will most strongly influence the shadow price of factor j, then the operating rate of that process will increase more elastically than the operating rate of other processes when there is an increase in the permitted quantity y_j of the factor j. (However its elasticity is not necessarily greater than unity.)

In the above, we have assumed that C, the matrix of technical coefficients concerning non-free goods (including quasi-free goods) of the processes employed, is square. In the general case of the rectangular matrix, it goes without saying that even the above 'correct Stolper–Samuelson theorem' and the 'correct Rybczynski theorem' will be subject to substantial amendment.

5

The behaviour of the household

A. The independence of households

In modern society places of work (government offices, enterprises, etc.) are separated from households. Not merely are official money and materials distinguished from the private property of the head of the enterprise and his staff, but no confusion is permitted between decisions relating to the running of the enterprise and the decisions of households. That, in almost all cases, the workplace and the private dwelling-place are in different places is a reflection of this fact.

This separation is one of the important features of modern society. In the patrimonial state and the feudal state, for example, there was no distinction between the national administration and the sovereign's household. The government officials of these states were family servants who disposed of matters which really pertained to the sovereign's household (the Head of the Royal Household, the Comptroller of the Household, the Master of Horse, the Butler, the Secretary, the Chancellor, etc.).[1] In Japan in the early modern period, farming by large farmers (*Ōtakamochibyakushō*), depended in the main on the labour of hereditary servants (*fudai genin*) and indentured servants (*Shichimono hōkōnin*).[2] Even in the middle and late modern period, when these servants were replaced by the general use of employed agricultural workers, who were engaged for a fixed period of time for wages, these latter lived under the roof of the employer, were supplied with clothing as well as food by him, and were put to work cultivating or at other tasks at his command. This confusion and lack of differentiation still occurs in a modern society. The director of a limited company which has developed from a private shop often has to consider the family circumstances of the original owner of the shop in running the company. It is not unusual for a ship's captain to take his wife and children on his voyages, nor for the English vice-chancellor's family to live on the university campus.

From the point of view of economics, the failure completely to separate the enterprise and the household is most note-worthy in the case of agriculture and the private business. Because of the fragile basis on which the farmer and the owner of the private firm conduct their businesses, it is difficult for them to resort to the modern capital market for finance, and they must therefore supply the greater part of their needs for finance from their own savings. They differ from company officials, government officials and workers; they are not in a position to make large consumption decisions until they have considered the disposal of the funds relating to their business operations.[3] Their household consumption plans and their business investment plans are mutually interlinked and determined simultaneously, and in this sense the household is not independent of the business. Consequently, we ought to construct a theory to explain the behaviour of these households which is different from the one which explains the behaviour of the normal household. However, I shall not attempt this here; I shall continue the discussion on the supposition that all households are independent of enterprises. Households which do not fulfil this assumption exist in actual modern societies; but we make the assumption in order to analyse modern societies in their ideal, typical form.

However, even though households are independent of enterprises in the above sense, yet there are cases where the decisions of the head of the household are influenced by the decisions of the enterprise to which he belongs. Where the wages or the salary the enterprise pays to the household change, then needless to say the household is greatly affected. Therefore, in what follows, we shall treat wages paid to households by enterprises as fixed. If we assume that the consumption of the household is proportional to its income, and that there is no difference in the rate of consumption (the propensity to consume) between households, then a transfer of income between households will have no net effect on total consumption, so that we can expect the total consumption of all households to be independent of the distribution of wages.

However, even in this case, the consumption of the household still depends on the wages structure employed by the enterprise. Let us assume, for example, that workers are homogeneous, and consider the case where all workers are paid identical wages, and the case where a seniority system is operated, with wages of less than the average paid to young workers, and wages greater than the average paid to older workers. Where the average wage in the latter case equals the wage in the former case, the total wages which the firm has to pay are the same whichever wages system is adopted; and so from the firm's point of view they can be considered the same. However, the household will regard a monthly income of £100 received under a seniority system as being better than the same monthly income received under the other system, for the former is an income which, it is promised, will increase next year. Consequently when we look at two households with the same income, other things being equal, the propensity to consume of the household head who works for a firm which employs a seniority system will be higher. Also, the total of savings over the lifetime of the household is not the same in the case where a fixed income is received year by year as it is where the same discounted total is received in instalments which rise with the age of the income receiver. If we assume that young people are more inclined to consume than middle-aged or old people, then under a seniority system of wage payments, the consumption of young people is suppressed and the savings of middle-aged or old people have ample scope to materialise. However, as we have just seen, other things being equal, the propensity to consume of a head of household who is employed under the seniority system will tend to be higher when he reaches the age at which he receives the average wage than that of one who is not. But if we take into account the inertia which affects his propensity to consume because he has previously become accustomed to low consumption out of a low income, then, even in this case, we can imagine that his propensity to consume when he reaches the age of average income may be lower than that of someone of the same age who is employed under the non-seniority system, and who has a customarily high propensity to consume. Since the propensity to consume is thus not higher for young, middle-aged or older people under the seniority system, it is conceivable that, even where the total of wages paid out to households is the same, the total savings of the entire household under the seniority system may be greater. At all events, it is clear that the wages structure of the firm will influence the decisions of each household.

The conduct of the household is influenced by the way in which enterprises distribute their profits. As we have already seen, in a capitalist society all the profits go to capital, and in a socialist society they are distributed to the workers and staff who contribute to production. However, we cannot say that these custom-determined, normal methods of distribution are necessarily scientific. With a scientific distribution — that is where profits are distributed using shadow prices which correspond to a rational production plan — profits in a capitalist society ought to be distributed to labour as well as to capital; in a socialist society profits ought to be distributed to the state as supplier of capital, as well as to workers and staff. The twice-yearly bonus which has become customary in postwar Japan is not necessarily based on such a rational distribution of profits; it is a fact, however, that it forms a sizeable part of the annual income of wage-earners and other staff. In the case of certain kinds of employees (for example civil servants), the bonus is determined more or less as a proportion of the monthly salary and is hardly influenced by the economic climate. However, in the majority of enterprises, the bonus depends on total profits, and consequently is a markedly uncertain income for the household. Where the household receives both certain permanent and uncertain transitory income, it can be regarded as having a different way of consuming each of these incomes.

According to Friedman, the household can be regarded as permanently consuming a fixed percentage of its permanent income (the size of this proportion may be seen as depending on the rate of interest, the ratio of assets to income, the propensity to save, etc.). Besides this permanent consumption there is transitory consumption, which changes from time to time, but the latter can be regarded as having no correlation with permanent and transitory income.[5] This permanent income hypothesis of Friedman may well be regarded as containing too strong an assumption. In fact, we may rather more realistically say that it is perfectly possible for transitory consumption to be proportionate to transitory income, or else positively correlated with transitory income. However, if we generalise the permanent income hypothesis and assume that the propensity to consume out of transitory income is less than the propensity to consume out of permanent income; or else generalise even further and assume no more than that each form of income will yield a different propensity, then there is scarcely room for dissension. For present purposes this generalised permanent income

hypothesis is sufficient. That is, from this hypothesis it is immediately clear that the conduct of the household will differ according
to whether enterprises adopt the bonus system, or dispense with it
and raise wages instead.

Thus the propensity to consume of each household, and consequently the quantity of each good which it demands, will be
directly affected by the wages structure and the bonus system of
the firm in which the head of the household is employed. But the
decisions of the household will also depend, indirectly, on the
publicity and the advertising carried out by firms, the state, regional
bodies, etc.; they will also be influenced by the consumption
decisions of neighbours, friends, workmates, relatives, etc., and
the size of the household's income in relation to these peoples'. It
would be hard to deny that our consumption decisions are affected,
consciously and unconsciously, by the 'buy-home-produced-goods'
movements which take place when the balance of payments is unfavourable, and by appeals for donations to charitable organisations.
In an era in which a revolution in consumption has been rapidly
ushered in by the appearance on the market of many kinds of
sophisticated goods — the products of new chemical and machine
technologies — it must be said that advertising and other forms of
information dissemination are indispensable for the formation of
consumers' tastes. Advertising has great significance in modern,
highly developed capitalist societies; as a result of it, production in
these societies is not undertaken because a demand exists, but rather
a state of affairs has developed where publicity and advertising
occur in order to induce a demand for production which has already
taken place. 'The woman next door has a diamond ring so why
can't you buy one for me' is a common technique for persuading
husbands; and besides this kind of inter-household straight (good
to the same kind of good) propagation of wants (the so-called demonstration effect), it is clear that there is cross (good to another
kind of good) propagation, as is shown by the experience of the
household which installed double glazing because the boy next
door had bought an electric guitar. Furthermore, when subsocieties
are formed within a society, as with whites and blacks in the
United States, the influence exerted by a person's relative position
within the subsociety is greater than that exerted by his position in
the larger society. Consequently, we may imagine that the savings
propensity, or rate, of a well-off American black man is at the

same level, relatively, as that of a well-off white, because he is a rich man amongst blacks, even though his absolute income is low compared with incomes in white society (the so-called 'relative income hypothesis').[6]

As we saw above, a household is always a household within a society, and, in various senses, it cannot remain isolated. However, I assume as a rule that private lives and working lives are entirely separate. Nevertheless, the income which the household receives is not an abstract sum of money. It is a concrete sum that is paid as wages under a seniority system, as a bonus or as profits; and though the sum itself may be the same it will have a different meaning for the household depending on the way in which it is received. The formation of wants is also socially interlinked. Consequently, to treat income as abstract income and to assume that wants are formed in isolation, autonomously and purely subjectively (as do Walras, Hicks, and others in their traditional theories of demand), is somewhat unrealistic. However, the traditional theory of demand is useful as first approximation towards a more satisfactory, concrete theory, and below I shall consistently assume the independence of households. In the next two sections I shall give a general outline of traditional demand theory, after which I shall deal with comparatively new problems such as the demand for money and points-rationing systems.

B. Traditional demand theory

Among traditional theories of demand there are: (1) those which assume the existence of a utility function; (2) those which assume the existence of indifference surfaces (or an indifference map); (3) those which do not assume the existence of indifference surfaces, but which do assume the existence of a marginal rate of substitution between all goods; and (4) those which make only a few basic assumptions relating to the choice of goods. Thus, a variety of theories exist, but in the broad sense they all belong to the same family of theories, and differ only according to whether they make strong or weak assumptions. Below I shall outline Samuelson's theory (the so-called theory of revealed preference), which may be regarded as the one with the weakest assumptions.

Let me begin by explaining the notation which I shall use. Suppose there are n goods, and a household or an individual demands $x_1, \ldots, x_n$ respectively of these goods. The problem of how much of each good is bought can be thought of as the problem of what combination of goods to buy. or what vector

$$x = \begin{pmatrix} x_1 \\ \cdot \\ \cdot \\ \cdot \\ x_n \end{pmatrix}$$

to choose. We use superscripts to show specific vectors such as x^0, x^1, x^2. Next let $p_1, \ldots, p_n$ be the prices of goods, and write a general price vector as

$$p = (p_1, \ldots, p_n)$$

and specific price vectors as p^0, p^1, p^2 with superscripts. Since x is a column vector and p a row vector, their inner product (scalar product) px shows total expenditure $p_1 x_1 + p_2 x_2 + \ldots + p_n x_n$.

Let us assume that when prices are p^0 the household chooses the combination x^0, and that when they are p^1 the same household chooses the combination x^1. These choices are given as facts or data. If we assume here that the household's scale of preferences for the various x's is the same whether prices are p^0 or p^1, we can construct the following axiom.[7]

The Revealed Preference Axiom   If $p^0 x^0 \geqq p^0 x^1$ for $x^0 \neq x^1$, then $p^1 x^0 > p^1 x^1$.

That is, the first inequality of the axiom means that, if an expenditure of $p^0 x^0$ is made when prices are p^0, then either x^0 or x^1 can be bought. But since the household chose x^0 when prices were p^0, this inequality implies that, when it compares x^0 and x^1, the household prefers x^0. By assumption this order of preference is also preserved when prices are p^1. Consequently, when x^0 and x^1 are valued at prices p^1, x^1 must be cheaper. The reason is that, where $p^1 x^0$ is the same as or less than $p^1 x^1$, the preferred combination x^0 is not more expensive than the other, and therefore there is positively no reason for choosing x^1, the one which is lower in the scale of preferences. Therefore we would expect x^0 to be purchased when prices are p^1 too. Nevertheless, according to the data this household buys x^1 when prices are p^1, so that x^0

must be more expensive than x^1 at p^1. We can thus obtain the second inequality of the axiom. That is, when the household compares x^0 and x^1 it will prefer the former; nevertheless when prices are p^1 it determines not to spend $p^1 x^0$ and therefore actually chooses x^1. On the other hand, when prices are p^0 it resolves to spend $p^0 x^0$ and therefore chooses x^0.

The above axiom does not hold when prices change from p^0 to p^1 and the household's scale of preferences for combinations of goods changes correspondingly. But the premising condition of the axiom — namely that the scale of preferences is independent of prices — is an unrealistic assumption which only holds in the most exceedingly strict, pure, cultivated conditons. A well-known exception is the demand for luxury goods, such as precious stones. The reason a woman wants diamonds is not because of their material utility, but because of the price. It is the fact of wearing an expensive diamond ring which gives her satisfaction, and thus she would probably cease to want one were its price to fall. Apart from the case where the price itself is a source of satisfaction, there is the case where the consumer judges the quality of the good by its price. When my friend was invited to a Chinese restaurant he was unable to guess at the contents of the menu from the names of the dishes, and so he choose the most expensive dish. He told me it was delicious, and so thereafter I resolved, if invited out, to order the most expensive dishes I possibly could (however, this requires courage, and also some skill if you are not to be thought a mean fellow). Besides this comparatively unimportant, exceptional case, there are more important examples, and with modernisation and industrialisation they will cease to be exceptional.

According to economic theory, the price of a good reflects its scarcity. When demand exceeds supply, prices rise and vice versa. As we shall see in the following chapter, this relationship between demand—supply and price is valid in a market where competitive buying and selling occurs; it does not, however, hold for the great majority of modern industrial products, such as cars and television sets. As for the price of these goods, their costs of production are calculated at the factory, a 'normal' profit is added, and the goods are passed on to a retailer. The retailer then sells them to the final consumer at a fixed price (or at a 'recommended' price given him by the factory). Of course, the actual price may differ from the 'recommended' price, so reflecting scarcity even in this case; but this divergence is rarely great, and the difference between demand and supply is mainly absorbed not through price, but through regulation of the quantity of output. That is, where there is an excess demand, output increases with price unchanged; where there is an excess supply, output decreases with price unchanged. Thus what generally determines price is not scarcity, but costs of production.

Consequently when firms change the prices of their products (especially when they increase prices), they attempt to justify the new prices technically. In the case of cars for example, the manufacturers try to include some sort of technical 'improvement' in their new models so that the increase in price due to wage increases can be camouflaged by the increase in price due to the improvement in the quality of the good. As a result, consumers often take price as an indicator of quality. Thus a change in price comes to signify a change in quality, so that the scale of preferences, or the want-pattern, differs before and after the price change, and the revealed preference axiom becomes inappropriate. If the preference ordering between two sets of goods is reversed due to a change in prices, then although on the basis of both the old and the new prices both x^0 and x^1 can be bought, the paradoxical situation will come about where x^0 is bought at the old prices and x^1 at the new. I have called this change in demand, based on a change in the scale of preferences for goods, the 'want-pattern effect'; it is always regarded as zero in the traditional theories of demand.[8]

As I have already indicated, it is assumed in the revealed preference axiom that when prices are p^0 the household decides to spend $p^0 x^0$, and when they are p^1 *not* to spend $p^1 x^0$. That being the case, how does it decide how much to spend? I shall discuss this question again in section D; traditional demand theory dismisses the problem from consideration through the following assumption. When prices are p^0 and p^1 let the totals of income be respectively M^0 and M^1, and assume that the household uses up the whole of its income. In which case

$$M^0 \ = \ p^0 x^0 \quad \text{and} \quad M^1 \ = \ p^1 x^1 \tag{1}$$

and thus by the assumptions of revealed preference

$$M^0 \geqq p^0 x^1, \qquad M^1 < p^1 x^0. \tag{2}$$

Consequently, when prices were p^0 the household was able to purchase either x^0 or x^1, but when prices were p^1 the household became unable to purchase x^0 due to an insufficiency of income. Thus, under the assumption of equality between income and expenditures of (1), the problem of why the household was unable to determine on an expenditure of $p^1 x^0$ is provided with the self-evident answer that there was insufficient income to encompass such an expenditure.

However, if the household had been provided with sufficient income to purchase x^0 with price of p^1, that is

$$M^2 = p^1 x^0, \tag{3}$$

would it in fact have purchased x^0? Here let X^0 be the set of x which this household can purchase with income M^0 and prices p^0; that is all the x which satisfy the inequality

$$M^0 \geqq p^0 x. \tag{4}$$

Also let X^2 be the x which our household can buy with income M^2 and prices p^1; that is the set of x which satisfy

$$M^2 \geqq p^1 x. \tag{5}$$

Since by (1) and (3) x^0 satisfies both inequalities, x^0 is a common point in X^0 and X^2. There may be other common points, and in some special cases X^0 and X^2 may coincide. Since x^0 is the most preferred point amongst the x which belong to X^0, we would expect the same x^0 to be chosen under prices p^1 and income M^2 when X^0 and X^2 coincide (on the assumption that the order of preference is independent of price changes). However, when X^0 and X^2 do not coincide, there may be a point higher in the scale of preferences than x^0 among the x which are not included in X^0 but are included in X^2. If there is such a point, the household will discard x^0 and choose this new, most preferred point.

Next let x^2 be the highest point on the scale of preferences in X^2. It may be equal to x^0 but this is not a problem here. $p^1 x^2$ must not, of course, exceed M^2, and again is probably not less than M^2. The reason for this is that, if it were less than M^2, the household could purchase x^2 and still have some income remaining. As long as the household is not already satiated with x^2, then if it purchases further goods with this remaining income, it is clear that its degree of satisfaction will have risen. Consequently, the highest point on the scale of preferences in X^2 must be on the boundary. That is for x^2 the equality

$$M^2 = p^1 x^2 \tag{6}$$

holds. When a price change from p^0 to p^1 is accompanied by a parallel change in income from M^0 to M^1, the demand for goods will change from x^0 to x^1, and when income changes from M^0 to M^2 along with a change in prices, there is a change from x^0 to x^2. But these two changes in income which occur in parallel with price changes are very different. Firstly, where income changes from M^0 to M^1, the household is no longer able to purchase the quantity x^0 at the new prices p^1. (See the second inequality of (2).) Consequently, we may consider that income M^1 with prices p^1 is, in real terms, less than income M^0 with prices p^0. That is, a decline in real income has accompanied a change in prices. Against this, where income changes from M^0 to M^2, we can see from (3) that, if the household wanted to buy the original combination x^0 at prices p^1, it could do so. (But since it became possible for it to buy the preferred combination x^2, its demand changed from x^0 to x^2.) Thus, if we take x^0 as the basis for calculating real income, M^0 with prices p^0 and M^2 with prices p^1 are the same in real terms. Therefore the fact that income changed from M^0 to M^2, parallel with a change in prices, means that a compensatory variation in income took place at the same time as price changed, so that real income remained the same.[9+]

Thus income changed from M^0 to M^1 with the change in prices from p^0 to p^1, and as a result demand changed from x^0 to x^1. In order to analyse this observed change, we adopt the method of splitting up the actual change into two hypothetical changes, and then, conversely, treating the actual change as a resultant of the hypothetical changes. If, we suppose on the one hand, a change in prices from p^0 to p^1 which is accompanied by a compensatory variation in income of M^0 to M^2, and, on the other hand, a pure change in income whereby prices remain fixed as p^1 and income change from M^2 to M^1, then when these take place successively the change which occurs accords with that actually observed — prices change from p^0 to p^1 and income from M^0 to M^1 (passing through M^2). When the first hypothetical change takes place, the quantity demanded changes from x^0 to x^2, and when the second occurs the quantity demanded changes from x^2 to x^1. The change which is actually observed is the combined sum of these two changes. That is

$$x^1 - x^0 = (x^2 - x^0) + (x^1 - x^2). \tag{7}$$

The first term on the right-hand side of this expression shows the change in demand when a compensatory variation in income has accompanied a price change (we call this the 'substitution effect'). The second shows the change in demand which occurs when prices remain fixed and income alone changes (this we call the 'income effect'). Thus, under the axiom of revealed preference, actual changes in demand are analysed into substitution and income effects; but in the general case where the scale of preferences for goods changes when prices change, what I have elsewhere called the 'want-pattern effect' is added.[10]

C. The substitution and the income effects

The reason why we analyse the total effect into the substitution effect and the income effect is that each obeys its own characteristic rules. Let us first consider the substitution effect. Firstly, where x^2 differs from x^0, x^2 is the highest point on the scale of preferences which ranks all the x which belong to X^2, and x^0 is a point belonging to X^2. Therefore it is clear that x^2 ranks higher in the scale of preferences than does x^0. For precisely this reason x^2 was chosen despite the fact that, with prices p^1 and income M^2, the household could have purchased x^0. On the other hand, when prices were p^0 and income M^0 it chose x^0. Thus by the revealed preference axiom

$$M^0 < p^0 x^2. \tag{8}$$

If this were not so, it would also be possible to purchase x^2 and therefore we would expect our household to have chosen x^2 even when prices were p^0 and income M^0, contradicting the fact that it actually chose x^0. Thus we obtain $p^0 (x^2 - x^0) > 0$ from the first equation (1) and from (8), and

$$p^1 (x^2 - x^0) = 0 \tag{9}$$

from (3) and (6). Therefore,

$$(p^1 - p^0)(x^2 - x^0) < 0. \tag{10}$$

That is, we obtain the rule whereby, if we assume that there is any sort of substitution effect whatsoever (if $x^2 \neq x^0$), the sum of the products of the substitution effects and the price changes is always negative. This means either that a negative substitution effect

$(x_i^2 - x_i^0 < 0)$ must occur in the demand for at least one good among those whose prices have risen $(p_i^1 - p_i^0 > 0)$; or else that a positive substitution effect must occur in the demand for at least one good among those whose prices have fallen. Of course this rule does not make the strong assertion that the demand for a good whose price has risen must fall, and that the demand for one whose price has fallen must rise. Nevertheless, it is a generalised version of this strong proposition, and therefore (10) is often called 'the generalised law of demand'.

However, it is only in this case that (10) holds as a pure inequality, and needless to say, where $x^2 = x^0$, (10) becomes zero. This being so, in what cases will the substitution effect be zero (that is $x^2 = x^0$)? There are two noteworthy cases where the substitution effect is zero. The first is where prices change proportionally; that is, where the prices vector p^1 is α times p^0. In this case M^2 is α times M^0 from the first equation of (1) and from (3). Where prices and income have increased by the same multiple α, it is possible to purchase the same x as formerly. Thus $X^0 = X^2$, and since x^0 is the highest point on the scale of preferences in X^0, the same x^0 is the highest point on the scale of preferences in X^2. Hence $x^0 = x^2$; that is there is no substitution effect when relative prices do not change.

Perfectly complementary goods are the second case. For example, overseas travel and visas are perfect complements. In this case it is ridiculous to envisage an increase in demand through the substitution effect when the cost of acquiring visas falls with the cost of overseas travel remaining unchanged.[11+] This is because it is pointless simply collecting visas for a large number of countries without intending to go there, however cheap they may be. However, even in this case, when the cost of acquiring a visa falls there is a slight reduction in the total cost of overseas travel, and the surplus from this source may generate a new demand for various goods, including travel. However, an increase in demand generated in this way is not the substitution effect; it is the income effect to which we shall shortly turn. Again, if we allow for the possibility that our travel schedule may be altered later, we may acquire visas for countries we do not intend to visit if they are cheap (or free). However, such conduct is only justified where the travel schedule is uncertain. In the present example, where we have ignored the problem of uncertainty, there is no need to consider this possibility.

Next equation (9), which was obtained as a supplementary

proposition to the generalised law of demand (10), itself reveals a proposition relating to the substitution effect. In fact Hicks counted (9) as one of the four rules relating to the substitution effect. That is, (9) shows that, when the substitution effects for all goods weighted by the new prices p^1 are totalled, the result is 0. This cancelling-out characteristic of the substitution effect should certainly occasion no surprise, in view of our definition of it as the effect on demand of a change in prices which is accompanied by a compensating change in income.

The income effect (that is the second term of the right-hand side of (7), fulfills the following conditions. If we subtract (6) from the second formula of (1) and divide both sides by $M^1 - M^2$, we obtain

$$p^1 \frac{x^1 - x^2}{M^1 - M^2} = 1. \tag{11}$$

Here $(x^1 - x^2)/(M^1 - M^2)$ is a vector obtained by dividing each component of vector $(x^1 - x^2)$ by $(M^1 - M^2)$. Consequently, these components show the increase in the quantity demanded of each good per unit increase in income. If we multiply each of them by its respective price, we can obtain coefficients which show what proportion of the unit increase in income is spent on each good — in other words Engel coefficients. (11) signifies that the sum of the Engel coefficients is equal to 1. Engel coefficients are not necessarily positive. When my total income changes, so will my demand for different goods. For example, if I have to go from Osaka to Tokyo, I will probably go by bus if my income is small. When I enter the middle-income bracket, I will probably go by express train, and when I become rich I will probably go by plane. Thus as I move from the low-income to the middle-income bracket, the Engel coefficient for bus journeys is negative and for train journeys positive. Economists refer to goods whose Engel coefficient is negative as 'inferior goods'. However, the total of the Engel coefficients is positive, as we saw from (11), and therefore it is seen that the broader we make our classifications of goods, the more will negative coefficients be cancelled out by positive ones. Therefore, there is little possibility that broad classifications of goods will be inferior goods; but where classifications are very narrow ones, there will be many inferior goods. As income increases, consumers scramble up through the classes of goods.

Suppose the price of good i alone changes. Also, suppose there is no change in income, i.e. $M^0 = M^1$; we then obtain

$$\frac{x_j^1 - x_j^0}{p_i^1 - p_i^0} = \left[\frac{x_j^2 - x_j^0}{p_i^1 - p_i^0}\right] + \frac{x_j^1 - x_j^2}{M^1 - M^2} \cdot \frac{M^0 - M^2}{p_i^1 - p_i^0}$$

from equation (7). We put the first term of the right-hand side of the above equation into square brackets in order to show clearly that it is the substitution effect. Furthermore, when we consider the fact that the prices of goods other than i are unchanged, we obtain

$$M^0 - M^2 = -(p_i^1 - p_i^0)x_i^0$$

from the first equation of (1) and from (3). Thus we obtain

$$\frac{x_j^1 - x_j^0}{p_i^1 - p_i^0} = \left[\frac{x_j^2 - x_j^0}{p_i^1 - p_i^0}\right] - x_i^0 \frac{x_j^1 - x_j^2}{M^1 - M^2} \cdot \qquad (12)$$

This is known as the Slutsky equation, and it reveals the change in demand per unit change in price when the price of good i alone changes.[12+]

The first term on the right-hand side of (12) shows the substitution effect which good i has on good j. Following Hicks, when it is positive we may define j as substitutable for i, and when negative as complementary with i.[13+]

As we saw above, $x^2 - x^0$ is the general substitution effect when the prices of various goods change at the same time, and

$$\left[\frac{x_j^2 - x_j^0}{p_i^1 - p_i^0}\right]$$

the partial average substitution effect when the price of good i alone changes. This being the case, what is the relationship between the general substitution effect and the partial average substitution effect? Is the former not shown as some weighted sum of the partial average substitution effects produced by their respective price changes? If it is possible to do this, the general or total substitution effect on good j would be the weighted sum of the partial average substitution effect on good j from (a change in the price of) good 1, the partial average substitution effect from good 2 and so on. Consequently, if we know that good j is either a substitute for each good or is complementary with them, and we know the weight of each partial effect, we can calculate the total substitution effect.

Evidently it will be useful when we come to estimate demand to have obtained these relevant relationships in explicit formulae. Let $p^0 = (p^0_1, p^0_2, \ldots, p^0_n)$ be prices before a change, and $p^1 = (p^1_1, p^1_2, \ldots, p^1_n)$ prices after a change. Since we are thinking of a general change in prices, p^1_i is generally different from p^0_i, except for the final good n, which is taken as the base good in our price calculation (the numéraire), its price being constant, say at p^0_n, in the case of both p^0 and p^1. By interpolating prices such as $p^{(1)}, p^{(2)}, \ldots, p^{(n-1)}$, we can analyse the change from p^0 to p^1 as a sequence of simple price changes. That is we define

$$
\begin{aligned}
p^{(1)} &= (p^1_1, p^0_2, \ldots, p^0_n), \\
p^{(2)} &= (p^1_1, p^1_2, p^0_3, \ldots, p^0_n), \\
&\cdots \\
p^{(n-1)} &= (p^1_1, p^1_2, \ldots, p^1_{n-1}, p^0_n) = p^1
\end{aligned}
\tag{13}
$$

When the price of good 1 alone changes we arrive at $p^{(1)}$ from p^0, when the price of good 2 alone additionally changes we arrive at $p^{(2)}$, and so on thereafter until, when the price of the final good $n - 1$ changes, we arrive at p^1 from $p^{(n-2)}$.

If when prices change from p^0 to p^1 we adapt income so as to make it $M^{(1)} = p^{(1)}x^0$ instead of M^0, then despite the fact that price p^1 has changed, the household can still buy the original combination x^0, and therefore there has been a compensatory variation in income. When there has been an income change accompanying a price change in this fashion, let the household choose the combination $x^{(1)}$. Since $x^{(1)}$ has to be a point where income and expenditure are equal, we have $M^{(1)} = p^{(1)}x^{(1)}$. Next suppose that there is a compensating variation in income corresponding to the change in prices from $p^{(1)}$ to $p^{(2)}$; that is a change which enables the household to purchase $x^{(1)}$ at prices $p^{(2)}$. Income after the change is $M^{(2)} = p^{(2)}x^{(1)}$, and with this income and at prices $p^{(2)}$ we let the household choose the combination $x^{(2)}$. The new equilibrium point $x^{(2)}$ satisfies $M^{(2)} = p^{(2)}x^{(2)}$. Continuing in the same fashion thereafter, prices finally change from $p^{(n-2)}$ to $p^{(n-1)}$ (that is p^1). With prices $p^{(n-2)}$ and income $M^{(n-2)}$ the household chooses $x^{(n-2)}$, and in order to be able to purchase this $x^{(n-2)}$ with prices $p^{(n-1)}$, income has to be $M^{(n-1)} = p^{(n-1)}x^{(n-2)}$. Let us assume that with prices $p^{(n-1)}$ and income $M^{(n-1)}$, the household chooses $x^{(n-1)}$.

Now the final $p^{(n-1)}$ which we arrived at in this way is p^1, but $M^{(n-1)}$ is not necessarily M^2. $M^{(n-1)}$ is the amount of income adjusted so as to enable the household to purchase the combination $x^{(n-2)}$ at prices p^1, and M^2 is the adjusted income which allows the purchase of x^0 at prices p^1. If $M^{(n-1)}$ is by chance equal to M^2, then $x^{(n-1)}$ is the same as the combination x^2 which is chosen when prices are p^1 and income M^2. If they are not equal, $x^{(n-1)}$ and x^2 are not the same. In order to arrive at x^2 we must fix prices at p^1 and adjust income anew from $M^{(n-1)}$ to M^2. By doing so we can obtain the equality

$$x^2 - x^0 = (x^{(1)} - x^0) + (x^{(2)} - x^{(1)}) + \ldots$$
$$+ (x^{(n-1)} - x^{(n-2)}) + (x^2 - x^{(n-1)}). \tag{14}$$

That is, the general susbtitution effect is shown as the sum of the $(n-1)$ partial substitution effects (the parts within the first $(n-1)$ pairs of brackets in the above equation) *and* the income effect from the supplementary adjustment in income from $M^{(n-1)}$ to M^2 (the part in the final pair of brackets). In particular for a good j, (14) can be written

$$x_j^2 - x_j^0 = (p_1^1 - p_1^0)\left[\frac{x_j^{(1)} - x_j^0}{p_1^1 - p_1^0}\right] + (p_2^1 - p_2^0)\left[\frac{x_j^{(2)} - x_j^{(1)}}{p_2^1 - p_2^0}\right]$$
$$+ \ldots + (p_{n-1}^1 - p_{n-1}^0)\left[\frac{x_j^{(n-1)} - x_j^{(n-2)}}{p_{n-1}^1 - p_{n-1}^0}\right]$$
$$+ (M^2 - M^{(n-1)})\frac{x_j^2 - x_j^{(n-1)}}{M^2 - M^{(n-1)}} \tag{15}$$

by dividing each substitution term and the income term by their corresponding respective price changes and the income changes. The content of each pair of square brackets of the right-hand side of (15) is the partial average substitution effect of its corresponding price change upon good j. That is, leaving aside the supplementary income effect at the end of (15), the total substitution effect is the weighted sum of the partial average substitution effects with price changes as weights.

Thus formula (15) shows that the total substitution effect is not entirely analysable into partial average substitution effects, but that it must include an income effect based on a supplementary adjustment in income as a residual term. This being so, what sort of status does this remaining term have in the formula? Can we in fact regard the weighted sum of the partial average substitution effects as the basically important part, and ignore the residual term? In order to confront this problem, we will consider

$$M^2 = p^1 x^0,$$

$$M^{(i)} = p^{(i)} x^{(i-1)} = p^{(i)} x^{(i)} \quad (i = 1, \ldots, n-1)$$

(provided $x^{(0)} = x^0, p^{(n-1)} = p^1$), and transform $M^2 - M^{(n-1)}$ as follows:

$$M^2 - M^{(n-1)} = (M^2 - M^{(1)}) + (M^{(1)} - M^{(2)}) + (M^{(2)} - M^{(3)})$$

$$+ \ldots + (M^{(n-2)} - M^{(n-1)})$$

$$= (p^1 - p^{(1)})x^0 + (p^{(1)} - p^{(2)})x^{(1)} + (p^{(2)} - p^{(3)})x^{(2)}$$

$$+ \ldots + (p^{(n-2)} - p^{(n-1)})x^{(n-2)}$$

$$= (p^1 - p^{(1)})x^0$$

$$+ (p^{(1)} - p^{(2)})x^0 + (p^{(1)} - p^{(2)})(x^{(1)} - x^0)$$

$$+ (p^{(2)} - p^{(3)})x^0 + (p^{(2)} - p^{(3)})(x^{(2)} - x^0)$$

$$+ \ldots + (p^{(n-2)} - p^{(n-1)})x^0 +$$

$$(p^{(n-2)} - p^{(n-1)})(x^{(n-2)} - x^0)$$

$$= (p^1 - p^{(1)})x^0 + \sum_{i=1}^{n-2} (p^{(i)} - p^{(i+1)})x^0$$

$$+ \sum_{i=1}^{n-2} (p^{(i)} - p^{(i+1)})(x^{(i)} - x^0).$$

In the extreme right-hand side of this equation the sum of the first and second terms is 0. The reason is that their sum is $(p^1 - p^{(n-1)})x^0$ when terms which mutually cancel out are excluded; but, since $p^1 = p^{(n-1)}$, this remaining term also cancels itself. Consequently we obtain

$$M^2 - M^{(n-1)} = \sum_{i=1}^{n-2} (p^{(i)} - p^{(i+1)})(x^{(i)} - x^0). \qquad (16)$$

The meaning of this equation is as follows. Let us assume that the price change is only a very small one, and thus that the change in the quantity demanded will be very small. Since in (16) both $p^{(i)} - p^{(i+1)}$ and $x^{(i)} - x^0$ are vectors of small absolute values, their products and $M^2 - M^{(n-1)}$, which is the sum of them, are all infinitesimals of a higher order. For that reason, we can see that, when we substitute (16) in (15), the residual term is a higher order minute number than the other terms. Thus if we restrict the scope of the price change within sufficiently narrow confines, we can ignore the residual term and write (15) as

$$x_j^2 - x_j^0 \cong \sum_{i=1}^{n-1} (p_i^1 - p_i^0) \left[\frac{x_j^{(i)} - x_j^{(i-1)}}{p_i^1 - p_i^0} \right], \tag{17}$$

where $x_j^{(0)} = x_j^0$. If we substitute (17) in (9) and (10) we obtain

$$\sum_{j=1}^{n} \sum_{i=1}^{n-1} (p_i^1 - p_i^0) \left[\frac{x_j^{(i)} - x_j^{(i-1)}}{p_i^1 - p_i^0} \right] p_j^1 \cong p^1(x^2 - x^0) = 0 \tag{18}$$

and

$$\sum_{j=1}^{n-1} \sum_{i=1}^{n-1} (p_i^1 - p_i^0) \left[\frac{x_j^{(i)} - x_j^{(i-1)}}{p_i^1 - p_i^0} \right] (p_j^1 - p_j^0)$$

$$\cong (p^1 - p^0)(x^2 - x^0) < 0. \tag{19}$$

(Note that in (19) $p_n^1 = p_n^0$)

(18) and (19) are, respectively, generalisations of what Hicks called the third and fourth rule of substitution effects; of his four rules they play the most basic roles. In fact when all other prices are unchanged and a very small change takes place in the price of a certain good k, (18) and (19) are reduced to

$$\sum_{j=1}^{n} \left[\frac{x_j^{(k)} - x_j^{(k-1)}}{p_k^1 - p_k^0} \right] p_j^1 \cong 0, \tag{20}$$

and

$$\left[\frac{x_k^{(k)} - x_k^{(k-1)}}{p_k^1 - p_k^{0\,'}} \right] (p_k^1 - p_k^0)^2 < 0 \tag{20'}$$

respectively, because $p_i^1 = p_i^0$ for all i except k.

From (20') we find that the substitution effect for itself $[(x_k^{(k)} - x_k^{(k-1)})/(p_k^1 - p_k^0)]$ is always negative; that is, considering the substitution effect alone, the demand curve for each good will be downward sloping to the right with respect to its own price (Hicks' second rule). (20) shows that the substitution effect for a good with respect to its own price and the substitution effects upon other goods of the same price change operate in total so as to cancel each other out, so that there must not be a strong negative substitution relationship (i.e. strong complementarity in Hicks' sense) with other goods.[14+]

D. A simple model of the demand for money

We assumed in the last section that the household spent

the whole of its income or holdings of money. But in fact it will probably spend only part of the money at its command in the current period, and hold the rest for the future. What proportion it consumes in the current period is the result of the household's decision. Although in some cases it does actually spend the whole of its income, as we assumed in the previous section, the theory which assumes that the whole of income is consumed by command from above is no more than a partial theory. In other words, the proportion of income which is currently spent must itself be a variable in the theory.

The reverse side of the decision to consume is the decision to preserve the power to purchase. Consequently, in a society where it is technically impossible to preserve purchasing power, this power is immediately used to the full. In the normal modern society, the power to purchase is preserved in the form of money, bonds, shares, land and other forms of immovable assets, books, pictures, antiques and durable consumer goods; but the power to preserve which they possess is neither uniform nor certain. For example, in a society where there is no well-developed secondhand market, the costs of reselling consumer durables will be high and they will not be an effective means of preserving the power to purchase for the future. And the disadvantage of books, pictures and antiques in this respect is that the resale price may be uncertain and unstable. In the same way uncertainty dogs the heels of shares, immovable assets, bonds with guaranteed interest, and money. Even money — where you might think that a dollar will always be a dollar — cannot be said to be a certain means of preserving purchasing power, since future prices are uncertain.

Which of the various means of preserving value the household chooses (its so-called portfolio selection) is determined depending upon: (i) the returns (interest and others), (ii) the prices of assets at the time they are realised (cashed), (iii) the costs of realising them, (iv) the future level of prices, and so on. Since these proceeds, prices, costs, etc., actually materialise only in the future, and are not fixed at the time of the portfolio-selection decision, the latter also depends on the kind of subjective probability distribution the household has in mind regarding them, and again on the attitude it takes towards risk and uncertainty (whether it will avoid risk and take the safe road, or whether it will accept some risk and go for a big coup).

But even this is not the whole story. Portfolio selection is also influenced by the time when the necessity for realising each asset arises. Where cash is needed in the near future, should interest-bearing bonds be chosen, the interest earned over a short period is unlikely to outweigh the costs of realising the asset (transactions costs); and therefore, money will probably be the form chosen. Thus, portfolio selection depends on the time structure of future cash needs, but these cash sums which will be necessary depend on future revenues and future consumption, and these in turn depend on future prices. Because future prices for consumer goods and future wages are uncertain, and, more basically, because future wants themselves are uncertain, the time structure of future needs for cash is uncertain, and the most which we can obtain is a subjective probability distribution of cash-needs on each future occasion. At this stage in the discussion, whether households like or dislike risk becomes relevant. Furthermore, there are two ways of purchasing future consumer goods. The first is to buy the goods needed on the actual market at the time in the future when they are intended to be consumed. The second is to buy them in advance from the futures market, and have them delivered at a promised time in the future. The second method is only possible where futures markets exist, but once trading in futures is possible, short-selling, hedging (by buying or selling), speculation and so on occur, and insolvency is the result of failure to succeed.

As could be anticipated from the above explanation, a full theory of money or portfolio selection would first require the preparation of a multi-period theory of consumption; secondly it would necessitate consideration of consumer durables, second-hand goods markets and futures markets; thirdly, account would have to be taken not only of uncertainty regarding prices, interest and selling costs, but even of uncertainty regarding utility functions; fourthly, it would have to deal with the difficult problems of short-selling, hedging by buying and selling, speculation and bank-ruptcy. Here I shall forgo any attempt to develop such a compli-cated theory, and content myself with considering an exceedingly simple money model.[15]

Simplicity is achieved by laying down the following strong assumption. The consumer in question here (let us make him a wage-earning labourer) is assumed to live from the present period until period T in the future, and he firmly believes that he has perfect knowledge of the future. Consequently, there is no consideration of uncertainty and risk on his part, and his plans for the future are deterministic. Next, in this economy the only instrument for storing value is money (fiat money), and for that reason there can be no problem of the choice between instruments for storing value. However, we assume thirdly that this is a money economy, and that barter is impermissible. If we make the length of each period short enough that money will not change hands twice within a single period, then money earned by working in a given period cannot be used in that same period, expenditure of it only beginning in the following period. For this reason our labourer has to hold, at the beginning of each period, a sum of money not less than the sum to be spent in the period.

We call x the vector of the quantities of consumer goods demanded in the current period (a column vector), p the vector of their prices (a row vector), y the labour supplied, w the wage rate, and M the quantity of money held at the beginning of the period. The sum which remains after px has been subtracted from M we call H, which is held in the form of money, and combined with the sum of money $J = wy$ which is received as wages, it forms the quantity of money $M(1)$ held at the beginning of the next period (period 1). As for the future (for example future period t), $M(t)$ is the quantity of money held at the beginning of the period, $x(t)$ the vector of the quantities of consumer goods demanded in period t, $p(t)$ the vector of anticipated prices, $y(t)$ the quantity of labour supplied, $w(t)$ the expected wage rate, $H(t)$ the sum which remains after $p(t) x(t)$ is subtracted from $M(t)$, and $J(t) = w(t) y(t)$ the total sum paid as wages. $M(t + 1)$, which is the quantity of money held at the beginning of period $t+1$, is equal to the sum of $H(t)$ and $J(t)$. This relationship holds from period 1 to period T. If we assume that our consumer leaves no money when he dies, then $M(T + 1) = 0$, and thus both $H(T)$ and $J(T)$ are 0. Consequently, he will spend in period T all the money he held at the beginning of the period, and he will do no work during period T. The above relationship can be shown algebraically as follows, bearing in mind that $M(T+1) = 0$,

$$M = px + H, \qquad wy = J, \qquad H + J = M(1), \qquad (21)$$

$$M(t) = p(t)x(t) + H(t), \qquad w(t)y(t) = J(t),$$
$$H(t) + J(t) = M(t + 1) \qquad (t = 1, \ldots T). \tag{22}$$

Let us here introduce the utility function, which did not explicitly appear at all in the discussion of the previous section. Now our consumer has the capacity to compare series of various possible expenditures and series of different amounts of labour which he can supply, and to draw up a scale of preferences among them. We give higher index numbers to more preferred series of expenditures and labour supplies so as to render the scale of preferences in index form, and by so doing, translate the problem of choosing the most preferred series into that of choosing that series with the highest index number.[16] We call these index numbers utilities, and the relationship of correspondence between index number and series, the utility function. We can show the utility function in our case as

$$u = U(x, y, x(1), y(1), \ldots, x(T)). \tag{23}$$

(Since $y(T)$ is always 0, there is no need to show it in the utility function.) In order to prescribe the utility function even more closely, we divide the variables into two classes. In the first class we place variables relating to the present, and in the second those relating to the future. But although the labour y which is supplied at the present time is a variable relating to the present, it is supplied in order to purchase consumer goods in the next period. Therefore, the amount of labour y which the worker undertakes to supply will probably depend a great deal on $x(1)$. For this reason, despite the fact that y is a variable relating to the present, we shall put it into the second class. Thus we obtain x as variables of the first class, and $y, x(1), y(1), \ldots, y(T-1), x(T)$ as variables of the second class. If we assume here that the variables in both classes are separable[17+] (that is, the scale of preference for the various x is independent of the variables of the second class, and conversely, the scale of preferences for the various $(y, x(1), \ldots, x(T))$ is independent of x), u is shown as a function of both the utility function $\phi = \phi(x)$ specific to x and the utility function specific to $(y, x(1), \ldots . x(T))$. That is, under the assumption of separability the utility function (23) can be written as

$$u = U[\phi(x), f\{y, x(1), y(1), \ldots, x(T)\}]. \tag{24}$$

The consumer wants the most desirable combination of present and future goods $x, y, x(1), \ldots x(T)$ under the restriction of (21) and (22). Since by 'most desirable' we mean a situation where utility takes on a maximum value, the problem of determining the consumption plan can be formulated as a problem of conditional maximisation of the utility function over T periods (24). If we then substitute the values of $x, y, x(1), \ldots, x(T)$ at the maximum point so derived into conditions (21) and (22), we can obtain the quantities of the demand for money $H, J, H(t), J(t)(t = 1, \ldots, T-1)$ and consequently $M(t)(t=1, \ldots, T)$. This is the direct method of solving this problem.

E. The simultaneous determination of consumption, earnings and money holdings

We can solve this problem in the following roundabout manner. Instead of maximising u at once under (21) and (22), we maximise the future utility function f under (22) only, as a first preparatory stage. At this point we fix an arbitrary value for y. This preparatory problem determines $x(1), y(1), \ldots, x(T)$. Their values depend upon $y, M(1), p(1), \ldots, p(T), w(1), \ldots, w(T-1)$, which we have regarded as data. But if we assume that expected prices $p(t)$ and expected wage rates $w(t)$ are functions of present prices p and the present wage rate w, then ultimately $x(t)$ and $y(t)$ are shown to be functions of $y, M(1), p, w$. If we further substitute these $x(t), y(t)$ into the original utility function for future goods f, we obtain, in view of $M(1) = H + J$,

$$f = F(y, H + J, p, w). \tag{25}$$

This function can be interpreted in the following way. The two ultimate factors (ultimate arguments), which guarantee the future life of our consumer, are his supply of labour and his holdings of money. We can think of the f thus obtained as the index which shows his scale of preferences for the various combinations of these — that is, the utility function for labour and money holdings. We ought to note here that the utility function for labour supply and money holdings derived in this form as an indirect utility function depends, naturally enough, on prices and on wages. Consequently, we cannot apply the revealed preference axiom, which assumes that the scale of preferences for them is independent of prices and wages. Thus, as we shall see later, the want-pattern effect comes to have a decisively important significance in the analysis of money demand. If we substitute (25) into (24), we obtain[18]

$$u = U[\phi(x), F(y, H + J, p, w)]. \tag{26}$$

These second stage in the maximisation problem is to maximise
(26) under the conditions of (21). Let us write L for $H + J = M(1)$
for the sake of simplicity. Making no distinction between H and J
we combine the three conditions of (21) as

$$px + L = M + wy, \qquad x \geqslant 0, \qquad y \geqslant 0, \qquad L \geqslant 0 \tag{27}$$

We find that this problem has often been dealt with as that of maximising

$$u = U[\phi(x), F(y, L, p, w)] \tag{28}$$

subject to (27). However, it is difficult to assert that sufficient consideration is being given by this traditional form of analysis to the
fact that, in our economy, money is the sole means of payment.
For example, let the solution to the traditional problem be x^0, y^0,
L^0; it is possible that px^0 is smaller than $M + wy^0$, but larger than
M. Consequently our consumer will not have enough money at the
beginning of the period to enable him to buy all his consumer goods,
and he will have to make up the deficiency by passing over some of
the money which comes in as wages from the right to the left.
Because we defined a period as the interval during which money
circulates once, money cannot change hands twice within a period,
and hence it is not possible to assign wages from the right to the
left for the purchase of goods. But let us not raise this objection
here, so that the traditional consumption plan remains both legitimate and feasible. In the extreme case, which is where our consumer
has no money whatsoever at the beginning of the period, he can still
formulate his consumption plan for the current period in anticipation
of the wages he is likely to earn in the current period. Once we
allow this sort of thing to occur, we cannot exclude the possibility
that the extreme case will occur for all people and all firms except
one. The money which the exceptional person holds circulates time
and time again within the society in the settlement of transactions.[19]
Since there is equilibrium in the demand and supply of money, there
must be a consumer or a firm wishing to hold money. If the money
which is circulating in the market comes into the hands of such an
individual or firm last of all, no trouble is caused; but since there is
no guarantee of this, it is likely that it may reach such a person

before long and will not thereafter re-emerge into the market. In this case the remaining demand and supply transactions will have to be settled by barter. That is, if we accept that the traditional theory applies to all individuals and organisations, we shall have to accept the possibility of barter, and thus the paradox arises whereby the need to lay aside money as a means of payment disappears.

The budget equation (27) cannot be a precise formulation of the fact that money is the sole means of payment. Thinking along these lines, Clower[20] was the first to advocate decomposing (27) into a form such as (21). Not only that, he divided the quantity of money into H and J and wrote the utility function as

$$u = U(x, y, H, J, p, w),\tag{29}$$

and maximised it subject to the expenditure equation

$$px + H = M, x \geqslant 0, H \geqslant 0,\tag{30}$$

and the income equation

$$wy - J = 0, \qquad y \geqslant 0, \qquad J \geqslant 0.\tag{31}$$

Since $L = H + J$, Clower's utility function (29) may formally be considered as a generalisation of our utility function (28). But Clower tacitly assumes that $\partial U/\partial H \neq \partial U/\partial J$ and hence the case with which he is dealing must be regarded as different from ours. However, the assumption that $\partial U/\partial H$ (the marginal utility of money in the case where money which was held at the beginning of the period continues to be held), and $\partial U/\partial J$ (the marginal utility of money received as wages) are different is very strange in a model such as Clower's, where the element of uncertainty is excluded. On the assumption that the labourer behaves rationally, the dollar which was kept back at the beginning of the period and the dollar which was earned by working ought to possess the same utility — a dollar is a dollar, after all. Therefore, conclusions which he derived on the premise that $\partial U/\partial H \neq \partial U/\partial J$ cannot be applied to the real world. Then, in the case where $\partial U/\partial H = \partial U/\partial J$ or where the utility function is given by (28), let us examine the significance and the effects of dividing the budget equation into the income equation and the expenditure equation.

In the expenditure equation (30) we have $x \geqslant 0$ and $H \geqslant 0$; hence it implies that consumption in the current period will not exceed the total of money holdings at the beginning of the period (that is, consumption expenditure cannot be made in anticipation of wages to be received in the current period). Similarly, the income equation (31) shows that wages cannot be spent in the current period; the whole must be held in money form and spent in the next period and thereafter. (In our simple model, borrowing and lending are not possible.) But where (28) is maximised under (30) and (31), two cases are possible. Let the solution be x^0, y^0, H^0, J^0; the first case is where $H^0 > 0$, and the second is where $H^0 = 0$.

In the first,case, we can see that our solution is the same as the one obtained in the conventional way by maximising (28) subject to the single budget equation (27). In order to prove this let a denote the combination (x^0, y^0, H^0, J^0), and a' the combination (x^0, y^0, L^0), where $L^0 = H^0 + J^0$. First, a satisfies (27) as well as (30) and (31), and, points in the neighbourhood of the a which satisfies (30) and (31) satisfy (27). As $H^0 > 0$, the converse is also true; that is, points in the neighbourhood of the a' which satisfies (27) also satisfy (30) and (31). Thus when $H^0 > 0$, the condition (27) and the two conditions (30) and (31) are equivalent in the neighbourhood of points a, a'. Consequently, the two conditional maximisation problems give the same maximum point. That is, even though we followed Clower in dividing the budget equation into the income equation and the expenditure equation, the same conclusion has been reached up to this point as with the conventional method of analysis.

Next let us turn to the second case, where $H^0 = 0$. In this case the points in the neighbourhood of a' do not necessarily satisfy (30) and (31). Point a is on the boundary of the set of points which satisfy (30) and (31), but its corresponding point a' is not a boundary point, with respect to L, of the set of the points which satisfy (27) (while $J^0 > 0$). Points in the neighbourhood of point a' to one side of a' (the side which makes $L > wy = J$), satisfy (30) and (31) (since $H > 0$); but because $H < 0$ with neighbouring points on other sides, these do not satisfy (30). In the conventional analysis which does not divide the budget equation into two, we look for a maximum point under the weak condition (27); this maximum point will not come within the limits of the strong conditions (30) and (31), and hence cannot be achieved in our model which divides income and expenditure. In this case the solution yielded by the conventional analysis is a point of higher utility than the true solution, and in order to put such a consumption plan into practice, money earned as wages would have to be defrayed from the right to the left. This is not possible, since the period is made sufficiently brief to prevent it. Consequently, the consumption plan is restricted by the limits imposed by the expenditure condition, and the consumer has to be satisfied with a second best plan which satisfies individually the two budget conditions (30) and (31). Thus the Clower suggestion for separating the income—expenditure condition into two is only significant where the maximum point is on the boundary, and $H^0 = 0$.

However, in this second case we have $px^0 = M$ from (30). Similarly, from (31) $w^0 y^0 = J^0$. These points must give the maxima for $\phi(x)$ or $F(y, J, p, w)$ subject to $px = M$ or $wy = J$ respectively. The reason for this is that, if $\phi(x^0)$ is not a maximum and if $\phi(x)$ becomes a maximum with another point x' where $px' = M$, then it is clear that x', y^0, J^0 will satisfy (30) and (31) with $H = 0$, and moreover that it will give a larger u than x^0, y^0, J^0.[21] This conclusion contradicts the fact that, under (30) and (31), x^0, y^0, J^0 ($H^0 = 0$) is the maximum point of u. Thus x^0 must be the point which maximises $\phi(x)$ under $px = M$. The same can be said for $F(y, J, p, w)$.

Thus in the second case, our problem of the simultaneous determination of the demand for consumer goods, the supply of labour and the demand for money can be divided into two parts; that is, into the problem of the determination of the demand for consumer goods, and the problem of the demand for labour and the demand for money. The former can be formalised as maximising $\phi(x)$ under

$$px = M \tag{32}$$

the latter can be treated as the problem of maximising

$$f = F(y, J, p, w) \tag{33}$$

under

$$wy - J = 0. \tag{31}$$

The former is nothing other than the traditional theory of consumer demand discussed in the previous section. The latter is a variation of the classical theory of money, because, if we sum (31) for all individuals, we obtain a formula to the effect that the total demand for money equals total income. This is identical with the case where, in the classical cash balance equation $M = kY$, the reciprocal k of the velocity of circulation is put at 1. When we

consider the fact that, in our model, the period was made sufficiently short to prevent money changing hands more than once, and
the fact that, in the second case, all the money which the consumer
has at the beginning of the period is used and none remains in his
pocket, then it is natural that k is 1. At all events the complete
separation of consumer theory and monetary theory which holds
in this case can be regarded as the condition necessary for the
validity of the dichotomy in economics between real theory and
monetary theory, discussed by Patinkin.[22]

Now the consumer theory and monetary theory which apply in
the second case are not novel, and neither is the demand theory of
maximising (28) under (27) which is regarded as applying in the
first case. That is, Clower's new proposition has not produced a
new third theory. However, the result of constructing a new model
to take into consideration his suggestion is to determine the respective places of the existing ordinary theories, and to unite them
within a larger framework. Besides, it has been made clear that
traditional consumer theory, and consequently the revealed
preference axiom, is valid only in the special case of $H^0 = 0$. In
maximising either (26) under (21), or (28) under (27), the scale of
preferences for combinations (x, y, H, J) or that for (x, y, L)
depends on prices and the wage rate. For that reason, it is not
possible in this case to apply the revealed preference axiom which
assumes that the scale of preferences for combinations of goods is
independent of prices. In this analysis, the want-pattern effect, to
which little importance has so far been attached in demand analysis
becomes exceedingly important.[23]

Finally, let me point out that it is possible to understand the
problem of maximising (26) or (28) under (21) — the simultaneous
determination of consumption, the labour supply and the demand
for money plans — as a two-stage problem which first formulates
the consumption plan on the one side and the labour supply and
demand for money plan independently on the other, and then
secondly adjusts the two. To do so let us consider the problems of
maximising $\phi(x)$ under

$$px = E,$$

and maximising $F(y, L, p, w)$ under

$$M - E = L - wy,$$

where total consumption expenditure E is a parameter of both problems. When we take the quantity of money at the beginning of the period M, prices p and the wage rate w as given, the maximum point x of the first problem and the maximum point (y, L) of the second are both functions of E. Thus we obtain $u = U(\phi(E), F(E))$. Since E can take on any value within the scope of $0 \leqslant E \leqslant M$, E can be adjusted so as to maximise u in the second stage of the planning operation. Looked at from the point of view of this sort of two-stage demand plan, the case we have seen, where consumer theory and the theory of money are entirely separate, can be regarded as the special case where E is determined at M. Traditional consumer theory solves the first stage of the problem — namely, that of choosing the combination of consumer goods highest in the scale of preferences under a given E. It is seen that this has nothing to do with solving the second stage problem, to find the best value of E. Unless E hits the ceiling of M before and after a price change, E generally depends upon prices, and we cannot apply the conventional Slutsky equation, which has as its premise that E is independent of changes in price. We must add the effects due to changes in E (the income effect), and traditional consumer theory was unable to make clear how E changes. We have to expand the Slutsky equation so as to make it capable of including an analysis of the supply of labour and the demand for money. But in a Slutsky equation thus expanded, a third, want-pattern effect will be added to the income and substitution effects.

F. Points rationing systems

When a large part of a country's resources have to be reserved for the production of military goods, as we experienced during the war; or when in a socialist society consumption has to be restrained in order to build that society, various controls are put into effect. These range from weak functional controls whose sole aim is the fostering or the restraining by the state of the free movement of the economy, to powerful organisational controls whereby the state exercises its authority to completely reform economic organisations in order to prosecute a war or to construct the desired society. One example of organisational control is the 'readjustment of enterprises' (*kigyō seibi*) experienced in Japan during the war.[24] Controls are not necessarily aimed against the 'free enterprise economy'. There is also the case where, without government intervention, competition becomes unmanageable, so that larger monopolies are established as a result of the survival of the fittest. Prices are then manipulated according to the will of the monopolists, and the economy turns into something vastly different from the 'free enterprise economy' (the monopoly capitalism economy of the Marxists, for example). In this sort of situation, the state may work towards the maintenance of the competitive system by enacting anti-monopoly legislation and enforcing the dissolution of 'financial empires' (*zaibatsu*) and large enterprises.

Amongst functional controls, there are price controls and quantity controls.[25+] Price controls range from strict controls which require that a single, official price be established for every individual good (or a number of goods), and that all trading in these goods takes place at these prices, to slack controls whereby maximum or minimum prices (or both) are fixed for a group of goods, and trade in these goods within the permitted price range is acceptable. Furthermore, there is the dual price system where a middle-man (a state organisation) is introduced between the buyer and the seller, and the price at which he buys from the producer and that at which he sells to the consumer are made to differ. If the difference between the price at which the state sells and the price at which it buys is positive, it can be regarded as a kind of taxation; if it is negative, it may be regarded as a subsidy. There is no need for the purchase price to be a uniform one. It is possible to give large subsidies to weak, high-cost enterprises by buying from them at high prices. Quantity controls include distribution controls, where a fixed quantity of a good is allocated to each individual or organisation, and points rationing systems, which we shall consider below. The most strict version of distribution controls is where a good is given an allocation of zero — that is it becomes a prohibited commodity. These quantity controls can occur at various stages. It is possible to have a completely free market in producer goods while instituting distribution controls only for finished goods; or to have a free market in finished goods while allocating producer goods (including labour) to each enterprise. Moreover, if political circumstances permit, both distribution controls and points rationing systems can be discriminative. As in fact happened in wartime, allocations, or the total of points, can differ according to age, sex, occupation, etc.

In a society where a fairly large part, or even most, of limited resources has to be reserved for the prosecution of a war or the building of a society, it is unlikely that price inflation, due to the necessity for dividing the small output of consumer goods between a large number of households, can be avoided. It is also possible under these sorts of circumstances for people of means to use their wealth to buy up the available supply, so that poor people can buy hardly anything. Therefore the state will have to consider distributing these goods as fairly as possible to each household. A variety of methods of control must be studied as price stabilisation policies, or as methods of fair distribution; we shall here evaluate points rationing systems.

Under a system of distribution controls, each household is allocated a fixed quantity of each good, and there is almost no freedom of choice among consumer goods. In contrast to this, under a rationing system, as long as the total of points used by the household on the goods which it has purchased does not exceed a specified number, it can choose freely. Rationing systems are termed general (or total), or partial (or restricted) according to the breadth of the area to which they are applied. The systems which have actually been applied (like the points rationing system for clothing in wartime Britain and Japan) are usually partial rationing systems. Naturally, it is possible to use a number of partial rationing systems at once. However, I shall consider below the case where a general rationing system is applied to all consumer goods.

Forms of economic control have always to be tested in two stages. The first stage is to examine whether the method of control is effective in achieving its objective where all the constituent parts of the economy conform with the controls. The second is to consider whether the method in question is still an effective one, on the assumption that the constituent individuals and organisations of the economy will not necessarily conform with the controls and will engage in illegalities (black-market dealings). The government will hope that no black-market dealings will take place; but since this is unlikely, the method of control must be effective up to a point even though illegal dealings are condoned.

Now let M be the quantity of money a given household can spend on consumer goods in a given period, and N its total of points.[26+] There are n kinds of goods, and we denote the money price of the ith good by p_i, its points by q_i, and the quantity of the

ith good which the household purchases by x_i. The household will choose the highest x in its scale of preference from those x which satisfy both the constraints

$$p_1 x_1 + \ldots + p_n x_n \leqq M, \tag{34}$$

and

$$q_1 x_1 + \ldots + q_n x_n \leqq N. \tag{35}$$

This being the case, what sort of x will it choose? In order to deal with this question we think first of an economy without the points rationing system, where we have our household choose its most preferred combination of goods under the money conditon (34) only; let this combination be x^0. Next we calculate the total of points needed to acquire x^0 as qx^0.[27] Having done this, it is poss-ible for the three cases to occur: (i) qx^0 is smaller than N; (ii) qx^0 is equal to N; (iii) qx^0 is greater than N. In cases (i) and (ii), no difficulty arises in acquiring x^0 under the points rationing system because (35) is satisfied. Since x^0 is the most preferred x of all those which satisfy (34), then naturally it is the most preferred x of those which satisfy both (34) and (35). Consequently, x^0 will in fact be purchased by this household, and thus in cases (i) and (ii) the introduction of a points rationing system will have no influence on the household. It will behave exactly as it did under a free market economy. That is, x^0 is determined only by p and M, and is independent of q and N. In case (ii), (35) is an equality, and so the household uses up all its points; but in case (i) there is an excess of points, and the household will probably keep the unused pages of the ration book on one side while they are still current, and there-after discard them.

In contrast, because of an insufficiency of points, the household cannot acquire x^0 in case (iii). Consequently, the household has to aim at a second-best strategy. It is points and not money which our household lacks, and therefore it may choose its most preferred combination x^1 under (35), which is the formula which expresses the points limitation, multiply this by p and then claculate the total of money needed to purchase this x^1. As before, there exist three possibilities: (i $'$) px^1 is smaller than M; (ii $'$) px^1 equals M; (iii$'$) px^1 is greater than M. In cases (i$'$) and (ii$'$) x^1 satisfies the money condition and so will in fact be chosen. Leaving aside the problem of whether points rationing controls are effective in achieving their objective, in these cases they do influence house-hold behaviour. x^1 is determined by q and N, and is independent of

p and M. Particularly in case (i'), our household possesses an excess of money, but since there is no limit to the period in which money can be used, it is not thrown away but probably put into a safe and kept.

The simultaneous occurrence of (iii) and (iii'), that is, the case where the most preferred combination chosen when considering only the money constraint of (34) fails to meet the points constraint of (35), and vice versa, should occasion no surprise. For example, let us consider a case where the money price of good 1 is much higher than that of good 2, but the points price of good 1 is much lower than that of good 2. When only the money constraint is taken into account, the household will probably purchase a little of good 1 and a good deal of good 2. It is perfectly possible that the points total of such a combination will be large and will exceed the given points constraint. Similarly, when only the points constraint is taken into account, the household will probably demand a good deal of the low-points good 1 and only a little of the high-points good 2. Since the money price of good 1 is high and that of good 2 low, the amount of money required to purchase this combination of goods is large, and it is perfectly possible for it to exceed the money the household possesses. In this case, the household ought not to choose the most preferred combination from among those which satisfy one or other of (34) and (35), and then see whether this combination satisfies the other constraint; it ought instead to choose the most preferred combination from those which simultaneously satisfy (34) and (35). In this case, both (34) and (35) are satisfied as equalities at the most preferred point,[28+] and therefore both the money and the points constraints operate effectively as limits when demand is determined. The equality (34) shows one $(n-1)$ dimensional plane, and equality (35) shows another plane of $(n-1)$ dimensions. Consequently, the set of x which satisfies both equalities forms an area of intersection of two planes; that is, a plane of $(n-2)$ dimensions. The household chooses the most preferred, non-negative point in this plane. If a money price or a points price changes, the slopes of these planes alter. If the quantity of money M or the total of points N changes, then the money plane or the points income plane shows a parallel movement corresponding to these changes. Consequently, the two planes come to intersect at different places, and as a result the household probably chooses a different, most preferred point. That is, in this case the most preferred point x is not only a function of money prices p and money income M, but also of points prices q and points income N.

Thus there are the three cases, where (a) there is an excess of points, (b) there is an excess of money, and (c) there is an excess neither of points nor money, and both the money constraint and the points constraint work effectively as limitations on demand. But since the distribution of points is perfectly (or more or less perfectly) even between households, case (a) will probably arise for households where money income is small, and conversely case (b) will probably arise for households where money income is large.[29+] Thus no restrictions are placed on the demand of poor people, while that of rich people is restricted, so that the gap between the real living standards of the rich and the poor is reduced, and the rationing system makes a contribution to a fairer distribution of scarce goods. Case (c) will arise for the majority of households which are neither rich nor poor. In case (c), despite the fact that, in terms of the total amount of money spent, they are in the same position as they were when no rationing system was in effect, their real consumption is influenced by the system. The state can encourage households of the type (b) and (c) to purchase goods in comparatively plentiful supply, or goods whose elasticity of demand is high, by giving them a small number of points. That is, it can mitigate price inflation as far as is possible by so manipulating the points as to increase the demand for substitutes for scarce goods, and to disperse the pressure of demand over a large number of goods. Thus, if households abide by the points rationing system, it is also effective as a policy for restraining inflation.

G. The black market

We assumed above that the points rationing system was observed perfectly by all consumers. But if an exchange of points for money takes place between the rich and the poor when the well-to-do have an insufficiency of points and an excess of money, while the poor have ample points but insufficient money, then both can lead a better life. That is, if the poor sell a part of their surplus points to the well-to-do, they can then use the remainder in combination with the money they have acquired; the well-to-do can use the points they have bought, with their remaining money, to buy more goods. Thus, if there are sellers and buyers for the scarce good 'points', it is certain that no matter how the law tries to prevent buying and selling of them, a hidden trade in them will take place. Unless the state is excessively coercive, it will resign itself to the appearance of a black market; it will anticipate the circumstances likely to arise when black-market dealings occur, and, if it dislikes them sufficiently, it should not introduce a points rationing system in the first place.

Suppose the black market price of 1 point is r cents and P is the total number of points which the household purchases. (More precisely, if P is positive the household purchases P points; if P is negative it sells $-P$ points.) Since rP cents must be paid out in money for the purchase of P points, the total of money our household is able to use for the purchase of consumer goods is $M - rP$; on the other hand it now holds $N + P$ points. The household will attempt to choose the most preferred combination of goods x which will satisfy the two constraints

$$p_1 x_1 + \ldots + p_n x_n \leqq M - rP, \tag{36}$$

and

$$q_1 x_1 + \ldots + q_n x_n \leqq N + P. \tag{37}$$

How will it adjust P, and what sort of x will it choose? In order to solve this problem, we first of all multiply both sides of (37) by r and add them to each side of (36) respectively. We then obtain

$$(p + rq)x \leqq M + rN. \tag{38}$$

The x which satisfies (36) and (37) must satisfy (38), and it is therefore not possible for the most preferred point from among the x which satisfy (38) (we call it x^0), to be any less desirable than the most preferred point from among the x which satisfy both (36) and (37). It is clear that at x^0 (38) will be satisfied as an equality. That is, we obtain

$$(p + rq)x^0 = M + rN. \tag{39}$$

If a number of points qx^0 needed to purchase x^0 exceeds the points income N, then the deficiency has to be supplied from the black market. Our household does in fact possess the money needed to buy these points P^0, because

$$M - px^0 = rP^0 = r(qx^0 - N) \tag{40}$$

from (39). The first equality of (40) shows that with x^0, P^0 (36) holds as an equality; the second equality of (40) shows that (37) holds as an equality. Thus x^0, P^0 satisfies both (36) and (37), and since no more preferred point than x^0 exists amongst the x which simultaneously satisfy the two constraints, x^0 is the most preferred point.

Thus, when a black market exists, the point of demand of the household is the same as the point of maximum utility under the single constraint (38), and it is therefore formally exactly the same as the result reached by traditional consumer theory. That is, apart from substituting total income $M + rN$ for money income M, and overall prices $p + rq$ for money prices p, there is nothing in the traditional theory that requires amendment. We can write the demand function of each good i as

$$x_i = x_i(p + rq, M + rN), \qquad i = 1, \ldots, n \qquad (41)$$

while we write the function for the demand for points on the black market as

$$P = \Sigma q_i x_i(p + rq, M + rN) - N \qquad (42)$$

This conclusion should cause no surprise. Where there is a black market, it is possible to formulate one's behaviour plan by converting everything into cash terms without being worried by an insufficiency of points. First, total income is $M + rN$ when the household's holdings of points are recalculated in money terms. Next the household will calculate in money terms the prices which it has to pay for its purchases of each good. To purchase good i it has to pay p_i in money and q_i in points, but if we assume it has to go to the black market for all of these points, then it has to pay a total of money $p_i + rq_i$. Thus we obtain (38) as the budget equation when everything is converted into money (or when all transactions are settled on the black market). The quantity of goods demanded is determined as (41) without consideration of a shortage of points, and the deficiency of points which must be supplied from the black market is as shown in (42). (In exactly the same way we can explain the case where money is lacking and points have to be sold.)

With appropriate emendations, all the laws of demand dealt with in section C are valid here. We can divide the effect of prices (money or points prices) on demand into the income effect and the substitution effect. If we take the demand function as being differentiable and write $\partial x_i / \partial M$ for the money-income effect,

$\partial x_i/\partial N$ for the points-income effect, $[\partial x_i/\partial p_j]$ for the substitution effect of money prices and $[\partial x_i/\partial q_j]$ for the substitution effect of points prices, then

$$r\frac{\partial x_i}{\partial M} = \frac{\partial x_i}{\partial N}, \qquad r\left[\frac{\partial x_i}{\partial p_j}\right] = \left[\frac{\partial x_i}{\partial q_j}\right], \tag{43}$$

and we obtain two rules in respect of the income effects:[30+]

$$\sum_i p_i\frac{\partial x_i}{\partial M} + r\sum q_i\frac{\partial x_i}{\partial M} = 1, \tag{44}$$

and

$$\frac{1}{r}\sum p_i\frac{\partial x_i}{\partial N} + \sum q_i\frac{\partial x_i}{\partial N} = 1. \tag{45}$$

From $\sum q_i x_i - N = P$ we obtain $\sum q_i \partial x_i/\partial M = \partial P/\partial M$, and therefore (44) implies that, when money income increases by one unit, money expenditure will increase by only $\sum p_i \partial x_i/\partial M$, and the remainder will be spent on the black market to purchase the points necessary to increase the demand for each good by $\partial x_i/\partial M$. We can explain (45) in a similar way. That is, (45) implies that, when points income increases by 1 unit, the household will increase its demand for each good by $\partial x_i/\partial N$ and itself expend only $\sum q_i \partial x_i/\partial N$ points; it will probably then sell the remainder on the black market in order to acquire the money $\sum p_i \partial x_i/\partial N$ needed for the increase in its demand for each good.

The four rules previously adumbrated are valid for the substitution effects. The most important of them are

$$\left[\frac{\partial x_i}{\partial p_i}\right] < 0, \tag{46}$$

and

$$\sum_{j=1}^{n} \sum_{i=1}^{n} \left[\frac{\partial x_i}{\partial p_i}\right] z_i z_j < 0. \tag{47}$$

(47) corresponds to rule (19) of the traditional theory of demand, and is valid for arbitrary z_i which are not proportional to $p + rq$[31+] (46) means that, as far as the substitution effect is concerned, an increase in the money price of a good will cause its demand to decrease. If we consider (43), we can obtain $[\partial x_i/\partial q_i] < 0$ from (46). That is, an increase in the points price of a good gives its demand a negative substitution effect. This shows us that, even when there is a black market, a points rationing system has the effect of restraining demand.

Putting $z_i = q_i$ in (47), we obtain

$$\sum_{j=1}^{n} \sum_{i=1}^{n} \left[\frac{\partial x_i}{\partial p_j} \right] q_i q_j < 0, \tag{48}$$

provided that q is not proportional to $p + rq$; that is, as long as it is not proportional to p. On the other hand, it can easily be proved from the demand function for points (42), that the left hand side of (48) is equal to the substitution effect on the black market demand for points of an increase in the black market price of points $[\partial P/\partial r]$. Consequently, (48) means that if the black-market price increases, the black-market demand for points will decrease (ignoring the income effect).

Finally, admitting that there is a black market for points, let us examine the effectiveness of a rationing system in restraining demand, in promoting equity and in restraining price inflation. As we have already seen, a household which has a money income over and above that needed to use up its allocation of points from the state, will appear in the black market for points in order to buy points, and will purchase goods with the points so acquired. Hence, the demand for goods by an affluent household is not subjected to such strong limits as when no black market exists. However, part of money income has to be spent on the purchase of black-market points, and so, compared with a free market economy with no rationing, the demand for goods from the affluent household is restricted. In contrast to this, the poor household which does not spend the whole of its allocation of points from the state, will sell a part of its holdings of points on the black market, and thus supplement the deficiency in its money income. Therefore, the poor household's demand for goods is likely to be greater than when there is no black market, or when there is a free economy. Thus, compared with a free market economy, the rich household's demand is restricted and the poor household's demand is promoted under the black market which accompanies a points rationing system. Such restriction and promotion is based on the transfer of money income from rich to poor households which occurs via the black market. For this reason, if we assume that there are no differences in taste for goods between these households, restriction and promotion will cancel out, and we may consider that, overall, the demand for goods will be little different from the free market economy case. Of course, even in this case it is possible by assigning a high points price to goods which are in short supply, to induce households to demand instead goods which are in comparatively plentiful supply, or goods whose demand is elastic. Therefore, we may consider that the demand for each good under the rationing system accompanied by a black market does not put pressure on the supply of these goods to the extent which occurs under a free market economy. Furthermore, it is not impossible to make the demand for each good smaller than the corresponding one in the free economy by assigning points prices in such a way that their ratios to the corresponding money prices are all greater than the ratio of the issued points income to the money income. However, we ought to conclude that, compared with the case where there is no black market, the rationing system's effect in restraining demand is markedly curtailed.

In contrast, we have no need for such pessimism over the effect on equity. The distribution of money income is not equal, but points are distributed equally to households. As a result of buying and selling points on the black market, the number each household actually uses is not equal; but since money is redistributed in a way favourable to poor households through the black market for points, the level of consumption of each household is markedly more equal when compared with what happens under a free market economy. Seen from this point of view, points rationing is a kind of subsidy to poor households.

We assumed above that, despite the institution of a points rationing system, money prices were the same as under a free market economy. However, this is not possible. As we have already seen, consumers' demand for goods is greatly changed, both absolutely and relatively, by the operation of a rationing system. Indeed it is precisely because such a large change was anticipated that this form of control was employed. This being the case, how do prices change when demand functions shift so markedly?

We cannot discuss this question in a strict or general sense at this stage. We have not yet discussed the way in which prices are determined in a perfectly competitive economy where no controls exist. The problem of whether a general equilibrium solution exists is the main subject of chapter 6, and I shall analyse the effects which changes in demand functions have on equilibrium prices on pp. 250–7. Logically speaking, the questions of how the introduc-

tion of various controls exerts pressure on the equilibrium conditions, and of the direction and extent of the movement of the
equilibrium point, can only be dealt with after we have clarified
the laws of free market economies with no controls. Thus, we have
to take many of the conclusions of chapters 6 and 8 as premises in
order to be able to discuss this question here, and for simplicity we
have to make many extreme assumptions.

First, the household's demand function for goods is a function
of overall prices $p + rq$ and total income $M + rN$, as we have
already seen. We shall assume below that the income effect for
rich people is the same as that for poor people, and consequently
that, even though income is transferred from the rich to the poor
through the intermediary of the black market, demand does not
change overall. We show the total demand for good i (that is the
sum of the demand for good i of each household) by X_i, and total
money income and total points income of all households respectively, by M and N which have so far signified the money income
and points income for a single household; but this will cause no
confusion. Thus we obtain the total demand function for all goods

$$X_i = X_i(p + rq, M + rN), \qquad i = 1, \ldots, n, \qquad (49)$$

and the excess demand function for black-market points

$$P = \Sigma q_i X_i(p + rq, M + rN) - N. \qquad (50)$$

Next, although the aggregate supply of all goods S_i depends not
only on the money price of commodities p, but also on the price
of producer goods, among other things, we assume here that there
are no repercussions on the prices of producer goods; so we may
think of S_i as being a function of p only, and regard all other
variables as being unchanged. That is

$$S_i = S_i(p), \qquad i = 1, \ldots, n. \qquad (51)$$

An important point here is that the points rationing system is not
operated for producers, and thus S_i is independent of q.

A proportional change in total composite income $M + rN$ and
composite prices $p + rq$ means that there is no change in real terms
in the budget condition (38), and hence no influence on the quantity demanded of each good — that is, the demand function (49)
is a homogeneous function of degree zero of $p + rq$ and $M + rN$.
Each X_i is independent of the absolute level of $p + rq$ and $M + rN$,

and depends only on their relative proportions. Consequently, we may write

$$X_i = X_i\left(\frac{p + rq}{1 + r\alpha}, M\right), \qquad i = 1, \ldots, n, \qquad (49')$$

and

$$P = \Sigma q_i X_i\left(\frac{p + rq}{1 + r\alpha}, M\right) - N, \qquad (50')$$

where $\alpha = N/M$, and $(49')$ and $(50')$ are obtained by dividing each variable of (49) and (50) by $1 + r\alpha$. In contrast to this, we cannot regard supply S_i as a homogeneous function of degree 0 of consumer good prices. It is true that, where all prices change proportionally, the volume of production and consequently the quantity of consumer goods supplied will be unchanged; but since we have ignored the effects on producer good prices and assumed them to remain unchanged, we can generally regard the volume of supply as changing when commodity prices p change (even though the change may be proportional). As I shall explain in more detail in chapter 6, prices are determined in such a way that demand and supply are in accord, and therefore we obtain the equilibrium conditions for demand and supply

$$X_i\left(\frac{p + rq}{1 + r\alpha}, M\right) = S_i(p), \qquad i = 1, \ldots, n \qquad (52)$$

and

$$\Sigma q_i X_i\left(\frac{p + rq}{1 + r\alpha}, M\right) = N \qquad (53)$$

as the equations of price determination. $n + 1$ of these equations determine n money prices $p_1, \ldots, p_n$ and the black-market price for points r. [32+]

Finally, in general terms the demand function X_i and the supply function S_i depend not only on the price of good i, but on other consumer good prices. However, for the sake of simplicity, I shall assume below that the influence which other consumer good prices exert on X_i and S_i is small enough to be ignored. Furthermore, I shall assume that demand X_i is a decreasing function of its composite price $(p_i + rq_i)/(1 + r\alpha)$, and that supply S_i is an increasing function of money price p_i.

The solution p obtained when we put $q = 0$, $\alpha = N = 0$ in (52),

(53) gives free market prices. Assuming free market prices to be p^0, then

$$X_i(p^0, M) = S_i(p^0), \qquad i = 1, \ldots, n$$

and, of course, (53) is automatically satisfied with $0 = 0$. But if points are issued at a ratio (to money income) greater than the ratio of points prices to money prices, then a points rationing system is not at all effective in restraining demand, so that we now assume that all the ratios β_i of q_i to p_i^0 are greater than the ratio α of N to M. Then

$$1 + r\beta_i > 1 + r\alpha$$

for all positive r; and if we take into consideration the fact that X_i is a decreasing function of $(p_i + rq_i)/(1 + r\alpha)$, then

$$X_i\left(\frac{p_i^0 + rq_i}{1 + r\alpha}, M\right) = X_i\left(\frac{1 + r\beta_i}{1 + r\alpha}p_i^0, M\right)$$
$$< X_i(p_i^0, M) = S_i(p_i^0),$$
$$i = 1, \ldots, n \tag{54}$$

for an arbitrary r. Consequently, whatever black market price for points is established, an excess supply will occur under free market prices, and to eleiminate this excess supply all money prices will have to be reduced.

Here let us make p^1 the prices which bring about equilbrium in the demand and supply of all goods under a given black market price r^1. Then,

$$X_i\left(\frac{1 + r^1\beta_i}{1 + r^1\alpha}p_i^1, M\right) = S_i(p_i^1), \qquad i = 1, \ldots, n \tag{55}$$

and $p^1 < p^0$. The larger is r^1 the larger is $(1 + r^1\beta_i)/(1 + r^1\alpha)$ and therefore the deficiency in demand in (54) will become larger and the fall in prices needed to eliminate this deficiency will become greater. That is, p_i^1 is a decreasing function of r^1. But the excess demand for black-market points is

$$P = \Sigma q_i X_i - N = \Sigma q_i S_i(p_i^1) - N$$

when (55) holds; and so we can think of it as a decreasing function of r^1. This is because if r^1 increases p_i^1 decreases, and if each p_i^1 decreases, S_i too will decrease. Consequently, when the black-market price is extremely high an excess supply of points will arise, and when it is 0 an excess demand will occur, as is proved in the note.[33+] Thus there must be a positive price between these two which will establish an equilibrium in the demand and supply for points in the black market. As we have already proved, the money price for each good corresponding to an arbitrary positive black-market value is smaller than the free market price; therefore, even where a black market for points comes into being, a points rationing system has the effect of restraining prices and is effective as a counter-inflationary policy.

Part 2: The market mechanism and planning

6 The flexprice economy

A. Two methods of determining prices

In part 1 we explained how each constituent part of the economy (firms and households) decided on its demand for goods and on its supply. If we aggregate the individual demand and supply quantities for each good for all firms and households, we can obtain the total demand and supply for society as a whole. Where a society's total demand and supply are equal, all demands are satisfied; where they are not equal unsatisfied demands arise, or else goods will be supplied for which there is no demand. That is, a state of affairs occurs where there is either dissatisfaction or waste. Thus it is most important for the efficient operation of the national economy, be it under socialism or capitalism, that the demand and supply of each good are made to coincide, and that conditions of general equilibrium materialise.

As we shall consider in detail below, there are two ways of equating demand and supply: there is the method whereby prices are adjusted, and the method whereby the quantity of output is adjusted. If returns to the scale of output are diminishing with respect to the production of a certain good, its price will have to increase in order to increase the quantity of output; therefore, where there is an excess demand, adjusting by means of increasing output and adjusting by means of raising the price take place in parallel. However, where returns are constant with respect to scale, it is possible to leave price unchanged and adjust the quantity of output, and therefore demand and supply can be equated purely by regulating the quantity produced and without revising prices. Since returns to scale are constant chiefly in modern manufacturing industries, we can regard the area within which the equating of demand and supply is done by altering supply as widening with the development of these industries, and the regulating function of prices as having atrophied in the economy.

It is very important to recognise this fact. Prices of products are determined according to the 'full-cost rule' or 'mark-up' system in modern manufacturing industries, and not in relation to the scarcity of the good. Consequently, even if the demand for a product increases, its price remains unchanged so long as wages and other costs do not rise, and excess demand is absorbed through expanding output. But in industries with decreasing returns to scale (such as agriculture, certain small and medium-scale enterprises etc. in the case of Japan), excess demand is eliminated by means of an increase in prices, which stimulates supply and at the same time reduces demand. Following Hicks, I have decided to call the former a fixprice economy and the latter a flexprice economy.[1] Actual economies are neither pure fixprice economies nor pure flexprice economies but a mixture of the two, so that where, for example, an economy is expanding through an increase in exports, one group of goods (the products of the modern manufacturing sector) will have their production increased with more or less fixed prices, while the prices of other goods (agricultural commodities and the rest) will increase rapidly. This sort of contrasting movement in prices and increases in the volume of output was a most marked feature of the process of rapid growth in postwar Japan.[2] In this chapter I shall analyse the demand–supply regulating function of prices on the assumption of a pure flexprice economy; in the next chapter I shall analyse the demand–supply regulating function of changes in output on the assumption of a pure fixprice economy. Such pure economies do not, of course, actually exist; but there is no way of discovering the whole ecology of the sytem except by such artificial cultivation.

In part 1, whether discussing the enterprise or the household, we took prices to be data of fixed values to which the household and enterprise had to adapt. Even if the price of a certain good was fixed at a low value, the individual firm had no power directly to revise that price. All it was able to do was to reduce (or suspend) production of that good, change course and seek a more favourable direction. The same circumstances confronted the individual household. That is, we assumed that the enterprise and the household were neither monopolists nor monopsonists, and consequently that it was not possible for any individual or enterprise to be a price-maker. They were price-takers who could do no more than determine their own attitudes after prices were decided.

Of course, in an actual economy many enterprises exist which are large enough to influence prices directly through their own decisions, despite anti-monopoly legislation. Therefore our assumption of an economic system made up only of price-takers is unrealistic, and at the very least can be regarded as far removed from the reality of this era of oligopoly or monopoly capitalism. However, we shall continue to assume below that the market is not monopolised by a single firm or individual, nor dominated by a small number of firms or individuals. In doing so we have to resign ourselves to a degree of unreality, but the need for the ideal conditions of the experimental laboratory is not confined to the natural sciences; it exists in economics too. The neoclassical method of a two-stage approach to reality, by first setting up conditions of pure competition and explaining the theory, and afterwards introducing elements of monopoly, is as persuasive as ever it was. Besides, the neoclassical theory of perfect competition not only guarantees theoretically the attainment of a Pareto optimum, but also offers a theoretical basis for competitive socialism.

When the enterprise or the household passively formulates its own plan of behaviour under given prices, there is no problem if these prices happen to be appropriate and accurately reflect the scarcities of goods. If they do not do so and are determined incorrectly, they will send the economy off in a wrong direction. For example, assume that the central planning authorities of a socialist country fix a high price for an unnecessary good (or one for which the demand is deficient), and a low price for a good which is needed (or one for which supply is insufficient). Under this sort of price system, enterprises will probably try to produce a lot of the unnecessary one; households will not demand the good for which demand is deficient, but the one for which supply is insufficient. Consequently, the conditions of excess supply of the unnecessary good and excess demand for the necessary one will not be eliminated; on the one hand a mountain of stocks will accumulate, while on the other a huge queue of would-be purchasers will form. In the case where the central planning authorities maintain their right to fix prices and have these prices adhered to by enterprises and households, the socialist economy will not function properly unless the authorities have the flexibility to continually revise prices, perseveringly and unabashedly, until they discover the appropriate ones. That is, it will not function properly while the authorities simply cling to their own authority and balk at rectifying the mistakes which they themselves have caused. Thus, giving the enterprise and the household the freedom to adapt to prices, and charging the central planning authorities with the duty of adapting prices, are two sides of the same coin. In fact, in the Soviet Union, the theory of price adjustment put forward by Nemchinov and Volkov, etc., is closely related with the Liberman proposal for making enterprises independently responsible for their efficiency.

How, then are prices made appropriate? Before examining this question, let us first consider how prices are determined under a system of negotiated transactions and under a system of competitive buying and selling, which are the two typical methods of price determination in a capitalist economy. Let us take the Tokyo stock market (before the war) as an example of a typical market in a capitalist economy. The stock exchange day is divided into the morning and afternoon sessions. The morning session and the afternoon session both start with competitive trading, but thereafter negotiated transactions take place until finishing competitive buying and selling occurs once more at the end of the sessions.

Dealings in the market can be seen as a kind of game played by the dealers (or jobbers), and advanced by its custodians, the caller, the watcher and the recorder. When the appointed time for the opening of competitive dealing arrives, these people take up fixed positions on the floor of the exchange, and the opening of trade is signified by the caller. Dealers who wish to buy and those who wish to sell indicate their intentions (who they are, what, how much, and at what price they wish to buy or sell) by waving their arms and shouting. Thus the custodians know the demand and supply coming on to the market, and the caller chooses a price which he thinks is appropriate, and has the first business take place under this first quote. Under the quote shouted out by the caller, the dealers hoping to transact business seek out their opposites; when they find them the two strike hands to signify that a deal has been made. The watcher informs the recorder of the deal which has been made, and the latter makes a record of it.

When this record is made it is worth noting that the following method of entering it up is employed. A record of a transaction only comes to have a definite meaning after five essentials are specified: (i) the parties to the transaction, (ii) the object of the transaction, (iii) the quantity changing hands, (iv) the price of the transaction, and (v) whether the transaction involves selling or buying. The record made during the course of competitive dealing involves only the entering up of essentials (i) to (iii), and (v). That is, there is no record made of the price which was called at the time the transaction took place. This is because competitive buying and selling is a 'single agreed-price' method of price determination; this recording procedure reflects the fact that the price shouted out during the course of these dealings are no more than quotes (or interim prices) and that only the sale price (or equilibrium price) which rules at the end of the process of competitive dealing is valid. In fact, where dealings are not actually carried out at the price which was being called at the time the first agreement was made, it is meaningless to record each and every quote. Furthermore, although it seems at first sight unnatural to actually conclude transactions at the price which holds finally rather than at the price quoted when the inital agreement is reached, this trick is not only necessary in order to discover the equilibrium price; it is also in no way unfair to either sellers or buyers. This is because a dealer who wishes to cancel an agreement made under a different quote can redeem his position completely without any loss whatsoever by buying or selling in the opposite direction. It is a rule of competitive buying and selling that the original transaction and the opposite transaction are settled at the same final price.

If all buyers and sellers are able without exception to 'strike hands' under the quote shouted by the caller, demand and supply are equal at that price, and it is an equilibrium price. But if either a buyer or a seller cannot find someone with whom to make a deal and his demand or supply remains on the market unsatisfied or not taken up, then the caller changes the quote. That is, if a seller is left in the market (an excess supply) the caller lowers the quote; if it is a buyer (an excess demand) he raises the quote. This process continues until finally no excess of either kind exists. In the meantime, needless to say, redemption (short-covering) and selling-up of the kind referred to earlier take place. Where dealers would still like to redeem or sell up, they remain in the market as buyers or sellers, and in these circumstances there is therefore no question of terminating proceedings. When the auctioning has finished and the final quote is recorded as the sale price, all dealers wishing to redeem have redeemed, all those wishing to sell up have sold up, and a state of affairs has been reached where all dealers are completely satisfied with their own trading.

While transactions by competitive buying and selling establish a single agreed price for each commodity, a number of sale prices will be formed through the process of negotiated transactions. As already stated, this occurs in the interval between the opening and the closing competitive buying and selling of the session. Assuming one dealer is waving his arms and shouting that he would like to buy ten thousand shares in company A at one hundred dollars each, and another wishes to sell six thousand shares in company A at one hundred dollars, then six thousand shares at one hundred dollars apiece will change hands between them. This transaction is, of course, recorded by the appropriate official; but in contrast to what happens under competitive buying and selling, a detailed record of all five essentials is made, including the price. The price at which the agreement is made is made public as the sale price, and the deal actually takes place at that price.

However the dealer still remains in the market, now saying 'I buy four thousand company A at one hundred dollars.' Unless a new supplier comes forward, he will have no-one with whom to do business and his demand will go unsatisfied. At this point he changes his stance and, for example, raises his arm with the offer 'I buy three thousand company A at one hundred and ten dollars.' Once the price has risen from one hundred to one hundred and ten, a third dealer emerges who wishes to sell five thousand shares in company A at that price, and so a deal is made. This latter dealer now raises his hand and voice with 'I sell two thousand company A at one hundred and ten', which is his excess supply. Thus the price has risen by ten dollars. This is known as the negotiated method of buying and selling, and the price which is established is known as the negotiated price. A negotiated price, unlike the sale price in competitive buying and selling, is not generally an equilibrium price. This is because, as the above example shows, there was an excess demand on the market at a negotiated price of one hundred and ten dollars. Thus it is not an equilibrium price, but neither is it a quote, or an interim price, necessary for discovering the equilibrium price. Negotiated prices are not quotes shouted out by the caller, but sale prices corresponding to which there actually exist agreements transacted at those prices.

B. Competitive trading and negotiated transactions

As stated above, there are two methods of price determination — the competitive-trading method and the negotiated-transactions method. If we except trading which occurs in special exchanges, trade which takes place in most actual markets is by negotiated transaction. Competitive trading, which is able to eliminate excess demand or supply in a short period, is only possible in a well-constituted market. Leaving aside the exchanges, actual markets are not as perfect as this, and therefore price determination via the competitive method is hardly possible in them. Looked at from this practical point of view, analysis of the negotiated transactions process ought to precede that of the competitive trading process. However, we shall assume below that the prices of all goods are determined competitively. The reason for this assumption is that we shall be seeking equilibrium prices which correspond to a given initial distribution of goods between individuals and organisations; that is, we shall be seeking a price system which makes mutually compatible the behaviour of each individual and organisation, provided that, under a given distribution, each behaves rationally. If we refer to the state of affairs where under a given distribution each component of the economy behaves rationally, and moreover the activity of each contradicts that of no other component, so that the whole is mutually compatible, as a Walrasian equilibrium, then what we are seeking is a Walrasian equilibrium corresponding to a given initial distribution. Even if the initial distribution of goods is determined by the past or by the central planning authorities, this of course does not necessarily mean that a Walrasian equilibrium materialises at once. If prices are given, each component will make its own particular decisions rationally; but when mistaken prices are given them, the decisions of each individual and organisation will not be mutually compatible.[3+]

While groping for the prices which will produce a Walrasian equilibrium, we have to assume that the initial distribution of goods is fixed. Otherwise, even if we assume we can finally discover equilibrium prices, these will be no more than equilibrium prices corresponding to a different initial distribution of goods. If the initial distribution of goods changes, the Walrasian equilibrium state will change correspondingly. For this reason, we can find the Walrasian equilibrium corresponding to an initial distribution of goods under a mechanism such as the competitive-trading market, whereby it is guaranteed that the initial distribution will be held unchanged; but we cannot find the Walrasian equilibrium corresponding to the very earliest distribution of goods in a market where negotiated transactions rule and the distribution of goods changes moment by moment. The best we can do in the latter market is to find the Walrasian equilibrium corresponding to the final distribution of goods. Moreover, where an excess supply (or demand) arises in the midst of the negotiated transactions process, it is more or less a matter of chance which supplier (demander) goes unsatisfied (who most quickly finds a trading partner, etc.,); therefore, the change in the distribution of goods during the negotiated transaction process is uncertain. Consequently, the Walrasian equilibrium, even if it is finally established, is also uncertain. The most we can obtain from analysis of the negotiated transactions process is the conclusion that one of a number of Walrasian equilibrium states from within given confines will finally materialise.[4+]

The comparative-statics analysis of individual supplies and demands, which we employed up to the last chapter, fits neatly with analysis of the process of determining equilibrium prices by the competitive method, but does not harmonise with analysis of price changes under the negotiated transactions rule. To show this let us compare alterations in demand and supply which occur within these two processes of change. Let $p_1 p_2, \ldots, p_n$ be prices at time t, and $p_1, p_2, \ldots, p_{n-1}, p_n + \Delta p_n$ prices at the next point of time $t + 1$.[5] Let us assume that, instead of the money and goods (respectively $\bar{M}, \bar{x}_1, \ldots, \bar{x}_n$) which the consumer held at time t, he would, if prices were given by $p_1, \ldots, p_n$, want to hold $M, x_1, \ldots, x_n$. The budget equation requires

$$\bar{M} + p_1 \bar{x}_1 + p_2 \bar{x}_2 + \ldots + p_n \bar{x}_n = M + p_1 x_1 + \ldots + p_n x_n \qquad (1)$$

Suppose now that our consumer agrees to purchase (or sell) goods in a competitive market, and, as a result, the quantity of goods he possesses becomes $x'_1, \ldots, x'_n$.[6] At time $t + 1$ these goods are valued at the prices of time $t + 1$, which are $p_1, \ldots, p_{n-1}, p_n + \Delta p_n$ (assuming only p_n changes). The quantity of money he holds at this time is derived by subtracting the sum to be paid for the goods which he agreed to purchase at time t, from the sum made up by adding the money deriving from the sale of goods at time t to the quantity of money held at time t. These sums ought to be calculated on the basis of the new prices ruling at $t + 1$, and not at the prices which ruled at t when the agreements were arrived at. (As already stated, this follows naturally from the fact that the competitive system of buying and selling is a formula for trading by the single, agreed-price method.) The money acquired by thus calculating sales, minus the expenditure for purchases, is

$$\Delta \bar{M} \equiv p_1(\bar{x}_1 - x'_1) + p_2(\bar{x}_2 - x'_2) + \ldots$$
$$+ p_{n-1}(\bar{x}_{n-1} - x'_{n-1}) + (p_n + \Delta p_n)(\bar{x}_n - x'_n).$$

Therefore money holdings at time $t + 1$ are the same as $\Delta \bar{M}$ added to the money held at time t. On the other hand, the goods which our customer holds at time $t + 1$ have a value of

$$A \equiv p_1 x'_1 + p_2 x'_2 + \ldots p_{n-1} x'_{n-1} + (p_n + \Delta p_n) x'_n$$

Therefore, we can easily see that his total purchasing power at time $t + 1$, which is the sum of $\bar{M}$, $\Delta \bar{M}$ and A, is the same as the left hand side of (2) below. If we write $M + \Delta M$, $x_1 + \Delta x_1$, $\ldots$, $x_n + \Delta x_n$ for the quantity of money and goods which he wishes to hold at $t + 1$, his budget equation for that time is

$$\bar{M} + p_1 \bar{x}_1 + \ldots + p_{n-1} \bar{x}_{n-1} + (p_n + \Delta p_n) \bar{x}_n$$
$$= M + \Delta M + p_1(x_1 + \Delta x_1) + \ldots + p_{n-1}(x_{n-1} + \Delta x_{n-1})$$
$$+ (p_n + \Delta p_n)(x_n + \Delta x_n) \tag{2}$$

If we compare the right-hand side of (1) with the right hand side of (2), we can see at once that in both only prices change, and that holdings of money and goods $\bar{M}, \bar{x}_1, \ldots, \bar{x}_n$ are unchanged. At first glance this seems to contradict the fact that, in the process of competitive buying and selling, claims on goods are transferred along with the making of trading agreements, and that a record of these transfers is made by the recorder. But if the point is given further consideration, it is seen, as has been made clear above, that in the competitive buying and selling process what is paid as recompense for the transfer of claims or goods is not the price which ruled when the agreement was made; the payment is made at the price then current (consequently, ultimately at the equilibrium price). Therefore, the increase due to price increases in what has to be paid against agreements to buy made in the past, is exactly cancelled by the increase in the price of the stock of goods purchased in the past. As a result, purchasing power remains the same as if no transfer of goods at all had taken place. This characteristic of the method of competitive buying and selling lightens considerably the work of the caller in the competitive market itself.

In fact, if the market were constituted in such a way that prices proposed by the caller influenced various people's purchasing power through the transactions which were made at these prices, then the calling of a mistaken price would have significant effects on future transactions and the responsibility of the caller would be heavy. As we shall see later in more detail, where prices are formed by the negotiated transaction method, equilibrium prices depend on the course of preceding transactions, and consequently in any strict sense negotiated transactions cannot be a *neutral* trial for finding equilibrium prices. When attempts are made to find equilibrium prices by trial and error, the equilibrium price arrived at ought not to be influenced by the trials made; therefore we have inevitably to rely on the competitive method of price formation. Even if, under this system, the caller calls out a somewhat wild price, influence is exerted only on the time needed to arrive at an equilibrium price, and not on the equilibrium price itself. Thus, the neutrality of the role of the caller is guaranteed within the rules of competitive pricing themeslves, and he is absolved from any heavy responsibility.

If we subtract (1) from (2) and rearrange terms, we obtain

$$\bar{x}_n - x_n = \frac{\Delta M}{\Delta p_n} + p_1 \frac{\Delta x_1}{\Delta p_n} + \ldots + p_n \frac{\Delta x_n}{\Delta p_n}. \tag{3}$$

We assume that the size of the change in the price of good n, Δp_n, is sufficiently small that the changes induced in the demand and supply $\Delta M, \Delta x_1, \ldots, \Delta x_n$ are also small. The values of each of these individually may themselves be ignored, but their ratios $\Delta M/\Delta p_n$, $\Delta x_1/\Delta p_n$, etc. cannot necessarily be disregarded.[7+] As we have seen from (1) and (2), which are budget equations before and after a change in prices, $\Delta M, \Delta x_1, \ldots, \Delta x_n$ are equal to the changes in the quantities of money and goods demanded in the case where the price of good n alone has changed, and the initial quantities of money and goods are held constant. In the competitive market, as changes in an individual's holdings of money and goods are independent of the progress of his transactions agreements, we can regard his demand function as a function of prices only, with the initial holdings of money and goods being fixed at the values at the beginning of the period, just as we did in the comparative-statics analysis of consumer demand of the preceding chapter; we may totally ignore the historical progress of agreements which have arisen between the beginning of the transactions period and that moment.

It is thus possible to use knowledge of the demand functions derived from comparative-statics analysis to analyse the process of price formation (or price change) in the competitive process. In order to show that this is not possible in the negotiated transactions process, let us consider what kind of changes in demand do take place there. Let us first think of a consumer who is unable to make an agreement for any good in a market where negotiated transactions rule. Since he holds the same quantity of money and goods before and after the price change, needless to say his budget equation before the price change is (1), while that for after the change is (2). Therefore his demand function has to satisfy the condition (3). However, assume also that our consumer made agreements to buy or sell when prices were $p_1, \ldots, p_n$ and that as a result his holdings of goods became $x'_1, \ldots x'_n$. These holdings will be valued at the new prices $p_1, \ldots, p_{n-1}, p_n + \Delta p_n$, and in a market where negotiated transactions are the rule, these agreements to buy or to sell will be settled at the prices ruling when the agreement was concluded (that is at the old prices). For this reason, the net acquisition of money from having sold or purchased is

$$\Delta \bar{M} = p_1(\bar{x}_1 - x'_1) + \ldots + p_n(\bar{x}_n - x'_n). \tag{4}$$

Consequently, our consumer's budget equation after the price change is written as

$$\bar{M} + \Delta \bar{M} + p_1 x'_1 + \ldots + p_{n-1} x'_{n-1} + (p_n + \Delta p_n)x'_n$$
$$= M + \Delta M + p_1(x_1 + \Delta x_1) + \ldots + p_{n-1}(x_{n-1} + \Delta x_{n-1})$$
$$+ (p_n + \Delta p_n)(x_n + \Delta x_n). \tag{5}$$

If we take (4) into consideration we can derive

$$x_n' - x_n = \frac{\Delta M}{\Delta p_n} + p_1 \frac{\Delta x_1}{\Delta p_n} + \ldots + p_n \frac{\Delta x_n}{\Delta p_n} \tag{6}$$

from (1), the budget equation before the price change, and from (5), the budget equation after the price change. As will be seen from a comparison of (3) and (6), they are not the same. That is, the quantity held of good n, which appears on the left-hand side of these equations, remains at $\bar{x}_n$ as in (3), where the consumer was unsuccessful in negotiating transactions in this good; where a transaction is made the quantity held becomes x_n', which replaces $\bar{x}_n$, as in (6). Thus by comparing the case where, in the past, a consumer made agreements to buy or to sell in a negotiated transactions market with the case where he did not make any agreements, we find that the change in the volume of demand cannot be the same. This tells us that the demand function in the negotiated transactions market at any particular time is not simply a function of holdings of goods and money at the beginning of the period and prices; it depends also on the progress of agreements to buy or to sell between the beginning of the period and that time. Therefore we must conclude that comparative-statics analysis, which regards demands for goods as being functions only of prices and the initial holdings of goods and money, ignoring those historical effects on demand which are exerted by the dynamics of the change in holdings during the course of transactions, cannot be applied to analyse price changes under the negotiated-transactions process, though it can be applied to the analysis of the competitive process.[8+]

C. The price-adjustment equation and the numéraire
Let us assume now that all dealers are price-takers, and that the custodians of the market or the central planning authorities determine prices so as to equate the total quantity demanded and the total quantity supplied for each good. These quantities were determined by suppliers and demanders adapting passively to given prices; if they are unequal for some goods, then their prices are adjusted according to the competitive formula. For a good whose demand exceeds its supply, the caller or the authorities will propose a higher price, while for a good with an excess supply, a lower price. Economists normally refer to such a market as a perfectly competitive market.

In order to show how excess demand is determined we shall analyse the quantity of demand and the quantity supplied. We deal first with the enterprise. In the case of the socialist economy, as we have already seen, if the enterprise once fulfils its output norm, then, under the restrictions imposed by its state allocation of capital, raw materials and labour, it is allowed to pursue the maximisation of profits. (There may be free markets for labour and raw materials, for which each enterprise can make demands without restriction.) In the case of the capitalist economy, there is no restriction placed on the volume of output, raw materials and labour, while capital goods, if they are immobile, are subject to restriction in the short period. Where prices are given, the enterprise works at its full capacity even in the case of the socialist economy. The level of activity at which the enterprise meets the limit of full capacity depends on the techniques employed, and since the choice of techniques depends on prices, ultimately the volume of production of the enterprise and its demand for factors of production are a function of prices.

Thus where there is a fixed limit on production, a firm's supply of output and demand for factors can be expressed as a function of prices alone. However, in a capitalist economy, if there is perfect mobility of capital goods, or if they increase or diminish freely in quantity (this can always occur if we take a fairly long period); or, in a socialist economy, if the central planning authorities make the allocation of productive factors to enterprises a flexible one, the quantities demanded and supplied by the enterprise will not be predetermined even though prices are determined. Thus the analysis which follows is not appropriate in such a case. I shall consider the mechanism of adjustment of demand and supply in the case where the volume of production is freely flexible separately in chapter 8.

Next we deal with the demand for each good and the supply of labour (or the services of managers) made by the household of the ordinary worker (and of the head of the enterprise). These depend on the prices of goods, wages, salaries and bonuses, and on the quantities of these goods held by workers and managers at the time. But bonuses depend on profits, and thus eventually on prices; thus we can think of the quantities demanded and supplied by the household as being functions of prices and the quantities of goods held. While competitive buying and selling goes on, the quantities of goods held by each individual change from time to time. However, as we explained in detail in the preceding section, while transactions take place according to the competitive formula, we can simply disregard movements of goods between the beginning and the end of the process of competitive dealing, and can take the households' demand and supply as a function of prices alone.

Finally, we turn to the state. We shall think of it as always aiming for a balanced budget, but as not levying taxes.[9+] This implies that we totally ignore the economic activity of the capitalist state, where taxation is the origin of state revenue. In the socialist economy the state levies a rental on capital goods from each enterprise, and therefore it has a revenue. But we assume that the state does not vary its allocation of capital goods to each enterprise, so that the income of the state is a function of the rentals on capital goods and the bonuses to capital goods. Since the latter depend on prices, ultimately they are a function only of prices. With the revenue thus acquired, the state purchases various goods. I am assuming that the quantity demanded of these goods is also a function of prices alone.

According to the above, the quantities demanded and supplied of all goods by all individuals and organisations in the economy are functions of prices alone, and therefore the excess demand for each good is also a function of prices alone. Now let $p_1(t)$, $p_2(t)$, $\ldots$, $p_n(t)$ be the prices shouted out by the caller at time t during one session of competitive trading, and $E_i(t)$ the excess demand for good i corresponding with these prices; then

$$E_i(t) = E_i(p_1(t), p_2(t), \ldots, p_n(t)).$$

If we assume that the caller raises and lowers prices in proportion to the quantities of excess demand, the price of good i shouted out at time $t + 1$ has to satisfy the formula

$$p_i(t+1) - p_i(t) = aE_i(t). \tag{7}$$

Here the proportional coefficient a is a fixed positive number, and shows how sensitively the price of good i reacts to the excess demand for it. This coefficient (Lange called it the degree of price flexibility) will generally be different for every good, since there is no reason why the degree of price flexibility should be the same for strawberries as for steel.[10] But in order to simplify the analysis below, I shall assume that a is the same for all goods.

The equation (7) holds not only with respect to a specific good i, but for all i where $i = 1, \ldots, n$. When prices shouted at time t are given, the corresponding $E_i(t)$ is determined, and consequently, by (7), the prices $p_i(t+1)$ shouted at time $t+1$ are determined for all goods i. It seems at first glance that this process can be repeated without limit and not come to a deadlock. However, (7) implies that the price $p_i(t+1)$ shouted at $t+1$ is the sum of the prices $p_i(t)$ shouted at t and $aE_i(t)$. Consequently, where there is an extreme excess supply of good i, that is where $aE_i(t)$ takes on a large enough negative value, the $p_i(t+1)$ determined by formula (7) becomes negative. Clearly negative prices are meaningless, and in practice the caller never shouts a negative price for a good (unless it be sewage

or waste of some sort). In such a case, were the caller to call out a
negative price calculated according to the formula, he would only
throw the market unnecessarily into confusion. Therefore he will
not lower prices until they are negative, but will probably call out
a price of zero, which can be thought of as the lowest limit. When
the sum of $p_i(t)$ and $aE_i(t)$ is greater than 0, the caller shouts out
the price according to the formula, and consequently the price
called on occasion $t + 1$ is the same as the sum of $p_i(t)$ and $aE_i(t)$.
But when this sum is negative, he will call out 0, which is larger
than this sum. Thus the caller compares the sum of $p_i(t)$ and $aE_i(t)$
with 0 before shouting the price, and he calls the larger as the price
at time $t + 1$. If we show the operation of comparing x and y and
taking the larger by max $[x, y]$, we may write the equation of price
formation, after the amendment described above has been carried
out, as

$$p_i(t+1) = \max\ [p_i(t) + aE_i(t), 0], \qquad i = 1, \ldots, n \qquad (7')$$

Even when competitive trading is conducted by the caller in this
way according to the revised formula $(7')$, there is a case where
eventually a standstill is reached. It occurs for the following reason.
Firstly, what is meant by the price of good i is the rate of exchange
between good i and a good which forms a standard — the numéraire.
Therefore, the price of good i is relative to the standard good or
numéraire. In the normal case of the money economy, money
becomes the numéraire; but in the pure, barter economy (in which
money does not exist), which we have constructed to avoid the
various difficulties surrounding money, we can take unskilled labour
or a representative consumer good (wheat for example) as our
numéraire. Behind the formula $(7')$ there is the premise that some
good or other has been chosen as the numéraire, so that $p_i(t)$ and
$p_i(t+1)$ are prices of good i which have been expressed in terms of
this numéraire. For this reason, where good i is itself the numéraire,
it is evident that $p_i(t)$ and $p_i(t+1)$ are always equal to 1. (All goods
exchange with themselves at a rate of 1.) Consequently, providing
$E_i(t)$ is not equal to 0, we know that formula $(7')$ is not valid for
the standard good or numéraire. By this reasoning, as long as we
take a specific good as the numéraire, this good lies outside the
range of goods 1 to n; we must regard formula $(7')$ as being appropriate only for goods other than the numéraire.

Let us proceed now on this basis. That is, we take some good or

other, for example money or perhaps wheat, as our numéraire
good, and measure the price of each good as a rate of exchange
with the numéraire. We tacitly premise this with the assumption
that money and wheat are never free goods. However, this is not
self-evident. Even if we assume that the demand for money and
wheat is not less than the supply under the prices which prevail at
the opening of competitive dealing, if prices change with the
progress of competitive trading, it may happen that demand will
fall below the supply of money or wheat at the new prices. The
price of money or wheat in terms of money or wheat is 1 and not
0, and therefore, by the Walras law which I shall deal with in detail
later, there must arise an excess demand for some good other than
money or wheat. Consequently, according to formula (7'), the
price of that good will rise. If an excess supply of money or wheat
arises even on the basis of the new prices, and if these circumstances
persist, the prices of the other goods will increase more and more.
Eventually they will become limitlessly high, and it will become
either impossible or meaningless to express the prices of these goods
in terms of money or wheat. That is, the numéraire or standard
good will cease to perform the function of a standard, and will become a free good, no better than the sands of the seashore or the
air in the sky for this purpose. Of course, as a practical possibility,
the chances of such exceptional circumstances occurring are small;
but in theory there is no guarantee against them. (In fact, the mark
became essentially a free good after the First World War, and in the
United States it would cause no astonishment if wheat became
virtually a free good, were the government not to support its price.)
This is the same for whatever good becomes the numéraire. The
existence or otherwise of the possibility that an excess supply of
the numéraire good will persist, and that it will lose its ability to
function as a numéraire because it becomes virtually a free good,
cannot be determined without discovering the quantities demanded
and supplied of the good in question under all price conditions. As
a result of such an exhaustive investigation we may find out, even
at this stage, that unfortunately the worst case will occur — where
the possibility outlined above exists for every good and there is no
good suitable to function as a numéraire.

   In these circumstances what good should the caller choose in
order to further the process of competitive dealing? The most
certain way of preventing the process of competitive dealing

coming to a halt in mid-stream because the numéraire becomes a
free good, is to take one unit of each good and make an artificial
good out of the whole set, and to use this as the numéraire. By
doing so, as long as only some and not all goods become free goods,
the artificial composite good which is the numéraire will contain
some non-free goods, and therefore will not itself become free. (Of
course, in the extreme case where all goods become free goods, the
numéraire too will be a free good; but in that case there would be
no scarcity, the economic problem would cease to exist and there
would be no need to continue with the process of competitive
buying and selling.) That is, we ought not to view the price adjustment equation $(7')$ as being valid for the remaining n goods after
one specific good has been taken as the numéraire, but as holding
for all goods. The prices of all goods should be regarded as being
measured in terms of a standard which is an artificial good made
up of a bundle comprising one unit of every good. Where the
caller furthers the course of competitive trading in accordance
with this rule for normalising prices, it is not possible for the
process to be halted by the failure of the standard good to function
as such. (We are proposing that the numéraire be formed this way
in theory, and not that the practical problem should be tackled
thus.)

I shall now explain price formation in a barter economy. We are
interested in such an economy because we want to avoid the problems surrounding money. Since the standard good (numéraire) is a
composite good made up of one unit of every existing good, its
price is the sum of the prices of all goods; that is

$$p_1(t) + p_2(t) + \ldots + p_n(t).$$

Since it is the price of the standard good it must always be equal to
1. But, since the sum of the $p_i(t+1)$ determined according to $(7')$
is not necessarily equal to 1, we ought to regard $p_i(t+1)$ as prices
which have not yet been made subject to a standard in the above
sense. In order to obtain prices in terms of the composite good, we
must further transform $p_i(t+1)$ into the $q_i(t+1)$ defined as

$$q_i(t+1) = \frac{p_i(t+1)}{\sum_j p_j(t+1)} \tag{8}$$

By doing so, the sum of the $q_i(t+1)$, $i = 1, \ldots, n$, will be equal to 1,
and prices at $t+1$ will come to satisfy our normalisation condition.

By substituting (7') in (8) we obtain

$$q_i = \frac{\max[p_i + aE_i, 0]}{\sum_j \max[p_j + aE_j, 0]}. \tag{9}$$

Here, needless to say, for simplicity's sake we have omitted the $t+1$ which ought to be attached to q_i, and the t which ought to be affixed to p_i, E_i. This equation of price adjustment satisfies (i) the condition for normalisation of prices, and (ii) the non-negative conditions where by prices will fall no further than 0 even if there still exists an excess supply when prices are 0. However, it does not necessarily satisfy the conditions of flexibility in an upward or downward direction where prices are positive. That is, even if there is an excess demand for a good it is possible for its price to fall; it is also possible for it to rise where there is an excess supply. At first sight this seems to contradict the upward and downward flexibility in (7) which was the point of departure for obtaining (9); but on closer examination it ceases to be a cause for surprise. If, even when there is an excess demand (or supply) for a certain good i, there is a good j with an even greater deficiency in its supply (or demand), the price of good i will not rise (or fall) as much as that of good j. Consequently, in its relationship with the artificial numéraire good which contains good j as one of its components, it is possible for circumstances to occur where the price of good i can fall (or rise) in this seemingly perverse fashion. Hereafter, I shall refer to the system in which prices are determined according to (9) as the neoclassical system.[11+]

D. The existence of equilibrium prices

Let us think of the caller as raising and lowering prices in accordance with (9), the equation for adjusting prices, and thus groping towards equilibrium prices. This groping process makes sense where the existence of equilibrium prices is guaranteed; but where it is not, it is as meaningless as buying a ticket in a lottery which has no prizes. Therefore, before dealing with the problem of whether we can arrive at an equilibrium by adjusting prices according to (9), we have to ask whether, in fact, equilibrium prices exist. I shall discuss the problem of arriving at equilibrium prices (or the analysis of the stability of equilibrium) in the next section; in this section I shall consider only the question of their existence.

First, we have to make clear what equilibrium prices are. There are two definitions of equilibrium prices. The first is that they are stationary prices; the second is that they are prices which balance demand and supply. Let us begin by explaining the first definition.

If we assume competitive buying and selling, excess demand is a function of prices alone. As I have already explained in some detail, the quantity of goods held by individuals and organisations changes during the competitive process, but, nevertheless, in the excess demand function we can regard the quantities of goods held by these individuals and organisations as unchanged. If prices $p_1, p_2, \ldots, p_n$ are given, the quantity of excess demand is determined and thus the value of the right-hand side of the equation for price adjustment (9) is ascertained, and the prices $q_1, q_2, \ldots, q_n$ which ought to be called out next are determined. In this way the transformation from prices $P = (p_1, p_2, \ldots, p_n)$ to $Q = (q_1, q_2, \ldots, q_n)$ is obtained. Accordingly, if $P \neq Q$ (that is, if for at least one good $p_i \neq q_i$), we say that P is a moving point; if $P = Q$ (that is if $p_i = q_i$ for all goods), we say that P is a fixed point or a stationary price system. Stationary prices defined in this fashion are, according to the first definition, equilibrium prices.

Next, according to the second definition of equilibrium, we say that the market for good i is in a state of normal equilibrium if the demand and supply of good i are equal (that is, if the excess demand for good i is zero). Besides this, we can imagine a state of anomalous equilibrium, where supply exceeds demand but the price of the good is already 0, so that it is already a free good. The suppliers, far from trying to bid down the price to get rid of all their unsold goods, renounce all claim to the ownership of the goods, and hand them over gratis to anyone who wants them. (However, there is an excess supply and so no demand for these goods, and they are left to lie before the public.) We can lump normal and anomalous states of equilibrium together, and show them formally as

$$E_i(p_1, p_2, \ldots, p_n) \leqq 0, \qquad i = 1, \ldots, n \qquad (10)$$

(with $p_i = 0$ if $E_i < 0$).

The equilibria of these two definitions are, however, identical under Walras' law. This can easily be proved. First, we prove in the following fashion that the point of equilibrium in demand and supply is a fixed point of prices. In a state of normal equilibrium, E_i is 0, and therefore max $[p_i + aE_i, 0] = p_i$; where the equilibrium is abnormal, E_i is negative and p_i is 0, and so again max $[p_i + aE_i, 0]$ $= 0 = p_i$. Therefore, at the point of equilibrium in demand and supply,

$$q_i = \frac{\max[p_i + aE_i, 0]}{\Sigma \max[p_j + aE_j, 0]} = \frac{p_i}{\Sigma p_j}, \quad i = 1, \ldots, n.$$

Consequently, if we take into consideration that prices p_i are set such that $\Sigma p_j = 1$, we obtain $q_i = p_i$ and prices are stationary.

Next let us prove the converse: that a fixed point is the point of equilibrium in demand and supply. Firstly, as I shall explain in detail later, by Walras' law is meant that the identity with respect to prices,

$$p_1 E_1(p_1, \ldots, p_n) + p_2 E_2(p_1, \ldots, p_n) + \ldots$$
$$+ p_n E_n(p_1, \ldots, p_n) = 0, \quad (11)$$

holds not only at fixed points (the equilibrium points), but also at all moving points (non-equilibrium points). I shall explain later for what sorts of society Walras' law is valid; here I simply mention that it is derived from the budget equations of households and the profits equations of enterprises.

P is a fixed point. Therefore $P = Q$, and so we obtain

$$p_i = \frac{\max[p_i + aE_i, 0]}{\Sigma \max[p_j + aE_j, 0]}, \quad i = 1, \ldots, n. \quad (12)$$

But from Walras' law (11) above, we must have

$$\sum_j \max[p_j + aE_j, 0] = 1 \quad (13)$$

at a fixed point. The reason for this is that, if and only if the p_i of the left-hand side of (12) is positive, the numerator on the right-hand side, $p_i + aE_i$, must be positive. Thus for all i with positive p_i we have

$$p_i = \frac{p_i + aE_i}{S}, \quad (12')$$

where $S = \sum_j \max[p_j + aE_j, 0]$. Consequently we obtain

$$E_i = \frac{1}{a} p_i(S - 1)$$

from (12'). Since this equation holds for all i with positive p_i, and

p_i is 0 for all other i, then

$$p_1 E_1 + \ldots + p_n E_n = \frac{1}{a}(\Sigma p_i^2)(S-1).$$

Since at least one price is positive, Σp_i^2 is always positive, and thus to establish Walras' law we must have $S = 1$. That is, (13) holds. Consequently (12) becomes

$$p_i = \max[p_i + aE_i, 0], \quad i = 1, \ldots, n. \tag{12''}$$

If p_i is positive, the right-hand side of (12'') also has to be positive. For this sort of p_i, (12'') becomes $p_i = p_i + aE_i$ and therefore we obtain $E_i = 0$. That is, the market for good i must be in normal equilibrium. In contrast to this, if p_i is 0, the $p_i + aE_i$ which appears in the right-hand side of (12'') is zero or negative, and of these terms p_i is zero and therefore E_i must be zero or negative. That is, an excess supply of i may occur, but since its price has fallen to zero, we are in a state of anomalous equilibrium. Thus it is plain that at a fixed point of prices, the market for every good is in a state of normal or anomalous equilibrium.

Thus, since the identity of the fixed point for prices with the point of equilibrium of demand and supply is proven, the question of whether a point of equilibrium in demand and supply exists is reduced to whether a fixed point exists. That a fixed point exists can be confirmed using the theorem of fixed points; but since it is difficult to prove the theorem for the general case, let us illustrate it for the case where $n = 2$. Here, letting $n = 2$, we write the right-hand side of (9), the price adjustment equations, as

$$f_1(p_1, p_2) = \frac{\max[p_1 + aE_1, 0]}{\max[p_1 + aE_1, 0] + \max[p_2 + aE_2, 0]},$$

$$f_2(p_1, p_2) = \frac{\max[p_2 + aE_2, 0]}{\max[p_1 + aE_1, 0] + \max[p_2 + aE_2, 0]}.$$

If we assume that E_1, E_2 are continuous functions of p_1, p_2, it is proved that the denominator of the right-hand side of the above equations will never be 0, and therefore f_1, f_2 will be continuous functions of prices.[12+]

We can write (9) as

$$q_1 = f_1(p_1, p_2),$$
$$q_2 = f_2(p_1, p_2).$$

We now have a two dimensional plane with axes X and Y, and can take a distance of one unit in length on the X axis and the Y axis respectively. Then p_1 is measured from the origin along the X axis, and p_2 from the point 1 on the X axis back towards the origin. Since $p_1 + p_2 = 1$, p_1 and p_2 will meet at the same point. Similarly q_1 is measured from the origin on the Y axis, and q_2 downwards from point 1 on the Y axis. q_1 and q_2 will also meet at the same point. Since the point $Q = (q_1, q_2)$ so obtained is a continuous function of $P = (p_1, p_2)$, then $[P, Q]$ will trace out a continuous curve in the square of one unit on the XY plane (see fig. 2). Since this curve contains no discontinuous points, it will certainly meet a diagonal from the origin (a 45° line) at least once.

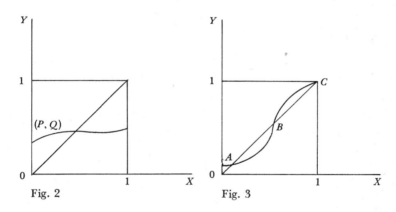

Fig. 2   Fig. 3

However, there is not necessarily only one point of intersection. Two or more points of intersection are possible, as is shown in fig. 3. But at all events, $P = Q$ at the point of intersection (since it is a point on the 45° line). Therefore all points of intersection are fixed points and are equilibrium points. Where the point of intersection is an interior point (such as A and B in fig. 3), all prices are positive and equilibrium is normal. But in the case of an extreme point (such as C for example), there will be a state of anomalous equilibrium in a few markets (in the market for good 2 in this case). Since there may be more than one point of intersection, a number of equilibria can exist, and in the extreme case they can be infinite in number.[13] The above geometrical analysis guarantees the existence of equilibrium for the two-good case, and we can obtain the same conclusion for the general case of three or more goods. While

Walras' law applies, a fixed point certainly exists for (9), and at that fixed point, the rule to the effect that if p_i is positive the demand and supply of good i are equal, and that if there is an excess of supply over demand p_i is 0, is satisfied. We call this the rule of free goods. Each consumer and enterprise merely pursues the maximisation of its own utility or profits under given market prices from the caller, ignoring the conduct of other individuals or organisations. By adjusting prices in the manner of (9) in accordance with the aggregate values of quantities of demand and supply determined in a decentralised fashion, prices are amended when they are inappropriate, and they remain unamended only when they are equilibrium prices. Since equilibrium prices are within the square (of figs. 2 and 3) we search this region until they are found. If we eliminate all moving points by subjecting all feasible prices to the test of the price adjustment functions (9), fixed points (that is, equilibrium prices) will be discovered.

E. The process of price formation

Normally, in competitive buying and selling, the caller shouts out as his first quotation either the last negotiated prices before competitive dealing began, or the closing (equilibrium) prices of the end of the previous session. If these happen to be the equilibrium prices for that session, competitive trading ends at once; but in fact it is almost impossible for this to be the case. Ordinarily there will be an excess demand or supply of some good, and therefore the second quotation $Q = (q_1, q_2, \ldots, q_n)$ corresponding to the first quotation $P = (p_1, p_2, \ldots, p_n)$ will be obtained through the price adjustment functions (9) and bargaining will be tried under Q. That is, the $p_1, p_2, \ldots, p_n$ of the right-hand side of (9) will be replaced by $q_1, q_2, \ldots, q_n$ and the excess demands or supplies under Q will be obtained. If these are not 0, then once again a new Q (that is, a third quotation) will be determined. This process is repeated until equilibrium prices are found.

Thus the time-sequence of quotations, which continues until we arrive at the equilibrium prices, is produced by (9), and consequently this process of groping for equilibrium prices can be made clear by solving the difference equations (9). However, I shall first of all transpose (9) into differential equations in order to facilitate mathematical analysis. For the sake of simplicity, I shall confine the discussion within the neighbourhood of equilibrium prices $p_1^0, p_2^0, \ldots,$

p_n^0. We assume that all these prices are positive. Consequently there is a normal equilibrium for all goods, and there are no free goods.[14]

Since $p_i^0 > 0$, $E_i(p_1^0, \ldots, p_n^0) = 0$. The scope of price changes is confined within a sufficiently small neighbourhood of $p^0 = (p_1^0, \ldots, p_n^0)$, and therefore the absolute value of $E_i(P)$ is sufficiently small. As p_i and p_i^0 are sufficiently close, we may assume

$$p_i + aE_i(P) > 0, \quad i = 1, \ldots, n.$$

Thus

$$\max[p_i + aE_i(P), 0] = p_i + aE_i(P), \quad i = 1, \ldots, n$$

and consequently we may write the price adjustment equations as

$$p_i(t+1) = \frac{p_i(t) + aE_i(P(t))}{1 + a \sum_j E_j(P(t))}, \quad i = 1, \ldots, n. \tag{14}$$

The 1 of the denominator here occurs because $\sum_j p_j(t) = 1$. In the above adjustment equations we think of prices being adjusted each time t becomes a whole number; a is a corresponding coefficient of adjustment, i.e. the one where the period of adjustment is unity. Therefore, when we think of a more general case of the period of adjustment being h, the $p_i(t+1)$ on the left-hand side of (14) is replaced by $p_i(t+h)$, and the a on the right-hand side by $a(h)$. The longer the period of adjustment, the larger will be the influence of a given volume of excess demand for a good upon its price, and so we ought to assume $a(h)$ to be an increasing function of h. If, for the sake of simplicity, we think of $a(h)$ as being proportional to h, then $a(h) = ah$. Thus we can write (14) as

$$p_i(t+h) = \frac{p_i(t) + ahE_i(P(t))}{1 + ah \sum_j E_j(P(t))}, \quad i = 1, \ldots n. \tag{14'}$$

If we subtract $p_i(t)$ from both sides of (14'), divide the result by h and approximate h to zero (the normal procedure for differentiation), we obtain

$$\frac{dp_i}{dt} = a[E_i(P(t)) - p_i(t) \sum_j E_j(P(t))], \quad i = 1, \ldots, n, \tag{15}$$

which is what Nikaido called the Brown–von Neumann differential equation. If $\sum_i p_i(t) = 1$, we obtain $\sum_i dp_i/dt = 0$ from (15). For this reason, if the initial prices of competitive trading are given in terms of an artificial standard-good made up of one unit of every good, the prices determined by (15) satisfy the condition $\sum_i p_i(t) = 1$ pertaining to the standard throughout the process of competitive dealing.

Will the course of the change in prices obtained through solving (15) eventually lead to or approximate to equilibrium prices? If we can answer this question in the affirmative, we say that equilibrium prices p^0 are stable; otherwise, they are unstable. Generally speaking, we cannot affirm theoretically whether or not equilibrium prices are stable. This depends on the price adjustment functions which are assumed, and at the same time on the excess demand functions. I shall show below that, when the price adjustment functions are of the form (15), if we assume (i) that the excess demand functions are homogeneous of degree 0 in prices, and (ii) that the income effects are small, p^0 is stable; that is, the solutions to (15) have the property $\lim_{t \to \infty} p_i(t) = p_i^0$, $i = 1, \ldots n$.

That an excess demand function is homogeneous of degree zero in prices means that the quantity of excess demand is unchanged when all prices change proportionately. If we here take as our numéraire not an artificial good made up of 1 unit of every good, but one made of λ units of each good, the price of each good will be $(1/\lambda)p_i$. Here the p_i are prices when the numéraire is composed of 1 unit of every good; consequently, when we change the numéraire good to one made up of λ units of every good, all prices simultaneously increase $1/\lambda$ times. However, to change the numéraire in this way is only to change the method of expressing prices and exerts no real influence on the economy whatever; therefore the volume of excess demand of any good remains unchanged when the numéraire changes. That is

$$E_i\left(\frac{1}{\lambda}p_1, \frac{1}{\lambda}p_2, \ldots, \frac{1}{\lambda}p_n\right) = E_i(p_1, p_2, \ldots, p_n),$$

$$i = 1, \ldots, n. \tag{16}$$

This is what is meant by an excess demand function which is homogeneous of degree 0, and it is a very reasonable assumption; excess demand functions derived from utility theory and the theory of the firm satisfy this assumption.[15] (It should be noted that a barter economy rather than a money economy is assumed, so that there is no problem of money illusion.) If we differentiate both sides of (16) with respect to λ, for each i we obtain

$$\frac{\partial E_i}{\partial p_i}p_1 + \frac{\partial E_i}{\partial p_2}p_2 + \ldots + \frac{\partial E_i}{\partial p_n}p_n = 0 \qquad \text{(Euler's formula)}. \qquad (17)$$

Next, we divide the total effect of a change in prices on excess demand into the income and substitution effects. If we ignore the income effects we obtain Hicks' rule concerning substitution effects,

$$\Sigma\Sigma X_{ij}\xi_i\xi_j \leqq 0, \qquad (18)$$

which is valid for arbitrary $\xi_1, \ldots, \xi_n$. Here X_{ij} represents the substitution effect which a marginal change in the price of good j exerts on good i, and (18) holds with equality when $\xi_1, \ldots, \xi_n$ are proportional to prices $p_1, \ldots, p_n$, or, of course, if all ξ_i are 0; in all other cases it necessarily holds with inequality. When there are income effects, an equation similar to (18) and including the income effects will not necessarily be valid; but when the income effects are negligible

$$\Sigma\Sigma\frac{\partial E_i}{\partial p_j}\xi_i\xi_j < 0 \qquad (19)$$

will be valid for arbitrary $\xi_1, \ldots, \xi_n$, provided that at least one of $\xi_1, \ldots, \xi_n$ is not 0, and that they are not proportional with $p_1, \ldots, p_n$.

The test for whether or not quoted prices converge to equilibrium prices is made either, as is customary, by the method whereby we solve the differential equation (15) and ascertain directly whether

$$\lim_{t \to \infty} p_i(t) = p_i^0, \qquad i = 1, \ldots, n$$

or not; or by the method whereby we introduce the Liapounoff function and show that it is always diminishing with respect to time. Here we mean by the Liapounoff function one which becomes zero only at the equilibrium point, and which has a positive value at all non-equilibrium points; if it is always a diminishing function with respect to time at points other than the equilibrium point,[16] then the value of the function will eventually diminish to zero, even if its value was positive to begin with. That is, the variables will eventually converge with the respective equilibrium values. Often the distance between quoted prices and equilibrium prices is employed as the Liapounoff function; for example

$$(p_1(t) - p_1^0)^2 + \ldots + (p_n(t) - p_n^0)^2 .$$

However, here I shall take the distance between actual excess demands and equilibrium excess demand as the Liapounoff function. Since the excess demand for each good is 0 at equilibrium, it is given by

$$V = \sum_i [E_i(p_1, p_2, \ldots, p_n)]^2.$$

V is 0 in equilibrium, and positive where we are not in equilibrium (we assume that the equilibrium is normal.) Consequently, if we can prove that dV/dt is always negative, then equilibtium prices are stable.

Now

$$\frac{dV}{dt} = 2\sum_i E_i\left(\sum_j \frac{\partial E_i}{\partial p_j} \cdot \frac{dp_j}{dt}\right).$$

Therefore, using (15), we obtain

$$\frac{dV}{dt} = 2a\sum_i \frac{\partial E_i}{\partial p_j} E_i E_j - 2a\left\{\sum_i E_i\left(\sum_j \frac{\partial E_i}{\partial p_j} p_j\right)\right\}\left\{\sum_k E_k\right\}.$$

If we here use the assumption that the excess demand functions are homogeneous of degree 0, what appears inside the round brackets on the right-hand side of the above equation becomes 0 by Euler's formula (17). Consequently

$$\frac{dV}{dt} = 2a\sum_i \sum_j \frac{\partial E_i}{\partial p_j} E_i E_j.$$

If we take into consideration the second assumption, which is that the income effects are negligible, dV/dt is negative as long as E_1, $\ldots$, E_n are not proportional to $p_1, \ldots, p_n$. At the equilibrium point we have $E_i = 0$ $(i = 1, \ldots, n)$ and so dV/dt is 0. However, in a non-equilibrium state at least one E_i is not 0; and if there is a positive (negative) excess demand for some good, there has to be another good for which there is a negative (positive) excess demand. This is because Walras' Law would not otherwise be valid. Consequently, it is impossible for all the E_i to be positive or all negative. Thus it is not possible for the E_i to be proportional to prices, and consequently in a non-equilibrium situation $dV/dt < 0$, and equilibrium is therefore stable.

We assumed in the above that the first quotation called was sufficiently close to the equilibrium prices; but this depends on the **premise** that the caller has a fairly correct knowledge of equilibrium prices beforehand. Where the caller has no such knowledge, and thus the first quoted prices are fairly far from the equilibrium prices, the price adjustment functions in the differential equation form do not assume as simple a form as that of (15). In order to prevent prices becoming negative, they must remain at 0 and not fall further, even when E_i is negative at a point where p_i is 0. Thus at a point where p_i is 0, we switch from (15) to

$$\frac{dp_i}{dt} = 0.$$

The analysis of global stability has to consider this switch and proceed rather more delicately; but this will not alter the general outline of the argument. While we can ignore the income effects, equilibrium points are, as formerly, stable.[17+]

Thus an equilibrium point is arrived at through competitive buying and selling. There is, of course, the possibility of instability when the income effects are not sufficiently small, and where instability occurs quoted prices will not converge on equilibrium prices. The market will be thrown into confusion and a state of affairs will arise where commodities are unquotable. This happens occasionally, but only in exceptional cases. Normally, equilibrium prices are discovered through competitive trading. However, equilibrium prices are solutions to the equations which make all excess demands equal zero. Therefore it is not necessarily the case that equilibrium prices must be found through competitive dealing; we can imagine an alternative method whereby the central government sets up a price determination bureau, estimates the excess demand equation for each good and, through the use of a computer, obtains the solutions which simultaneously satisfy all these equations. But this sort of central supervision of prices is frequently inefficient; however efficient the bureaucratic mechanism may be, it is impossible promptly to calculate new equilibrium prices corresponding to a sudden change in the excess demand functions. In a modern state it is certainly essential for economic administration to be conducted through the application of advanced econometric techniques, using large-scale computers and with a first-class bureaucracy; but it is even more important to have a highly efficient market mechanism. This has not one gear or electric wire, but is an extremely elaborate computing machine for arriving at equilibrium prices. In an economy where the market mechanism is imperfectly formed the self-interested plans-of-behaviour of each individual and organ-isation will not be adjusted one to the other, and shortage and waste will continually appear at all points in society. In such a society, information regarding excess demand functions is disas-trously lacking, and it is very difficult to discover through the computer how prices should be revised. The market provides in-formation to the society on what is desired, by whom, in what quantities and with what degree of intensity; it performs the func-tion of preventing the economy from falling into a state of dis-harmony. However, as we shall see in the chapters which follow, such a market mechanism has unfortunately ceased to exist in a complete form in actual modern societies.

7

The fixprice economy

A. The advent of Keynes

As we have already seen, in a competitive market where
Walras' law holds, equilibrium is eventually established (except in
special cases). At equilibrium, demand and supply will be equal as
long as price is positive, and demand can be less than supply only
where price is zero. Looked at in relation to the market for labour,
an equilibrium which is accompanied by unemployment can occur
only in the anomalous case where labour is a free good with a zero
price. In the normal case equilibrium must be a full-employment
equilibrium, and unemployment is impossible.

But in reality, unemployment frequently occurs. Moreover it
occurs when wages are positive. From the point of view of the neoclassical economics referred to above, this implies that the market
for labour is not in equilibrium. Through the identity of equilibrium
in demand and supply on the one hand, and stationary prices (the
fixed point) on the other, prices must be moving in a situation
where there is an excess supply. Therefore, where unemployment
occurs with positive wages, it will eventually be eliminated by
changing wages. Thus, unemployment is regarded as a transitory
phenomenon on the road towards equilibrium, and not as a permanent feature of the situation.

This way of looking at things emerges inevitably from neoclassical analysis, but it is out of keeping with the fact that, in reality,
unemployment is a continuing phenomenon. Confronted by the
Great Depression of the 1930s, Keynes saw clearly that the mechanism for eliminating unemployment did not work (see table 7.1);
it is also possible to see the full employment of the post-war
period purely as the result of the strong fiscal policies which were
followed. What we have been able to observe in practice is the
fact that, even when unemployment exists, wages maintain a fixed

positive value and show no tendency to fall to zero. We may regard the economies of the real world (particularly in the 1920s and 1930s), as being in a kind of fixed state which is accompanied by unemployment and is achieved under positive wage rates. This does not signify an equilibrium point, in the sense that demand and supply are equalised, but a fixed point of wages — a kind of paradoxical state which violates the neoclassical identity between equilibrium point and a fixed point. Thus from the neoclassical point of view we have the contradiction whereby we cannot regard what has actually occurred either as an equilibrium or as a non-equilibrium state.

This means that, although the neoclassical theoretical system is effective for proving the existence of Walrasian equilibrium in a competitive socialist economy or a capitalist economy, it is inappropriate for explaining what actually occurs in the labour markets of capitalist economies. We have first to break down the neoclassical theorem of identity between equilibrium in demand and supply and the fixity of prices, and then discover the new market-mechanism whereby the system of prices and wages may become stationary even though unemployment exists. At a fixed point in such a new system, a new type of equilibrium, that is, an equilibrium which is accompanied by unemployment and hence leaves demand and supply unequalised, will be established. In this way the identity between a fixed point and an equilibrium point will be re-established at a revised level. In this chapter, I shall attempt to show the theoretical basis for Keynes' views.[1] The new Keynesian model which I shall present is, as you will probably see later, entirely different from the neoclassical one. By making clear the logic of this system, I hope to show in what way Keynes sought to change economic thinking.

I shall express my own opinions in the last section, and before that I shall closely examine the ideas of Glustoff, as a recent representative of a group whose ideas are regarded by those who prize their pure Keynesian blood as bastard Keynesian.[2] Glustoff's analysis is somewhat difficult, and moreover, since it is a mathematical form of analysis which abbreviates many of the economic explanations, l shall restate it in a somewhat changed form. Nevertheless the presentation which follows in no way interferes with the essential nature of his argument. Since I shall be supplying many supplementary economic explanations, the exposition will take up

Table 7.1. Weekly wages (£p) and the unemployment rate (%) in the UK

year	1925	1926	1927	1928	1929	1930	1931	1932	1933	1934
unemployment rate	11.3	12.5	9.7	10.8	10.4	16.0	21.3	22.1	19.9	16.7
wages	4.09	4.08	4.06	4.05	4.04	4.03	3.97	3.90	3.90	3.93

year	1935	1936	1937	1938		1955	1956	1957	1958	1959
unemployment rate	15.5	13.1	10.8	13.5	...	1.2	1.3	1.6	2.2	2.3
wages	3.97	4.01	4.04	4.08	...	14.04	15.88	16.24	16.69	17.79

year	1960	1961	1962	1963	1964	1965	1966	1967	1968	1969
unemployment rate	1.7	1.6	2.1	2.6	1.7	1.5	1.6	2.5	2.5	2.5
wages	18.91	19.75	21.06	22.32	23.33	25.51	26.59	27.71	29.45	31.72

Source: *The British Economy Key Statistics, 1900–1970*, published for the London and Cambridge Economic Service by Times Newspapers Ltd.

a good deal of space, but the virtues of this will be clear later, when I come to deal with the ideas of the legitimate Keynesians, and it should become easy for us to understand the true intentions of Keynes.[3+]

As will soon be seen, at first glance Glustoff's analysis appears to be equipped with Keynesian tools. By revealing the essential oneness of the three pillars of Keynesian theory — namely (i) acceptance of the downward rigidity of wages, (ii) denial of Walras' law (or Say's law), (iii) denial of the rule of free goods — he has built up a skilful image of Keynes. However, although these three pillars have imposed a restriction on the function of prices as conceived by the neoclassicals, as we shall see later, this restriction is not serious enough to fundamentally hinder the function of prices as regulators of supply and demand. The system is as before essentially a neoclassical one, and, once the Keynesian mask is stripped from it, is revealed as no more than traditional, neoclassical general equilibrium theory. What Keynes himself had in mind was not this sort of a quasi-neoclassical system, but a situation where the price system had even further lost its ability to function as formerly conceived. Such a state of affairs has been referred to by Hicks as a fixprice economy, and in such an economy the principle of effective demand operates in place of the lost function of prices.[4] Neoclassical theory is applicable only in the case of the flexprice economy, and the laws of operation of the fixprice economy have to be explained by economic theory based on the principle of effective demand. What was stressed by Keynes was the changeover from adjustment by prices to adjustment through effective demand or outputs. Glustoff's interpretation of Keynes is devoid of all consideration of the principle of effective demand, and he regards the core of Keynes' theory as being merely a revision of the price adjustment mechanism. One of the purposes of this chapter is to correct this sort of mistake made by the illegitimate offspring of Keynes, and to build up a general equilibrium theory on the basis of the principle of effective demand.

B. The downward rigidity of wages

The next three sections are devoted to a recapitulation of Glustoff's theory with added critical comments. First of all, neoclassical economists assert that the price of each good is adjusted in accordance with the volume of excess demand for it, with the exception of unusual cases where a straightforward application of this formula produces negative prices. Therefore, as long as prices are positive, they will fall when there is an excess supply. Looked at in terms of the market for labour, this means that when there is unemployment there will be pressure for lower wages, and wages will be cut as a result. However, in actual labour markets, as a result of trade union activity or the existence of a social security system, or else because the unemployed worker himself values his own dignity, wages will not be forced down despite the existence of unemployment. Therefore an excess supply of labour will not cause a lowering of wages. This would not be the case if actual labour markets were competitive in the manner conceived of by the neoclassicals, for, seeing the existence of an excess supply, the caller would adjust wage rates.

At this point let us classify goods into two kinds. The first kind comprises goods $i = 1, \ldots, m$ for which adjustment of prices in the neoclassical fashion occurs, and in the stage before standardisation-of-prices through the choosing of a numéraire occurs, prices change in accordance with the formula

$$p_i(t + 1) = \max[p_i(t) + aE_i(t), 0], \quad i = 1, \ldots, m. \qquad (1)$$

(Here a is the coefficient of adjustment and is positive. E_i is the volume of excess demand for good i, and p_i is its price.) An excess demand will cause an increase in the prices of the second kind of good $i = m + 1, \ldots, n$, but an excess supply will not cause a fall in their prices. That is, if $E_i(t) > 0$, then $p_i(t + 1) > p_i(t)$; but if $E_i(t) < 0$, then $p_i(t + 1) = p_i(t)$. Prices are not symmetrically flexible with respect to both negative and positive excess demand; they are flexible in an upward direction, but rigid in a downward direction. We may express this sort of adjustment in prices by means of the following formula.[5+]

$$p_i(t + 1) = p_i(t) + a \max[E_i(t), 0], \quad i = m + 1, \ldots, n. \qquad (2)$$

It goes without saying that since $\max[E_i(t), 0]$ expresses the larger of $E_i(t)$ or 0, when $E_i(t)$ is positive the above expression is $E_i(t)$, and when $E_i(t)$ is negative it is 0.

The numéraire problem still exists even where there is this second kind of good. Since the prices of the second kind of good do not fall nominally, they remain positive throughout the process of the formation of prices if they were set at some positive value at the start. For this reason, it seems certain, at first glance, that the second kind of good (for example, labour) can be taken as the numéraire. However, even in this case, if the prices of all other goods rise without limit and wages alone are left with a finite price, the bothersome state of affairs will arise where something which is infinitely great has to be measured against a finite yardstick. That is, labour becomes effectively a free good.

In order for the measuring-rod to increase in length as the things to be measured become larger, we must include elements of what are to be measured in the measuring-rod. Since it is uncertain which of the things to be measured will get larger, the measuring-rod has to include a little of each. Thus, as previously, an artificial composite good is constructed out of 1 unit of each good. Since the price of the composite good at time $t + 1$ is $\Sigma p_j(t + 1)$, the relative prices of goods in terms of the composite good are

$$q_i(t + 1) = \frac{p_i(t + 1)}{\Sigma p_i(t + 1)}, \quad i = 1, \ldots, n. \tag{3}$$

The prices $p_i(t)$ at time t are the prices of goods already themselves expressed in terms of the composite good, provided they are taken so that $\Sigma p_i(t) = 1$. When we take (1) and (2) into consideration and rewrite (3), we obtain the equations for the change in relative prices in terms of the composite good

$$q_i(t+1) = \frac{\max[p_i(t) + aE_i(t), 0]}{\sum_i^m \max[p_j(t) + aE_j(t), 0] + \sum_{m+1}^n (p_j(t) + a\max[E_j(t), 0])}$$
$$i = 1, \ldots, m, \tag{4}$$

and

$$q_i(t+1) = \frac{p_i(t) + a\max[E_i(t), 0]}{\sum_i^m \max[p_j(t) + aE_j(t), 0] + \sum_{m+1}^n (p_j(t) + a\max[E_j(t), 0])}$$
$$i = m + 1, \ldots, n. \tag{5}$$

where (4) applies to normal neoclassical goods, and (5) to a Keynesian type of good such as labour, whose price is rigid in the downward direction.

Where the composite good is taken as the numéraire, the price of a good is not necessarily rigid in the downward direction even if it is a good of the second kind. It is true that, where there is an excess supply of the second kind of good i, we have $\max[E_i(t), 0] = 0$ in the numerator and the denominator of the right-hand side of (5), so that such an excess supply will not directly cause $q_i(t + 1)$ to become less than $p_i(t)$. But this certainly does not mean that once $p_i(t)$ has risen it can never fall again. If an excess demand for another good arises, the price of that good will rise and therefore the denominator of (5) will become larger: as a result $q_i(t + 1) < p_i(t)$ is possible. This parallels the fact recognised by Keynes in respect of money and real wages. That is, trade unions oppose the lowering of money wages, so that they do not fall even though there is an excess supply of labour (that is, unemployment). However, trade unions are not so sensitive to increases in the price of consumer goods, and there is no effective brake against a fall in wages expressed in terms of consumer goods — that is, real wages — as a result of such price increases, so that such a fall is perfectly possible.[6+] Put in terms of equation (5), as a result of a rise in consumer good prices, the price of the composite good will rise, and wages expressed in terms of the composite good will fall.

The system made up of the price adjustment equations (4) and (5) includes the neoclassical system and Glustoff's Keynesian system as two special cases. Where $m = n$ in (4) the second term in the denominator of the right-hand side of (4) vanishes, and (4) is reduced to the neoclassical adjustment equation. In this case there are no goods governed by (5). In contrast, Glustoff is concerned with the case where there is only one kind of good to be governed by (5). That is, according to him, the neoclassical system has $m = n$, while the Keynesian system has $m = n - 1$. More generally, we may think of m as being any positive integer not exceeding n.

C. A generalisation of Walras' law

The rule of free goods which Keynes criticised so severely depends, on the one hand, on simple price adjustment functions which ignore the downward rigidity of prices (wages), and on the other on Walras' law. As I explained earlier, what is meant by Walras' law is, in mathematical terms, that the sum of the products of prices and excess demands, $\Sigma p_i E_i$, will identically vanish, irrespective of whether prices are equilibrium prices or not. In this section I should like first to derive Walras' law for a purely private enterprise economy; and then, while explaining in what circumstances it ceases to meet the conditions for its validity, I hope to show how the law may be amended.

I shall assume with Walras a pure capitalist economy made up of workers, capitalists and entrepreneurs. The area of land is very large in proportion to population and production activity, and hence land prices and land rents are zero; that is, we assume land is a free good. This is an assumption made merely for the sake of simplicity, and is not essential to the discussion which follows. Even when the area of land is limited and its price and rents from it are high, an argument in the same form as that which follows is still valid.

Needless to say workers live by selling their labour, and capitalists obtain their income by hiring out the various capital goods they own to enterprises (that is, they sell the services of capital goods to enterprises).[7+] The enterprise makes its payments for the services of capital from the total left over after payments have been made out of sales revenue for raw materials, labour and so on (i.e. the surplus over costs, or gross profits). The reward for one unit of the services of capital (the rental on capital) has to include depreciation, insurance charges and interest. That is, capital is subject to wear and tear each time it is used, and furthermore capital goods (machinery) are constantly exposed to danger; therefore the rental of capital has not only to cover interest but also depreciation and insurance charges. What is left out of profits on capital after payments to capitalists have been made is the income of entrepreneurs in the form of enterprise profits. This can be regarded as the reward to the entrepreneur for making decisions relating to the use of capital; it is not a fixed amount, but what is left after all payments have been made. In some cases it can be very small, in others large.[8]

In many cases people do not fit neatly into the categories worker, capitalist, entrepreneur. There are a good many labourers who are capitalists, and capitalists who are entrepreneurs. However, in the society we are considering workers are thoroughbreds, though capitalists and entrepreneurs are intermingled, so that we assume society to be sharply divided into two classes — those who own property and those who do not. Workers own no capital goods and live by selling their labour, while capitalists obtain a livelihood by hiring the capital goods they themselves own to the enterprises and at the same time receive enterprise profits for acting simultaneously as entrepreneurs and carrying out the decision making function in enterprises.

Each household spends its own income. Here we arrange goods so that $i = 1, \ldots, h$ are consumer goods, $i = h + 1, \ldots, l$ are capital goods, $i = l + 1, \ldots, m$ are the services of capital goods and

$i = m + 1, \ldots, n$ are various kinds of labour (assuming labour is heterogeneous).[9] The varieties of capital goods are, of course, the same in number as the services of capital goods. Since workers do not own capital goods, the budget identity for workers contains no term relating to capital goods either on the income or on the expenditure side, and thus is

$$\sum_{i=1}^{h} p_i D_i^j = \sum_{i=m+1}^{n} p_i S_i^j, \tag{6}$$

where D_i^j shows the demand for consumer good i of worker j and S_i^j the quantity of labour i he is willing to supply. Worker j will, under the constraints of (6), determine D_i^j and S_i^j so as to maximise the value of his utility function. Therefore, these are functions of both sets of prices $p_1, \ldots, p_h$ and $p_{m+1}, \ldots, p_n$. There is no necessity that these be equilibrium prices. Since the demand functions and the supply functions are determined so as to satisfy (6),

$$\sum_{i=1}^{h} p_i D_i^j (p_1, \ldots, p_h, p_{m+1}, \ldots, p_n)$$

$$= \sum_{i=m+1}^{n} p_i S_i^j (p_1, \ldots, p_h, p_{m+1}, \ldots, p_n) \tag{6'}$$

is valid as an identity for any prices.

Let us next consider a capitalist k. We denote the quantity of capital good i which he already owns by K_i^k, and the entrepreneurial profits he receives by Π^k. The capitalist will consume a part of his total income, devote another part to replenishing the capital goods which are consumed, and with his remaining net savings will plan to increase the quantity of capital goods he owns. The *raison d'être* of the capitalist is the ownership of capital goods, and therefore savings are essential to him. Let H_i^k be the quantity of capital good i he would like to acquire (H_i^k is gross investment and includes the part needed to replenish what was consumed of K_i^k); then we may write the capitalist's budget identity as

$$\sum_{i=1}^{h} p_i D_i^k + \sum_{i=h+1}^{l} p_i H_i^k = \sum_{i=l+1}^{m} p_i K_i^k + \Pi^k. \tag{7}$$

He will attempt to maximise his utility function under (7). As we shall see later, H_i^k has to be flexibly adjustable in order that equilibrium be established. However, let us assume for the time being that gross investment H_i^k for each capital good has a fixed value. The capitalist's demand functions for consumer goods are derived in the same way as were those of the worker, but they are not simply functions of price. They also depend upon H_i^k, K_i^k, Π^k. By assumption the values of H_i^k are fixed, and each K_i^k takes on a fixed value determined by the savings activity of the capitalist in the past. Therefore the only arguments of the demand functions which are variable are prices and enterprise profits. With such demand functions we obtain the indentity

$$\sum_{i=1}^{h} p_i D_i^k(p_1, \ldots, p_m, \Pi^k) + \sum_{i=h+1}^{l} p_i H_i^k = \sum_{i=l+1}^{m} p_i K_i^k + \Pi^k. \qquad (7')$$

Next, if we make S_i^f the quantity of consumer good i or capital good i supplied by enterprise f, and D_i^f its demand for labour of type i or the services of capital good i, then the definitional equation of the enterprise's profits is

$$\sum_{i=1}^{l} p_i S_i^f - \sum_{i=l+1}^{n} p_i D_i^f = \Pi_f, \qquad (8)$$

where Π_f represents the total of entrepreneurial profits earned by enterprise f. Normally enterprise f is not a totally integrated enterprise and does not produce all consumer goods and capital goods, so that a number of the S_i^f are 0. The enterprise will attempt to maximise profits on the basis of given technical possibilities, but here we assume that, because of limits on the supervisory capacities of entrepreneurs, returns to scale diminish for each enterprise when it enlarges its scale of production beyond a certain point. Where returns to scale are constant, only the proportions between outputs and inputs are determined, with their absolute level being left indefinite, even when prices are given. However, where there are diminishing returns to scale, the optimum level of production needed to maximise profits is determined in correspondence with prevailing prices, and consequently the volume of outputs (the quantities supplied) and the volume of inputs (the quantities demanded) are each given as a function of prices alone.[10+] Thus we obtain the identity

$$\sum_{i=1}^{l} p_i S_i^f(p_1, \ldots, p_n) - \sum_{i=l+1}^{n} p_i D_i^f(p_1, \ldots, p_n) = \Pi_f. \qquad (8')$$

Entrepreneurial profits Π_f will be distributed to the capitalists who worked as entrepreneurs in firm f at a fixed rate in accordance with their individual contributions. Since a single capitalist may be related with a number of enterprises, the entrepreneurial profits Π^k which capitalist k receives are the sum of the profits he receives from all the enterprises with which he is connected. Since by (8') the entrepreneurial profits Π_f of each firm are also a function of prices, and since the rates of distribution are fixed, the entrepreneurial profits Π^k received by individuals are also a function of prices. Therefore in (7′), the capitalist's demand functions for consumer goods ultimately depend on prices alone. If we here take the sum of the budget equations (6′) and (7′) over all workers and all capitalists respectively, and deduct from it the profits equation for each enterprise, then Π^k and Π_f drop out of the right-hand side because $\sum_k \Pi^k = \sum_f \Pi_f$; the result may be written as

$$\sum_{i=1}^{n} p_i E_i(p_1, \ldots, p_n) = 0, \tag{9}$$

where E_i shows the volume of excess demand for each good. In the case of consumer goods it is

$$E_i(p_1, \ldots, p_n) = \sum_j D_i^j(p_1, \ldots, p_h, p_{m+1}, \ldots, p_n)$$
$$+ \sum_k D_i^k(p_1, \ldots, p_n) - \sum_f S_i^f(p_1, \ldots, p_n);$$

in the case of capital goods it is

$$E_i(p_1, \ldots, p_n) = \sum_k H_i^k - \sum_f S_i^f(p_1, \ldots, p_n);$$

in the case of the services of capital it is

$$E_i(p_1, \ldots, p_n) = \sum_f D_i^f(p_1, \ldots, p_n) - \sum_k K_i^k;$$

and in case of labour it is

$$E_i(p_1, \ldots, p_n) = \sum_f D_i^f(p_1, \ldots, p_n) - \sum_j S_i^j(p_1, \ldots, p_h, p_{m+1}, \ldots, p_n).$$

Note that the capitalist's demand functions for consumer goods D_i^k are written in the ultimate form which eliminates Π^k, and by assumption H_i^k, K_i^k have fixed values. Equation (9) thus obtained is an identity with respect to prices, and is called Walras' law.

I should like here to make one comment. As we saw in the previous chapter, if the price adjustment functions are given by

$$q_i = \frac{\max[p_i + aE_i, 0]}{\sum_j \max[p_j + aE_j, 0]}, \qquad i = 1, \ldots, n, \tag{10}$$

equilibrium exists under Walras' law. At this point, and apart from free goods, the demand for each good equals its supply and only the supply of free goods can exceed their demand.

Our system includes capital goods and their services, but the prices of capital goods and their services determined in the above fashion are not necessarily those which will produce equilibrium rates of profit between capital goods. If we assume that there are g kinds of capital good, there are the same number of kinds of service rendered by capital goods, and $g = l - h = m - l$. If we number capital goods and the services of capital goods in the same order, the number of the service rendered by capital good i is $j = i + g$. Next, since one unit of capital good i renders one unit of the service $i + g$ per unit period, the ratio of p_{i+g} and p_i is the gross rate of return per unit period when capital good i is owned. But if capital good i is hired to an enterprise for one period, it is returned one period later having been partially consumed. Moreover, in order to ensure that it is returned in this form, insurance charges have to be paid. Therefore the returns p_{i+g} from the services of capital good i must cover the depreciation allowance and insurance charges. Let us assume that the total of depreciation allowances and insurance charges for each capital good is a constant fraction δ_i of the price of that capital good. Thus $p_{i+g} - \delta_i p_i$ is the net return after subtracting depreciation allowances and insurance charges, and

$$(p_{i+g} - \delta_i p_i)/p_i = r_i \tag{11}$$

is the net rate of return.

In equilibrium the net rate of return has to be equalised for each capital good. For example, when $r_i > r_j$, taking into account depreciation and insurance charges, owning capital good i is more profitable than owning capital good j; and therefore no-one will attempt to own good j. Thus from (11) we obtain

$$\frac{p_{h+1+g} - \delta_{h+1} p_{h+1}}{p_{h+1}} = \frac{p_{h+2+g} - \delta_{h+2} p_{h+2}}{p_{h+2}} = \ldots$$
$$= \frac{p_{l+g} - \delta_l p_l}{p_l}, \tag{12}$$

i.e. the conditions which prices of capital goods and their services must fulfil to be equilibrium prices.

According to the neoclassical school, prices are determined by (9) and (10) if gross investment H_i^k is given for each capital good in each enterprise. However, prices of capital goods and capital services determined in this manner do not necessarily satisfy the conditions, (12), of equal rates of profit between capital goods. If rates of profit on capital goods are unequal, many capitalists will invest in those capital goods whose profit rates are relatively high, while investment in those whose profit rates are low will cease. That is, as long as the investment plan we assumed initially is not a special one whereby investment is by chance concentrated on capital goods with the highest profit rates, then no capitalist will attempt to execute his original investment plan under these prices, but will instead revise it. New prices are obtained under new investment plans, and the process of adjusting investments will continue until, eventually, the prices of capital goods and capital services will fulfil the equalisation-of-profit-rates conditions (12).

In order to obtain the perfect equilibrium solutions which also satisfy (12), we should have to analyse a more general process of iteration which expressly took into account the investment adjustment function.[11+] However, this is not the problem here. Our present subject for discussion is whether or not Walras' law is valid for the kind of economy Keynes had in mind; and if the answer to this question is no, how this law must be amended.

We obtained the identity (9) above by simply adding the budget identities for workers (6'), those for capitalists (7') and the profits equations for enterprises (8'). However, if we take into account the possibility of the unemployment of workers, this kind of simple addition is inappropriate. The quantity of labour supplied $S_i^j(p_1, \ldots, p_h, p_{m+1}, \ldots, p_n)$ in the right-hand side of (6'), is the supply of labour i which the worker j voluntarily offers when the prices of consumer goods are $p_1, \ldots, p_h$ and wages are $p_{m+1}, \ldots, p_n$. The volume of demand on the left-hand side represents the purchases he wants to make when he is fully employed. However, the aggregate total of labour voluntarily supplied may exceed the demand for labour by enterprises. Where such a state of affairs arises under the neoclassical system, wages will fall until full employment results; but in the kind of economy which Keynes envisaged where strong trade unions prevent falls in wages, wages are rigid in a downward direction, and therefore the whole of labour voluntarily supplied is not necessarily demanded by enterprises.

Thereupon unemployment can occur. When he is unemployed, our worker is, as before, willing to supply the amount of labour $S_i^j(p_1, \ldots, p_h, p_{m+1}, \ldots, p_n)$; however, his demand for consumer goods is not $D_i^j(p_1, \ldots, p_h, p_{m+1}, \ldots, p_n)$ but less than this. Of course in reality even when he is unemployed he demands consumer goods, and therefore his demand is not zero; but provisionally, for the sake of simplicity, we shall assume the quantity he demands when fully employed to be $D_i^j(p_1, \ldots, p_h, p_{m+1}, \ldots, p_n)$, and that when he is unemployed to be 0. Therefore, the total value of the demands for consumer goods by workers is equal to the sum actually paid out in wages to employed workers; where unemployment is a possibility this can be less than the total value of the supply of labour offered voluntarily. That is, where unemployment may occur, we obtain

$$\sum_{i=1}^{h} p_i(\sum_j D_i^j(p_1, \ldots, p_h, p_{m+1}, \ldots, p_n))$$

$$\leqq \sum_{i=m+1}^{n} p_i(\sum_j S_i^j(p_1, \ldots, p_h, p_{m+1}, \ldots, p_n)) \qquad (13)$$

in place of the budget identity for workers (6′). In (13) the sum of the supplies of labour is a total sum for all workers, but the sum of the demands for consumer goods is for employed workers only. (Obviously, this is based on the assumption that there is no demand for consumer goods from unemployed workers; such a strong assumption is not strictly necessary, since, as long as the demand for a consumer good of a worker is less when he is unemployed than it is when he is employed, an inequality which is the same as (13) is valid.) Needless to say (13) is only valid as an equality when there is full employment, or in the special case where the workers' demands for consumer goods are totally uninfluenced by unemployment.[12+]

If we add to (13) the sum of the budget identities for capitalists (7′), and subtract the profits equations for the enterprises (8′), we obtain the inequality

$$\sum_{i=1}^{n} p_i E_i(p_1, \ldots, p_n) \leqq 0, \qquad (14)$$

which will be valid identically. We define excess demand E_i in the same way as before. In particular, the excess demand for labour is the difference between the demand for labour by enterprises and the quantity of labour voluntarily supplied by all workers; the excess demand for each consumer good is the difference between the total demand of workers and capitalists and the total quantity supplied by enterprises. On the assumption that the unemployed do not consume, the total demand of workers for a consumer good is the total demand of those in employment. Thus (14) resolves itself into the original statement of Walras' law in (9) only when full employment is achieved, or in the special case where, despite being unemployed, workers have the same demand for consumer goods as

when they are employed. Therefore we can regard (14) as a generalisation of Walras' law, and we shall call it the extended Walras'
law, or Keynes' law.

D. Bastard Keynesian unemployment theory

We saw previously that there are two methods of adapting
prices. First, there is the normal case where, as long as prices are
positive, they are flexible both upwards and downwards. Secondly,
there is the asymmetrical case where prices are flexible upwards but
rigid downwards. I shall assume in this section that the prices of
consumer goods, capital goods and capital services are adaptable as
in the normal case, and that only the adaptability of the prices of
various kinds of labour is asymmetircal. Taking an artificial composite good made up from 1 unit each of every good as our numéraire, these two cases can be formulated in the manner of (4) and
(5). (4) is valid for all consumer goods, capital goods and services of
capital goods, and (5) holds for all labour.

The price adjustment functions (4) and (5) have an equilibrium
point under (14), which is Keynes' law (or the extended Walras'
law). This point satisfies the rule of free goods for goods governed
by (4) (consumer goods, capital goods, capital goods' services), but
not for goods (labour) governed by (5). That is, it is possible that
wages will remain stationary at some positive level even though
there exists an excess supply of labour. The existence of an excess
supply of labour means that there is labour which is not actually
employed even though it is seeking employment, and therefore
there is so-called Keynesian involuntary unemployment. Thus, in
this kind of system, it is possible for a stationary equilibrium with
involuntary unemployment to be established.

We may prescribe such a Keynesian equilibrium point by

$$E_i(p_1, \ldots, p_n) \begin{cases} = 0, & p_i > 0, \\ \leqq 0, & p_i = 0, \end{cases} i = 1, \ldots, m \qquad (15)$$

$$E_i(p_1, \ldots, p_n) \leqq 0, \qquad i = m+1, \ldots, n \qquad (16)$$

We attach to (15) the proviso that excess demand can have a negative value only when prices are 0, because the goods concerned
satisfy the rule of free goods. However, the same sort of proviso is
not attached to (16), because the rule of free goods does not apply
to it.

At such an equilibrium point prices are stationary. We can see this in the following fashion. First, the numerator on the right-hand side of (4) is

$$\max[p_i + aE_i, 0] = p_i, \qquad i = 1, \ldots, m \tag{17}$$

by (15). (As we saw previously, when $E_i = 0$ (17) is self evident, and when $E_i < 0$ then, since $p_i = 0$, again (17) holds.) Similarly, by (16) the numerator of (5) becomes

$$p_i + \max[aE_i, 0] = p_i, \qquad i = m+1, \ldots, n. \tag{18}$$

We can see that by (17) and (18) the denominator on the right-hand side of (4) and (5) is

$$\sum_{i=1}^{m} \max[p_i + aE_i, 0] + \sum_{i=m+1}^{n} [p_i + \max(aE_i, 0)] = \sum_{i=1}^{n} p_i = 1.$$

At such an equilibrium point the numerator of the right-hand side of (4) and (5) is p_i and the denominator 1, and therefore the q_i of the left-hand side is equal to p_i. Consequently, prices do not change at the equilibrium point. That is the equilibrium point is a fixed point.

Conversely, a fixed point in the sytem which takes the downward inflexibility of wages into account is a Keynes-type equilibrium point. Let D be the denominator of (4) and (5), i.e.

$$D = \sum_{i=1}^{m} \max[p_i + aE_i, 0] + \sum_{i=m+1}^{n} [p_i + \max(aE_i, 0)]; \tag{19}$$

then at a fixed point we have

$$p_i = \frac{1}{D} \max[p_i + aE_i, 0], \qquad i = 1, \ldots, m, \tag{20}$$

$$p_i = \frac{1}{D} [p + a \max(E_i, 0)], \qquad i = m+1, \ldots, n. \tag{21}$$

By definition D is non-negative, and it can be proved that it will never become zero.[13+] Therefore by (20), if the p_i on the left-hand side is positive, the numerator of the right-hand side is also positive. That is $\max[p_i + aE_i, 0] = p_i + aE_i$, and consequently we obtain

$$(D-1)p_i = aE_i, \qquad i = 1, \ldots, m. \tag{22}$$

From (21) we obtain

$$(D-1)p_i = a \max(E_i, 0), \qquad i = m+1, \ldots, n. \tag{23}$$

Suppose $D > 1$. Then (22) and (23) imply that $E_i > 0$ as long as $p_i > 0$. Consequently we have $\Sigma p_i E_i > 0$ which contradicts the extended Walras' law of (4). Thus at a fixed point we must not have $D > 1$.

Next, if $D < 1$, (23) holds only at $p_i = 0$. This is because if we were to have $p_i > 0$, we would have a contradiction whereby the left-hand side of (23) would become negative, and the right-hand side 0 or positive. If all wages were zero, the income of workers would be zero whether or not they were employed, and therefore their demand for consumer goods would be zero whether or not they were employed. In this case, unemployment does not cause $\sum_i p_i E_i < 0$, and therefore whether or not there is unemployment we always have [14]

$$\sum_{i=1}^{n} p_i E_i = 0. \tag{24}$$

On the other hand where $D < 1$ we see that, if by (22) $p_i > 0$, then $E_i < 0$, $i = 1, \ldots, m$. From this, and since wages are zero, we obtain $\sum p_i E_i < 0$, and a contradiction arises between this and (24). Therefore we cannot have $D < 1$.

If D is neither greater nor smaller than one, then it is clear that it equals one. When $D = 1$ we can obtain the respective equilibrium conditions (15) and (16) from the fixed-point conditions (20) and (21). That is, a fixed point is a Keynesian equilibrium point.

A Keynesian equilibrium point is therefore a fixed point of the amended price adjustment functions (4) and (5), and vice versa. Thus the identity of equilibrium points with fixed points is once again established. However, at a Keynesian equilibrium point it is possible to have an excess supply of labour (or involuntary unemployment) with positive wages. The reason why a state of affairs is possible which violates the rule of free goods in this way is that we did not accept Walras' law, but replaced it with the extended Walras' law or Keynes' law. Wages are able to remain unchanged while an excess supply exists because we amended the neoclassical price adjustment functions by taking account of the downward inflexibility of wages. Thus the negation of the rule of free goods is linked on the one hand with the rejection of Walras' law in its original form, and on the other with the acceptance of the downward rigidity of wages. It is this trinity which guarantees the existence of Keynesian equilibrium.

At all events equilibrium points are once again fixed points. Therefore we can find equilibrium points by finding fixed points. This being so, we may apply the fixed point theorem to (4) and (5) which transpose $P = (p_1, \ldots, p_n)$ into $Q = (q_1, \ldots, q_n)$. This is what Glustoff did.)[15+] But to treat the problem in this mechanical fashion will be to miss the connection which exists at a higher level between neoclassical equilibrium and what we have called Keynesian or bastard Keynesian equilibrium. Therefore, in what follows we adopt a somewhat more roundabout method of thinking, and, at the same time as we prove the existence of a Keynesian equilibrium, I should like to show that this equilibrium is no more than a variant of neoclassical equilibrium and is not a surprising new variation at all. Such a method of proof has great significance, because it will demonstrate either that there is no essential difference between Keynesian theory and neoclassical theory, or that Glustoff's formulation of Keynesian theory is not the true Keynesian theory.

Let us now assume that there are N workers in our economy. We pick out N_1 of these and isolate the rest — in prison for example — for the meantime. Which workers we put in which group is not a problem. It is sufficient to designate them appropriately. The N_1 workers who have been picked out are taken to a neoclassical labour market. This means that not only the price adjustment functions for consumpton goods, capital goods and the services of capital goods are of neoclassical form, but also those for labour; that is

$$q_i = \frac{\max[p_i + aE_i,\, 0]}{\sum_j \max[p_j + aE_j,\, 0]}, \qquad i = 1, \ldots, n. \tag{25}$$

Furthermore it is the original Walras' law which is valid and not the extended version. We can then demonstrate the existence of full-employment equilibrium without the need for any new theory, by simply using the existing theorem for the neoclassical equilibrium system of chapter 6 as it stands. Let us assume such a situation was to come about. The chosen N_1 workers would be employed and positive wages would be paid. The demand and supply of other goods, too, would be equal (leaving aside free goods), and prices would remain stationary.

At the same time as this state of affairs comes about, let us have our workers form a trade union, and then let us release our hitherto incarcerated individuals. They will probably descend on the labour market. But the labour market is now of a Keynesian type. Under the established system of prices and wages, industry's demand for labour has been satisfied; there is no industry which will absorb the

newly released addition to the labour supply. For them to obtain
employment the prices and wages structure must alter, but since
the labour market is of Keynesian type, wages cannot change. These
workers will be unemployed. If they are unemployed, then their
demand for consumer goods is not an effective demand since it is
not backed with money. Therefore the demand for consumer goods
of the released individuals disappears from the market. The demand
and supply of consumer goods will continue in equilibrium and
there is no opportunity for price changes here either. Thus, such
a state of affairs is indisputably a Keyneisan underemployment
equilibrium in the sense of Glustoff; that is, it is a fixed point of
the price adjustment functions (4) and (5).[16+]

In this way we have obtained an underemployment equilibrium;
but what is important here is that we needed no special theory to
do so. If we simply employ the device of dividing existing workers
into two groups and temporarily incarcerating the members of one
group, we can easily bring about Keynesian equilibrium using the
neoclassical price adjustment functions, which are flexible both
upwards and downwards. Thus, if this is the logic by which Keynes
discovered underemployment equilibrium (in the next section I
shall show that it was not) it is by no means an essential contribution to economic theory, but merely a skilful application of neoclassical theory. The relationship between Keynes' own economics
and the (neo)classical school has been likened to the relationship
between non-Euclidean and Euclidean geometry; but to make
such a claim for Keynes must mean that there is a substantial
difference between the logic of Keynes and that of classical school.
If this is so, why was Glustoff only able to develop a neoclassical
version of Keynesian theory?

E. The principle of effective demand

Glustoff was unable to get at the core of Keynes' theory
because he lost sight of the principle of effective demand, which is
the mainstay of Keynes' logic. This being so we must find an
appropriate status for this principle, and to do so we assume that,
at our point of departure, prices and wages have a given, specific
value.

If prices and wages are given, each enterprise will choose that
technique which will yield maximum profits under the given price—
wage structure. If we now assume that there are constant returns

to scale, what is determined in accordance with the price—wage system is the quantity of each producer good required per unit of main product, or the quantity of by-products per unit of main product (that is the so-called input coefficient or output coefficient); it is not the absolute level of output. Thus the levels of output remain undetermined in the analysis of individual enterprises. They are determined by the demand and supply conditions of the market, so as to bring the two into equilibrium.

Let us compare this relationship of cause and effect with that of the neoclassical school. First, according to the neoclassical school, when the price—wage system is given, the quantities of outputs and inputs are determined in accordance with this system, and prices and wages are adjusted so that outputs and inputs thus determined are equalled by the demand and supply for them. Against this, in Keynes' theory all that is determined in accordance with prices and wages are production coefficients, and the volume of output is seen as changing freely so as to equate demand and supply in the market. That is to say, for the one prices and wages perform the function of regulating demand and supply, while for the other the volume of output regulates market excess demand or supply. Thus a fundamental difference exists between the two in their view of the adjustment mechanism of the market. The difference between the neoclassicals and Keynesians is not whether the price mechanism is perfect or imperfect; that is a difference of degree, as Glustoff saw it to be. It is a decisive difference over whether adjustment takes place via prices, or whether it takes place through an entirely different mechanism altogether (that is, the principle of effective demand).

˙ In order to get a clear perspective, we shall here assume that each enterprise produces only one kind of product. As before, we arrange goods in the order: consumer goods). $= 1, \ldots, h$, capital goods $i = h + 1, \ldots, l$, capital services $i = l + 1, \ldots, m$ and labour $i = m + 1, \ldots, n$. Each enterprise is classified into one of l industries according to its product (h industries are consumer goods industries, $l - h$ industries produce capital goods). Firms which belong to the same industry operate under the same technical constraints (that is, they possess the same book of blueprints), and, moreover, are confronted with the same prices and wages system. We assume, therefore, that they employ the same production techniques, as a result of the principle of maximising profits, and consequently that their production coefficients (input coefficients) do not differ. Needless to say, the volume of output of each industry is equal to the aggregate sum of the output of each firm belonging to that industry. The industry made up of enterprises making product i is called industry i; its input coefficients are $a_{l+1, i}, a_{l+2, i}, \ldots, a_{mi}$ with respect to the services of capital goods, and $a_{m+1, i}, \ldots, a_{ni}$ with respect to labour. Its output is X_i. Since input coefficients depend only on prices and wages, they do not change as long as prices and wages are unchanged.

Next, when prices and wages are given, each worker determines his consumption and the labour he is willing to supply, so as to maximise his utility in accordance with these prices and wages. The total demand by workers for consumer good i is shown by $\sum_j D_i^j(p_1, \ldots, p_n)$, and the total supply of labour i by $\sum_j S_i^j(p_1, \ldots, p_n)$.

However, these totals of demand and supply apply only in the case where there is full employment of labour. Since this is not necessarily realised, the volume of effective demand will not necessarily reach the full-employment level of demand. Therefore let us compare the quantity of labour supplied with industry's demand for labour. The total demand for labour i is given by $N_i = \sum_{r=1}^{l} a_{ir} X_r$, so that if $\sum_j S_i^j(p_1, \ldots, p_n)$ is less than N_i, there will be a shortage of labour, and in the opposite case the demand for labour is deficient. In the circumstances which were the object of Keynes' analysis, no producer good constituted a bottleneck, and therefore

$$N_i = \sum_{r=1}^{l} a_{ir} X_r \leqq \sum_j S_i^j(p_1, \ldots, p_n), \qquad i = m+1, \ldots, n. \quad (26)$$

Consequently, the total actual income of workers is

$$W = \sum_{i=m+1}^{n} p_i N_i. \quad (27)$$

Workers purchase consumer goods with their incomes. If workers' preferences differ, the total demand for each consumer good will differ, depending on who is employed, even if the level of employment overall is the same. Therefore, in order to avoid the difficulties caused by this fact, we assume all workers have the same preferences. Thus the actual total of consumer good i demanded by workers is shown by $D_i^w(p_1, \ldots, p_n, W)$.

As in the previous section, capitalists are also thought of as entrepreneurs. Therefore they earn enterprise profits as well as income from the capital goods they own; but as I shall explain later, capital goods as well as labour are not necessarily fully employed in the Keynesian system, and therefore income from capital goods depends not only on prices, but also on the degree to which they are used. The demand for the services of capital good i is given by $\sum_r a_{ir} X_r$ in the same way as the demand for labour. At the time the demand is made, $\sum_k K_i^k$ is the total quantity of usable capital services i within the system (k stands for the capitalist who owns capital good i, and we assume that each unit of capital good i can yield one unit of services i per period). Therefore, where there is no excess demand for the services of capital goods we have

$$N_i = \sum_{r=1}^{l} a_{ir} X_r \leqq \sum_k K_i^k, \qquad i = l+1, \ldots, m. \tag{28}$$

The right-hand side of this equation shows the supply of the services of capital goods and the middle term shows the effective demand. Therefore the N_i of the left-hand side shows the quantity of capital services actually supplied. Since the return to a capitalist from supplying one unit of the services of a capital good is p_i, $i = l+1, \ldots, m$, the total earnings from capital are $\sum_{s=l+1}^{m} p_s N_s$. Next, let b_i be the entrepreneurial profits per unit output of industry i; then the total of entrepreneurial profits from industry i is $b_i X_i$, and therefore $\sum b_r X_r$ are the total of entrepreneurial profits for all industries. b_i depends on the prices and wages system and on production techniques. However, under a given technology, the same method of production is always employed with specified prices and wages, and hence b_i depends ultimately on prices and wages alone. Where these are unchanged b_i is unchanged.

The total income of the capitalist class is

$$\Pi = \sum_{s=l+1}^{m} p_s N_s + \sum_{r=1}^{l} b_r X_r. \tag{29}$$

This is distributed to capitalists in accordance with the capital goods they own, and in proportion to their contribution to the management of enterprises. Each capitalist applies to consumption what is left after he has deducted savings from income (savings are applied to the purchase of new capital goods). His demand for consumer goods depends on prices and his income; but if the preferences of all capitalists are the same, we can ignore the distribution of the total income, Π, among individual capitalists and regard the demand for consumer good i of the entire capitalist class, D_i^k, as depending on prices and the income of the capitalist class as a whole. That is

$$D_i^k = D_i^k (p_1, \ldots, p_n, \Pi).$$

In market equilibrium the demand and supply of each product must be equal. Therefore for consumer goods,

$$X_i = D_i^w (p_1, \ldots, p_n, W) + D_i^k (p_1, \ldots, p_n, \Pi), \qquad (30)$$
$$i = 1, \ldots, h,$$

and for capital goods,

$$X_i = \sum_k H_i^k, \qquad i = h + 1, \ldots, l. \qquad (31)$$

In the formulae for W and Π, the demand for labour N_s, $s = m + 1$, $\ldots, n$, and the demand for the capital services N_s, $s = l + 1, \ldots,$ m, are functions of outputs $X_1, \ldots, X_l$, that is $\sum_{r=1}^{l} a_{sr} X_r$, as long as they do not exceed the quantities supplied (that is as long as the inequalities (26) and (28) are satisfied).

It is now easy to see the progress of Keynes' logic. If gross investment in capital goods is given, the $\sum_k H_i^k$ of the right-hand side of (31) takes on a specific value. Outputs of the capital goods industries adjust to these given demands, so that (31) is valid. Therefore $X_{h+1}, \ldots, X_l$ take on a specific value in (26) − (29); and the remaining variables are the outputs of consumer goods $X_1, \ldots, X_h$, which are determined so as to equal the effective demand for each consumer good (see (30)). It is the propensity to consume of workers and capitalists and the level of investment which determine effective demand. If investment is fixed at a high level, then the wages and profits of the investment goods industry will take on a high value in (30), and the outputs of consumer goods will, accordingly, be determined at a high level (the so-called Kahn multiplier theory).

We must note that, in this theory of the determination of output, all prices and wages are regarded as being given. (If wages and prices are determined, the input coefficients of (26) and (28) and the profits coefficient b_r of (29) are determined, and (30) ultimately depends on outputs alone.) Therefore we must provide a theoretical basis for the determination of prices and wages, and the major departure of our interpretation of Keynes from the bastard

Keynesian interpretations (Glustoff's for example) relates to this point. These Keynesians take into account the downward rigidity of wages and amend the wage-rate adjustment functions, but they do not differ basically from the neoclassical school. That is, it is prices which are regarded as regulating the demand and supply of goods, and these are seen as being determined by the equations of demand and supply. However, if we adopt this viewpoint there is no way to accommodate the principle of effective demand, or formula (30), which recognises the relationship of mutual adjust-ability between the demand and supply of goods on the one hand, and the quantity of output on the other. If we assume this principle too, equilibrium conditions (that is, when the excess demand for goods is zero) will on the one hand determine prices, while on the other hand simultaneously determining outputs, and the trouble-some situation arises whereby we have to determine two unknowns by one formula. Glustoff and the rest therefore ignored the prin-ciple of effective demand; but we shall, instead, keep (30) and get rid of the neoclassical price adjustment functions relating to prod-ucts. This decision is an essentially Keynesian one. After all, a Keynesian system without the principle of effective demand, and thus without a theory of the multiplier, no matter how consistently and skilfully it was operated, would be like Hamlet without the Prince of Denmark, and would no longer merit the appellation 'Keynesian'.

We shall think of the prices of products as being determined by the addition of per unit normal profits to costs per unit of prod-ucts.[17] Prices now no longer perform the function of regulating demand and supply (this function has been assigned to outputs); instead they regulate profits. If profits are above normal the price of products will fall so as to return them to normal, and if profits are less than normal, prices will rise to restore them to normality. Equilibrium prices of products which equal the sum of costs and normal profits are obtained at the end of a process of trial and error (this process will be explained later, on pp. 240–2); but as far as equilibrium prices are concerned, the prices of products will not change unless prices of producer goods change. That is, in the equations of product prices, per unit production costs and the coefficients of normal profits depend on prices of producer goods as well as product prices; if prices of producer goods are given, the equilibrium prices of producte are determined as the solutions to these equations.

In contrast to these products, we assume with Glustoff that the prices of producer goods are flexible upwards in respect of an excess demand, and inflexible downwards in respect of an excess supply. We differ from him on one point, which is that, while he assumed the presence of this asymmetry only in the price adjustment function with respect to every kind of labour, we assume it with respect to all kinds of producer goods, and particularly with respect to capital services. Therefore, not only can labour be underemployed at equilibrium; capital goods too can be underutilised. That is what Keynes was really emphasising when he referred to 'poverty in the midst of plenty'.[18+] We can write these sorts of price adjustment functions for producer goods as

$$q_i = \frac{p_i + a\max[E_i, 0]}{1 + a \sum\limits_{r=l+1}^{n} \max[E_r, 0]}, \qquad i = l+1, \ldots, n, \ (32)$$

if we choose as our numeraire for measuring prices a composite good made up of 1 unit each of all producer goods. Here p_i and q_i are prices before and after adjustment, the excess demand function E_i for the services of capital goods is

$$E_i = \sum_{r=1}^{l} a_{ir}X_r - \sum_k K_i^k, \qquad i = l+1, \ldots, m,$$

and for labour it is

$$E_i = \sum_{r=1}^{l} a_{ir}X_r - \sum_j S_i^j(p_1, \ldots, p_n) \qquad i = m+1, \ldots, n.$$

I would ask you to note that the excess demand functions are not functions of prices alone, as they are with Glustoff, but also include outputs as independent variables.

The Keynesian system we have described above has the following system of transmission between its parts. First, suppose that prices of factors of production are given arbitrarily or historically. The prices of products are determined so that they satisfy the equation: prices = costs + normal profits. Now all prices are given, and therefore the income of workers and capitalists per unit of product is determined, and we can determine the remaining unknowns, l individual outputs, by the equations of the theory of effective demand, (30) and (31), since we take the gross investment in capital goods as given. Outputs thus determined decide the demand for labour and the services of capital goods. When these demands do not exceed the existing quantities of capital goods and the supplies of various kinds of labour corresponding to given prices and wages, then there is no excess demand for producer goods. Therefore we have $E_i \leqq 0$, $i = l + 1, \ldots, n$, and from (32) we obtain $q_i = p_i$, $i = l + 1, \ldots, n$. That is to say, prices are stationary because of the downward rigidity of wages and the prices of capital services, and we have an underemployment equilibrium accompanied by idle capital or unemployment.

In contrast to this, if excess demand exists for capital services or for labour, the prices of producer goods will change according to the adjustment functions (32). The change spreads in turn to product prices, the outputs of each good and the excess demands for producer goods, and then back once again to the point of departure, namely the prices of producer goods. The process of price adjustment is repeated until full-employment equilibrium or underemployment equilibrium is eventually established.

This is our version of Keynesian theory, and, as is clear from the above explanation, whether or not underemployment equilibrium is established is determined in relation to the price system for producer goods which is given at the point of departure, and the given quantity of gross investment $\sum_k H_i^k$. Even where the overall volume of investment is unchanged, we can arrive either at an underemployment equilibrium or at a full-employment equilibrium, depending on the prices of producer goods from which we start. Similarly, in the case of underemployment equilibrium, it is possible for the degree of seriousness of unemployment to differ along with the difference in producer good prices, even though the volume of gross investment is unchanged. Thus to establish a better system of producer good prices is important even in the above system; however, the effect of these prices on unemployment is the most remote, becoming apparent only after the repercussions have been felt by product prices and outputs. Consequently, it is possible that it may be counterbalanced or weakened in the process of development by opposite effects, and it is difficult to conclude exactly what sort of influence on unemployment will be produced by what sort of adjustments in producer good prices. On the other hand, however, the shortest distance is that between the volume of gross investment and unemployment, and this effect is precisely known. Therefore, as we know, Keynes insisted on the importance of investment in his measures against unemployment. I shall discuss this subject in detail in chapter 9.

Finally, I must say something more about a condition which I have neglected to some extent in the above discussion, but which I ought to have considered more strictly. As stated previously, the net rates of return on each capital good have to be equal at equilibrium. This means that if there are g kinds of capital goods, the $g-1$ individual equalitites of (12) must hold ($g = l - h = m - l$). In order to find a place within the system for these additional conditions, we have to add $g-1$ degrees of freedom. To do this we must assume either that $g-1$ kinds of capital goods are variable in the gross investment $\sum_k H_i^k$, $i = h+1, \ldots, l$, which was hitherto assumed fixed, or that, although the total of gross investment $\sum_{i=h+1}^{l} p_i(\sum_k H_i^k)$ is given, its distribution among the various capital goods is completely free. The case which Keynes considered was that where underemployment equilibrium came about as a result of limiting total investment to a sufficiently low value.

Again, we held in the above that returns to scale were constant in all industries, and that the demand and supply of products were regulated by increasing or decreasing outputs and not by adjusting prices. However, in an actual economy part of industry will have decreasing returns to scale, and therefore the decision as to how much to produce will depend on prices. In such an industry the quantity of output cannot be an independent variable, and the demand and supply of products are adjusted by changing product prices.

Thus in an actual economy, one group of industries (for example the manufacturing sector) will constitute a fixprice economy, while another group of industries (for example, agriculture and mining) will constitute a flexprice economy. The economy as a whole can be seen as an amalgam of the neoclassical and the Keynesian economy. As a result, the principle of effective demand does not apply overall in an actual economy, but holds within a limited area. Similarly, the neoclassical price mechanism functions only imperfectly. However, the broad trend of history is on the side of Keynes, and in advanced capitalist countries the fixprice sectors of the economy have come to dominate the flexprice sectors.

8

Decentralised economic planning

A. A socialist allocation of capital goods and labour

In chapter 6 we analysed the process of price adjustment in the situation where a part or all of natural resources, capital goods and labour had already been allocated in fixed amounts to each enterprise. This process can be interpreted as a process leading towards equilibrium in a capitalist economy, and as a process of adjusting plans in a socialist economy. Needless to say an economic plan determined in this fashion is dependent on the initial fixed allocation to firms of natural resources, capital goods and so on, and does not necessarily produce an equilibrium state in the true sense (that is not merely a state where the demand and supply of goods are in equilibrium, but one where all enterprises are earning normal profits). Differences in productivity may arise among firms; that is to say, enterprises which have received an advantageous distribution of natural resources and so forth will probably make excess profits. Where the profit rates of different enterprises are not equal, total profits, and hence the income of the state, can be increased by transferring resources from low-profit to high-profit enterprises. If the increased income of the state is distributed to workers, they will gain greater satisfaction.[1+] Therefore we can regard the equilibrium which comes about when natural resources, capital goods and labour are mobile as being generally better than that which occurs when the distribution of these to enterprises is fixed. In this chapter we shall presume a socialist economy, and investigate how natural resources, capital goods, labour and so on, ought to be allocated amongst enterprises.

Before considering this problem, we must explain what kind of socialist economy we have in mind. A variety of different models or blueprints of socialist economies have been presented in the past,[2] but the one I shall assume below is specified as follows.

(i) The means of production are all state-owned, and therefore there is no class which gets its income from the ownership of these means (capitalist class). (ii) The state is exceedingly large and the central planning authority is aware that completely centralised planning is out of the question. The planning of production (the choice of production techniques) is left to each individual enterprise. (iii) In the many planning models so far produced, the planning authority has an objective function which is constructed from individual utility functions by assigning them equal or unequal weights, and the models determine not only the production plan but the consumption plan of each individual so as to maximise the value of the objective function.[3+] However, in our model the central planning authority is modest and does no more than allocate capital goods and labour to each enterprise so as to comply as far as possible with the demand determined voluntarily by individuals. If we evaluate the state attained as a result of the actions of such a modest and passive planning authority (a state where the voluntarily determined demands of the individual are satisfied as completely as possible) according to the standards of a particular welfare function, welfare is not necessarily maximised. In order to maximise welfare, or in order to maintain equity amongst individuals, the central planning authority will have to pursue additional policies of giving subsidies to particular types of people, levying taxes on others, and providing state-built community facilities. In this sense, the plan I shall discuss in this chapter is not an optimum plan; but since the analysis of the effect of additional measures designed to maximise welfare is barely different from the capitalist case, we can apply the analysis of public finance policies in a capitalist economy developed in the next chapter to the model in this chapter, with appropriate amendments and reinterpretations.

Let us here consider an economy where prices of factors of production are all supervised by the central planning authority, but the choice of techniques is left to the individual firm. For the sake of simplicity, we shall first of all consider the case where consumer goods and producer goods are made by labour and machines only. We shall leave until later the analysis of the general case where part of what is produced is used as raw materials. The central planning authority has to establish an adequate price system when it formulates the Economic Plan, and as a first step it chooses appropriate values $p_{l+1}(0), \ldots, p_n(0)$ for the wages of labour and the rentals on capital goods, and transmits these to each enterprise. The enterprise chooses a technique of production which will minimise unit costs under these prices, and then reports the unit cost of products produced with these techniques to the central planning authority. (Throughout the following, we assume that each enterprise produces only one product and constant returns to scale prevail.)

The central planning authority picks out from those which produce the same product the firms which have reported the lowest prices, and allocates capital goods and labour to these firms only. An enterprise r, which has earned the right to an allocation of capital goods and labour, reports to the central planning authority the quantity of labour and capital services $a_{l+1,r}(0), \ldots, a_{n,r}(0)$ which it needs per unit of product. Let f be the total number of firms which have earned this right, and write the matrix of input coefficients and the matrix of output coefficients as

$$
B(0) = \begin{bmatrix} a_{l+1,1}(0) & a_{l+1,2}(0) & \cdots & a_{l+1,f}(0) \\ a_{l+2,1}(0) & a_{l+2,2}(0) & \cdots & a_{l+2,f}(0) \\ \cdot & \cdot & & \cdot \\ \cdot & \cdot & & \cdot \\ \cdot & \cdot & & \cdot \\ a_{n,1}(0) & a_{n,2}(0) & \cdots & a_{n,f}(0) \end{bmatrix},
$$

$$
J(0) = \begin{bmatrix} 1 & 1 & \cdots & 0 \\ 0 & 0 & \cdots & 0 \\ \cdot & \cdot & & \cdot \\ \cdot & \cdot & & \cdot \\ \cdot & \cdot & & \cdot \\ 0 & 0 & \cdots & 1 \end{bmatrix}.
$$

$$(1)$$

Here $J(0)$ is a matrix of l rows and f columns. When enterprise r produces product j, then the jth element of column r is 1; all other elements are 0. The $J(0)$ illustrated above shows that enterprise 1 and enterprise 2 produce product 1, and that enterprise f produces product l.

Between the vector of factor prices $p_{II}(0)$ presented by the central planning authority, and the vector of lowest product prices $p_{I}(0) = (p_1(0), \ldots, p_l(0))$ reported by each enterprise, there is the relationship

$$p_{I}(0)\,J(0) = p_{II}(0)\,B(0). \qquad (2)$$

The prices of factors of production are proposed by the central planning authority, but since each enterprise determines its own respective column of matrix $B(0)$, the determination of product prices is decentralised. Where there is no competition between enterprises, each enterprise will report to the central planning authority a product price which is higher than the actual production price. However, in our economy an enterprise will lose its right to an allocation of capital goods and labour if its product price is higher than that of other enterprises, and therefore each enterprise chief has to report his prices honestly. But where all enterprices which produce the same product collude, each will report a price higher than the actual one; and since, moreover, they are still able to receive their allocation of capital goods and labour, the central planning authority will have to supervise firms to ensure that such collusion does not occur.

In this way the list of enterprises which ought to receive an allocation of capital goods and labour is determined. Enterprise r included in this list will produce $x_r(0)$ of product r, so that its allocation of factor of production i will be $a_{ir}(0) x_r(0)$. Therefore the total quantity of factors to be allocated to enterprises is $B(0)X(0)$. ($X(0)$ is a column vector of f dimensions whose components are the outputs of all producing enterprises.) Since these allocated factors must not exceed the total quantity $\overline{Z}$ of capital goods and labour which the society possesses ($\overline{Z}$ is a column vector of $(n - l)$ dimensions having components $\bar{z}_{l+1}, \bar{z}_{l+2}, \ldots, \bar{z}_n$), then

$$B(0) \, X(0) \leqq \overline{Z} \tag{3}$$

must hold.[4+] $J(0) \, X(0)$ is the total output of goods when each enterprise produces at $X(0)$.

When wages and prices are determined, workers' demand for consumer goods j, which is $D_j(p(0), \overline{Z}), j = 1, \ldots, h$, is determined. Next we show the state's demand for capital good k by D_k, $k = h + 1, \ldots, l$. Let $D(p(0))$ stand for the vector of the total demand for consumer goods and capital goods,

$$D(p(0)) = \begin{bmatrix} D_1(p(0), \overline{Z}) \\ \vdots \\ D_h(p(0), \overline{Z}) \\ D_{h+1} \\ \vdots \\ D_l \end{bmatrix} \tag{4}$$

Let ϕ_i be the proportion of the output of good i to its total demand, and ϕ the smallest value of ϕ_i, $i = 1, \ldots, l$. Then we obviously have

$$\phi D(p(0)) \leqq J(0) \, X(0). \tag{5}$$

We now assume that the central planning authority allocates capital goods and labour to enterprises so as to maximise ϕ, the lowest of the degrees of satisfaction of the demand for goods. Then the problem which confronts the authorities is to maximise ϕ under the inequalities (3) and (5). (Naturally we must have $X(0) \geqq 0$.)

I have to say something at this point about the relationship between the prices $p_{m+1}(0), \ldots, p_n(0)$ assigned to labour and workers' earned incomes. (Here I shall regard the services which entrepreneurs supply as directors as a kind of labour, and count them among the $n - m$ varieties of labour.) As already stated, each enterprise calculates its costs on the basis of the factor prices assigned by the central planning authority. However, this does not mean that workers receive incomes exactly equal to these prices, nor that they have a right to receive them. But the enterprise has to pay to the central planning authority, at these prices, the 'cost' of the factors of production which it uses. Therefore, when there is full employment, the central planning authority is able to anticipate an 'income' of $p_{\text{II}}(0) \, \bar{Z}$, which it can distribute among the workers. Let us assume here that there are v workers and that any worker j offers the amount $\bar{z}_{ij}$, $i = m + 1, \ldots, n, j = 1, \ldots, v$, of each type of labour $i = m + 1, \ldots, n$. (Most workers are only able to offer one kind of labour, and therefore all but one of the $\bar{z}_{ij}$ are zero). If we make q_{ij} the income worker j acquires by offering one unit of labour i, the total income of j is

$$Q_j = \sum_{i = m+1}^{n} q_{ij} \bar{z}_{ij}, \, j = 1, \ldots, v.$$

This is not necessarily equal to the income which results when the $\bar{z}_{ij}$ are valued at $p_{\text{II}}(0)$, i.e. $\sum_{i=m+1}^{n} p_i(0) \bar{z}_{ij}$. According to the capitalistic way of looking at it, when the former is smaller (larger) than the latter, we may think of worker j as getting an income which is equal to the latter, but as being taxed (subsidised) by the amount of the difference. However, in a socialist society 'as a matter of common sense, it would clearly be absurd for the central board to pay out incomes first and, after having done so, to run after the recipients in order to recover part of them';[5] therefore the central planning authority does not pay $\sum_{m+1}^{n} p_i(0)\bar{z}_{ij}$ to the worker, and his income is always Q_j. The income left in the hands of the state when all workers have received their incomes is $p_{II}(0)\bar{Z} - \sum_{j=1}^{v} Q_j$, and the central planning authority will probably use this for replacement investment and new investment in capital goods. Therefore the budget equation of the state is

$$\sum_{i=h+1}^{l} p_i(0)D_i = p_{II}(0)\bar{Z} - \sum_{j=1}^{v} Q_j.$$

The budget equation for each individual worker is

$$\sum_{i=1}^{h} p_i(0)d_{ij} = Q_j, j = 1, \ldots, v,$$

subject to which each decides his d_{ij} so as to maximise his utility function. Therefore d_{ij} is a function of the prices of consumer goods and of Q_j. If we sum the d_{ij} for all j we obtain

$$D_i(p_1(0), \ldots, p_h(0), Q_1, \ldots, Q_v) = \sum_{j=1}^{v} d_{ij}(p_1(0), \ldots, p_h(0), Q_j).$$

Given that the central planning authority distributes incomes among workers according to the total income of the state, then $Q_1, \ldots,$ Q_v is a function of $p_{II}(0)\bar{Z}$. Therefore we may put the above equation in the form,

$$D_i(p(0), \bar{Z}) = \sum_{j=1}^{v} d_{ij}(p_1(0), \ldots, p_n(0), \bar{Z}).$$

If we now add the budget equation for the state and those for each individual worker, we obtain

$$\sum_{i=1}^{h} p_i(0)D_i(p(0), \bar{Z}) + \sum_{i=h+1}^{l} p_i(0)D_i = p_{II}(0)\bar{Z}.$$

This formula is valid no matter what prices may happen to be put forward by the central planning authority. The amounts of capital goods demanded by the state must always satisfy the state's budget equation, and therefore when prices change they must also change. Consequently the $D_i(i = h + 1, \ldots, l$, of the above formula are also a function of prices, and we may generally write the above equation as

$$p_{\mathrm{I}}D(p) = p_{\mathrm{II}}\bar{Z}. \tag{6}$$

This is an identity which is valid for all prices, and it expresses Walras' law for a socialist society.[6]

If we take into account the fact that $p_{\mathrm{I}}(0) \geqq 0$, and $p_{\mathrm{II}}(0) \geqq 0$, we can obtain from (2), (3) and (5),

$$\phi p_{\mathrm{I}}(0)D(p(0)) \leqq p_{\mathrm{I}}(0)J(0)X(0) = p_{\mathrm{II}}(0)B(0)X(0) \leqq p_{\mathrm{II}}(0)\bar{Z}.$$

Therefore, by (6) we have $\phi \leqq 1$. That is, if the factor prices which the central planning authority initially regards as being appropriate are not really appropriate, then $\phi < 1$, and there are goods for which the demand is only imperfectly satisfied. In order to satisfy all consumers and the state itself, the central planning authority has to revise factor prices so as to ensure that $\phi = 1$.

How then are prices determined so as to ensure $\phi = 1$? As a preparation for solving this problem, let us first show that among those $X(0)$ which maximise ϕ subject to (3) and (5), there is one which satisfies (5) with equality. This is easily seen. Suppose now that (5) holds with an inequality sign for a certain good. In this case there is no direct effect on ϕ even if the volume of output of that good is made to decrease (the reason being that we assume each individual enterprise produces only one kind of good). However, if we reduce output, the quantities of labour and capital goods which that enterprise used will also decrease. As a result, it may be possible to raise the output of other enterprises, so that the possibility arises that ϕ will increase. In any case we can reduce the level of activity of industries producing goods where an inequality sign appears in (5) without any unfavourable consequences for the value of ϕ. Therefore in all cases there is a maximum solution which satisfies (5) as an equality.

Let $X(0)$ be such a solution, and define $X'(0) = (1/\phi)X(0)$; then

$$D(p(0)) = J(0)X'(0).$$

That is, if enterprises carry out production activities $X'(0)$, workers' demands and the demands of the state will be completely satisfied.

However, the amounts $B(0)X'(0)$ of capital goods and labour will be needed in order to maintain this level of production activity, and therefore an excess demand for factors

$$E = B(0)X'(0) - \bar{Z} \tag{7}$$

will arise. This is because, since (3) has to be satisfied with equality for at least one factor of production at the solution $X(0)$ to the maximisation problem confronting the central planning authority, there must occur a positive excess demand for at least one factor when each enterprise is operated at a level of activity $X'(0)$ with $\phi < 1$. Hence there is no excess demand for any factor (i.e. $E \leqq 0$) only when $\phi = 1$.

Thus the problem of satisfying the demand of workers and of the state (that is of obtaining factor prices which will make $\phi = 1$) is converted into the problem of producing an equilibrium in the demand and supply of factors (that is, of obtaining factor prices such that $E \leq 0$ will be established). This being the case, how are such equilibrium factor prices obtained? First, E depends, apart from $\bar{Z}$, upon $B(0)$ and $X'(0)$. $B(0)$ is determined as soon as factor prices $p_{II}(0)$ are given, and so is a function of $p_{II}(0)$. Next, $X'(0)$ is determined by ϕ and $X(0)$, but since both of these depend on the parameters of the maximisation problem $D(p(0))$, $J(0)$ and $B(0)$, it depends ultimately on $p_{II}(0)$. Therefore E, which is the excess demand for factors, is a function of the prices of factors, and moreover by Walras' law (6) we have

$$p_{II}E(p_{II}) = p_{II}(BX' - \bar{Z}) = p_I JX' - p_{II}\bar{Z} = p_I D(p) - p_{II}\bar{Z} = 0.$$

Therefore the central planning authority can, for example by adjusting prices according to the neoclassical price adjustment formula (9) of chapter 6, find equilibrium prices by following the process explained on pp. 190–6.[7]

That is to say, where at $p_{II}(0)$ an excess demand arises for some factors of production and an excess supply for others, the prices of the former are raised and those of the latter lowered. The new prices $p_{II}(1)$ are then presented to enterprises. Enterprises will re-evaluate their production techniques under the new prices and will choose those which will minimise unit costs; they will then inform the central planning authority of the likely prices of the products produced with these techniques. The authority will allocate capital goods and labour only to those enterprises which are most efficient (that is, to those whose product prices are lowest). The tables of input coefficients and output coefficients of firms chosen in this fashion are, respectively, $B(1)$ and $J(1)$. We make $p_I(1)$ the product prices corresponding to the new factor prices $p_{II}(1)$, and $D(p(1))$ the workers' demands for consumer goods and the state's demands for capital goods after their prices $p(1) = (p_I(1), p_{II}(1))$ have been publicly announced. The central planning authority determines $X(1)$ so as to maximise ϕ subject to

$$\phi D(p(1)) \leqq J(1) X(1),$$

$$B(1) X(1) \leqq \overline{Z}.$$

If $\phi < 1$, then $B(1) X'(1)$, the capital goods and labour needed to satisfy completely the demand $D(p(1))$, is calculated. (Note that $X'(1) = (1/\phi) X(1)$.) A factor of production for which there is an excess demand will have its price raised further, and one for which there is an excess supply will have its price lowered. A process exactly similar to the above will be continued until we have $\phi = 1$. When $\phi = 1$, workers' demand for consumer goods and the state's demand for capital goods will be completely satisfied, and the supply of and demand for factors will be in equilibrium.

B. The Walrasian process and the Keynes—Leontief process

In order to compare the above mechanism for adjusting prices with the two typical price adjustment mechanisms of the capitalist economy (namely the Walrasian mechanism and the Keynes-Leontief mechanism), I shall in this section consider what conditions are necessary for the process of change in the prices and outputs generated by these two mechanisms to be a stable one. Under the Walrasian or neoclassical mechanism the prices of products and factors are made to rise when there is an excess demand for them, and to fall when there is an excess supply. According to this mechanism the output of products is increased when the industries which make these products earn excess profits; when they are earning negative excess profits it is decreased. In contrast to this, the prices of factors of production are fixed under the Keynes—

Leontief mechanism, and the prices of products are adjusted in a direction which will eliminate excess profits (that is, when excess profits are positive the prices of the products of those industries are reduced, and when excess profits are negative they are raised). Under this mechanism outputs of goods are increased when there is an excess demand for them and decreased when there is an excess supply. The analysis of these mechanisms has so far been mainly conducted presupposing a capitalist economy; but it can also be applied to a socialist economy, as long as prices and outputs are adjusted by the methods assumed.

For simplicity of analysis, I shall make the following assumptions. (i) Each firm always employs the same method of production whatever prices are given, and moreover production by this method yields constant returns to scale. Therefore production coefficients are always fixed. This means that we ignore the process whereby the techniques employed change in accordance with price changes and as a result production coefficients change. Such neglect is permissible only in the case where each enterprise really only has one method of production, or where changes in prices are insignificant (price changes are confined locally). (ii) Factors of production (the services of capital goods and labour) are mobile, and the production plan is formulated on the assumption that the enterprise can buy the factors it needs in the market, or will receive them through its central allocation. The total quantity of each factor possessed by society is limited, but from the point of view of the individual enterprise, the existing quantity is large enough to be, to all intents and purposes, unlimited. Consequently, there is no reason why output should hit a ceiling. Therefore, the volume of output X_i is, like prices, flexible — an independent variable in the economy.

In the past a variety of stability conditions have been put forward. The first is the Walras—Hicks stability condition where, put in simple terms, we distinguish between stability and instability according to the way demand and supply react to changes in price. This condition was later expressed in more precise terms by a number of people (Samuelson, Arrow, Hurwitz, etc.). The next is the Keynes stability condition, which distinguishes instability according to whether the marginal propensity to consume is greater than one. The third is the Leontief stability condition, which hinges on whether the matrix of input coefficients is productive or not.[8] Normally these stability conditions are discussed in parallel in relation to different systems, and their mutual relationships are not inquired into. However, I hope to show below that the stability condition which applies in an economy will be either the Hicks stability condition or the Keynes-Leontief stability condition, according as the mechanism of adjustment differs. Therefore, which of these stability conditions is the correct one depends on which adjustment mechanism applies in that economy.

As in the previous section, we think of $1, \ldots, h$ as consumer goods, $h + 1, \ldots, l$ as capital goods, $l + 1, \ldots, m$ as the services of capital, and $m + 1, \ldots, n$ as labour. But in this section we assume that consumer goods can be used not only purely as consumer goods, but also as raw materials. The same applied to capital goods. a_{ij} is the quantity of good i which is used as a raw material in the production of one unit of good j. Since both the subscript i and the subscript j can take on values (natural numbers) of from 1 to l, the production coefficients a_{ij} form an l by l matrix (the Leontief input-coefficient matrix).

First, in the neoclassical or Walrasian mechanism, both product prices and factor prices are regarded as being flexible. That is to say, in the capitalist case workers and capitalists sell the labour and the capital services at their disposal and buy consumer goods. It is understood that when they do so, they form their consumption plans on the assumption that the productive services they supply will be demanded in their entirety. In the case of socialism, capital goods, and hence the services of capital goods, are provided by the state and not by capitalists. The state receives rentals for them from enterprises, and with the income so acquired it carries on its own undertakings (including investment in capital goods). Transactions made before the demands and supplies for productive services and products are in equilibrium are assumed to be settled at the final prices and not at the prices ruling when the contractual obligation was undertaken (the assumption of a competitive process of buying and selling). That is, each individual component of the economy formulates his, her or its individual demand and supply plans on the assumption of full employment, and where the aggregate totals of these demands and supplies are not in equilibrium, prices — which are flexible — are adjusted, either in the market or by the central planning authority.

Under such a market or planning mechanism we can think of

the supplies of factors and demands for consumer goods as depending on prices alone. It is true that the demands and supplies decided upon by households depend on the quantities of factors of production initially owned by them; but, under the assumption of competitive buying and selling, we may treat the quantities of factors owned at the beginning of the period as if they were unchanged throughout the process of *tâtonnement* (or groping) which lasts until equilibrium is finally reached (see chapter 6 for a detailed account). Consequently both the quantities of consumer goods demanded and the quantities of factors of production supplied become functions of prices alone. We now denote the demand function for consumer good i by

$$D_i = D_i(p_1, \ldots, p_n), \qquad i = 1, \ldots, h, \tag{8}$$

and the supply function of factor of production i by

$$S_i = S_i(p_1, \ldots, p_n), \qquad i = l+1, \ldots, n. \tag{9}$$

In the socialist case (9) will hold only for labour $i = m+1, \ldots, n$, individuals cannot own capital goods. The following holds for the services of capital

$$S_i = K_i, \qquad i = l+1, \ldots, m, \tag{9'}$$

where K_i is the total quantity of capital good i possessed by the state, which is assumed to be constant.

Now let X_i, $i = 1, \ldots, l$, be the output of product i (consumer good or capital good). Since consumer goods and capital goods can be used as raw materials, the total demand for consumer good i is $D_i + \sum_{r=1}^{l} a_{ir}X_r$, and that for capital good i is $H_i + \sum_{r=1}^{l} a_{ir}X_r$. Hence H_i shows investment demand for capital good i by capitalists or by the state, and we shall assume below that it is a constant. On the other hand, the supply of good i is X_i. Therefore, if we assume that its price p_i is adjusted in proportion with the excess demand for it, we have the price adjustment equations

$$\alpha_i \dot{p}_i = D_i(p_1, \ldots, p_n) + \sum_{r=1}^{l} a_{ir}X_r - X_i, \quad i = 1, \ldots, h, \tag{10}$$

and

$$\alpha_i \dot{p}_i = H_i + \sum_{r=1}^{l} a_{ir}X_r - X_i, \qquad i = h+1, \ldots, l, \tag{11}$$

where the α_i are the proportionality coefficients, and are called the adjustment coefficients. The dot above p_i shows that it is the differential derivative of price with respect to time. That is $\dot{p}_i = dp_i/dt$. Similar adjustment functions are assumed for producer goods. The demand by enterprises for productive service i is $\sum_{r=1}^{l} a_{ir}X_r$. Therefore, in the case of the capitalist economy, we obtain the adjustment equations for wages and the prices of capital services

$$\alpha_i \dot{p}_i = \sum_{r=1}^{l} a_{ir}X_r - S_i(p_1, \ldots, p_n), \quad i = l+1, \ldots, n-1. \quad (12)$$

However, in the socialist case, for capital services we have

$$\alpha_i \dot{p}_i = \sum_{r=1}^{l} a_{ir}X_r - K_i, \quad i = l+1, \ldots, m, \quad (12')$$

in place of the corresponding equations in (12). The reason why (12) does not hold for labour n is that we take it as our standard of value, and hence its price is always 1. We assume that n will never become a free good.

Since, in the above, outputs X_r are independent variables, we must have equations for adjusting X_r. Following Walras, we assume that where excess profits are obtained from the production of good i, the output of good i is increased, and where less-than-normal profits are obtained (negative excess profits), it decreases.[9] Even in the socialist case, under a system where profits are used as an incentive for enterprises, they are able to determine their outputs autonomously, and will probably decide whether to increase or decrease outputs according to whether excess profits are positive or negative. Excess profits are given by the difference between product prices and unit costs (including normal profits). The unit costs (including normal profits) of producing good i are shown by $\sum_{s=1}^{n} a_{si}p_s$. Here the total sum from $s = 1$ to l is the cost of using consumer goods or capital goods as raw materials; the sum from $l+1$ to m is the part paid to the state or to capitalists as normal profits, and the sum from $m+1$ to n shows wage costs. If we denote the adjustment coefficient for the volume of output by β_i, we may write the adjustment equations

$$\beta_i \dot{X}_i = p_i - \sum_{s=1}^{n} a_{si}p_s, \quad i = 1, \ldots, l. \quad (13)$$

The values for prices and outputs which will make the right-hand sides of the adjustment equations (10) to (13) zero are the general equilibrium values. If we designate these p_i^0, X_i^0 (note that $p_n^0 = p_n = 1$), we have

$$D_i(p_1^0, \ldots, p_n^0) + \sum_{r=1}^{l} a_{ir} X_r^0 - X_i^0 = 0, \qquad i = 1, \ldots, h,$$

$$H_i + \sum_{r=1}^{l} a_{ir} X_r^0 - X_i^0 = 0, \qquad i = h+1, \ldots, l,$$

$$\sum_{r=1}^{l} a_{ir} X_r^0 - S_i(p_1^0, \ldots, p_n^0) = 0, \qquad i = l+1, \ldots, n-1,$$

$$p_i^0 - \sum_{s=1}^{n} a_{si} p_s^0 = 0, \qquad i = 1, \ldots, l.$$

If we add these to both sides of (10) to (13) respectively and rearrange terms, we obtain[10]

$$\alpha_i \dot{p}_i = \Delta D_i + \sum_{r=1}^{l} a_{ir} \Delta X_r - \Delta X_i, \qquad i = 1, \ldots, h, \tag{10'}$$

$$\alpha_i \dot{p}_i = \sum_{r=1}^{l} a_{ir} \Delta X_r - \Delta X_i, \qquad i = h+1, \ldots, l, \tag{11'}$$

$$\alpha_i \dot{p}_i = \sum_{i=1}^{l} a_{ir} \Delta X_r - \Delta S_i, \qquad i = l+1, \ldots, n-1, \tag{12'}$$

$$\beta_i \dot{X}_i = \Delta p_i - \sum_{s=1}^{n-1} a_{si} \Delta p_s, \qquad i = 1, \ldots, l. \tag{13'}$$

In the socialist case K_i is fixed, and hence ΔS_i, which is the change in the supply of the services of capital good i, is always zero.

If the Liapounoff function which shows the distance from an equilibrium point is here defined as

$$V = \sum_{i=1}^{n-1} \alpha_i (p_i - p_i^0)^2 + \sum_{i=1}^{l} \beta_i (X_i - X_i^0)^2, \tag{14}$$

then $V = 0$ at an equilibrium point and at all other points $V > 0$. If we differentiate V with respect to t, we have

$$\frac{dV}{dt} = 2\left(\sum_{i=1}^{n-1} \alpha_i \dot{p}_i \Delta p_i + \sum_{i=1}^{l} \beta_i \dot{X}_i \Delta X_i \right).$$

Substituting (10') to (13') for $\alpha_i \dot{p}_i$, $\beta_i \dot{X}_i$ in the right-hand side of the above formula, the terms ΔX_i, Δp_i, $\Sigma a_{ir} \Delta X_r$, $\Sigma a_{si} \Delta p_s$ in (10') to (13') cancel out and we finally obtain

$$\frac{dV}{dt} = 2\left(\sum_{i=1}^{h} \Delta D_i \Delta p_i - \sum_{i=l+1}^{n-1} \Delta S_i \Delta p_i \right).$$

Therefore, if

$$\sum_{i=1}^{h} \Delta D_i \Delta p_i - \sum_{i=l+1}^{n-1} \Delta S_i \Delta p_i < 0 \qquad (15)$$

always holds, dV/dt is always negative, and the distance from the equilibrium point is always decreasing. Consequently, where the point given initially was distinct from the equilibrium point, there will emerge a tendency to approach the equilibrium point. As long as this distance is positive, there will always be this tendency. Therefore the ever diminishing distance from the equilibrium point must finally become zero. That is, the above process of adjustment will finally lead the economy to a state of equilibrium.

Thus (15) is a stability condition for equilibrium. The first thing to note is that it is the household (the worker's, the capitalist's or the state) which determines both D_i and S_i in (15), and the enterprise is unrelated with (15). If (15) is not satisfied and equilibrium is unstable, we may say that households are to blame for instability. Since workers have to work to live, they will always attempt to supply the whole of their labour when wages are low, and hence we should have $\Delta S_i = 0$, $i = m + 1, \ldots, n - 1$. Again, in the case where capitalists leave none of the capital goods they own lying idle, but always supply the whole of the existing capital services in an attempt to earn every dollar they can, then $\Delta S_i = 0$, $i = l + 1, \ldots, m$. Under these assumptions of inelasticity in the supply of factors of production, (15) is reduced to

$$\sum_{i=1}^{h} \Delta D_i \Delta p_i < 0. \qquad (15')$$

This is a condition which we may derive from the analysis of household behaviour of chapter 5. That is, where we may ignore the the income effects, an inequality which is the same as (15′) will hold for every consumer, and hence we may think of (15′) as the aggregate sum of these individual inequalities.[11] Furthermore, since we can extend the analysis of chapter 5 to include the supply of factors of production as well, we may interpret (15) as being valid when the income effects on demands and supplies are negligible. Since Hicks was the first to show that (15) or (15′) are stability conditions, they are usually known as Hicks' stability conditions.[12]

Next let us consider an economy which is a little more flexible than the fixprice economy of the last chapter. We assume that product prices are flexible, while wages and the prices of capital services are fixed, as previously. The fixed values for wages and the prices of capital services, p_i^*, $i = l + 1, \ldots, n$, will not necessarily produce full employment of labour and capital services. I shall continue the analysis below on the presupposition of a capitalist economy; but as will easily be seen, with the amendment that the state receives all rentals on capital goods, the analysis can be applied in exactly the same form to a socialist economy with fixed wages and rentals on capital goods, and exactly the same conclusions will emerge.

We assume that the equilibrium corresponding to the fixed prices of factors of production p_i^*, $i = l + 1, \ldots, n$, is an underemployment equilibrium, and moreover we shall consider only movements in the neighbourhood of equilibrium. Consequently, the economy is in a state of underemployment throughout the process of change. Therefore, as for consumer goods, we ought not to assume neoclassical demand functions which presuppose full employment of factors of production; we should instead regard the demands for consumer goods as being functions of prices and the actual incomes of individuals, which are now at their respective underemployment levels. Income (wages and profits) is determined depending on outputs. Wages are given by

$$\sum_{r=1}^{l} \left(\sum_{s=m+1}^{n} p_s^* a_{sr} \right) X_r,$$

normal profits by

$$\sum_{r=1}^{l} \left(\sum_{s=l+1}^{m} p_s^* a_{sr} \right) X_r,$$

and excess profits by

$$\sum_{r=1}^{l} \left(p_r - \sum_{s=1}^{l} p_s a_{sr} - \sum_{s=l+1}^{m} p_s^* a_{sr} - \sum_{s=m+1}^{n} p_s^* a_{sr} \right) X_r.$$

Therefore total income, which is the sum of wages, normal profits and excess profits, is

$$Y = \sum_{r=1}^{l} \left(p_r - \sum_{s=l}^{l} p_s a_{sr} \right) X_r. \tag{16}$$

If, for the sake of simplicity, we assume that each worker and each capitalist has the same propensity to consume, we may think of the total demand function for each consumer good as depending on the size of total income Y, but not on the distribution of Y to individuals.[13] We thus obtain the demand functions

$$D_i = D_i(p_1, \ldots, p_l, Y), \qquad i = 1, \ldots, h. \tag{17}$$

Although demand also depends on wage rates and the prices of the services of capital goods, there is no need to show them explicitly, since they are fixed.

Next, we turn to the mechanism for adjusting product prices and outputs. In the neoclassical system, which we considered previously, prices are adjusted in correspondence with excess demands and outputs in correspondence with excess profits; in what follows we consider prices to be determined so as to equal unit costs, including normal profits (the full-cost principle), and outputs so as to equal demands (the principle of effective demand). But prices determined so as to equal unit costs are not necessarily the prices which were taken as the basis for calculating costs, and hence costs have to be recalculated at the new prices. Prices have then to be readjusted so as to equal the recalculated costs. The case is similar with outputs. Demands depend on outputs and therefore adjusting outputs will cause demands to change, and as a result outputs must once again be adjusted. Now let the prices and outputs of the tth round of adjustment be p_{st} and X_{rt} respectively. Then we have the adjustment equations[14]

$$p_{i,t+1} = \sum_{s=1}^{l} p_{st} a_{si} + \sum_{s=l+1}^{n} p_s^* a_{si}, \qquad i = 1, \ldots, l, \tag{18}$$

$$X_{i,t+1} = \sum_{r=1}^{l} a_{ir} X_{rt} + D_i(p_{1t}, \ldots, p_{lt}, Y_t), \; i = 1, \ldots, h, \tag{19}$$

$$X_{i,t+1} = \sum_{r=1}^{l} a_{ir} X_{rt} + H_i, \qquad i = h+1, \ldots, l. \tag{20}$$

We may call these the Keynes–Leontief adjustment mechanism.[15]

Let us first obtain the stability condition for prices. If we write w_i for $\sum_{l+1}^{n} p_s^* a_{si}$, which is the value added per unit of production of good i, we can write (18) as

$$P_{t+1} = P_t A + w, \tag{18'}$$

where A is the l by l matrix of input coefficients, P the prices vector, and w the vector of unit value added.[16] If we are given the initial price vector P_0, then P_1 is determined as

$$P_1 = P_0 A + w. \tag{18''}$$

When P_1 is thus determined, P_2 is determined as

$$P_2 = P_1 A + w = P_0 A^2 + wA + w$$

by (18″). Similarly, by repeatedly using (18′), we obtain the general solution

$$P_t = P_0 A^t + wA^{t-1} + wA^{t-2} + \ldots + wA + w$$

Therefore price movements are convergent when

$$\lim_{t \to \infty} A^t = 0 \tag{21}$$

is satisfied. In fact in this case, if the adjustment is made an infinite number of times, prices will finally converge on

$$P^* = w(I + A + A^2 + \ldots) = w(I - A)^{-1}.$$

This value is the stationary solution to the price adjustment equations (18), and, therefore, a partial equilibrium value of our system.

This being so, in what sort of case is the price stability condition (21) satisfied? To consider this problem let P be a certain vector of product prices; then PA gives the raw material costs needed to produce one unit of a product. By assumption, consumer goods and capital goods are also used as raw materials to produce other goods, and thus A is the matrix of raw material input coefficients for them. If there is at least one set of positive prices P such that raw material costs for all goods are less than product prices, we say that A is *productive*. That is, the condition for productiveness may be written as

$$P > PA, \qquad P > 0. \tag{22}$$

(Of course, (22) need not hold for arbitrary prices even though A is productive.)

The condition that A be productive is the condition for price stability. In order to prove this let $\bar{P}$ be a positive price vector which satisfies (22). If we take σ less than 1 but sufficiently close to 1, $\sigma\bar{P}$ will be between $\bar{P}$ and $\bar{P}A$, so that

$$\bar{P} > \sigma\bar{P} > \bar{P}A. \tag{23}$$

Since the input coefficients are all either positive or 0, the sense of the inequalities in the above formula will not change when we multiply it by A. Hence

$$\sigma\bar{P}A > \bar{P}A^2.$$

Since the $\bar{P}A$ which appears on the left-hand side is smaller than $\sigma\bar{P}$ by (23), we have

$$\sigma^2\bar{P} > \sigma\bar{P}A > \bar{P}A^2. \tag{24}$$

If we further to multiply this formula by A and take account of (23), we obtain $\sigma^3\bar{P} > \bar{P}A^3$, and so on. Thus we see that

$$\sigma^t\bar{P} > \bar{P}A^t \tag{25}$$

is valid for an arbitrary t. Since we have $1 > \sigma > 0$, as t becomes large σ^t eventually approaches zero. On the other hand, since A is a non-negative matrix and $\bar{P}$ is a positive vector, $\bar{P}A^t$ is always non-negative. By (25) as t becomes large $\bar{P}A^t$ must converge on 0. A^t is non-negative and $\bar{P}$ is positive, and therefore there are no elements which cancel out. Consequently, all the elements of A^t will converge on 0. That is to say, we obtain the price stability condition (21).

According to the above, prices will eventually be stabilised at the equilibrium value P^*, but even during this process of adjustment outputs are adjusted according to (19) and (20). When prices approach sufficiently close to P^* we can ignore the effects on demands of a very small change in prices which takes place in the neighbourhood of P^*, and hence there is probably no danger of reaching a wrong conclusion even if we fix prices at P^* in (19) in the final stages of the adjustment process. If we here fix prices at P^* in (16) and (17), and for the sake of simplicity assume that demand D_i is a linear equation with respect to total income Y, we obtain[17]

$$D_i = c_i Y_t + d_i = c_i P^*(1-A)X_t + d_i.$$

Here X_t is the output vector of the tth round of the adjustment process. If in addition we define

$$c = \begin{bmatrix} c_1 \\ \cdot \\ \cdot \\ \cdot \\ c_h \\ 0 \\ \cdot \\ \cdot \\ \cdot \\ 0 \end{bmatrix}, \quad H = \begin{bmatrix} d_1 \\ \cdot \\ \cdot \\ \cdot \\ d_h \\ H_{h+1} \\ \cdot \\ \cdot \\ \cdot \\ H_l \end{bmatrix},$$

we may put the output adjustment equations (19) and (20) in simple form as

$$X_{t+1} = [A + cP^*(I-A)] X_t + H. \qquad (26)$$

Mathematically (26) is a system of equations of the same structure as (18'). That is, A is a non-negative matrix, c a non-negative column vector and $P^* (1-A)$ a positive row vector, and hence $A + cP^* (I-A)$ is a non-negative matrix.[18] Therefore if

$$M = A + cP^*(I-A)$$

is productive, (26) is stable.

However, it is not possible to prove the productiveness of M only from the assumption that A is productive. This being so, we make the additional assumption that the marginal propensity to consume $\gamma = P^*c$ is less than 1. Thus we have $w > \gamma w$, from which, in view of $\gamma = P^*c$ and $w = P^*(1-A)$, we obtain

$$P^* > P^*[A + cP^*(I-A)].$$

Since P^* is positive, this inequality means that M is productive.[19] That is, if A is productive and the marginal propensity to consume is less than 1, M becomes productive, and the output adjustment process is stable. In other words the condition for an underemployment equilibrium to be stable in a system where wages and the prices of capital services are fixed is that (i) the Leontief condition (that A be productive), and (ii) the Keynes condition (that the marginal propensity to consume be less than one) are simultaneously satisfied. The Hicks stability condition is not a guarantee of stability in this system. Whether prices are stable is determined by the technical coefficients of production and is unrelated to consumers' demand. Even if prices are unstable, this is not the fault of the consumers, but is the result of the fact that the techniques employed by enterprises are not productive. If prices are unstable outputs will also be unstable, but even if prices are stable outputs are not necessarily stable; only when the additional condition is met that the marginal propensity to consume of households as a whole is less than one, is the movement of outputs a stable one. Apart from extremely exceptional cases, the Leontief and Keynes conditions will be fulfilled. Hence, in a system where prices are adjusted according to the full-cost principle and outputs according to the principle of effective demand, we can conclude with more or less certainty that an underemployment equilibrium will be stable.

C. The long-term Keynes—Leontief process and decentralisation of planning

In the second of the two adjustment mechanisms above, the prices of factors (wages and the prices of capital services) were thought of as fixed and unchanging. We can only make this assumption of rigidity about the short-term process of adjustment; in the long period, factor prices will probably fall if there is an excess supply and rise if there is an excess demand. In the capitalist case this must happen in the face of market pressure, and in the socialist case prices will have to be revised so that factors will be used effectively. This being the case, the real time necessary for one round of the short-term adjustment which takes place under fixed factor prices is extremely short compared with the long-period process of adjustment just mentioned. Consequently, from the long-term point of view, we may ignore the time-lag in the adjustment equations (18) to (20). Therefore, when the prices of factors of production are given, product prices will immediately adjust themselves to the partial equilibrium values which correspond to those prices. That is, the equation

$$P = PA + w \tag{18*}$$

which says that product prices equal unit costs (including normal profits), materialises immediately and without a time-lag. When product prices are determined, the quantities of output are the only variables in the output adjustment equations (19) and (20). We assume that this adjustment is also complete, so that outputs adapt instantaneously to the solutions to the static, no-lag equations

$$X_i = D_i(p_1, \ldots, p_n, Y) + \sum_{r=1}^{l} a_{ir}X_r, \qquad i = 1, \ldots, h, \tag{19'}$$

$$X_i = \sum_{r=1}^{l} a_{ir}X_r + H_i, \qquad i = h+1, \ldots, l. \tag{20'}$$

That is to say, since the Y in (19′) has to satisfy (16), (19′) ultimately includes only prices and outputs as variables. The determination of prices has already been completed, and hence only outputs remain undetermined. (19′) and (20′) are a so-called Keynes—Leontief system, which contains the same number of unknowns as there are equations. Thus, outputs which are determined in this fashion are, ultimately, functions of factor prices alone. That is, if factor prices change, product prices determined according to (18*) also change; and if factor and product prices change, outputs determined according to (19') and (20') will also change.

Similarly, the quantities of factors of production supplied can be shown ultimately as functions of factor prices alone. The quantities of factors supplied are functions of product prices and not merely factor prices, but since product prices are functions of factor prices the latter are the ultimate variables in the supply functions for factors of production. Thus we obtain

$$X_r = X_r(p_{l+1}, \ldots, p_n), \quad r = 1, \ldots, l,$$
$$S_i = S_i(p_{l+1}, \ldots, p_n), \quad i = l+1, \ldots, n.$$

The demand for factor of production i is $\sum_{r=1}^{l} a_{ir}X_r$, and hence, if we assume an adjustment mechanism whereby factor prices rise or fall in proportion to the excess demand for factors, we obtain

$$\alpha_i \dot{p}_i = \sum_{r=1}^{l} a_{ir}X_r - S_i, \quad i = l+1, \ldots, n-1 \quad (27)$$

where α_i is the coefficient of adjustment. However, the above equation is not valid for labour n, because it has been adopted as the numéraire.

In order to test the stability of general equilibrium prices $p^0_{l+1}, \ldots, p^0_{n-1}$, let us now introduce the Lapounoff function

$$V = \sum_{i=l+1}^{n-1} \alpha_i(p_i - p^0_i)^2.$$

Differentiating V with respect to time t, we have

$$\frac{dV}{dt} = 2 \left(\sum_{i=l+1}^{n-1} \alpha_i \dot{p}_i \Delta p_i \right). \quad (28)$$

Since under general equilibrium prices there is no excess demand for factors of production, we have $\sum_{r=1}^{l} a_{ir}X_r(p^0) - S_i(p^0) = 0$, and therefore we can write (27) as

$$\alpha_i \dot{p}_i = \sum_{r=1}^{l} a_{ir}\Delta X_r - \Delta S_i, \quad i = l+1, \ldots, n-1, \quad (27')$$

with $\Delta X_r = X_r(p) - X_r(p^0)$ and $\Delta S_i = S_i(p) - S_i(p^0)$. If we substitute (27′) into (28), we obtain

$$\frac{dV}{dt} = 2\left[\sum_{r=1}^{l}\left(\sum_{i=l+1}^{n-1}\Delta p_i a_{ir}\right)\Delta X_r - \sum_{i=l+1}^{n-1}\Delta S_i \Delta p_i\right].(29)$$

If we take (18*) into account,[20] then

$$\sum_{i=l+1}^{n-1}\Delta p_i a_{ir} = \Delta p_r - \sum_{i=1}^{l}\Delta p_i a_{ir}, \qquad r = 1, \ldots, l, \qquad (30)$$

and in addition we have

$$\Delta X_i - \sum_{r=1}^{l} a_{ir}\Delta X_r = \Delta D_i, \qquad i = 1, \ldots, h, \qquad (31)$$

$$\Delta X_i - \sum_{r=1}^{l} a_{ir}\Delta X_r = 0, \qquad i = h+1, \ldots, l, \qquad (32)$$

by (19′) and (20′).[21+] If we take (30), (31) and (32) into account, then ultimately we can write (29) in the form

$$\frac{dV}{dt} = 2\left[\sum_{i=1}^{h}\Delta D_i \Delta p_i - \sum_{i=l+1}^{n-1}\Delta S_i \Delta p_i\right].$$

This formula is formally of the same kind as the one we obtained earlier for a neoclassical system. Therefore, as in the neoclassical case, general equilibrium is stable under the Hicks condition

$$\sum_{i=1}^{h}\Delta D_i \Delta p_i - \sum_{i=l+1}^{n-1}\Delta S_i \Delta p_i < 0. \qquad (33)$$

But if we examine the case in more detail we see that despite the fact that (15) and (33) are formally identical, they differ on two points. First, in (15) product prices do not have a fixed relationship with the prices of factors of production, and as long as they satisfy the adjustment equations (10) or (11), they can move freely. In contrast to this, in (33) there must always be a fixed relationship between product prices and the prices of factors of production. That is to say, (33) has only to be valid for those product prices which satisfy the partial equilibrium condition (18′). In respect of this point, the assumption (15) is stronger than (33). On the other hand, however, the demands for consumer goods in (15) always assume full-employment, while the demands for consumer goods of (33) do not. Consequently, (33) must be valid not only for the full-employment level of income, but also for a variety of levels of income which may change, and hence (33) is more

restrictive than (15). Therefore we are unable to give an uncon-
ditional answer to the question whether (15) or (33) imposes the
strictest conditions. However, what is important is that once again
households have emerged as having the major responsibility for
the stability of the economy in our long-period model. Enterprises
or technology determine product prices through the full-cost
principle, and they are also concerned in the determination of
outputs through the principle of effective demand. However,
their role in the achievement of economic stability is never more
than the secondary one of determining the range within which
(33) must be true, and they cannot be regarded as having any
major part to play in the long-term stability problem.[22+]

We assumed in the above that each good can be produced by
only one method of production. It is extremely simple in this case
for the central planning authority of a socialist economy to solve
equations (18*), (19′) and (20′). It is indeed true that the number
of equations will be very large, but there is no difficulty in finding
their solution in principle. If we are satisfied with more or less
approximate solutions, we can aggregate the elements of matrix A
and reduce its scale, and we can reduce the number of equations
until they meet the capacity of the computer which the authorities
have installed.

In contrast, in the case where there are a number of alternative
techniques for producing a product, we cannot immediately discover product prices through the full-cost principle. In order to
grope towards equilibrium product prices a large number of notifications and reports have to be exchanged between the central
planning authority and individual enterprises. Assume that the
prices of factors of production are fixed at $p_{II}(t)$, and that product
prices are initially given by the central planning authority as $p_I^1(t)$.
Each enterprise will choose a technique which will minimise costs
under $p_I^1(t)$ and $p_{II}(t)$, and report this cost to the central planning
authority. The authority communicates this vector of minimum
product prices $p_I^2(t)$ collected from enterprises back to enterprises
as the second round of provisional prices. Each enterprise will
again choose a production technique under prices $p_I^2(t)$, $p_{II}(t)$
and communicate its cost to the authority. The authority will
prepare the new product prices vector $p_I^3(t)$ from these reports in
the same way as it did previously, and notify enterprises of them.
This exchange of notifications and reports will be continued until

the state of affairs is finally reached in which $p_I^s(t) = p_I^{s+1}(t)$.[23] '
When this situation comes about, the authority instructs each
enterprise to report the technical coefficients it will choose under
$p_I^s(t), p_{II}(t)$.

At time t let them be the matrix of input coefficients of raw
materials $A(t)$, and the matrix of input coefficients of factors
(labour and the services of capital goods) $B(t)$; then we have

$$p_I^s(t) = p_I^s(t)A(t) + p_{II}(t)B(t)$$

which is the equation of full cost pricing (18*). If we substitute
the prices and production coefficients determined in this manner
into (19′) and (20′) we can solve them using the central planning
authority's computer. Since product prices $p_I^s(t)$ and production
coefficients $A(t)$ and $B(t)$ are determined according to factor prices
$p_{II}(t)$, the ultimate independent variables on which outputs depend
are factor prices. Again the S_i, which are the quantities of factors
supplied, also depend ultimately on factor prices alone. Therefore
the factor price adjustment function

$$\alpha\dot{p}_{II}(t) = B(t)X(p_{II}(t)) - S(p_{II}(t)) \qquad (34)$$

is also given as a function of factor prices. Here α is a diagonal
matrix of the coefficients of adjustment α_i, and S is a column vector of the supplies of factors S_i, $i = l + 1, \ldots, n$. The solution to
(34) shows how equilibrium factor prices are established. This
process of adjustment is, on the one hand, the long-term Keynes—
Leontief process discussed above; on the other hand, it also de-
scribes that process of decentralised planning in a socialist economy
which we discussed in section A for the case where the supplies of
capital goods and labour are variable.[24] That is, the formal identity
of the long-period Keynes—Leontief process and our decentralised
planning process has been confirmed.

We have now obtained the stability conditions for three mechanisms of adjustment. In the capitalist economies of the real world
these three mechanisms do not exist in parallel, in an interchangeable
way, without any reference to time; they are in fact bound together
in a sequential relationship. First, in early capitalism there was a
freely competitive market for factors of production as well as
products, and we can regard prices as having functioned well in
adjusting supply and demand. New enterprises were established
where profit rates were high, and industries contracted where they

were low. Consequently, we can regard the economy at that stage as having possessed the neoclassical adjustment mechanism previously outlined. However, when oligopolies came about in product markets and prices came to be determined according to the full cost principle, prices ceased to function as a mechanism of adjustment, and market supply and demand came to be equated by adjustments in outputs. At the same time social security systems were introduced and trade unions became stronger, so that wages became inflexible in a downward direction, and there was a decline in the ability of prices to act as a mechanism for adjusting demand and supply in the markets for factors of production. As a result a 'free labour market', which was the precondition for the development of capitalism, now only exists imperfectly, and a situation of underemployment can arise and become chronic. Capitalists do not employ more workers, despite the fact that such workers are available to be exploited. Therefore a situation occurs in which such people are shut out of the labour market, as the involuntarily unemployed. We can explain this state of affairs by use of the short-term Keynes—Leontief adjustment mechanism.

Even though the constitution of capitalism has changed in this fashion, it perhaps remains true that, in the long period, unemployment will exert a downward pressure on wages. However, this pressure is extremely weak and its effects will appear only after the passage of a long period of time. From such a long-period point of view, we may regard all the time lags which appear in the short-run Keynes—Leontief adjustment process as being of a magnitude which is negligible. Our third mechanism can therefore explain such long-period movements, but needless to say, since we are concerned with long-period phenomena, we have to reconstruct our theory to take into account such long-term factors as population growth and capital accumulation. The formulation of such a theory is the problem of the theory of economic growth. In the realm of growth theory too there are the neoclassical and the anti-neoclassical schools, which either affirm or deny the flexibility of the prices of factors of production. Even if we accept the point of view of the neoclassical school, we have to recognise that the stabilising effects produced by wage adjustments are extremely weak, and that a very long passage of time is required before the economy is sufficiently close to the equilibrium growth path.[25]

In a socialist economy, so long as it is more or less decentralised, adjustments in the plan are unavoidable. In what we know as socialist states, the demands and supplies of some goods (for example a part or all of consumer goods) have been freed and adjustments in their prices are left to the market. Even where there are no free markets, the central planning authority dictates alterations in prices after taking excess supply or excess demand into account. In this case the economy is regulated in the neoclassical manner, and the Hicks condition is the condition for stability of equilibrium. In contrast to this, if the planning authority constructs an input—output table for industry, and determines product prices so that they equal unit costs and outputs so that they equal final demand, then the economy is likely to show more or less the same movements as a Keynes—Leontief capitalist economy. That is, where the planning authority has wrongly prescribed the wage structure and the structure of rentals for capital goods, workers will be made to work involuntarily; or labour will be used wastefully within the enterprise even if unemployment as such does not emerge (what is called socialist-type disguised unemployment); or shortages of some capital goods will occur while others lie idle. In order for socialist economies to avoid disguised unemployment and succeed in allocating labour to all enterprises in an efficient way, it is necessary for the wage structure which the authority prescribes to be the same as that which would be likely to come about if labour were freed from central control. (A similar conclusion holds for capital goods.) Thus, revision of wages and the rentals of capital goods is likely to take place more or less according to the third method of adjustment described above or the planning procedure discussed in section A.

D. The rule for fixing official prices

We have already observed that the two basic types of mechanism for adjustment in prices and outputs can work under both capitalism and socialism. In mechanism (i) prices are adjusted according to the excess demands for products, and outputs are adjusted in accordance with excess profits. In mechanism (ii) prices are adjusted in accordance with excess profits, and outputs in accordance with excess demands. Furthermore, we have shown that for the economy to be efficient and for full employment to be maintained, a Walrasian general equilibrium of production has to be realised. That is to say, three conditions have to be fulfilled for all goods and factors: (i) there must be equilibrium in the demand and supply for consumer goods and for capital goods; (ii) the prices of consumer goods and capital goods must equal their costs (including normal profits); (iii) the demand and supply for factors of production must be in equilibrium.[26] In the socialist case the central planning authority must have no preconceptions regarding prices or the allocation of raw materials to enterprises; it must adjust official prices and allocations flexibly so as to establish these three conditions.

However, such a state of general equilibrium is relative to the demands for products (households' demands for consumer goods and capitalists' or the state's demands for capital goods) and the supplies of factors of production (households' supplies of labour and capitalists' or the state's supplies of capital services). Therefore, if for any reason the demands for goods or the supplies of factors change exogenously, equilibrium values will have to change accordingly. In the flexprice-economy period of capitalism, economies were furnished with an automatic mechanism whereby prices and outputs naturally adapted themselves to any exogenous change in demand or supply; but on entering the era of the fixprice economy, the prices of factors of production ceased to show a sensitive response to excess supplies. For this reason a chronic state of underemployment came about and economies were no longer in Walrasian equilibrium (consequently neither were they at a Pareto optimum). As we shall see in the next chapter, in order to remove this kind of inefficiency within the system of the fixprice economy, effective demand has always to be maintained at the full employment level by regulating state finance.

The same thing occurs in the socialist economy. Either the central planning authority has to exercise continuous surveillance over demands and supplies in the markets for factors of production and quickly adjust factor prices to their equilibrium values after any change, or else the state must maintain the factor markets in equilibrium by fiscal means. Therefore, where there is an exogenous change in the demand for products or the supply of factors, knowing how general equilibrium is affected by such a change is important not only for the analysis of capitalist economies, but also for the operation of socialist societies. I shall deal with this problem of comparative statics in this section, confining the analysis to the case where the demand for a consumer good increases. In exactly the same way, it is of course possible to analyse the case where the demand for a capital good or the supply of a capital service increases.

Let us assume that for some reason the demand function for consumer good h changes by δD_h. At a given price set p, the demand was $D_h(p)$ before the change and is $D_h(p) + \delta D_h$ after the change. The equilibrium prices and outputs before the change were $p_1^0, \ldots, p_n^0, X_1^0, \ldots, X_n^0$, while they become $p_1^1, \ldots, p_n^1, X_1^1, \ldots, X_n^1$ after the change. If we assume that when the price of a consumer good is zero, the demand for it is sufficiently great, then no consumer good can be a free good, so that any good (say, good 1) can be taken as the numéraire. Therefore in what follows we fix $p_1^0 = p_1^1 = 1$. In a state of general equilibrium, neither consumer goods nor capital goods are free goods, and hence the equilibrium demand–supply conditions for consumer and capital goods each hold as an equation. If we further assume that the input–output system is indecomposable, then the equilibrium outputs of all goods will be positive, so that there will be no unprofitable industries. Hence, in all industries, product prices will equal costs (including normal profits). However, factors of production may be free goods, and hence the equilibrium demand–supply conditions for factors of production may hold with inequality. Thus we have

$$p_r^0 = \sum_{i=1}^{n} p_i^0 a_{ir}^0, \qquad p_r^1 = \sum_{i=1}^{n} p_i^1 a_{ir}^1, \qquad r = 1, \ldots, l, \qquad (35)$$

$$\sum_{r=1}^{l} a_{ir}^0 X_r^0 \leqq S_i(p^0), \; \sum_{r=1}^{l} a_{ir}^1 X_r^1 \leqq S_i(p^1), \qquad i = l+1, \ldots, n, \qquad (36)$$

$$\sum_{r=1}^{l} a_{ir}^0 X_r^0 + D_i(p^0, X^0) = X_i^0, \; \sum_{r=1}^{l} a_{ir}^1 X_r^1 + D_i(p^1, X^1) = X_i^1,$$

$$i = 1, \ldots, h-1, \quad (37)$$

$$\sum_{r=1}^{l} a_{hr}^0 X_r^0 + D_h(p^0, X^0) = X_h^0,$$

$$(38)$$

$$\sum_{r=1}^{l} a_{hr}^1 X_r^1 + D_h(p^1, X^1) + \delta D_h = X_h^1,$$

$$\sum_{r=1}^{l} a_{ir}^0 X_r^0 + H_i = X_i^0, \; \sum_{r=1}^{l} a_{ir}^1 X_r^1 + H_i = X_i^1, \qquad i = h+1, \ldots, l. \qquad (39)$$

Here, on the assumption that production coefficients depend on prices, production coefficients corresponding to equilibrium prices before and after the change in demand are shown by a_{ir}^0 and a_{ir}^1 respectively.

We are assuming that returns to scale are constant. That is to say, with an unchanged method of production it is possible to increase the output in the same proportion that the inputs have been increased. Therefore production coefficients only change when the method of production changes. Suppose that there are two methods of production, A and B, and that despite the fact that each could produce the same output at the same money costs before the change in prices, the enterprise has adopted method A. Where such a tied (equally profitable) pair of production methods exist before a price change, it is possible that B may become more profitable than A even after a very small change in prices, and that the method adopted by the enterprise will change. However, where there is an order given to A and B before a price change (for example, A is more profitable than B), then this order will not change unless the price change is of an appreciable magnitude. Therefore, after only a small price change it is likely that A will still be more profitable than B. Even in this case a very small price change may give rise to a change in the method of production adopted, but for this to happen there must be an infinite number of methods of production between A and B. Where there is a limit to the number of methods, a very small price change does not induce a move from method A to the method nearest to A unless they were tied before the change. In what follows we assume that: (i) δD_h, the change in the demand for good h, is very small and hence the induced change in price is small; (ii) there is a limited number of production methods; (iii) there was a single, most-efficient method before the price-change and no tied methods. No change will occur in production coefficients under these assumptions, and $a_{ir}^0 = a_{ir}^1$ in formulae (35) and (36).

We may therefore ignore the superscripts 0,1 applied to a_{ir}. We then obtain from (35),

$$\Delta p_r = \sum_{i=1}^{n} \Delta p_i a_{ir}, \quad r = 1, \ldots l, \tag{40}$$

where $\Delta p_r = p_r^1 - p_r^0$. Since the price of the numéraire (good 1) is always equal to 1, we have $\Delta p_1 = 0$. Next if the factor of production i is a free good either before or after the price change, then the first or the second equation of (36) will correspondingly become an inequality. Therefore we have the following four possible cases.

(*a*) When factor i is not a free good either before or after the price change, then

$$\sum_{r=1}^{l} a_{ir} \Delta X_r = \Delta S_i, \qquad i = l+1, \ldots, n. \qquad (41a)$$

(*b*) When it is not a free good before but becomes a free good after the price change, then

$$\sum_{r=1}^{l} a_{ir} \Delta X_r < \Delta S_i, \qquad i = l+1, \ldots, n. \qquad (41b)$$

(*c*) When it is a free good before the price change but not afterwards, then

$$\sum_{r=1}^{l} a_{ir} \Delta X_r > \Delta S_i, \qquad i = l+1, \ldots, n. \qquad (41c)$$

(*d*) When it is a free good both before and after the price change, then

$$\sum_{r=1}^{l} a_{ir} \Delta X_r \gtreqless \Delta S_i, \qquad i = l+1, \ldots, n. \qquad (41d)$$

Note that in these expressions we write $\Delta X_r = X_r^1 - X_r^0$, and $\Delta S_i = S_i(p^1) - S_i(p^0)$. Moreover we obtain from (37)-(39)

$$\sum_{r=1}^{l} a_{ir} \Delta X_r + \Delta D_i = \Delta X_i, \qquad i = 1, \ldots, h-1, \quad (42)$$

$$\sum_{r=1}^{l} a_{hr} \Delta X_r + \Delta D_h + \delta D_h = \Delta X_h, \qquad (43)$$

$$\sum_{r=1}^{l} a_{ir} \Delta X_r = \Delta X_i, \qquad i = h+1, \ldots, l, \qquad (44)$$

where ΔD_i is defined in the same way as ΔS_i.

If we multiply both sides of (40) by ΔX_r and sum for all the r, we obtain

$$\sum_{r=1}^{l} \Delta p_r \Delta X_r = \sum_{i=1}^{n} \sum_{r=1}^{l} \Delta p_i a_{ir} \Delta X_r. \qquad (45)$$

Next let us multiply (41) by Δp_i and sum for all factors of production i. (41) is an inequality in cases (*b*), (*c*) and (*d*), but in case (*b*) i is not a free good before the price change ($p_i^0 \geqq 0$), while it is a free good afterwards ($p_i^1 = 0$); hence $\Delta p_i \leqq 0$. Similarly, in case (*c*) we have $\Delta p_i \geqq 0$, and in case (*d*) $\Delta p_i = 0$. If we take the signs of these price changes into account, we can see that we have

$$\Delta p_r \sum_{r=1}^{l} a_{ir} \Delta X_r \gtreqless p_i \Delta S_i$$

for each of (a) to (d). Therefore we have

$$\sum_{i=l+1}^{n} \sum_{r=1}^{l} \Delta p_i a_{ir} \Delta X_r \gtreqless \sum_{i=l+1}^{n} \Delta p_i \Delta S_i. \tag{46}$$

Furthermore, from (42), (43) and (44),

$$\sum_{i=1}^{l} \sum_{r=1}^{l} \Delta p_i a_{ir} \Delta X_r + \sum_{i=1}^{h} \Delta p_i \Delta D_i + \Delta p_h \delta D_h = \sum_{i=1}^{l} \Delta p_i \Delta X_i. \tag{47}$$

Consequently, from (45)–(47),

$$\sum_{i=1}^{h} \Delta p_i \Delta D_i - \sum_{i=l+1}^{n} \Delta p_i \Delta S_i \gtreqless - \Delta p_h \delta D_h. \tag{48}$$

ΔD_i and ΔS_j show, respectively, the changes in the demand for consumer good i and the supply of factor of production j when prices alter from $p_1^0, \ldots, p_n^0$ to $p_1^1, \ldots, p_n^1$. At this time there are changes not only in the prices of consumer goods and of factors of production but also in those of capital goods. Hence, in the capitalist case ΔD_i and ΔS_j include the direct effect of price changes on consumer good i and factor of production j, and also the indirect effects through the repercussions of the original change in the prices of factors on capital goods, which give rise to a change in the total amount of investment and further induce a change in the real income of capitalists which affects D_i and S_j. (We assume, however, that the physical amount invested in each capital good remains the same.) The direct effects can be divided into the income and substitution effects. If we here assume that the income effects and the indirect effects (the latter clearly being a kind of income effect) are concentrated entirely on the numéraire, so that we can ignore both the income effects and the indirect effects on other consumer goods and factors of production, then the left-hand side of (48) is the sum of the products of the substitution effects and the changes in prices. The reason for this is that, although ΔD_1 includes the income and the indirect effects, it is multiplied by Δp_1, which is 0. Other ΔD_i and ΔS_i include only the substitution effects. Therefore, as we explained in chapter 5, the sum of these multiplied by the corresponding price changes is definitely negative. That is[27+]

$$\sum_{i=1}^{h} \Delta p_i \Delta D_i - \sum_{i=l+1}^{n} \Delta p_i \Delta S_i < 0. \tag{49}$$

Consequently from (48)

$$\Delta p_h \, \delta D_h > 0.$$

Therefore Δp_h is positive when δD_h is positive and negative when δD_h is negative. That is, when the demand for a certain consumer good h increases (diminishes), the price of that good will rise (fall) in the market economy case, and must be made to rise (fall) in the case of the planned economy. In exactly the same way, if the supply of an arbitrarily chosen factor of production rises (falls), we know that the price of that factor of production must fall (rise) as long as we can ignore the income effects and the indirect effects via the channel of a change in the prices of capital goods.

These two pricing rules are all we can know in general concerning changes in equilibrium prices which are caused by an exogenous change in the demand for (or supply of) a good. On the question of how the prices of other goods change (or how we ought to change them), we can in general say nothing whatever, unless we make very strict assumptions with respect to the substitute—complement relationship between goods (for example, that all goods are substitutes). Again, on the question of how outputs change we can say absolutely nothing, even about goods for which the demand has increased. If we define the flexibility of price p_h as the ratio of the rate of increase in the price of good h to the exogenously produced rate of increase in the demand for good h (that is $\Delta p_h / p_h$ divided by $\delta D_h / D_h$), and the elasticity of the demand D_h as the ratio of the rate of decline in induced demand to the rate of increase in price (that is $-\Delta D_h / D_h$ divided by $\Delta p_h / p_h$), then we can say that the output of good h will decline or increase according as the elasticity of demand for h is larger or smaller than the reciprocal of its price flexibility.[28+] Since *a priori* we can say nothing even about the relationship between elasticity and flexibility, and still less about their absolute values, we have no law concerning increases and decreases in outputs.

The rules of pricing which we derived above are the laws of prices of the neoclassical (Walrasian) school, and they are already familiar as the conclusions drawn from the general equilibrium theory of capitalist production.[29] It is, however, extremely interesting to see that they must also hold for socialist economies. In the above system, the full-cost principle, i.e. that price equals average cost (including normal profits), holds for all goods, and therefore prices are the same as Marx's production prices. However, even these prices must at the same time reflect scarcities. That is to say, if the demand for consumer good h increases and it becomes relatively scarce, then its production must increase. The expansion of production in industry h and its related industries will cause a change in the demand for factors of production, bringing about a rise in the prices of those factors which become relatively scarce, and a fall in the prices of those which are relatively plentiful in supply. This change in factor prices results in a change in the prices of those which are relatively plentiful in supply. This change in factor prices results in a change in the prices of products and, above all, a rise in the price of good h. Thus Marx's production prices are not determined purely by technology; they also reflect the scarcities of goods, as equilibrium production prices. The same thing can be observed in the case of the supply of a factor of production which has changed exogenously. That is, where a certain kind of labour becomes scarce, its reward (wage) must increase, and where it becomes abundant it must fall. When we come to consider the labour theory of value, we are confronted with the problem of converting heterogeneous labour into abstract labour. The quantity of abstract labour used by each industry, if it is calculated by taking wages as conversion rates, will depend on the scarcity of goods, because wages reflect factor scarcities, and each good's labour value itself will depend on scarcity — a result which is contrary to the intention of Marx.[30] At all events, in a socialist society as well as in a capitalist society, prices of factors of production must be set at levels which reflect relative scarcities — despite Marx's labour theory of value — as long as the intention is to make effective use of such factors.

Part 3: Control by the state

9 Finance and full employment

A. The economic conduct of the government

In part 2 we saw that when capitalist economies have left the flexprice and entered the fixprice stage the price mechanism does not work perfectly, so that full employment does not materialise automatically. We also saw that the economy will be afflicted with long-term or chronic involuntary unemployment. The price mechanism, especially in the labour market, is seen to become imperfect along with the ripening and ageing of capitalism. But if we reverse the movement of time and turn our eyes to the era which precedes capitalism, we see that a free market for labour is only imperfectly and partly formed, and that labour does not flow smoothly from sectors where there is an excess to sectors where there is a shortage. For that reason labour is not used efficiently in society, and consequently the full productive capacity of the society is not exhibited. This precapitalist phenomenon appears in capitalism too — the degree to which it is manifest corresponding to the precapitalist elements remaining in the labour market. Moreover these two types of unemployment, namely the unemployment of late capitalism, which is due to an insufficiency of effective demand, and precapitalistic unemployment, which stems from the fact that movement towards equilibrium in relative wages is prevented by considerations of status or other elements of discrimination, are different in principle even though it is possible for them to co-exist. In what follows we shall separate the two and consider them individually. In this chapter we consider how the unemployment of late capitalism can be eliminated through economic policies, and in the next chapter we shall investigate where and how precapitalistic unemployment occurs — mainly for the case of Japan.

So far this book has concentrated its attention on the household

and the enterprise and has totally ignored the economic activity
of governments. However, this does not mean that economies have
no governments, or that governments are inactive economically.
Even in our economy, where the government has made no direct
appearance, it exists and carries on economic activities. It is simply
that, because it was supposed that government activity was inflexible and that its demand for goods was unaffected by changes in
prices and wages, it was unnecessary to pay it particular attention
(in the same way as there is no point in giving separate consideration to the constant terms in firms' and households' demand and
supply functions).

However, with the advent of Keynes, economists' views of
government underwent a complete change. The passive, small-
scale government, carrying on the minimum of economic activity
consonant with a fixed level of official business, gave way to a
large-scale government acting positively (by raising and lowering
taxation, or by public expenditure measures) to create employment
or to damp down inflation according to the demands of necessity.
With this kind of government the demand for each good is not
unchanging but is a policy variable, which has to be determined so
as to achieve most effectively such objectives of the government
as the creation of employment or the control of inflation, etc. If
the effects of changes in public finance expenditures and rates of
taxation are analysed, governments will be able to determine these
so as to achieve the best overall results. In order to conduct an
analysis of these effects, the government must be placed explicitly
within the system, and the links between policy variables and
other economic variables must be made clear.

The public sector of an economy consists of public enterprises
(such as national railways) and general government, both central
and regional. Although public enterprises differ from private ones
in that the former do not seek profits as their only goal, they have
much in common in their operation (take, for example, public and
private railways). Hence there are public enterprises which resemble
their private counterparts very closely. Furthermore, the relationship between public enterprises and government is not a uniform
one. From the finance and decision making points of view, there
are government enterprises which are subjected to a very high
degree of government control; but there are also public corporations
which have obtained the right of independent operation from the

government and which take an independent profit system as their guiding principle. I shall therefore assume for the sake of simplicity in what follows that there are no public enterprises, and that public services are all provided by the government.

To maintain the welfare and the cultural life of the nation at a certain level, and to ensure that its economic life can be conducted safely and smoothly, the provision of a health service, education, defence, justice, police, a fire service and so on, is indispensible. Responsibility for the maintainance of these services lies with the government, but in order to maintain them it has to provide finance to purchase a variety of goods. Its income normally derives chiefly from the levying of taxes. These are divided into direct taxes (direct personal taxation and direct corporation taxes) and indirect taxation (consumption or excise taxes and commodity taxes, etc.). For simplicity we shall think of the government as not levying indirect taxes. (The proportion of direct taxes is greater in capitalist states, while indirect taxation is greater in socialist states.) For the same reason, we assume that the government makes no subsidies (we can think of them as negative direct or indirect taxes). The income and expenditure plans of our government have to be ratified by parliament.

Let us assume, as we did in chapter 7, that our society is capitalist, and that, therefore, all profits are distributed to capitalists. Since firms do not retain profits there is no direct company taxation. As for the two forms of direct personal taxation, let us denote the tax on income from employment by T_W and the tax on income from profits by T_Π; the total income of the government is then the sum of T_W and T_Π. Let $F_i, i = 1, \ldots, l$ be the government's demand for the ith good; government expenditure on consumer goods is $\sum_{i=1}^{h} p_i F_i$ and on capital goods $\sum_{i=h+1}^{l} p_i F_i$. If the government's expenditure exceeds its total income it will go into deficit; in the opposite case it will have a positive balance. Thus the deficit R is given by
R is given by

$$R = \sum_{i=1}^{l} p_i F_i - T_W - T_\Pi. \tag{1}$$

Our economy is the fixprice economy of chapter 7 and we assume it to be in underemployment equilibrium (that is equilibrium accompanied by an excess supply of factors of production). The numbering of goods is the same as before: 1 to h are consumer goods, $h + 1$ to l are capital goods, $l + 1$ to m are the services of capital goods and $m + 1$ to n are the various kinds of labour. Outputs of consumer goods are $X_1, \ldots, X_h$, of capital goods $X_{h+1}, \ldots, X_l$. If we make D_i^W the actual demand by workers for consumer good i, and D_i^K the demand by capitalists for consumer good i, then we have

$$D_i^W = D_i^W (p_1, \ldots, p_n, (1 - t_W) \sum_{s = m+1}^{n} p_s N_s), \quad i = 1, \ldots, h,$$

$$\tag{2}$$

$$D_i^K = D_i^K (p_1, \ldots, p_n, (1 - t_\Pi) \Pi), \qquad i = 1, \ldots, h, \tag{3}$$

where $N_{m+1}, \ldots, N_n$ show the actual amounts of the $n - m$ kinds of labour employed and $p_{m+1}, \ldots, p_n$ their wages, while t_W shows the marginal rate of taxation on income from employment (in the case of graduated taxation t_W is an increasing function of employment income, but in what follows I shall assume for simplicity that t_W is a fixed number less than 1);[1+] t_Π shows the rate of tax on income from profits, and we also assume that t_Π is a fixed number which is smaller than 1; Π shows the total profits income. Let $N_{l+1}, \ldots, N_m$ represent the actual amounts of the services of capital goods which are used; $p_{l+1}, \ldots, p_m$ their prices; $b_1, \ldots, b_h$ entrepreneurial profits per unit of product in consumer goods' industries, and $b_{h+1}, \ldots, b_l$ those for capital goods' industries; then total income from profits amounts to

$$\Pi = \sum_{s = l+1}^{m} p_s N_s + \sum_{r = 1}^{l} b_r X_r. \tag{4}$$

We can write the equality of demand and supply for consumer goods (including demand by the government) as

$$X_i = D_i^W + D_i^K + F_i, \qquad i = 1, \ldots, h, \tag{5}$$

and that for capital goods as

$$X_i = H_i + F_i, \qquad i = h + 1, \ldots, l. \tag{6}$$

Here H_i is the total gross investment undertaken by capitalists in capital good i (that is the $\sum_k H_i^k$ of chapter 7).

Next let $a_{l+1,r}, \ldots, a_{mr}$ be the quantities of the services of capital goods required to produce one unit of good r (consumer good), and $a_{m+1,r}, \ldots, a_{nr}$ the quantities of labour required.

Since we are assuming that profits are not retained by enterprises, but are all distributed to capitalists and entrepreneurs, we have[2+]

$$p_r - \sum_{i=m+1}^{n} p_i a_{ir} = \sum_{i=l+1}^{m} p_i a_{ir} + b_r, r = 1, \ldots, l. \tag{7}$$

Since production coefficients a_{ir} are functions of prices and wages, b_r is also a function of prices and wages. But since in a fixprice economy we can think of all prices and wage rates as being fixed, a_{ir} and b_r take on a fixed value. However, this fixity in prices and wage rates only arises under an underemployment equilibrium where the demand for each kind of capital service and each kind of labour is less than its supply. That is to say, only when under given prices and wage rates

$$\sum_{r=1}^{l} a_{ir} X_r < K_i, \qquad i = l+1, \ldots, m, \tag{8}$$

is true for all capital services, and

$$\sum_{r=1}^{l} a_{ir} X_r < S_i(p_1, \ldots, p_n), \qquad i = m+1, \ldots, n \tag{9}$$

is true for each kind of labour, does the prices and wages system remain stationary because of the downward rigidity of factor prices.[3] In (8) K_i shows the total quantity of the capital service i supplied (i.e. the $\sum_k K_i^k$ of chapter 7), and in (9) S_i shows the total quantity of labour supplied (the $\sum_j S_i^j$ of chapter 7). Where, as in (8) and (9), there is an excess supply of each factor, an amount of each factor is employed which is equal to the demand for it, while the rest lies idle in involuntary unemployment. That is, the relationships between $N_s, s = l+1, \ldots, n$, which are the quantities of capital services and labour actually employed, and the demands for them are

$$N_s = \sum_{r=1}^{l} a_{sr} X_r, \qquad s = l+1, \ldots, n. \tag{10}$$

In a system with explicit government economic activity, a state of underemployment equilibrium is determined by the above ten equalities and inequalities; but it may be that, when the government is satisfied with a minimal provision of the public services, such as education, health, the judiciary, defence, police, fire prevention etc., which is its primary responsibility, unemployment on a large scale will occur as a result of a deficiency in effective demand. In a flexprice economy, even under these circumstances, relative prices and wage rates will change and full employment will be automatically achieved, so that the government does not have the additional task of bringing it about; but in the case of the fixprice economy, the achieving of full employment becomes an important task of the government. That is, state activity has to make up for that part of the price mechanism which is deficient.

As I shall show in the next section and thereafter, employment will increase if government expenditure increases or if taxation is reduced. If unemployment results when the government formulates a budget which only provides for the minimum of public services, then in order to decrease or eliminate this unemployment it needs to provide these services on a rather larger scale. Conversely, when a budget which is too large is drawn up, not only will full employment be achieved but inflation will occur, and hence it is desirable that the budget, and consequently the scale on which public services are provided, be reduced. Thus the decision whether to increase or decrease the supply of public services is not taken as a result of an evaluation of the services themselves designed to show to what degree they are necessary and how much such provision would cost; rather it is based on an assessment of the effects on the national economy as a whole of a change in their supply. Thus, along with the change in its character which takes place as an economy becomes fixprice after being flexprice, the government comes to take on the important and hazardous task of the management of the national economy in addition to its primary duties.

The significance of allowing one political group to manipulate the levers which control the national economy is great. There is no longer any need for the economy to have a government which is, as far as possible, small scale and efficient (nor ought it to have such a government); the situation demands that it have a large-scale, dependable government. However, a strong government is not only able to achieve full employment; it can even alter the content of that employment. For example, it is perfectly possible for a strong government to create a totalitarian state and achieve quasi-wartime full employment, unless the political parties, the bureaucracy and the people possess a high degree of political self-restraint. That is not all. It may be that the full employment achieved by an expansion of government expenditure under a given system of prices and wages provides less satisfaction for individuals than full employment achieved by tightening control on government expenditure and rationalising the prices and wages system. When we are able to vary government expenditure and taxation, there is no longer only one full-employment equilibrium. If they are adjusted appropriately, full employment can be established under a variety of price—wage systems. These states of full employment vary in quality — that is, they differ in the degree of satisfaction they provide to individuals. Therefore it is natural for the government to aim to achieve the best of these states of full employment. However, Keynesian policy seeks only to achieve full employment under the existing prices and wages system, by regulating public expenditure and income, and is often apt to neglect efforts to achieve a better quality full employment by a positive revision of the structure of prices and wages. This makeshift nature of Keynesian policy, with its failure to correct the fundamental contradictions or disequilibria in the economy, is its weakness and danger. Just as the central planning authority of a socialist country cannot achieve an optimum state of the economy if it neglects efforts to arrive at appropriate prices, so it is possible that high satisfaction cannot be achieved — despite ostensible full employment — if, in a Keynesian fixprice economy, there is merely an acceptance of the given prices and wages system and no attempt is made to rationalise it.

B. The theory of the expenditure multiplier

On the assumption that prices and wages were flexible, and taking public expenditure and taxation to be endogenous variables, Pigou considered the question of what values these had to take on for the welfare of society to be at a maximum.[4] However I shall assume below (as did Keynes) that public expenditure and the (rate of) taxation are exogenous variables, and I shall attempt to analyse the effects of an increase in government expenditure for the case of a fixprice economy.

Let $\overline{F}_i$, $i = 1, \ldots, l$, be public expenditure before it is increased, and F_i, public expenditure after it has been increased. $\Delta F_i = F_i - \overline{F}_i$ expresses the amount of the increase. Prices and wages are unchanged; the economy is in an underemployment equilibrium both before and after the change. As far as taxation is concerned we can identify two cases: in the first it changes in proportion or in a graduated fashion corresponding to changes in income, and in the second taxation is fixed and unchanging even though income changes. However, the latter is no more than a special case of the former, where the marginal rate of taxation is zero. In what follows, we shall consider only the case where taxation is a linear function of income. As we stated earlier, t_W shows the tax rate for employment income and t_Π that for profits income. In the case where $t_W = t_\Pi$ and where the marginal propensity to consume of workers equals that of capitalists, the degree to which the consumption of workers depends on their tax-deducted disposable incomes equals the degree to which capitalists' consumption depends on their disposable incomes. Therefore in this case there is no need to divide consumers into workers and capitalists, and there is no objection to regarding total consumption as depending on the disposable income of society as a whole. If total consumption is independent of the distribution of income between the working class and the capitalist class, then the level of consumption is determined independently of the relative labour- or capital-intensities of industries. Consequently there is no need to disaggregate the economy into its individual industries, and we can undertake a macroeconomic analysis of the multiplier effect of investment on consumption and income, regarding the whole economy as one large industry.[5+]

Therefore behind macroeconomic multiplier theory there lie the assumptions that (i) the marginal propensity to consume of workers equals that of capitalists, and (ii) the tax rate on employment income equals that on profits income.

Later we shall derive a more general formula for calculating the multiplier by abandoning these two unrealistic assumptions, but we begin by considering this simplified, yet basic, case.

First, the total consumer demand of workers and capitalists is

$$C = \sum_{i=1}^{h} p_i(D_i^W + D_i^K) \tag{11}$$

and the total investment demand of capitalists is

$$I = \sum_{i=h+1}^{l} p_i H_i. \tag{12}$$

On the other hand the total expenditure of the government is

$$G = \sum_{i=1}^{l} p_i F_i. \tag{13}$$

Since the gross national product, Y, equals $\sum_1^l p_i X_i$, then in view of the above definitions we can obtain the well-known equation for equilibrium of GNP

$$Y = C + I + G \tag{14}$$

from the equilibrium conditions for consumer goods (5) and for capital goods (6). Since in equation (14) prices are fixed, I takes on a fixed value, G varies in accordance with the decision of the government, and C depends on after-tax employment income and profits income. If W is employment income before tax is deducted, then we have

$$W = \sum_{s=m+1}^{n} p_s N_s = \sum_{s=m+1}^{n} p_s \left(\sum_{r=1}^{l} a_{sr} X_r \right) \tag{15}$$

from (10), and profits,

$$\Pi = \sum_{r=1}^{l} \left(\sum_{i=l+1}^{m} p_i a_{ir} + b_r \right) X_r. \tag{16}$$

Therefore, taking (7) into account, we obtain

$$Y = \left(\sum_{r=1}^{l} p_r X_r \right) = W + \Pi \tag{17}$$

as the equation for the distribution of the gross national product.

Bearing in mind that workers' consumption depends on post-tax employment income, that capitalists' consumption depends on post-tax profits and that there is no need to take account of the price effect since the price structure is unchanged, we can discover the effect of changes in government expenditure on the gross national product in the following manner. First, differentiating (14) with respect to G, we have

$$\frac{dY}{dG} = c_W (1 - t_W) \frac{dW}{dG} + c_\Pi (1 - t_\Pi) \frac{d\Pi}{dG} + 1. \tag{18}$$

Here c_W and c_Π are, respectively, the marginal propensities to consume of workers and capitalists; that is,

$$c_W = \sum_{i=1}^{h} p_i \frac{dD_i^W}{dW'}, \qquad c_\Pi = \sum_{i=1}^{h} p_i \frac{dD_i^K}{d\Pi'}, \tag{19}$$

where W' and Π' show the post-tax values of W and Π. Taking into account the assumptions (i) that workers' and capitalists' propensities to consume are equal ($c_W = c_\Pi$), and (ii) that the tax rates for employment income and profits income are the same ($t_W = t_{\Pi}$), we can simplify (18) by writing

$$\frac{dY}{dG} = c(1-t)\left(\frac{dW}{dG} + \frac{d\Pi}{dG}\right) + 1, \tag{18'}$$

where c shows the common marginal propensity to consume of workers and capitalists, and t their common tax rate. Therefore, taking (17) into account, (18') can be further rewritten as

$$\frac{dY}{dG} = c(1-t)\frac{dY}{dG} + 1$$

and therefore we can obtain the famous formula for the macro-economic expenditure multiplier

$$\frac{dY}{dG} = \frac{1}{1 - c(1-t)}. \tag{20}$$

This formula holds irrespective of the good for which government expenditure increases. That is, whether it takes the form of an increase in the demand for consumer good i, or of an increase in the demand for another consumer good j or a capital good k, the effect on the gross national product will be determined by (20). Therefore, it is enough for the government merely to increase its expenditure by a sufficient amount to achieve the necessery increase in the gross national product, and it does not matter which goods the expenditure falls on. However, this conclusion can be reached only in the case where presuppositions (i) and (ii) of macroeconomic multiplier theory are satisfied. If the propensities to consume of capitalists and workers differ, or if their incomes are taxed at different rates, the two classes cannot be treated as one, and consequently we cannot rewrite (18) as (18'). As a result macroeconomic multiplier theory ceases to apply.

Where conditions (i) and (ii) do not hold, we have to calculate the multiplier using the whole system of equations (1)–(10). Moreover, the value of the multiplier will depend on the goods on which public expenditure falls (apart from an exceptional case, with which I shall deal later). Let us here look at the case where government expenditure on consumer good 1 increases. First, this increase will produce an increase in the production of good 1. Since we are considering an economy in an underemployment equilibrium, output of good 1 is increased simply by increasing the numbers employed to produce it, and profits too will increase in proportion. The increase in the volume of employment and in profits in the enterprises which produce good 1 induces a general increase in the demand for consumer goods by their workers and capitalists. Consequently the outputs of consumer goods other than good 1 have to increase, and, in addition, there is a further or secondary expansion in the output of good 1. This second expansion in the production of good 1 and the first expansion of the outputs of goods other than good 1 produce increases in employment and profits in these industries; as a result the demand of capitalists and workers for consumer goods must once again rise. In the same way we get a third expansion in the output of good 1, and a second expansion in the outputs of consumer goods other than good 1, and so forth. After these higher order repercussive effects have all worked themselves out, the economy will arrive at a new equilibrium. Since the old equilibrium was an underemployment equilibrium, we shall not arrive at full employment at the new equilibrium unless the increase in government expenditure on good 1 is sufficiently large. Otherwise, prices and wages will not change and there is, of course, no price effect on the multiplier.

This multiplier effect, produced by an increase in government expenditure on consumer good 1, can be analysed mathematically as follows. Since we think of the demand for capital goods as being unchanged during this process of diffusion in output increases, the increases in profits and employment caused by the increased government expenditure on consumer good 1 are confined to the consumer goods industries; there is no spreading of the effects to the capital goods industries. The demand—supply equations for capital goods, (6), are undisturbed, and we have only to consider the effects of an increase in F_1 on the demand—supply equations for consumer goods (5). If we differentiate both sides of (5) with respect to F_1 and take into account (2) and (3), which are the consumption functions of workers and capitalists, the total wages equation, (15), and the total profits equation, (16), then we obtain

$$\begin{bmatrix} \dfrac{\partial X_1}{\partial F_1} \\[2mm] \dfrac{\partial X_2}{\partial F_1} \\[2mm] \cdot \\ \cdot \\ \cdot \\ \dfrac{\partial X_h}{\partial F_1} \end{bmatrix} = \begin{bmatrix} m_{11} & m_{12} & \dots & m_{1h} \\ m_{21} & m_{22} & \dots & m_{2h} \\ \cdot & \cdot & \cdots & \cdot \\ \cdot & \cdot & \cdots & \cdot \\ \cdot & \cdot & \cdots & \cdot \\ m_{h1} & m_{h2} & \dots & m_{hh} \end{bmatrix} \begin{bmatrix} \dfrac{\partial X_1}{\partial F_1} \\[2mm] \dfrac{\partial X_2}{\partial F_1} \\[2mm] \cdot \\ \cdot \\ \cdot \\ \dfrac{\partial X_h}{\partial F_1} \end{bmatrix} + \begin{bmatrix} 1 \\ 0 \\ \cdot \\ \cdot \\ \cdot \\ 0 \end{bmatrix} \quad (21)$$

where

$$m_{ij} = \frac{\partial D_i^W}{\partial W'} (1 - t_W) \left[\sum_{s=m+1}^{n} p_s a_{sj} \right]$$

$$+ \frac{\partial D_i^K}{\partial \Pi'} (1 - t_\Pi) \left[\sum_{s=l+1}^{m} p_s a_{sj} + b_j \right]. \quad (22)$$

The first term inside square brackets on the right-hand side of (22) shows total wages per unit of product j, and the second term in square brackets shows total profits per unit of product j. If we multiply these respectively by $1 - t_W$ and $1 - t_\Pi$, we have post-tax wages and profits per unit of product j. Since $\partial D_i^W / \partial W'$ and $\partial D_i^K / \partial \Pi'$ show, respectively, workers' and capitalists' marginal propensities to demand consumer good i (with respect to their respective post-tax incomes), m_{ij} defined in (22) shows the increase in the demand for good i when the output of good j has increased by one unit. Solving the simultaneous equations (21) with respect to $\partial X_1 / \partial F_1, \dots, \partial X_h / \partial F_1$ and substituting these values into

$$\frac{\partial Y}{\partial G} = \frac{p_1}{p_1} \frac{\partial X_1}{\partial F_1} + \frac{p_2}{p_1} \frac{\partial X_2}{\partial F_1} + \dots + \frac{p_h}{p_1} \frac{\partial X_h}{\partial F_1}, \quad (23)$$

we obtain the rate of increase in the gross national product when government expenditure on good 1 increases by $dG = p_1 dF_1$. This is called the multiplier effect originating from consumer good 1.

The value of the multiplier thus obtained has to accord with the macroeconomic multiplier when the previously stated conditions (i) and (ii) are satisfied. That is, if we multiply successive rows of (21) by $p_1, p_2, \dots, p_h$ and sum each column, we obtain

$$\sum_{i=1}^{h} p_i \frac{\partial X_i}{\partial F_1} = \sum_{j=1}^{h} p_j m_j \frac{\partial X_j}{\partial F_1} + p_i. \quad (24)$$

Here m_j is

$$p_j m_j = p_1 m_{1j} + p_2 m_{2j} + \ldots + p_h m_{hj}, \qquad j = 1, \ldots, h. \qquad (25)$$

Let $\bar{m}$ be the average value of the $m_1, m_2, \ldots, m_h$ with

$$p_1 \frac{\partial X_1}{\partial F_1}, p_2 \frac{\partial X_2}{\partial F_1}, \ldots, p_h \frac{\partial X_h}{\partial F_1}$$

as their weights; then we have

$$\bar{m} = \frac{\sum\limits_{j=1}^{h} m_j p_j \frac{\partial X_j}{\partial F_1}}{\sum\limits_{j=1}^{h} p_j \frac{\partial X_j}{\partial F_1}} \qquad (26)$$

Considering (26) and (23), we may write (24) as

$$\frac{\partial Y}{\partial G} = \bar{m} \frac{\partial Y}{\partial G} + 1$$

and consequently

$$\frac{\partial Y}{\partial G} = \frac{1}{1 - \bar{m}}. \qquad (27)$$

On the other hand, when we take (19), (22) into account, $p_j m_j$ is written as

$$p_j m_j = c_W (1 - t_W) \left[\sum_{s=m+1}^{n} p_s a_{sj} \right] + c_\Pi (1 - t_\Pi) \left[\sum_{s=l+1}^{m} p_s a_{sj} + b_j \right]; \qquad (28)$$

if we assume in addition that (i) $c_W = c_\Pi$ and (ii) $t_W = t_\Pi$, then it becomes

$$p_j m_j = c(1 - t) p_j$$

by equation (7). Therefore in this case the average value $\bar{m}$ becomes equal to $c(1 - t)$; hence formula (27) comes to be the same as the macroeconomic multiplier formula (20) which we obtained earlier. Since the values of c and t are independent of the increase in government expenditure, the value of the multiplier is independent of the good on which the increase in government expenditure has fallen. However, where either (i) or (ii) alone, or neither, is satisfield, the average value $\bar{m}$ depends on the weights $p_1 (\partial X_1 / \partial F_1)$, $p_2 (\partial X_2 / \partial F_1), \ldots, p_h (\partial X_2 / \partial F_1)$ (apart from an exceptional case).

These are different from the weights $p_1 (\partial X_1 / \partial F_2)$, $p_2 (\partial X_2 / \partial F_2)$, $\ldots, p_h (\partial X_h / \partial F_2)$ in the case where another good, say good 2, is the recipient of an increase in government expenditure, and hence the value of the multiplier (27) is not fixed but will depend on which goods receive the increased government outlay. Consequently, in order to obtain the correct value of the multiplier, it is necessary to solve the simultaneous equations of (21) and determine these weights.

However, there is an exceptional case where no error will arise even if the weights are ignored. The ratio of the first square-bracketed term to the second square-bracketed term on the right-hand side of (28) shows the wages—profits ratio where consumer good j is being produced. If this ratio is the same for all consumer goods, the m_j for all consumer goods will be the same (even where conditions (i) and (ii) cannot be satisfied), and consequently the average value of the m_j will be independent of their weights. (That is, $\bar{m} = m_j$, $j = 1, \ldots, h$.) Thus there are two cases where we need not concern ourselves with the weights. The first is where the marginal propensities to consume of workers and capitalists are the same and their incomes are taxed at the same rate; the second is where the wages—profits ratio is the same in all consumer-goods producing industries. That is, if those doing the consuming are similar, macroeconomic multiplier theory holds good even though the rate of distribution differs between industries; and if those who do the producing are similar, it holds even though propensities to consume and tax rates may differ, provided that we make appropriate amendments to the value of the multiplier.

In the general case where these conditions do not necessarily hold, the sum of the first and second square-bracketed terms on the right-hand side of (28) is equal to p_j by (7), and since the marginal propensities to consume c_W and c_{Π} are less than one, m_j is less than one. Therefore $\bar{m}$, which is the average of the m_j, is less than one, and hence the value of the multiplier by (27) is greater than one. For example, suppose $c_W = 0.6$, $c_{\Pi} = 0.2$, $t_W = 0.2$ and $t_{\Pi} = 0.6$; also suppose that the weighted averages of the shares of wages and the shares of profits in prices are 0.75 and 0.25 respectively, provided $p_1 (\partial X_1 / \partial F_1), \ldots, p_h (\partial X_h / \partial F_1)$ are taken as weights. Then $\bar{m}$ will be calculated at 0.38 and the multiplier is about 1.6. That is, an increase in government expenditure of one unit will not just bring about an increase of the same value in the output of consumer goods; it will also produce an increase in the incomes of workers and capitalists, and as a result induce a further total increase of 0.6 units in consumption.

In the same way, we can analyse the effects on the gross national product of an increase in government expenditure on capital goods. In this case the income-creating effects will not spread to other industries making capital goods, but will spread to all consumer goods industries. We can obtain a formula for the multiplier similar in form to (27). However, note here that $\bar{m}$ is a weighted average which assigns weights of $p_1 (\partial X_1 / \partial F_l), \ldots, p_h (\partial X_h / \partial F_l)$ to the $m_1, \ldots, m_h$ of consumer goods and $p_l (\partial X_l / \partial F_l)$ to the m_l of the capital good l for which government expenditure has increased. In the general case this average value is not equal to the average value in the case where government expenditure on a consumer good has increased, so that the government investment multiplier and the government consumption multiplier differ. However, where the wages—profits ratio is equal for all industries (consumer goods industries and capital goods industries), the government investment multiplier equals the consumption multiplier, irrespective of the capital good for which the government increases its demand. This is true even if there are differences in propensities to consume and tax rates.

C. Efficient public expenditure

Where the size of the multiplier changes with changes in the goods on which public expenditure falls, the government is able to choose its value within a certain range. In a period of recession the government will wish to ensure that the multiplier effect is as large as possible, while in an inflation it will wish to keep the multiplier small. Since there is a limit to the total of government expenditure, the government has to make an efficient expenditure plan so as to maximise (or minimise) the total multiplier effect. In making public expenditure efficient, the question arises of how to make the whole of the expenditure efficient, as well as that of how to spend the additional marginal units efficiently when a given part of the total has already been determined. In what follows we shall consider these problems on the assumption that the economy is in a period of recession. Firstly, we shall discuss the efficiency of marginal expenditure.

Here a fixed marginal amount of government expenditure ΔG

is permitted, in addition to total government expenditure on l kinds of consumer and capital goods. Let ΔF_i be the increase in government demand for good i; we have

$$\Delta G \geqq p_1 \Delta F_1 + p_2 \Delta F_2 + \ldots + p_l \Delta F_l. \tag{29}$$

Since the government may decrease its demand for good i, ΔF_i may be negative. But since total government demand for any good must not be negative, we must have

$$F_1 + \Delta F_1 \geqq 0, \quad F_2 + \Delta F_2 \geqq 0, \quad \ldots, \quad F_l + \Delta F_l \geqq 0. \tag{30}$$

Next, since the demand and supply for goods must be equal both before and after the increase in government expenditure, the increase in the demand for each good must be equalled by an increase in its supply. Therefore

$$\Delta X_1 = m_{11} \Delta X_1 + \ldots + m_{1l} \Delta X_l + \Delta F_1$$
$$\vdots \qquad \vdots \qquad \qquad \vdots \qquad \vdots \tag{31}$$
$$\Delta X_h = m_{h1} \Delta X_1 + \ldots + m_{hl} \Delta X_l + \Delta F_h$$

must hold for consumer goods, and

$$\Delta X_{h+1} = \Delta F_{h+1}, \ldots, \Delta X_l = \Delta F_l \tag{32}$$

must hold for capital goods. As stated previously, ΔF_i may be negative in (31) and (32), but we assume that ΔX_i cannot be negative. That is, although the government wishes to make public expenditure efficient, it is not allowed to formulate a public expenditure plan which would adversely influence the outputs of industries. Thus in the following we assume

$$\Delta X_1 \geqq 0, \ldots, \Delta X_l \geqq 0. \tag{33}$$

The increase in the gross national product is given by

$$\Delta Y = p_1 \Delta X_1 + \ldots + p_l \Delta X_l. \tag{34}$$

The problem now is to maximise (34) subject to (29)–(33). To do so let us disregard (30) for the time being, and consider how to maximise (34) under (29) and (31)–(33). The solution derived in this way is the one which we are seeking if it also satisfies condition (30); and as I shall show later, the maximum solution obtained while ignoring (30) will in fact also satisfy (30).

In order to obtain the maximum value of (34) under all the

constraints apart from (30), we have to maximise the Lagrangian function

$$\sum_{i=1}^{l} p_i \Delta X_i + \lambda \left[\Delta G - \sum_{i=1}^{l} p_i \Delta F_i \right] + \sum_{i=1}^{h} \mu_i \left[\sum_{j=1}^{l} m_{ij} \Delta X_j + \Delta F_i \right.$$
$$\left. - \Delta X_i \right] + \sum_{i=h+1}^{l} \mu_i [\Delta F_i - \Delta X_i]$$

with respect to ΔX_i, ΔF_i, and minimise it with respect to λ, μ_i. Since, while we do so, ΔX_i cannot be negative by (33), the maximising conditions with respect to ΔX_i are given by a set of inequalities; that is,

$$p_i + \sum_{j=1}^{h} \mu_j m_{ji} - \mu_i \leqq 0, \qquad i = 1, \ldots, l, \qquad (35)$$

$$\text{where} \begin{cases} \text{if '<' then } \Delta X_i = 0 \\ \text{if '=' then } \Delta X_i \geqq 0. \end{cases}$$

On the other hand, ΔF_i can be either positive or negative, and hence the maximising conditions with respect to ΔF_i are simply

$$\mu_i - \lambda p_i = 0, \qquad i = 1, \ldots, l. \qquad (36)$$

We obtain (29), (31) and (32) respectively as the minimising conditions with respect to λ, μ_i, $i = 1, \ldots, h$, and μ_i, $i = h + 1$, $\ldots, l$. When (29) holds as an inequality the corresponding Lagrange multiplier λ is zero, and when it holds as an equality it is positive or zero.

First let us prove that $\lambda > 0$. From (35) and (36) we have respectively[6+]

$$\sum_{i=1}^{l} \left(p_i + \sum_{j=1}^{h} \mu_j m_{ji} - \mu_i \right) \Delta X_i = 0,$$

and

$$\sum_{i=1}^{l} (\mu_i - \lambda p_i) \Delta F_i = 0.$$

If we further add these two equations and take the equations of (31) into account, we have

$$\Delta Y \equiv \sum_{i=1}^{l} p_i \Delta X_i = \lambda \sum_{i=1}^{l} p_i \Delta F_i = \lambda \Delta G. \qquad (37)$$

Therefore λ shows the multiplier effect on the gross national product of an increase in government expenditure at the maximum point. However, as formula (27) shows, the multiplier effect is greater than 1, whatever the direction from which it originates (for example, take the effect in the case where government demand for consumer good 1 increases). Therefore the maximum multiplier effect λ must, of course, be greater than 1.

If we substitute (36) into (35) and take into account (25), which is the equation defining m_i, we obtain $p_i \leq \lambda \, (p_i - p_i m_i)$; that is

$$\lambda_i \leq \lambda, \qquad i = 1, \ldots, l, \tag{35'}$$

where $\lambda_i = 1/(1 - m_i)$. Since (35') has to hold with equality for at least one i,[7+] λ must be the maximum of $\lambda_i, i = 1, \ldots, l$. $\Delta X_i = 0$ for goods for which (35') holds as an inequality (i.e. goods for which λ_i is not a maximum). That is, in order to achieve efficient public expenditure the government should calculate λ_i for each good, and then, selecting those goods for which λ_i is a maximum, should determine its demand for consumer goods so that the outputs of the selected goods increase, while those of other goods remain unchanged.

Next let us confirm that a maximum solution such as the above also satisfies the condition (30), which we have so far disregarded. If we multiply each equation of (31) by $p_1, \ldots, p_l$ respectively, sum each side and, moreover, take (25), the definitional equation of m_i, into account, we have

$$(1 - m_1) p_1 \Delta X_1 + (1 - m_2) p_2 \Delta X_2 + \ldots + (1 - m_l) p_l \Delta X_l$$
$$= \sum_{i=1}^{l} p_i \Delta F_i.$$

By (29) the right-hand side of this equation will not exceed ΔG; ΔX_i is positive or zero, and $m_i < 1$. Therefore ΔX_i is bounded above and below. Therefore by (31), ΔF_i is also bounded above and below. Consequently, when the marginal increase in government expenditure ΔG is sufficiently small, the absolute value of the change in the government's demand for each good is also sufficiently small. Thus if we assume that the quantities of each good demanded by the government are positive before the increase, then they will remain so after the change. That is, (30) is satisfied.

Thus the maximum solution which we have obtained gives the maximum for the increment in the gross national product subject to all the constraints, including (30). This being so, what economic meaning does λ_i have? It is true that it appears in the criterion (35'), which decides for which goods ΔX_i is positive and for which zero in the maximum solution, but its meaning is not entirely clear. One way to clarify it is to consider a situation where the government's demand for good 1 has been increased by ΔF_i. Then the outputs of consumer goods $1, \ldots, h$ will clearly show a tendency to increase, so that in order to keep the outputs of consumer goods other than good 1 unchanged, we have to make a compensating decrease of ΔF_i, $i = 2, \ldots, h$ in the government's demand for good $2, \ldots, h$. Where this compensating reduction has taken place, the equations

$$\Delta X_1 = m_{11} \Delta X_1 + \Delta F_1,$$
$$0 = m_{21} \Delta X_1 + \Delta F_2,$$
$$\vdots \qquad \vdots \qquad \vdots$$
$$0 = m_{h1} \Delta X_1 + \Delta F_h$$

hold. Since we assume capitalists' demand for capital goods to be constant, the government's demand for capital goods must also be constant in order for the output of capital goods to remain unchanged; that is $0 = \Delta F_i$, $i = h + 1, \ldots, l$. When we multiply each of these equations by their corresponding prices and sum them, we obtain

$$\Delta Y = p_1 \Delta X_1 = p_1 m_1 \Delta X_1 + \sum_{i=1}^{l} p_i \Delta F_i = m_1 \Delta Y + \Delta G,$$

which is to say

$$\frac{\Delta Y}{\Delta G} = \frac{1}{1 - m_1} = \lambda_i.$$

Thus λ_i shows the multiplier effect of government expenditure when a compensatory change is made in the government's demand, so that the outputs of goods $2, \ldots, l$ remain unchanged when its demand for consumer good 1 increases. We refer to such a multiplier effect as the multiplier effect concentrated on consumer good 1, and we distinguish it from the multiplier effect originating from good 1 referred to above (that is, the multiplier effect where the government's demand for other goods is kept the same while only its demand for consumer good 1 increases). The other λ_i can be similarly interpreted. That is to say, they show the multiplier effect concentrated on good i. Thus efficiency of the marginal increase in government expenditure requires that expenditure be concentrated where the multiplier effects are at a maximum.

Let us next consider the question of the efficiency of total government expenditure. As before, we assume that the economy is in a recessionary period, and that the government consequently wishes to maximise the multiplier effect. For simplicity in what follows we assume

$$D_i^W + D_i^K > 0, \qquad i = 1, \ldots, h$$

no matter what the level of income; furthermore, let

$$H_i = \text{constant} > 0, \qquad i = h + 1, \ldots, l. \qquad (38)$$

Substituting (10) into (2) and taking into account the fact that prices and the employment income-tax rate are constant, we can express workers' demands for consumer goods as functions of outputs $X_1, \ldots, X_l$. Further, substituting (10) into (4) and the latter into (3), capitalists' demands for consumer goods will similarly become functions of the outputs of goods. Consequently we can write the conditions of equilibrium in the demand and supply of consumer goods in the form

$$X_i = D_i(X_1, \ldots, X_l) + F_i, \qquad i = 1, \ldots, h, \qquad (5')$$

where D_i shows the total demand of workers and capitalists for good i. We regard the government as aiming at efficiency in its total public expenditure G and hence pursuing the maximisation of the gross national product

$$Y = p_1 X_1 + \ldots + p_l X_l \qquad (39)$$

subject to the budget constraint,

$$p_1 F_1 + \ldots + p_l F_l \leq G, \qquad (40)$$

and the equilibrium demand–supply conditions for consumer goods (5') and for capital goods (6). We assume that all gross investments, H_i, appearing in (6) are constant. Since neither F_i nor X_i can be negative, the maximum point can be obtained by maximising the Lagrange function

$$\sum_{i=1}^{l} p_i X_i + \lambda \left[G - \sum_{i=1}^{l} p_i F_i \right] + \sum_{i=1}^{h} \mu_i \left[D_i(X_1, \ldots, X_l) + F_i - X_i \right]$$

$$+ \sum_{i=h+1}^{l} \mu_i \left[H_i + F_i - X_i \right]$$

with respect to X_i, F_i, and minimising it with respect to λ, μ_i.[8] Since at this time X_i, F_i cannot be negative, the maximising conditions with respect to X_i are

$$p_i + \sum_{j=1}^{h} \mu_j m_{ji} - \mu_i \leqq 0, \qquad i = 1, \ldots, l,$$

$$\text{where } \begin{cases} \text{if `<' then } X_i = 0, \\ \text{if `=' then } X_i \geqq 0, \end{cases} \tag{41}$$

and with respect to F_i they are

$$\mu_i - \lambda p_i \leqq 0, \qquad i = 1, \ldots, l,$$

$$\text{where } \begin{cases} \text{if `<' then } F_i = 0, \\ \text{if `=' then } F_i \geqq 0. \end{cases} \tag{42}$$

When we compare these conditions with (35) and (36), which are the conditions of efficiency for a marginal increase in government expenditure, (42) is more complicated than (36) because F_i must be non-negative, whereas formerly ΔF_i could either be positive or negative; (41) and (35) are similar.

The significance of the replacement of (36) by the complicated condition (42) is great. First, because of the simplifying assumption (38), the right-hand side of each equation of (5′) and (6) is always positive whatever happens to $X_1, \ldots, X_l$, and therefore we never have $X_i = 0$. Consequently, (41) always holds with equality. Thus we obtain

$$p = \mu[I - M]. \tag{43}$$

Here p is a row vector $(p_1, \ldots, p_l)$, and μ is a row vector $(\mu_1, \ldots, \mu_l)$. I is the l by l unit matrix and M is the l by l matrix of marginal demand coefficients

$$M = \begin{bmatrix} m_{11} & m_{12} & \cdots & m_{1l} \\ \cdot & \cdot & & \cdot \\ \cdot & \cdot & & \cdot \\ \cdot & \cdot & & \cdot \\ m_{h1} & m_{h2} & \cdots & m_{hl} \\ 0 & 0 & \cdots & 0 \\ \cdot & \cdot & & \cdot \\ \cdot & \cdot & & \cdot \\ 0 & 0 & \cdots & 0 \end{bmatrix}, \quad m_{ij} = \frac{\partial D_i}{\partial X_j}.$$

As can be easily ascertained, the elements of

$$p[I-M]^{-1}$$

show the multiplier effect of government expenditure originating from each good, mutiplied by its respective price.[9+] In other words, its ith element shows the increase in the gross national product when the government's demand for good i alone has increased by one unit, and when this is divided by $\Delta G = p_i$ we obtain the multiplier originating from good $i, i = 1, \ldots, l$. Thus we know from (43) that the Lagrange coefficient μ_i is equal to the multiplier originating from good i multiplied by p_i. If this is smaller than λ (the government expenditure multiplier at the maximum point) multiplied by p_i, then by (42) no government expenditure goes in that direction, and consequently the multiplier effect originating from that quarter is zero.[10] (42) implies that the government ought to compare the multiplier effects originating from each good, and direct its expenditure where the effects are greatest.

Thus the efficiency criteria for the government's marginal expenditure are different from those for total expenditure. First, the m_{ji} in the former is the marginal demand coefficient at the equilibrium point before government expenditure increases marginally; the m_{ji} in the latter is the marginal demand coefficient at the equilibrium point where government expenditure as a whole is efficient. Apart from the case where the demand function is linear, the two are not generally equal. Secondly, there is another difference, in that the multiplier effect *concentrated on* each good is compared in the case of the efficiency of marginal expenditure, whereas the multiplier effect *originating from* each good is compared in the case of the efficiency of total expenditure. This difference is unrelated to the question of whether or not the demand function is linear, and therefore it is more fundamental than the first. It originates in the fact that in the case of the efficiency of marginal expenditure it is possible to decrease government demand for certain goods, while in the case of the efficiency of total expenditure there is the restriction that government expenditure on no good can be negative. Thus, in the former case it is possible freely to change the marginal demand of the government so as to concentrate the multiplier effect on a certain good. In the latter case total government demand for a good cannot be negative, and hence the same freedom does not exist; the government will thus compare the multiplier originating from each good and demand only those goods which have the largest multiplier effect. Since the $\bar{m}$ which appears in the formula (27) of the multiplier effect originating from good i is the average of each m_j, the formula,

The multiplier effect originating from good i	$\leqq$	the multiplier effect concentrated on the good where it is a maximum,

must hold for all directions i, provided we disregard the difference between the m_{ji} in the efficient marginal expenditure programme and those in the efficient total expenditure programme. Therefore where the demand function is linear, we obtain the conclusion that the multiplier effect of efficient total expenditure cannot be larger than that of efficient marginal expenditure. Furthermore, since the government has to purchase at least a minimum quantity of certain goods, irrespective of the size of their multiplier effects, in order to perform those functions which it cannot avoid, the efficiency of overall expenditure is an impossible policy target, and in practice only marginal efficiency is meaningful. Moreover, there is a limit to marginal efficiency too (apart from some special cases). That is to say, in order to produce a multiplier effect concentrated only on certain goods, for the sake of marginal efficiency, the government demand for a number of goods must be reduced, and there are political and other limits to this process.

We have now considered the problem of maximising the multiplier effect on the gross national product, and it is possible, with suitable amendments, to deal in a similar way with the problem of the multiplier effect on employment.[11]

D. The multiplier effect of a reduction in taxation

It goes without saying that an increase in taxation has the opposite effect from an increase in government expenditure. We assume, as we did in the previous section, that taxation on employment income and taxation on profits income are each linear functions of those incomes. First, let us analyse the case where the marginal rate of taxation on employment income increases.[12+] An increase in t_W means a decrease in the disposable income of workers (as long as their incomes from employment do not change), and this will bring about a decrease in workers' demand for consumer goods. The outputs of consumer goods will decrease, and as a result employment in the industries producing consumer goods, and hence employment incomes and profits from them, will decrease. This will cause a decrease in the disposable incomes of workers and capitalists, so that there will be a further decrease in the demands for consumer goods and a corresponding fall in outputs. As this process repeats itself there will be a successive diminution in outputs, but since the effects emanating from the increase in taxation will successively weaken, the fall in outputs will become ever smaller, and eventually the decline will cease. That is, outputs of consumer goods will, after a tax increase, arrive at equilibrium at a lower level.

When the change is very small we can obtain the effects of a change in the marginal tax rate on the equilibrium outputs of consumer goods by differentiating the equilibrium conditions for consumer goods (5′) with respect to t_W . Since the influence on the output of capital goods is nil at this time, the equilibrium condition for capital goods (6′) is undisturbed by a change in t_W . If we differentiate both sides of (5′), we have

$$
\begin{bmatrix} \dfrac{\partial X_1}{\partial t_W} \\ \vdots \\ \dfrac{\partial X_h}{\partial t_W} \end{bmatrix} = \begin{bmatrix} m_{11} & \cdots & m_{1h} \\ \vdots & & \vdots \\ m_{h1} & \cdots & m_{hh} \end{bmatrix} \begin{bmatrix} \dfrac{\partial X_1}{\partial t_W} \\ \vdots \\ \dfrac{\partial X_h}{\partial t_W} \end{bmatrix} - \begin{bmatrix} \dfrac{\partial D_1^W}{\partial W'} \\ \vdots \\ \dfrac{\partial D_h^W}{\partial W'} \end{bmatrix} W . \tag{44}
$$

Here m_{ij} are the marginal demand coefficients, W is total employment income, and W' is total income from employment after tax has been deducted. We assume that an increase in taxation has no effect on prices and wage rates. If we multiply the rows of (44) by $p_1 , \ldots , p_h$, respectively, and total each column, we obtain

$$
\frac{\partial Y}{\partial t_W} \equiv \sum_{i=1}^{h} p_i \frac{\partial X_i}{\partial t_W} = \sum_{j=1}^{h} p_j m_j \frac{\partial X_j}{\partial t_W} - \sum_{j=1}^{h} p_j \frac{\partial D_j^W}{\partial W'} W
$$

in the same way as we derived formula (27) for the multiplier effects of government expenditure. Here m_j is defined in the manner of (25), as it was in the case of the expenditure multiplier. Let us now define m' as the weighted average of $m_1 , \ldots , m_h$ which are assigned weights of $p_1(\partial X_1/\partial t_W), \ldots, p_h(\partial X_h/\partial t_W)$; i.e.

$$m' = \frac{\displaystyle\sum_{j=1}^{h} m_j p_j \frac{\partial X_j}{\partial t_W}}{\displaystyle\sum_{j=1}^{h} p_j \frac{\partial X_j}{\partial t_W}}. \tag{45}$$

We then obtain

$$\frac{\partial Y}{\partial t_W} = \frac{1}{1-m'}(-c_W W). \tag{46}$$

Here c_W is the marginal propensity to consume of workers—that is $\Sigma\, p_j(\partial D_j^W/\partial W')$. Each m_j is less than 1 and so m' is also less than 1. Consequently $1/(1-m')$ is greater than 1. However c_W and W are positive in (46), and the total effect on the gross national product of an increase in taxation is thus a negative one.

In exactly the same way, we can obtain the effect on the gross national product of a change in the tax rate which is levied on profits income. If we write out only the conclusion, it is

$$\frac{\partial Y}{\partial t_\Pi} = \frac{1}{1-m''}(-c_\Pi \Pi), \tag{47}$$

where c_Π is the marginal propensity to consume of capitalists and m'' is the value of the weighted average of $m_1, \ldots, m_h$, i.e.

$$m'' = \frac{\displaystyle\sum_{j=1}^{h} m_j p_j \frac{\partial X_j}{\partial t_\Pi}}{\displaystyle\sum_{j=1}^{h} p_j \frac{\partial X_j}{\partial t_\Pi}} \tag{48}$$

The absolute levels of capitalists' and workers' marginal propensities to consume individual goods (respectively $\partial D_1^K/\partial\Pi', \ldots, \partial D_h^K/\partial\Pi'$, and $\partial D_1^W/\partial W', \ldots, \partial D_h^W/\partial W'$) are different. But if we assume their ratios to be the same, then although the weights of the weighted averages (48) and (45) will also differ in their absolute sizes, their ratios will be the same and therefore m'' will become equal to m'.

In order to compare the effect on the gross national product of the case where employment income taxation has risen with that where profits income taxation has risen, let us assume, as we did when we made an approximate estimate of the multiplier effect of public expenditure, that $c_W = 0.6$, $c_\Pi = 0.2$, $t_W = 0.2$, $t_\Pi = 0.6$ and $W/Y = 0.75$, while $\Pi/Y = 0.25$. If we assume that $m' = m''$ and moreover that these are the same as the $\bar{m}$ of the public expenditure multiplier, then we have $1/(1-m') = 1/(1-m'') = $ approximately 1.6.[13] In this case increases of 100% in the tax rate on employment income and on profits income will, ignoring the multiplier effects, produce the same increase in the government's income from taxation, and may be thought of as matching tax-rate increases. The multiplier effects of these increases in taxation are respectively

$$\frac{\partial Y}{\partial t_W} t_W = \frac{1}{1-m'} (-c_W W) t_W , \tag{49}$$

and

$$\frac{\partial Y}{\partial t_\Pi} t_\Pi = \frac{1}{1-m''} (-c_\Pi \Pi) t_\Pi , \tag{50}$$

and if we assign the values assumed above, the former is $-0.144Y$ while the latter becomes $-0.0487Y$. (If we divide these values by Y we obtain the elasticities of the gross national product with respect to employment income tax and profits income tax respectively.) That is, where matching increases are made in employment income taxation and profits income taxation, the reducing effect on the gross national product of the former is three times that of that latter. Put in terms of the opposite case of a reduction in taxation, where we attempt to expand the gross national product by reducing taxation, we may conclude that the income creating effect of a reduction in employment income taxation clearly exceeds that of a reduction in profits income taxation, even though the diminution in the direct revenue from taxation is the same in both cases.

Thus taxation influences the demand for each good and therefore the gross national product, but at the same time it affects the value of the public expenditure multiplier dY/dG. As we saw in the previous section, the main factors determining the value of the public expenditure multiplier are (i) the marginal propensities to consume c_W and c_Π of workers and capitalists, (ii) the marginal tax rates t_W and t_Π on employment and profits income, and (iii) the weighted averages of the wages and profits of industries. As long as the demand functions of workers and capitalists are not linear, their marginal propensities to consume depend on their disposable incomes, and hence on income-tax rates. Furthermore, the weights which we use when we average wages and profits in each industry for the whole economy also depend on income taxation. Therefore the government can regulate the value of the multiplier by changing the marginal rates of tax on income.

Musgrave and Miller proposed an index α as one which would show to what extent the public expenditure multiplier depends upon the marginal rate of income taxation.[14] This index is described as follows. The expenditure multiplier when the marginal rates of taxation on income are zero is calculated, and the difference between it and the multiplier under the actual marginal rates is thought of as the part of the multiplier ascribable to the actual marginal tax rates. Then this part is expressed as a percentage of the multiplier when the marginal tax rates are zero. Let $(dY/dG)_0$ be the multiplier when the marginal tax rates are 0. We can prove that this is larger than the multiplier under the actual, positive marginal tax rates dY/dG, so that the Musgrave—Miller index defined as

$$\alpha = \frac{(dY/dG)_0 - (dY/dG)}{(dY/dG)_0}$$

is always positive. Thus the marginal tax rates contribute to lowering the expenditure multiplier by $\alpha \times 100\%$ from $(dY/dG)_0$ and we can show that the higher the marginal rates of taxation the smaller dY/dG will become, and hence the larger the contribution of the tax rates to the lowering of the value of the multiplier.

If we gradually increase government expenditure, the gross national product will increase correspondingly and the economy will approach a state of full employment. The incomes of workers and capitalists will become correspondingly larger, and under a graduated system of income taxation the marginal tax rates will gradually increase. As a result, there will be a parallel increase in the restraining effect on the multiplier of the marginal tax rates, and the public expenditure multiplier will decrease in size. Therefore, as full employment is approached, it will become gradually more difficult to raise the gross national product through public expenditure. In contrast to this, incomes of workers and capitalists, and hence the marginal income tax rates, are low when there is high unemployment; therefore the multiplier is large and it is relatively easy to escape from this position by increasing public expenditure. Thus, under a system of graduated income taxation, the gross national product will not become very small as a result of public expenditure policy, nor very large. The economy is furnished with an automatic mechanism whereby the gross national product is stabilised within a given range of values.[15+]

Finally let us add some general numerical estimates for the value of α. Here we assume that the marginal propensities to consume do not depend on the level of income, and we shall also ignore changes in the weighted averages of wages and profits of industries. We assume the same numerical values for c_W, c_Π, W/Y and Π/Y as were used previously when we calculated, for purposes of illustration, the public expenditure multiplier and the elasticities of the gross national product with respect to changes in the tax rates. Putting $t_W = t_\Pi = 0$ and calculating $(dY/dG)_0$, we obtain a multiplier of 2.0. On the other hand dY/dG was 1.6, and hence we have

$$\alpha = \frac{2.0 - 1.6}{2.0} = 0.2.$$

This is more or less the same value as Goldberger obtained for the American economy, but it is smaller than the value of 0.358 obtained by Musgrave and Miller for the USA and larger than the one calculated by Morishima and Nosse for the British economy. Musgrave and Miller can be regarded as having overestimated the propensity to consume, and Morishima and Nosse as having underestimated the rates of taxation. In the normal case the value of α can be regarded as being in the range 0.1–0.25, although it will, of course, depend upon the values of the propensities to consume and the rate of taxation.

E. The catalytic effect of an increase in taxation

As we saw above, an increase in public expenditure produces a greater increase in the gross national product. An increase in the gross national product signifies an increase in employment and profits income, and therefore the income taxes from these increase. For that reason, part of the initial increase in public expenditure will be recouped as income from taxation, but the remainder will become part of the government deficit. In the normal case there is a limit to the deficit expenditure permitted to the government, so that, although there is an income-creating effect involved, the government cannot increase its expenditure without limit. Therefore, it looks for the moment as if an upper limit is put on public expenditure policy by the extent to which the government can run a deficit.

If the only policy available to the government is one of expenditure alone, then this is indeed the case. However, as we saw in the previous section, the government can increase its tax revenue from a given income by increasing the tax rates. Clearly an increase in taxation will eliminate a government deficit and the government will be presented with scope for a policy of further increases in public expenditure. The gross national product will further increase as a result of this policy of additional expenditure. But on the other hand, an increase in taxation will cause a diminution in the gross national product, and therefore the net effect of an increase in expenditure coupled with a policy of increasing taxation can be thought of as the sum of a positive and a negative effect. As long as the net effect is positive, a policy of combining public expenditure increases with taxation increases is the better one, for it is then possible, by putting an increase in taxation into effect, to achieve a larger increase in public expenditure with a given deficit, and a larger increase in the gross national product. An increase in taxation on its own causes a decrease in the gross national product; but linked with an expenditure policy it will form a source of revenue for that expenditure policy. If the linked expenditure policy produces an increase in income which exceeds the increase accompanying the pure expenditure policy, then increased taxation becomes, instead, the cause of an increase in the gross national product. The effect which an increase in taxation has in this respect we shall call the catalytic function of an increase in taxation.

The combined effect of an increase in taxation and in public expenditure was first discussed by Haavelmo for the case of a zero deficit — that is, the balanced budget multiplier effect.[16] However, his argument can be extended, needless to say, to the general case of deficit financing. In what follows I shall discuss generally the catalytic action of an increase in taxation, and derive, as special cases of the general solution, the Haavelmo and other propositions regarding the multiplier effect of a balanced budget. However it is necessary to establish one or two preparatory propositions in order to do this.

First, let us prove that an increase in public expenditure will bring about an increase in the deficit $R = G - T_W - T_\Pi$. If we think of the deficit R as a function of government expenditure and the tax rates t_W and t_Π and partially differentiate R with respect to G, then we have

$$\frac{\partial R}{\partial G} = 1 - t_W \frac{\partial W}{\partial G} - t_\Pi \frac{\partial \Pi}{\partial G}.$$

On the other hand by (18) we have [17]

$$\frac{\partial Y}{\partial G} = c_W (1 - t_W) \frac{\partial W}{\partial G} + c_\Pi (1 - t_\Pi) \frac{\partial \Pi}{\partial G} + 1.$$

If we here put $\dfrac{\partial W}{\partial G} \Big/ \dfrac{\partial Y}{\partial G} = \omega$ and $\dfrac{\partial \Pi}{\partial G} \Big/ \dfrac{\partial Y}{\partial G} = \pi$, then we obtain

$$\frac{\partial R}{\partial G} = 1 - (t_W \omega + t_\Pi \pi)\frac{\partial Y}{\partial G} \tag{51}$$

$$\frac{\partial Y}{\partial G} = \frac{1}{1 - \bar{m}} = \frac{1}{1 - c_W (1 - t_W)\omega - c_\Pi (1 - t_\Pi)\pi}. \tag{52}$$

If we substitute (52) into (51) we obtain

$$\frac{\partial R}{\partial G} = \frac{1 - [(1 - c_W)t_W + c_W]\omega - [(1 - c_\Pi)t_\Pi + c_\Pi]\pi}{1 - \bar{m}} \tag{53}$$

and since the denominator of the right-hand side is positive, a positive value of the numerator implies $\partial R/\partial G > 0$. But the numerator is necessarily positive because the terms in the square brackets of the numerator are all positive and smaller than 1,[18] and ω and π are of a positive numerical value such that their sum is 1.

Next let us prove that an increase in the tax rate t_W on income from employment will decrease the deficit. We shall assume that the tax on income from employment is proportional to the total of employment income after subtracting allowances against taxation (consequently T_W is a linear function of employment income), and that when the tax rate t_W increases, allowances against taxation are decreased so as to keep the constant term in the employment income tax function unchanged.[19]

If we partially differentiate the deficit R with respect to t_W we obtain

$$\frac{\partial R}{\partial t_W} = - W - t_W \frac{\partial W}{\partial t_W} - t_\Pi \frac{\partial \Pi}{\partial t_W}$$

Defining $\dfrac{\partial W}{\partial t_W} \Big/ \dfrac{\partial Y}{\partial t_W} = \omega'$ and $\dfrac{\partial \Pi}{\partial t_W} \Big/ \dfrac{\partial Y}{\partial t_W} = \pi'$ and considering (46), we have

$$\frac{\partial R}{\partial t_W} = - W \left[1 - \frac{(t_W \, \omega' + t_\Pi \, \pi')c_W}{1 - m'} \right]. \tag{54}$$

If we here take into account the fact that

$$m' = c_W(1 - t_W)\omega' + c_\Pi(1 - t_\Pi)\pi'$$

we obtain from (54)

$$\frac{\partial R}{\partial t_W} = - W \left\{ \frac{1 - c_W \, \omega' - [c_\Pi(1 - t_\Pi) + c_W t_\Pi]\pi'}{1 - m'} \right\}. \tag{55}$$

The value within the square brackets of the numerator of the fraction on the right-hand side is smaller than whichever is the larger of c_W and c_Π. Therefore, whichever is the larger, it is still less than 1. 1. Since ω' and π' are positive values such that their sum equals 1, the numerator of the fraction is positive. Since the denominator is also positive, it is proved that (55) is negative.

It can be proved with exactly the same procedure that an increase in the tax rate on profits income t_Π will cause a deficit. That is

$$\frac{\partial R}{\partial t_\Pi} = - \Pi \; \frac{1 - [c_W(1 - t_W) + c_\Pi t_W]\,\omega'' - c_\Pi \, \pi''}{1 - m'} \tag{56}$$

will have a negative value. Here $\dfrac{\partial W}{\partial t_\Pi} \Big/ \dfrac{\partial Y}{\partial t_\Pi} = \omega''$, and $\dfrac{\partial \Pi}{\partial t_\Pi} \Big/ \dfrac{\partial Y}{\partial t_\Pi} = \pi''$.

Provided with these, let us now discuss the catalytic effect on an increase in taxation on income from employment. $(\partial R/\partial G)\,\overline{dG}$ is the deficit which arises when government expenditure alone increases by $\overline{dG}$. If government deficit is increased up to $\overline{dR}$, which is the limit to the additional deficit allowed the government, then (60) below will hold. Next, when government expenditure and taxation are increased so that the resulting increase in the deficit reaches the permitted limit, then

$$\overline{dR} = \frac{\partial R}{\partial G} \, dG^* + \frac{\partial R}{\partial t_W} \, dt_W, \tag{57}$$

which means that, when the increase in expenditure is dG^*, taxation has to increase by dt_W. The total effect on the gross national product produced by such dG^* and dt_w is

$$dY^* = \frac{1}{1-\bar{m}} dG^* + \frac{1}{1-m'} (-c_w W) dt_w. \qquad (58)$$

If we eliminate dt_w from (57) and (58) we obtain

$$dY^* = \frac{1}{1-\bar{m}} dG^* - \frac{c_w W}{1-m'} \left[\frac{\overline{dR} - (\partial R/\partial G)\, dG^*}{\partial R/\partial t_w} \right], \qquad (59)$$

which is the overall effect of a mixed policy combining the increase in taxation dt_w with the increase in expenditure dG^*. On the other hand, where a policy is implemented of increasing expenditure alone, with no increase whatever in taxation, a limit will be imposed on this increase by the amount of the permitted deficit, and hence

$$\overline{dR} = \frac{\partial R}{\partial G} \overline{dG}. \qquad (60)$$

That is to say government expenditure can only increase by $\overline{dG}$.

Let us denote by $\overline{dY}$ the increase in the gross national product when a pure increase in expenditure $\overline{dG}$ has taken place. The difference between dY^* and $\overline{dY}$ expresses the surplus effect which may be expected when, with a given permitted deficit $\overline{dR}$, the government improves its income by increasing taxation by dt_w, and therefore is enabled to increase its expenditure by dG^* instead of the pure increase $\overline{dG}$ when there was no increase in taxation. That is, it shows the catalytic effect of an increase in taxation. We now substitute (60) into (59), take

$$\overline{dY} = \frac{1}{1-\bar{m}} \overline{dG} \qquad (61)$$

into account and obtain the difference

$$dY^* - \overline{dY} = \frac{1}{1-\bar{m}} (dG^* - \overline{dG}) - \frac{c_w W}{1-m'} \frac{\partial R/\partial G}{\partial R/\partial t_w} (\overline{dG} - dG^*). \qquad (62)$$

Consequently we can obtain the multiplier of the catalytic effect

$$\frac{dY^* - \overline{dY}}{dG^* - \overline{dG}} = \frac{1}{1-\bar{m}} + \frac{c_w W}{1-m'} \frac{\partial R/\partial G}{\partial R/\partial t_w}. \qquad (63)$$

The first term on the right-hand side of (63) is positive, while the second is negative since, as we have already proved, $\partial R/\partial G > 0$ and $\partial R/\partial t_w < 0$. Therefore, speaking extremely generally, the catalytic

effect can be either positive or negative. However, taking (53) and
(55) into account, we can easily prove that (63) is positive, provided
that $\omega = \omega'$ and $\pi = \pi'$.[20] From their definitions, ω and π are the
rates of distribution to wages and profits of the increase in the
gross national product caused by an increase in government expenditure, while ω' and π' are similar distribution rates obtained when
the rate of taxation on employment has been increased.

We can regard ω' and π' as having determined values. The reason
for this is that an increase in t_W means a decrease in the disposable
incomes of workers; corresponding to this there will be a given
proportional decline in workers' demands for consumer goods —
the proportions being $\partial D_1^W/\partial W', \ldots, \partial D_h^W/\partial W'$. Therefore there
will be a corresponding decrease of $\partial X_1/\partial t_W, \ldots, \partial X_h/\partial t_W$ in the
outputs of goods. Since ω' and π' are weighted averages of wages
and profits per unit of each good with weights of $\partial X_1/\partial t_W, \ldots,$
$\partial X_h/\partial t_W$, that is

$$\omega' = \frac{\sum\limits_{j=1}^{h} \left(\sum\limits_{s=m+1}^{n} p_s a_{sj} \right) \partial X_j/\partial t_W}{\sum\limits_{j=1}^{h} p_j (\partial X_j/\partial t_W)} \quad \text{and}$$

$$\pi' = \frac{\sum\limits_{j=1}^{h} \left(\sum\limits_{s=l+1}^{m} p_s a_{sj} + b_j \right) \partial X_j/\partial t_W}{\sum\limits_{j=1}^{h} p_j (\partial X_j/\partial t_W)}$$

ω' and π' are determined. On the other hand ω and π are not
determined. Since the government can increase its demand for
goods in any way whatsoever, the weights used for calculating ω
and π change according to the way the increase is made. However,
it is always possible for the government to increase its demand for
goods in proportion to $\partial D_1^W/\partial W', \ldots, \partial D_h^W/\partial W'$, and therefore it
is always possible to make $\partial X_1/\partial G, \ldots, \partial X_h/\partial G$ proportional to
$\partial X_1/\partial t_W, \ldots, \partial X_h/\partial t_W$. Consequently, it is possible to make ω
$= \omega'$ and $\pi = \pi'$. In this case the catalytic effect is positive, as we
saw above. Thus, in the case where there is a limit to the increase
in its deficit, it is always possible for the government to achieve a
positive catalytic effect by increasing taxation. That is, it can
achieve a larger multiplier effect on the gross national product
than in the case where there is a simple policy of increasing expenditure within the limits of the permitted increase in its deficit. In a

period of depression the government can make use of this catalytic action up to the point where further increases in taxation are politically impossible.

Since the importance of such a policy seems not to have been correctly understood by members of the Keynesian school, I shall, at the risk of tediousness, describe it again in more concrete form. We assume a fixprice economy which is in under-employment equilibrium. The Chancellor of the Exchequer will probably decide on an increase in the government deficit of a certain size in order to eliminate this unemployment. With this given limit to an increase in the deficit, the government should then decide how to increase the gross national product and what to do in order to achieve a greater increase in output. The available alternatives are: first, a simple increase in public expenditure; second, a reduction in taxation; third, an increase in public expenditure which uses an increase in taxation as a catalyst; and fourth, a reduction in taxation which uses a reduction in public expenditure as a catalyst. (This last can be regarded as the counterpart of the previous one.) Comparing the first and the second alternatives, the effect of the first is the greater,[21+] and comparing the first and the third alternatives, the latter is greater as long as the catalytic effect is positive (which is always possible). When we compare the third and fourth alternatives, we find that when the catalytic effect of the third is positive that of the fourth is negative, and vice versa. That is, it can be proved that, if the catalytic effect of the third alternative is positive (negative) when the government's demands for goods increase while preserving certain proportions, then the catalytic effect of the fourth alternative is negative (positive) when the government's demands for goods decrease keeping those same proportions. Since it is possible to ensure that the catalytic effect of an increase in taxation is always positive, it is always possible to ensure the reverse, which is that the catalytic effect of a diminution in expenditure is negative. Furthermore, since the catalytic effect is probably positive in all cases where taxation is increased, it may be that a positive catalytic effect resulting from a reduction in public expenditure is an impossibility.

Thus when only a given increase in the deficit is permitted, we ought to use an increase in taxation as a catalyst in order to increase the gross national product in an efficient way. However, the policy of an increase in taxation will only be supported when it is advocated by a strong government; so a straightforward policy of increasing public expenditure or reducing taxation may be rec- ommended as a second or third best alternative. Finally, we dealt above only with the case where taxation on income from employ- ment was used as the catalyst, but the catalytic effect of taxation on income from profits can be analysed in exactly the same way.

Equations (59) and (62) are the most general formulae of the multiplier. First, in the case where $dt_w = 0$ (that is where $dG^* = \overline{dG}$), we have $dY^* = \overline{dY}$ from (62). Thus, taking (61) into account, we obtain

$$\frac{dY^*}{dG^*} = \frac{\overline{dY}}{\overline{dG}} = \frac{1}{1 - \overline{m}} .$$ (64)

(64) is the multiplier (the pure expenditure multiplier) in the case where no use was made of the catalytic effect of an increase in taxation. Next, where $\overline{dR} = 0$, that is, where the government is not permitted to increase its deficit and additional expenditure has to be made on the basis of a balanced budget, then $\overline{dG} = 0$ by (60). Consequently we have $\overline{dY} = 0$, and therefore by (63) or by (59)

$$\frac{dY^*}{dG^*} = \frac{1}{1 - \overline{m}} + \frac{c_w W}{1 - m'} \frac{\partial R/\partial G}{\partial R/\partial t_w} .$$ (65)

This formula for the multiplier effect of a balanced budget has the following meaning. In this case, where there is no scope for ad- ditional government deficit expenditure, the government cannot pursue a policy of simply increasing expenditure; it has to pursue an equilibrium or balanced-budget expenditure policy. Therefore it has to increase taxation by an amount which will exactly com- pensate for the deficit arising from its increase in public expenditure, and such an equilibrium expenditure policy will, in fact, mean that it makes use of an increase in taxation as a catalyst. Where the government is able to run an additional deficit, the gross national product can be increased, by using an appropriate increase in tax- ation as a catalyst, by the sum of (61), which is the effect of the pure increase in expenditure corresponding to that deficit, and the catalytic effect. But in the balanced-budget case where the government cannot run an additional deficit, (61) is 0 and there- fore the total effect is the catalytic effect alone. The theory of the multiplier effect of a balanced budget which Haavelmo originated is important because it was the first to grasp the catalytic effect of an increase in taxation in its pure form.

It is assumed in the balanced-budget multiplier (65) that only taxation on income from employment is increased. If the rate of taxation on employment income and that on income from profits were increased proportionally, putting $dt_w/t_w = dt_\Pi/t_\Pi = dt$, we would obtain

$$\overline{dR} = \frac{\partial R}{\partial G} dG^* + \left[\frac{\partial R}{\partial t_w} t_w + \frac{\partial R}{\partial t_\Pi} t_\Pi \right] dt$$

$$dY^* = \frac{1}{1-\overline{m}} dG^* + \left[\frac{1}{1-m'} (-c_w W) t_w + \frac{1}{1-m''} \right.$$
$$\left. (-c_\Pi \Pi) t_\Pi \right] dt$$

in place of (57) and (58). Putting $\overline{dR} = 0$ and eliminating dt from these two equations we have

$$\frac{dY^*}{dG^*} = \frac{1}{1-\overline{m}}$$

$$+ \left[\frac{c_w W t_w}{1-m'} + \frac{c_\Pi \Pi t_\Pi}{1-m''} \right] \frac{\partial R/\partial G}{(\partial R/\partial t_w) t_w + (\partial R/\partial t_\Pi) t_\Pi}.$$

If we assume that in this equation $c_w = c_\Pi$, $t_w = t_\Pi$, $\omega = \omega' = \omega''$, and $\pi = \pi' = \pi''$, then $dY^*/dG^* = 1$. This is the conclusion reached by Haavelmo, but when these assumptions are not fulfilled it is not necessarily possible to reach his conclusion.[22]

F. The full-employment multiplier

We have so far assumed that the economy is in a state of underemployment equilibrium. Underemployment is as shown in the inequalities (8) and (9); that is, with respect to the services of capital goods the quantity used is less than the existing total, and with respect to labour the demand is less than the supply. The actual stock of capital goods is a fixed quantity which is hard to alter and which is determined by economic activity in the past. However, the quantity of labour supplied is a variable, since that part which the worker voluntarily decides not to supply depends on prices and wages. (The quantity of labour supplied is what remains of the existing quantity of labour — defined as the quantity available when all workers provide all the labour they have at their command — after subtracting the quantity forgone for the sake of leisure, etc.)

Now in an economy where certain capital services or certain kinds of labour are fully employed (we need not assume all capital services and labour to be so), additional expenditure by the government will give rise to an excess demand for them, unless prices and wages are altered. Such an excess demand can probably be eliminated taking one of the following two contrasting courses.

The first is a method of eliminating excess demand by means of movements in relative prices; full employment is restored to those producer goods for which there was an excess demand by altering the relative prices of goods. Take, for example, the case where an excess demand has arisen for a certain kind of labour. There will be an increase in the wage rate for that labour, and as a result workers will come to supply additional labour, at the expense of the time which they formerly devoted to leisure, etc. In addition, firms will economise on that kind of labour which is now comparatively high priced, and in these two ways the excess demand for labour will be eliminated. In order to be able to economise on the labour in question, firms will probably have to make more use of other kinds of labour or the services of capital. It may also be that, because the labour for which there is an excess demand has risen in price, the supply of other kinds of labour will decrease. (For example, if the salaries of mathematical economists increase, it may be that mathematicians will convert themselves into mathematical economists so that the supply of mathematicians will fall.) There will be no problem when those other kinds of labour or capital services whose demand (or supply) increases (or diminishes) are in a state of underemployment; but when they are not, there arises an excess demand for them, and there are, as a result, fresh price movements. These price movements may then spread outwards successively. However, when the repercussions have finally ceased, a situation will arise where there is no excess demand for labour or the services of capital.

The second method of eliminating excess demand is one with fixed relative prices. Assume here that the government has decided to increase public expenditure by ΔG, and that as a result the government's demand for goods has increased by $\Delta F_1, \ldots, \Delta F_l$. When this increase in demand produces an excess demand for certain kinds of labour and capital services, then first of all their prices will probably rise. However, there is also a proportionate rise in the prices of other kinds of labour and capital goods, such as will keep relative prices unchanged, then such a proportionate rise in the prices of all factors of production will raise the prices of products in proportion with the rise in production costs.

Now if all prices rise in proportion to the rate of increase in government expenditure, then after the price rise the government will only be able to buy out of its increased expenditure the same quantity of goods which it was able to buy before. Thus ΔF_1, ..., ΔF_l will be 0 after the increase in prices, and the pressure of government demand on production will cease. But product prices and producer good prices will have risen proportionately across the board. This proportionate increase will produce no technological substitution among products and producer goods, so that input coefficients will remain unchanged. Therefore the same quantities of factors of production will be necessary in order to produce the same volume of products before and after the increase in prices. Furthermore, if under a given level of employment the prices of products and those of production services show a proportionate increase, employment income and profits income will increase in the same proportion as prices. Since we may assume the demand function of workers D_i^W and that of capitalists D_i^K to be homogeneous functions of degree zero of prices and their respective incomes, neither demand will change at all as long as employment remains unchanged.[23+]

Where the prices of goods all increase in proportion with government expenditure in this fashion, there is no pressure of government demand on output, the same level of production takes place as before, employment is unchanged and consumption too is unchanged. There has simply been a nominal rise in the price of goods and services, and no real change whatsoever in the economy. That is, the multiplier effect of an increase in government expenditure on the real gross national product is zero. Keynes considered that this genuinely inflationary situation would only arise when a high degree of full employment was reached, and that until that time excess demand would be eliminated by the first method outlined above — that is by changes in relative prices. Thus, at the stage where full employment of all producer goods is established, and where, moreover, even that part of labour formerly withheld voluntarily for the sake of leisure and so on is almost all employed, it is no longer possible to meet the deficiency caused by an excess demand by contriving an increase in the supply of producer goods by altering relative prices. Again, even when attempts are made to economise on producer goods, those producer goods which ought to be substituted are already fully employed, and hence a rise occurs in the prices of all goods, so that, conversely, relative prices remain unchanged and genuine inflation occurs. It is, of course, possible to think of a transitional state between an underemployment situation with fixed (or more-or-less fixed) prices and a situation where there is a high degree of full employment with prices changing proportionately, in which the full employment which materialises in the markets for some factors is transmitted, with a movement in relative prices, to a larger number of factor markets, with the result that complete full employment gets closer and closer. Thus the multiplier theory discussed as far as the previous section is perfectly applicable where employment is less than full, but the multiplier effect cannot appear in its pure form during the transitional stage because of changes in relative prices. At complete full employment there is no real multiplier effect because of inflation.

However, it is no cause for concern that no real multiplier effect follows an increase in public expenditure in a state of full employment. Since the multiplier effect was originally employed to eliminate unemployment, there is no reason for its use when there is already full employment. The serious state of affairs is one where a proportionate increase in all prices occurs before full employment is achieved, and it is perfectly possible for this to happen. For example, the price of a certain kind of labour will probably rise if there is a further increase in government expenditure when that kind of labour is already fully employed. When this happens workers supplying kinds of labour for which there is no excess demand will adhere to those relative wages which have historically and by custom come to be accepted, and will also insist on a wage increase of the same proportion. If this happens with all kinds of labour, firms will raise prices in order to compensate for the rise in costs, and an overall increase in prices is likely to occur even though all kinds of labour are not yet fully employed. Thus there will be no real effect on the gross national product as the result of an increase in public expenditure because of the increase in prices, and we shall have arrived at a state of affairs where remaining unemployment is not amenable to remedy by public-expenditure policy.

This failure of Keynesian policy can occur at an even earlier stage. Let us here assume a serious depression where there is unemployment of every kind of labour. The government will probably plan an increase in public expenditure which ought to break the depression. The trade unions, which have learned sufficient economic theory, will probably conclude that where they cause an increase in wages at a rate which is equal to the increase in public expenditure, the multiplier effect will not be negative but zero, so that there will be no loss in existing employment. Thus wage increases will be demanded even in slumps, and when these are fully (or partly) achieved, the employment-creating effect of an increase in government expenditure will be rendered completely (or partly) nugatory. Consequently, the government will once again have to increase its expenditure, and prices and wages will once again rise correspondingly. Due to this vicious circle, increase in government expenditure and inflation will co-exist even where there is unemployment, and Keynesian policy will be ineffective for creating employment. It will simply become a policy for creating inflation.

We must give warning that Keynesian policy may thus be living out its tragic last days. The cure for tuberculosis kills some of the tuberculosis bacteria, while making the surviving ones stronger and immune to that cure, so that eventually a new cure is required. In the same way it is perfectly possible that Keynesian policy will change the problem of unemployment into one which is more difficult to solve. When Keynesian policy ceases to be a remedy for unemployment, our society will have to face a new test.

10
Unemployed and the dual structure of the economy

A. Disguised unemployment in Japan

Keynes in his *General Theory* classified unemployment into voluntary and involuntary unemployment. He analysed the cases in which involuntary unemployment would arise and the problem of how to eliminate it. Thus in Keynes' theory workers are either employed or unemployed. However, 'employment' and 'unemployment' are not in fact clearly separable; there is between the two an intermediate state where there is a mixed form which is regarded ostensibly as 'employment', but which ought essentially to be treated as unemployment. That is, we have the state of affairs known as latent or disguised unemployment. In a country which has an unemployment insurance system, workers can live on this insurance despite being unemployed; but in countries where society is poor in this sense, so long as there is work available the worker must take it, even though the wage may be incomparably lower than in the employment which he has lost. Therefore, if there is the opportunity for a worker to find employment for lower wages when he is dismissed from his original employment, he will not become one of the completely unemployed but will resign himself to the lower wage. But the employment he has acquired is latent or disguised unemployment. This being so, in what cases will disguised unemployment occur and how can it be eliminated? The purpose of the theoretical discussion which follows is the extension of Keynesian employment theory to enable it to analyse disguised unemployment.

Disguised unemployment does not only take the residual form exhibited by street match-sellers and the blackmarket ticket-touts outside a baseball stadium; it can occur on a larger scale and in more organised forms. Therefore we ought not to explain the phenomenon by means of the ostensible causes, such as the

absence of a system of unemployment insurance; there are cases
where it must be analysed fundamentally with resort to historical
or socio-economic theory as a phenomenon intrinsic to the
national economy. Japan is such a case. In March 1952 those
employed in Japan numbered 35,560,000, while those unemployed
were 530,000; but it is said that disguised unemployed at that time
numbered 6,700,000, or 19% of all those employed. It is difficult
to consider disguised unemployment on such a large scale as a
residual or as the result of temporary causes. As I stated on pp.
15—24 it can be thought of as the inevitable result of the dual
structure of the Japanese economy.

Since a free market for labour exists in the kind of competitive
society which is premised by economic theory, identical wages are
paid to homogeneous units of labour, while on the other hand, as
a result of competition among firms, the marginal productivity of
labour is made equal in all firms. The wage which is established in
the labour market is equal to this uniform marginal product.
However, the modern state built by the Meiji revolutionaries was
not of this simple construction. The Japan handed on to them by
the Edo (Tokugawa) government was a large country which it was
beyond their power to modernise at a stroke. They did not, however, adopt a plan requiring patience and slow modernisation;
they adopted a policy of creating a brand new 'modern Japan'
within the existing economy, and of quickly enlarging this core.
'Modern Japan', as a team playing for the whole of Japan, had to
be made especially strong. For it to be so, it was distinguished from
'premodern Japan' and a thorough preferential policy was adopted
towards it, so that it achieved an amazing rate of growth at the
expense of 'premodern Japan'. This process is normally indicated
by Marxist scholars as 'the criminal history of monopoly-capitalism
under a system of semi-feudal absolutism'. But since it was the
intelligentsia who controlled 'modern Japan', it can be thought of
as a process of expropriation by the intelligentsia directed against
the people in general. The offences complained of by Marxist
scholars show how cruel and merciless was the exploitation
undertaken by the intelligentsia.

'Premodern Japan' was differentiated from 'modern Japan' and
both Japans had to have their own labour markets. However, the
two were not on an equal footing. Marginal productivity theory
applied only to 'modern Japan', and the unemployed who could

find no work in 'modern Japan' descended on 'premodern Japan'.[1+] These people had to live. They had to be supported by parents, relatives or friends. Wages in 'premodern Japan' were thus fixed at an incomparably lower level than those of 'modern Japan'. The greater part of disguised unemployment in Japan arose from the fact that 'modern Japan' charged 'premodern Japan' with the role of being a reservoir of the disguised unemployed. This was a deliberate policy on the part of the ruling class.

This being so, what then was the range of variation in wages between 'modern' and 'premodern' Japan? For simplicity let us first of all think of 'modern Japan' as comprising the industrial sector only, and of 'premodern Japan' as the agricultural sector only. Let us then compare the range of variation between industrial and agricultural wages in Japan with the ranges in other countries. First, the monthly wages of permanent and seasonal agricultural workers in the United States in 1961 were 195 dollars, which was less than 49% of the 400 dollars earned monthly by workers in the manufacturing sector in that year. A difference of more or less the same size can be seen to have existed between agriculture and manufacturing in Japan too. There are exceptional cases, such as those of Cyprus and South Korea in the latter half of the 1950s, where the difference favoured agricultural workers; but as a rule they were at a disadvantage, and in the United States, Mexico, Peru, France, Norway, India, Japan, Finland, etc., agricultural wages were less than half the wages of industrial workers.[2] Of course, when we take into account such factors as differences in prices between the city and the agricultural village, the difference in the skills required of industrial and agricultural workers, pressure from trade unions and so on, it is natural for there to be a difference between the actual average wage in the agricultural sector and that of the industrial sector; nominal wages in agriculture cannot normally match those in industry.

However, in socialist countries like Bulgaria, Czechoslovakia, Hungary, Yugoslavia, etc., which are regarded as deliberately enforcing equal wages for equal work, and in capitalist countries such as Sweden, the United Kingdom, New Zealand, etc., where those regularly *employed* in agriculture form a high proportion of those actually engaged in agriculture, so that the proportion of unpaid family labour is low, agricultural wages are in the range 70–80% of industrial wages. When we take this into account, it must be that in countries where agricultural wages are less than 50% of industrial wages, workers in agriculture are being forced to accept wages which are less than normal.

We have so far been concerned with wage differentials between industry as a whole and agriculture. However, in Japan's case there are wage differentials within industry itself; there is, indeed, a very marked range of variation in wages between industries and between firms of different sizes (average wages in small-scale enterprises are less than half the wages in large-scale enterprises). In Japan small-scale enterprises are especially numerous in industries such as civil engineering and construction, in commerce and the service industry, in timber and sawmilling and the wood-products industries, and in quarrying, ceramics, glass and so on. There are almost no small-scale enterprises in the chemical and chemical-products industries, in the iron, steel and non-ferrous metals industries, or in the electric power industry. As a result in 1960, marked variations arise according to industry.[3+] For example, in 1960 average wages in timber and sawmilling and the wood-products industries were less than half of those in the electric power industry; they were also roughly half of those in enterprises employing more than 1000 people in the timber and sawmilling and wood-products industries. Therefore, there is no marked wage differential if we look only at large-scale enterprises. This means that the extent to which 'modern Japan' and 'premodern Japan' are intermingled varies according to the industry, that wage differentials between industries chiefly reflect differences in the degree of 'modernisation' achieved by industries, and that within the 'borders' of both 'modern Japan' and 'premodern Japan' wage differentials between enterprises are not large.

Even though high wages are welcomed by the workers of 'modern Japan', the capitalists of 'modern Japan' naturally prefer low wages, and hence it is surprising that very large wage differentials have continued to exist over the hundred years or so since the Meiji Revolution. This is something which cannot be explained completely by economic theory. But when we take into account Japan's sociological structure and her psycho-historical environment, such a phenomenon will not necessarily seem odd. That is to say, in Japan, where consideration of the 'whole' has always taken precedence over that of the individual, individualism has consistently been a vice, and therefore the entrepreneurs of 'modern Japan' would not employ workers who had deserted their masters and were attempting to leave the 'premodern' for the 'modern' sector. This was so even if these workers offered to work for very low wages. First, they were regarded as traitors to their masters and colleagues, and the entrepreneurs of 'modern Japan' did not want to betray their own workers by employing such people at low wages. Furthermore, the lifetime employment system and the system of promotion according to seniority are predominant in Japan. These extremely 'Japanese' systems have been evolved chiefly to preserve peace within the enterprise. The Japanese do not see competition in society as competition between individuals, as do Europeans and Americans. They always regard competition as being between groups — the competing unit being the family, the enterprise, the school or even the nation. Hence to the leader of the group, peace and harmony within the group are of paramount importance. The joy of victory is founded on the personal satisfaction which comes from sacrificing oneself for the sake of victory for one's beloved group. If a Japanese were to act in Japan with the same spirit as a westerner — whether it be in 'modern' or 'premodern Japan' — his every act would be regarded as a challenge to society and he would have no choice but to isolate himself as a lone wolf in an uninhabited wilderness.

Rationalisation in the western sense did not occur in Japan; but since there were many workers in 'premodern Japan' prepared to work for low wages, an attempt by the enterprises of 'modern Japan' to use them in some sense rationally was to be expected. In fact firms in the 'modern' sector controlled many firms in the 'premodern' sector by using them as subcontractors, and 'modern Japan' took full advantage of the benefits of low wages through this subcontracting system. Moreover, the managers and workers of these subcontracting firms were not citizens of 'modern Japan'. In a recession they were all discarded. By having subcontracting firms under their control, 'modern' firms were cushioned against the effects of a recession, and therefore the high wages paid in 'modern Japan' could be rationalised as a kind of cost of maintaining the subcontracting system, or as an insurance payment against recessions and depression.

However, as we have already observed (chapter 10 note 3), wage differentials between industries and between firms have recently begun to be eliminated. Correspondingly, disguised unemployment is also being reduced. This means that the dual structure so firmly embedded in the Japanese economy since the Meiji revolution is weakening, and that western principles of competition are at last beginning to be established in Japan. Why has Japan finally been compelled to go through this change in its physical constitution? In the most conventional explanation the reason advanced is that, because of the rapid growth which occurred after 1955, the labour market became permanently somewhat tighter. I myself think that the collapse of the intelligentsia in Japan ought to be cited as an additional cause and one which operates at a deeper level. After the second World War the education system was altered under the direction of the occupying forces. As a result, universities were set up without due foresight, so that at present the number of university students has reached roughly 1,800,000. This number is about eight times larger than Japan's standing army in the prewar period, and a further important fact is that no discipline is imposed on these students, so that they are able to live more or less as they wish for four years. I think that Japan can be proud of her junior, middle and high schools — both in their quality and quantity; but the disciplined attitude to life and the intellectual appetite instilled in pupils up till the time they leave high school is lost in the four years at university, and substantial numbers of students leave the university as persons whose intellects are, comparatively, inferior to those of their high-school days. The extent of this frightening ruination ought to be compared with Japan's apocalyptic industrial pollution.

As a result, what is occuring is the collapse of the intelligentsia. This is the inevitable result of the mass production of members of the intelligentsia without any control over their quality. They are now no longer a scarce good, and their quality is rapidly declining. They can no longer dream of a brilliant future as the ruling class. Many of them, in despair, have to queue impatiently for four years for a ticket to a life which is almost without meaning. Entrepreneurs, too, have finally come to realise that, when they are choosing their successors, a more important criterion is the substance (the capabilities of the individual) and not the form (as represented by the name of the university from which the individual comes). When they come to choose workers, and middle management too, they are becoming aware that the contribution made to the enterprise by unsophisticated high-school leavers is greater than that of university graduates who have lost their disciplined attitude to life. Thus in recent times, western individualism and the competitive principle have begun to operate in Japan. The conditions for the collapse of the system of control by the intelligentsia, which has continued throughout the 100 years since the Meiji Revolution, have finally been brought about in both the demand and supply of labour.

B. A Keynesian economy which includes agriculture

Let us think of the Japanese economy as being made up of the two sectors 'industry' and 'agriculture', in order that we may analyse theoretically the disguised unemployment which exists in Japan. We assume that the industrial sector comprises only firms and that there are no household enterprises; conversely, the agricultural sector is made up entirely of household enterprises and there are no firms as such. By household enterprises we mean producing units of the kind where the firm and the household are not differentiated, and whose activity is, as in the case of tenant and owner-farmers and others, the production of goods with the factors which they themselves own as the chief means of production, the sale of these products and the purchasing of the necessities of life with the proceeds.

In what follows we shall define disguised unemployment in the following way. If a worker in the agricultural sector earns real wages which are less than those of a worker in the industrial sector whose capacities are exactly the same, then we say that he is in disguised unemployment, even though he is actually employed.[4+] This definition is a complete parallel of the normal definition, according to which a worker is said to be in disguised unemployment if the income from his new employment is less than he received from the employment in which he had previously been engaged.[5] If, in this definition, we make agriculture his new place of employment and industry his previous place of employment, we arrive at our definition. The disguised unemployed can be divided into two broad groups. The first are in disguised unemployment because their working hours are short. The second are in disguised unemployment because their real wage rates, or the unit price of labour, is relatively low. In practice the two types co-exist, but in what follows I shall analyse only the second. Furthermore, for the sake of simplicity, I shall assume that workers in the same industry are paid identical wages, and that there is a difference only between industries — that is between agriculture and industry (the agricultural-wage—industrial-wage differential).

Let us next discuss the problem of how to measure the quantity of disguised unemployment. Now we are assuming that wages differ between our two industries, and that workers in the two industries have exactly the same capacities. Here all those employed in the industry with the lower wage rates are in disguised unemployment, but we ought not to use this total as a measure of the size of disguised unemployment. The reason for this is that, even if only a part of the disguised unemployed were eliminated, the quantity of output of that industry would decline. As a result the prices of the products of that industry would rise, the wage rate paid would increase, and the number of disguised unemployed would reach zero, since the wage in that industry would no longer be relatively low. Therefore, we measure the size of disguised unemployment by subtracting from the actual number of workers employed the number that would be employed if disguised unemployment did not exist (that is the number of workers employed if inter-industry wage differentials did not exist — hereafter called those 'normally' employed).

The net outputs of agriculture and industry will probably be disposed of in the following manner.[6+] (a) Part of the net product of agriculture will be sold to industry as raw materials, and the remainder will be appropriated for the consumption of non-farm households. (b) Part of the net output of industry will be sold to farmers, another part to non-farm households, and the remainder allocated for investment. Since it is only in equilibrium that the whole of the net product is demanded without anything left over, (a) states the equilibrium condition for agriculture, and (b) that for industry.

Let us write the above equilibrium conditions with symbols in the form of an equation. We show agriculture by A, industry by B and non-farm households by C. The net output of agriculture, x_A, is equal to the sum of industry's demand x_{AB} and the demand of non-farm households x_{AC}. The net output of industry x_B is the sum of farmers' demand x_{BA}, non-farm households' demand x_{BC} and investment I. Consequently, we can write the equilibrium conditions as

$$x_A = x_{AB} + x_{AC} \tag{1}$$

$$x_B = x_{BA} + x_{BC} + I. \tag{2}$$

Following the classical economists, let us take agricultural products as the numéraire. We show the price of industrial products and the wages of workers in industry, both of which are expressed in terms of agricultural products, as p and w respectively. The following assumptions are then not necessarily unrealistic ones. (i) The volume of farmers' demand for industrial products x_{BA} is positively proportional to farmers' purchasing power — that is to the real value x_A/p for farmers' net product. (ii) The demand by the industrial sector for agricultural products (as raw materials) x_{AB}, is positively proportional to the value of the net product of industry px_B. (iii) Non-farm households' demand for agricultural products x_{AC} is positively proportional to the total value of the real wages of workers in industry wN_B (N_B shows the number of workers employed in industry). (iv) The volume of non-farm households' demand for industrial products x_{BC} is positively proportional to the total of real wages wN_B/p in terms of industrial products.[7] We further assume there is sufficient idle capital in the industrial sector; that is, our economy is of a Keynesian type with surplus capital. Under this assumption, capital is not the limiting factor on industrial output, and consequently x_B, which is the physical volume of the net product of industry, can be thought of as a function of the number of workers employed (in industry) alone — the production function. On the other hand the size of the net product of agriculture, x_A, is an increasing function of the volume of agricultural labour N_A alone, as long as there is land which is idle. For the sake of simplicity, we assume that the net product of agriculture becomes inelastic as soon as there is no idle land. We also assume that until idle land is all fully used up, all land is used with a fixed degree of intensity.

With these premises let us consider the equilibrium conditions for agriculture and industry, (1) and (2) above. Let us assume that labour in agriculture and employment in industry are respectively determined at some or other quantity. This having been done, the physical quantities of the net outputs of agriculture and industry will be determined technically through the production functions corresponding to these values. But if we assume that the price of the net product of industry p, and the value of one unit of industrial labour w (the wage rate) are somehow or other already decided upon, then by our previous assumptions (i) to (iv) farmers' demand for industrial products, industry's demand for agricultural products, and non-farm households' demands both for agricultural and industrial products are all determined. If these satisfy the two conditions that the sum of industry's demand for agricultural products and non-farm households' demand for agricultural products equals the net product of agriculture, and that the total sum of farmers' demand for industrial products and non-farm households' demand for industrial products and investment (whose size we assume is already somehow or other exogenously determined) equals the net product of industry, then equilibrium conditions (1) and (2) are satisfied. Consequently, our economy is in equilibrium with these given quantities of agricultural labour and employment in industry. If they do not hold, the economy is not in equilibrium with these quantities, and until values such as will satisfy (1) and (2) are arrived at, the volume of labour in agriculture and employment in industry will change. That is to say, the equilibrium conditions determine the quantity of labour engaged in agriculture and the volume of employment in industry.

In the above we thought of the price of industrial products p and industrial wage rate w, both of which were expressed in terms of agricultural products, as taking on arbitrary given values. We continue to take agricultural products as the numéraire, so that their price is fixed at 1 throughout. Let us then consider the wage rate which is determined so as to equal the value of agricultural output per unit of agricultural labour x_A/N_A and call it the 'normal' wage rate. That is to say, the condition for the 'normal' wage rate is $w = x_A/N_A$. As the right-hand side of this equation represents the productivity of agricultural labour, or its value, the value of agricultural labour is the same as that of industrial labour when the industrial wage rate is 'normal'. Consequently, it makes no difference to the worker whether he is employed in the industrial sector or whether he is engaged in agriculture. Next we call the 'normal' wage rate divided by the marginal product in industry the 'normal' price of industrial products. (Therefore the marginal productivity of industrial labour is equal to the ratio of the 'normal' wage rate to the 'normal' price of industrial products.) The volume of agricultural labour and the volume of industrial employment which satisfy equilibrium conditions (1) and (2) when the 'normal' price and wage rate prevail, are called the 'normal' quantity of agricultural labour and the 'normal' volume of industrial employment respectively.

Taking the demand functions (i) to (iv) into account, we can write the equilibrium conditions (1) and (2) as

$$x_A = a_{AB}(px_B) + a_{AC}(wN_B), \qquad (3)$$

$$x_B = a_{BA}(x_A/p) \qquad\quad + a_{BC}(wN_B/p) + I, \qquad (4)$$

where a_{AB}, a_{AC} etc. are positive coefficients of the demand functions. Next let $g_A(N_A)$ be the agricultural production function and $g_B(N_B)$ the production function of industry; we have

$$x_A = g_A(N_A), \qquad (5)$$

$$x_B = g_B(N_B). \qquad (6)$$

The 'normal' value relationships are then given by

$$w = g_A(N_A)/N_A, \qquad (7)$$

$$w = pg_B'(N_B). \qquad (8)$$

Hence by solving (3)–(8), the 'normal' quantity of agricultural labour and the 'normal' volume of industrial employment are determined as functions of investment I.

However, under actual market prices the industrial wage rate is not necessarily at its 'normal' value, and consequently the value of one unit of agricultural labour is not necessarily equal to the value of one unit of industrial labour. At what levels will the quantity of agricultural labour and the volume of industrial employment be fixed when the industrial wage rate is 'non-normal'?

Since, by assumption, the industrial wage rate is 'non-normal', (7) will not hold. However, as long as we accept that the industrial sector operates according to the principle of maximising profits, equation (8), which is the statement of the marginal value productivity being equal to the wage rate, will certainly be true, and hence the relationship

$$wN_B/p = g_B'(N_B)N_B \qquad (9)$$

will always hold. Now despite the fact that industrial wage rates are 'non-normal', let us for the time being assume that the volume of employment in the industrial sector is 'normal'. If the volume of employment is once fixed at its 'normal' value, the volume of industrial output x_B, and the real purchasing power of industrial workers wN_B/p, are fixed by the production function (6) and by relationship (9) respectively at their corresponding 'normal' levels (whether or not the wage rate is 'normal'). Thus the supply of industrial products and the demand for them from non-farm households take on 'normal' values, so that what remains after this demand (as well as investment demand) has been satisfied is exactly sufficient to satisfy the 'normal' demand from agriculture. Hence farmers' purchasing power x_A/p must be 'normal'. It is thus seen that if the purchasing power of farmers is 'normal' when the volume of industrial employment is normal, equilibrium condition (4) is satisfied.

However, if the industrial wage rate w is above 'normal' (or below) when N_B is 'normal', we know from (8) that price p will be above (or below) 'normal' in proportion to the deviation of w from 'normal'. If p is above (or below) 'normal', x_A will also be above (below) 'normal'. (If this is not so x_A/p cannot be 'normal'.) That is, where the industrial wage rate is above (or below) 'normal' the net physical product of farmers will be above (or below) 'normal', and the volume of agricultural labour will be correspondingly above (or below) 'normal'. Such a 'non-normal' agricultural output will, under 'non-normal' prices and wage rates, satisfy another equilibrium condition (3). (In (3) x_B, N_B are 'normal' values, while w, p, x_A are 'non-normal' values in proportion to their 'normal' values.)

We may draw the following conclusions from the above. (*a*) The volume of employment in the industrial sector is always 'normal' regardless of the size of the wage rate w. That is to say, it is inelastic with respect to the wage rate w which is expressed in terms of agricultural products. It is only elastic with respect to the real wage rate w/p, which is expressed in terms of industrial products, and the quantity of investment. (*b*) If the industrial wage rate w, expressed in terms of agricultural products, is above (below) 'normal' (that is, if the price of agricultural products expressed in terms of industrial labour is below (above) 'normal'), then the volume of agricultural labour is above (below) 'normal'.

Provided with these results we are now able to tackle the problem of disguised unemployment.[8] We continue to assume (i) that the quantity of investment is exogenously determined, and (ii) that the statement of marginal productivity (8) applies to the industrial sector. The results (*a*) and (*b*) above then hold true, so that the volume of employment in the industrial sector is fixed at a 'normal' level in any case, while the quantity of agricultural labour is 'normal' only if the industrial wage rate is set at a 'normal' level. If the sum of the 'normal' employment in the industrial sector and the 'normal' quantity of agricultural labour exactly equals the number of those seeking employment, there will be full employment in the economy and this state of affairs will be maintained.[9+] However, if the equality is violated and the sum is less than the numbers seeking employment, unemployment will appear. As long as there is idle land, or as long as land can be used more intensively, these unemployed workers will combine with land to produce agricultural products and attempt to obtain a livelihood by so doing. The volume of agricultural output will rise above 'normal', and as a result its relative price will decline compared with other goods (industrial products and labour). Consequently, the industrial wage rate and the prices of industrial products, both of which are expressed in terms of agricultural products, will rise above 'normal'.

This rise in price and the wage rate will increase the purchasing power over agricultural goods of industry and non-farm households, and the demand for these products will rise above 'normal' and thus meet the above 'normal' level of supply. Thus a part of the unemployed will be absorbed as agricultural labour; but because the industrial wage rate expressed in terms of agricultural products is now above 'normal', the value of one unit of agricultural labour will become relatively low vis-á-vis that of one unit of industrial labour. Had we maintained the equality of these values, workers could not have been absorbed in agriculture in this fashion; they would instead probably have remained unemployed. It is only by being satisfied with an income which is less than that of industrial workers that they are able to earn a living at all in the agricultural sector, and hence, although they are 'employed', it is in fact disguised or latent unemployment. That is, when actual employment in agriculture exceeds 'normal' employment, the difference between the two gives the size of disguised unemployment.

Thus, when the relative price of agricultural products and consequently the industrial wage rate w are flexible, those who could not be employed in industry will, as long as land is available to them, be absorbed into agriculture in the form of disguised unemployment. Therefore, in an economy with a sufficient area of land, all the unemployed will be absorbed into agriculture as disguised unemployed, and open — that is revealed — unemployment will not exist. If, in such an economy, there were to be revealed unemployment, it would be the result of inflexibility in the relative price of agricultural products. In contrast to this, the quantity of labour which can be absorbed as the disguised unemployed is small when land is in limited supply. Hence, even when the relative price of agricultural products is flexible, there can still be revealed unemployment.

Finally, where the sum of the 'normal' volume of employment in industry and the 'normal' quantity of farm labour exceeds the total of those seeking employment, the numbers left after subtracting those employed in the industrial sector from the total seeking employment will be less than the 'normal' quantity of agricultural labour. If only this quantity of labour engages in agriculture, the relative price of agricultural products will rise above 'normal'. Therefore, in this case, the value of one unit of agricultural labour will exceed that of one unit of industrial labour, so that the industrial wage rate w is fixed at a lower level than agricultural income per man. The same will occur when the 'normal' volume of agricultural labour exceeds the maximum limit to the amount of labour which can be absorbed by the available land.

C. Keynesian policy and disguised unemployment

As I have already explained, the core of Keynesian policy is to increase effective demand by increasing investment, and thereby to increase production and employment and decrease unemployment. It goes without saying that a policy of this kind was conceived of on the presumption of an economic system which did not include agriculture.[10] Thus, the question is, what effect will a Keynesian policy of increasing investment have in the case where there is an agricultural sector which can absorb the unemployed as disguised unemployed?

Before addressing ourselves to this problem, some preparatory analysis is necessary. First, we discovered in the previous section that the quantity of labour engaged in agriculture and the volume of employment in industry will be fixed at values which satisfy the equilibrium conditions (1) and (2). Putting it the other way around, this means that we have made the implicit assumption that there is inherent in our system a mechanism whereby, if the amount of labour in agriculture and the volume of employment in industry do not satisfy the equilibrium conditions, they will be changed until finally they are made to attain values which satisfy these conditions. This being so, what conditions must our system in fact satisfy in order to have such a mechanism incorporated in it?[11]

First, for convenience of explanation, let us divide both sides of the equilibrium condition (3) by p and write it as

$$\frac{x_A}{p} = a_{AB}x_B + a_{AC}\frac{w}{p}N_B. \qquad (3')$$

As explained in the previous section, if the volume of investment is given, the volume of 'normal' industrial employment will be correspondingly determined. If the volume of industrial employment is above 'normal', the volume of industrial output x_B will also be above normal and hence the demand for agricultural products as industrial raw materials (the first term in the right-hand side of $(3')$) will also be above 'normal'. Taking (9) into account, whether or not wN_B/p will increase will depend on the elasticity of the marginal productivity curve for labour in the industrial sector. If this is less than unity, wN_B/p will be above 'normal' when the volume of industrial employment is above 'normal', and consequently the demand for agricultural products of non-agricultural households will be above 'normal'. (However, when the elasticity of the marginal productivity curve for labour in the industrial sector is greater than unity, the demand for agricultural products by non-farm households will be below 'normal' when the volume of industrial employment is above 'normal'.) Therefore, it is possible for the total demand for agricultural products (the right-hand side of $(3')$) to be above 'normal'. Farmers' net output, which is expressed in terms of industrial products (the left-hand side of $(3')$), must be either above or below 'normal' according to whether the total demand is above or below 'normal'. If this net output is above 'normal', farmers' demand for industrial products (the first term in the right-hand side of (4)) will be above 'normal'. On the other hand, a level of industrial employment which is above 'normal' will cause the demand for industrial products of non-farm households (the second term in the right-hand side of (4)) to be either above or below 'normal'. Therefore, it is possible for the total demand for industrial products also to be above 'normal'.

But, if the total demand thus determined falls short of the above-'normal' quantity of industrial products produced by the above-'normal' number of industrial employees, excess supply will arise in the industrial sector. If this happens entrepreneurs are likely to attempt to reduce output. Thus the volume of employment in the industrial sector will decline in the direction of its 'normal' value. That is, there is in fact an equilibrating mechanism within our system. I shall assume below that this is the case; that is, that the stability condition whereby an excess supply will appear in the industrial sector when the volume of industrial employment is above 'normal' is satisfied.

If we now solve the equilibrium conditions (3') and (4) with respect to the total demand for industrial products x_B, we have

$$x_B = \frac{a_{BA}\,a_{AC} + a_{BC}}{1 - a_{BA}\,a_{AB}}\frac{w}{p}\,N_B + \frac{1}{1 - a_{BA}\,a_{AB}}\,I \qquad (10)$$

If we take (9) into account and differentiate the right-hand side of (10) with respect to N_B, then we have

$$\frac{a_{BA}\,a_{AC} + a_{BC}}{1 - a_{BA}\,a_{AB}}\,(g'_B\,(N_B) + g''_B\,(N_B)N_B). \qquad (11)$$

On the other hand, according to the production function the slope of the supply curve is

$$g'_B\,(N_B). \qquad (11')$$

Since marginal productivity is diminishing, $g''_B\,(N_B)$ in (11) has a negative value. Thus if

$$\frac{a_{BA}\,a_{AC} + a_{BC}}{1 - a_{BA}\,a_{AB}} < 1, \qquad (12)$$

the slope of the demand curve (11) is less than the slope of the supply curve (11'), and an increase in the volume of industrial employment which takes the latter above normal will produce an excess supply of industrial products.

(12) is a sufficient condition for stability. There is no *a priori* reason why this condition should be fulfilled, but actual values of the coefficients a will almost certainly satisfy (12). For example, let us take workers as spending 40% of their incomes on agricultural products and 60% on industrial products (a_{AC} is 0.4, a_{BC} is 0.6). Even if industry assigns 30% of its net output to the purchase

of agricultural products as raw materials (a_{AB} is 0.3), and even if agriculture allots 40% of its net output to the purchase of industrial goods (a_{BA} is 0.4), the left-hand side of (10) is 0.86 which is less than 1. Besides this, if we take into account the fact that (12) is a sufficient though not a necessary condition for stability — that is that even though the left-hand side of (12) may be greater than one there still remains the possibility of stability — then we ought to conclude that instability is confined to exceedingly special and extreme cases.

On these premises let us now consider how the 'normal' volume of industrial employment will change when the volume of investment increases. Since we are assuming that the stability condition is satisfied, then before the increase in investment an excess supply of industrial products will arise, as a result of a level of industrial employment which is above the equilibrium level. Conversely, an excess demand for industrial products will arise as a result of a level of industrial employment which is below the equilibrium level. Since an increase in the volume of investment will mean an increase in the demand for industrial products, the supply of industrial products must be more than able to satisfy the demands of agriculture, non-agricultural households and the old investment demand, for this additional demand to be satisfied. That is, there has to be an excess supply of industrial products over the total demand for them associated with the old volume of investment. This is only possible if industrial employment is greater than the old 'normal' volume of industrial employment. Thus an increase in investment will produce an increase in 'normal' industrial employment, and consequently an increase in the actual volume of industrial employment.

The increase in the output of industrial products induced by a one unit increase in investment, i.e. dx_B/dI, is referred to as the investment multiplier with respect to industrial products. By (10) it is

$$\frac{dx_B}{dI} = \frac{1}{1 - a_{BA}\,a_{AB} - (a_{BA}\,a_{AC} + a_{BC})(1 - e)}$$

where e shows the elasticity of marginal productivity,

$$e = -(g''_B N_B)/g'_B.$$

Using the numerical examples given above the multiplier is 1.37 when $e = 0.8$, 1.14 when $e = 1$, and 0.97 when $e = 1.2$. Further, we know from stability condition (12) that, as long as the elasticity e is not negative (i.e. as long as marginal productivity is decreasing), the value of the multiplier is necessarily positive.

From the above we were able to reconfirm Keynes' thesis (which was, of course, derived ignoring the existence of agriculture) that an increase in investment will increase employment, while making the explicit assumption that there is an agricultural sector. What then is the effect of an increase in investment on the numbers 'normally' engaged in agriculture? This problem is analysed by transforming the equilibrium condition in the following way. First from (7), which is the condition for determining the 'normal' quantity of labour engaged in agriculture, and (8) which is the statement of marginal productivity, we can obtain

$$x_A / N_A = p g'_B (N_B), \quad \text{or} \quad x_A / p = g'_B (N_B) N_A,$$

and if we substitute this into (3') and divide both sides by $g'_B (N_B)$ then we obtain

$$N_A = a_{AB} (x_B / g'_B (N_B)) + a_{AC} N_B. \tag{3''}$$

An increase in investment will cause an increase in the volume of industrial employment, and hence at the same time as it causes an increase in the second term of the right-hand side of (3'') it will also cause an increase in the first term by increasing the x_B of that term (the production function) and decreasing g'_B (the law of diminishing marginal productivity). Thus we know that an increase in investment will cause an increase in the 'normal' quantity of labour engaged in agriculture.

Let us next analyse the effects of an increase in investment on open and disguised unemployment on the basis of the above results. If, after those employed in the industrial sector have been subtracted from the total seeking employment, more workers remain than the land can absorb, open unemployment of this amount will occur. The agricultural sector will absorb workers up to the limit imposed by the capacity of the land to absorb them, and when this number exceeds the 'normal' number engaged in agriculture, the excess number are the disguised unemployed. But if we now assume that a policy of increasing investment is adopted in an economy where there is simultaneously both open and disguised unemployment, then, as we have already seen, the volume of industrial employment and the 'normal' number of those engaged in agriculture will increase. Therefore the difference between the quantity of industrial labour and the quantity of labour which remains after as many workers as can be combined with the available land are subtracted from the total seeking employment, will diminish. At the same time, the difference between that maximum quantity of labour and the 'normal' quantity of labour engaged in agriculture will also decrease. That is, both open and disguised unemployment will diminish. Thus we are able to say that a Keynesian policy of increasing investment will eliminate both open and disguised unemployment.

In the sort of case where land is limited and can only absorb small quantities of labour, or where the effect of investment on the 'normal' quantity of labour engaged in agriculture is sufficiently greater than its effect on the volume of industrial employment, disguised unemployment will cease to exist even at comparatively low levels of investment. An increase in investment above this level will have no effect on the quantity of labour engaged in agriculture; the effect will be confined to increasing the volume of industrial employment and decreasing open unemployment. In the case where the quantity of labour engaged in agriculture has reached its upper limit and is no longer affected by an increase in investment, we may exclude agriculture (that is the household-industry sector) from consideration and think of the economy as if it consisted merely of an industrial sector (or a pure enterprise sector). We may then view the whole of the problem of unemployment simply as the problem of whether the excess of the total seeking employment over the maximum number of workers which can be combined with the available land does or does not exceed that of the volume of industrial employment. In this case there is no problem of disguised unemployment. From the above we can see that it is possible to apply Keynes' theory, which did not consider the agricultural sector and which disregarded disguised unemployment, almost unaltered to economies where the quantity of labour in the agricultural sector has already reached its upper limit. Hereafter I shall call these type I economies.

However, if land is not thus limited and a comparatively large quantity of labour can be combined with it in production, and if the multiplier effect of investment on the volume of industrial employment is sufficiently larger than its effect on the 'normal' quantity of labour engaged in agriculture, then open unemployment will be eliminated first by an increase in investment, while disguised unemployment will remain. Hereafter I shall refer to economies where there is no open but only disguised unemployment as type II economies. In the case of type II economies, disguised unemployment and an increase in investment are related in the following manner.

First, an increase in investment will cause an increase in the level of industrial employment. As a result, the labour hitherto absorbed in the agricultural sector in the form of the disguised unemployed will move to the industrial sector. Next, the increase in investment will cause an increase in the 'normal' quantity of labour engaged in agriculture. That is, of the agricultural labour which may be regarded as in disguised unemployment, part will be employed in industry and another part will join the (enlarged) 'normal' quantity of those engaged in agriculture. Thus disguised unemployment will diminish. In contrast with type I economies where workers are faced with the alternative of being employed or unemployed, in type II economies there is no 'complete' unemployment. All unemployment is partly eliminated by becoming disguised unemployment, and it is not possible to avoid a wage differential arising between the agricultural and the industrial sector. Such an employment—unemployment relationship cannot be analysed using Keynesian theory which disregards agriculture (household industry); we have to rely on a theory which explicitly takes into account the existence of agriculture.[12+]

As we saw above, the problem of open unemployment is more important than that of disguised unemployment in an economy where land is relatively scarce, while the reverse is true in an economy where land is plentiful. At first sight this conclusion would seem completely to contradict the actual experience of the Japanese economy with its limited land, where, at least until the 1960s, there was large-scale disguised unemployment. How then are we to explain Japan's case?

It was assumed throughout the above analysis that the degree of intensity with which land is used is fixed, and that as long as there is idle land the agricultural population can increase, whereas when there is no longer any idle land it ceases to increase. In practice, however, the intensity of land utilisation is not fixed, and when there is no longer any idle land it comes to be used more and more intensively. Let us here consider an economy which is comparatively poorly endowed with land. In such an economy a state of affairs arises which resembles that described above in relation to type I economies, and we would expect open unemployment to be preponderant. However, if family considerations govern the behaviour of the farmers of this economy, they increase the intensity with which land is used, and hence the maximum quantity of labour which can be combined with land will become larger; by means of the increased capacity to absorb labour into agriculture which thus results, the openly unemployed who originate from farms are likely to be absorbed back into agriculture as the disguised unemployed. Thus, in the case where the intensity with which land is used is high even though the physical area of land is limited, it is possible in economic terms for an economy to approximate to type II. In such an economy disguised unemployment is likely to preponderate over open unemployment.

However, increasing the intensity with which land is used also has the following effect. If there is no proportionate increase in the output of agriculture when land is used more intensively and a larger quantity of agricultural labour is combined with this fixed amount of land, then returns per worker will diminish. This will produce a fall in the unit value of agricultural labour and drive agricultural workers into a state of affairs which more closely resembles unemployment. That is, full unemployment is avoided by increasing the degree of intensity of land utilisation, but the disguised unemployment which acts as a cushion against this becomes, instead, more closely akin to full unemployment.

We should regard the mechanism which operated in the Japanese economy as the same as that described above. The reason why the Japanese economy appeared to resemble type II economies despite the fact that it has very limited land available, is that the intensity with which land was used was high, and that this intensity was reinforced by the predominance of familistic ideas among farmers. It must be said that the theory of type II economies described above is more appropriate than the Keynesian theory of type I economies for diagnosing and prescribing for the illness from which the Japanese economy suffered. We should note especially that in Japan the low unit value of workers engaged in agriculture and the resulting wage differential between industry and agriculture were bound up with the high intensity with which land is used.

The most basic assumption in the above analysis is that, while the industrial sector is composed entirely of firms, the agricultural sector is made up of household producing units. Firms look outside themselves for labour, but in household industry there is hardly any reliance on employed labour. Production proceeds with the head of the household himself or family labour as the chief means of production. But strictly speaking, this assumption is clearly unrealistic. In practice there are extremely modern agricultural enterprises, while there are also household or cottage industries within the industrial sector. If so, how practically applicable is our assumption? Is it properly permissible as an idealised abstraction from reality?

If, at this point, we examine the proportion of the total number engaged in agriculture in Japan which is made up of employed workers, we see that it was no more than 5.5% in 1960. In the same year, in almost all countries where the ratio of agricultural to industrial wages was less than 0.5, this same proportion was, at its highest, no more than 30% (in the United States, for example, it was 28%).[13+] Given this fact, and the fact that the proportion of employed workers among the total number engaged in industry is very high (e.g. 86% in Japan, 95% in the United States), we may consider our assumption that agriculture is organised on household-industry lines and industry is organised into firms to be entirely appropriate as an 'ideal' assumption for countries where the ratio of agricultural to industrial wages is less than 0.5, and especially for Japan.[14+]

In contrast, in Great Britain 66% of those engaged in agriculture are employed workers and the agricultural sector is highly capitalistic. Therefore, our basic premise that the industrial sector equals the firm sector and the agricultural sector equals the household industry sector is not appropriate. Rather we ought to regard both sectors as being made up of firms in the sense in which we use the word here. Consequently, when we think of the British economy in idealised, abstract form we should envisage it as not possessing an 'agriculture' in our sense, and we can see that Keynes' model was really developed for such an economy. Needless to say there is no disguised unemployment in an economy such as Great Britain's.

Thus there is a great deal of family labour in the agricultural sector of the Japanese economy, but it also has other sectors where the proportion of non-wage-earning family labour in the total engaged is high. The fact that it was 5.5% in manufacturing industry, 3.7% in building, 16.3% in trading and 4.8% in the service industry in 1960, is especially worthy of note. When we compare these figures with the corresponding ones for Great Britain and the United States, we see that they are very high. (Normally they are 1% in trading, 0.5% in the service industry and less than 0.1% in other sectors.) Thus, in Japan household industry exists outside the agricultural sector, and we ought to regard these industries, too, as being repositories of the disguised unemployed. This fact is often pointed out as an instance of the dual structure of the Japanese economy, and we do not need any special new theory in order to analyse this duality. We replace agriculture in the above analysis with the small-scale enterprise sector, and industry with the large-scale enterprise sector, and we may properly assume that the small-scale enterprise sector is more or less of the household-industry type. We have to make a few careful changes in the above analysis; but essentially we can use the theory without change not just to analyse the disguised unemployment concealed in small-scale enterprises and wage differentials between large and small-scale firms and so on, but also to explain the process whereby these wage differentials were eliminated with rapid economic growth.

Notes

Introduction

1 E.J. Mishan, *Growth: The Price we Pay* (Staples Press, 1969).

2 M. Morishima, Y. Murata, T. Nosse and M. Saito, *The Working of Econometric Models*, pp. 243–55 (Cambridge University Press, 1972).

3+ When dealing with socialist economies, theoretical constructions have often been formed giving careful consideration to the specific features of the economies of the Soviet Union, Poland, Czechoslovakia, Hungary, Yugoslavia, etc. Likewise when one analyses capitalist economies such as The USA and Japan, one has to construct a model which gives careful consideration to their respective distinctive features. Otherwise, theoretically at least, Japan's high growth rate, high employment rate and dualistic economic structure will not be explained.

4 J. A. Schumpeter, *Capitalism, Socialism and Democracy*, p. 169 (Allen & Unwin, 1961).

5 *Ibid.* pp. 198–9.

6 For example, A. Nove, *The Soviet Economy*, revised 3rd edn. pp. 111–23 (Allen & Unwin, 1969).

7 Max Weber, *Economy and Society*, ed. Guenther Roth and Claus Wittich, vol. 1, p. 225 (Bedminster Press, New York, 1968).

8+ Co-operative work is not peculiar to modern man; even chimpanzees co-operate when they have a common objective (see, for example, W. Kohler, *The Mentality of Apes*, 2nd edn. Routledge, 1956). However, it is only in modern society that mankind has come fully to reap the benefits of large-scale production based on the division of labour and co-operative effort.

9+ The above quotations from Marx come from *Capital*, vol. 1, pp. 186–90 and 834–6 (Charles H. Kerr and Co., Chicago, 1919). Exactly the same opinion was also asserted by Weber. For example, compare the following quotation: 'Persons must be present who are not only legally in the position, but are also economically compelled, to sell their labour on the market without restriction. It is in contradiction to the essence of capitalism, and the development of capitalism is impossible, if such a propertyless stratum is absent, a class compelled to sell its labour services to live; and it is likewise impossible if only unfree labour is at hand. Rational capitalistic calculation is possible only on the basis of free labour; only where in consequence of the existence of workers who in the formal sense voluntarily, but actually under the compulsion of the whip of hunger, offer themselves, the cost of products may be unambiguously determined by agreement in advance.' Max Weber: *General Economic History* (translated by Frank H Knight), p. 277 (Allen & Unwin, 1928).

10[+] 'The psycho-physical apparatus of man is completely adjusted to the demands of the outer world, the tools, the machines — in short, it is functionalised, and the individual is shorn of his natural rhythm as determined by his organism; in line with the demands of the work procedure, he is attuned to a new rhythm through the functional specialisation of his muscles and through the creation of an optimal economy of physical effort.' Max Weber (Introduction n7), vol. 3, p. 1156.

11[+] Whether they are used in the workplace or for leisure makes no difference to the fact that, when machines come to be used by human beings, the logic of the machine comes to dominate the human being. The car, the electric guitar, the transistor radio, the electric saw, the electric lawnmower — the head of the well-off family which is equipped with all of these is, by reason of these consumer durables, forfeiting riches. I recommended a reading of Mishan's work, (Introduction n1), to all those who dislike machines.

12 Weber (Introduction n7), vol. 1, pp. 944—5.

13 On the ubiquity of the bureaucratic form of organisation, see Weber (Introduction n7), vol. 1, part 1, chapter 3, especially 5 *Monocratic Bureaucracy*.

14[+] Weber insists that the 'eliminating from official business of love, hatred, and all purely personal, irrational, and emotional elements which escape calculation', and the possibility of calculating the results of work, were necessary conditions for the development of modern bureaucratic systems and modern, large-scale business management. Weber, (Introduction n7), vol.1, p. 975.

15[+] This two-way planning formula is an improved and simplified version of the 'there-back-there' formula of prewar Soviet Russia, whereby Gosplan drew up a draft plan along the lines laid down by the party or the government; each enterprise then devised a feasible 'response' plan along the lines of the draft plan, having considered and examined its own capacity in the light of the draft transmitted from Gosplan. These were then returned to Gosplan and co-ordinated, and a final plan fixed upon which was transmitted to all enterprises.

16 Nove (Introduction n6), cites a very interesting story relating to this point.

17 Eugen Slutsky is one of the best of the theorists who have objectively analysed rational consumption activity based on the principle of the maximum satisfaction of wants, 'Sulla Teoria del bilancia del consumatore', *Giornali degli Economisti*, 51 (July 1915), 1—26. This article was written before the accession to power of the Bolsheviks, but later he was elected a member of the Soviet Academy. This merits attention in view of the fact that Marxian economists have continued to criticise utility theory severely. (For example, see O. Lange, *Introduction to Econometrics*. Pergamon Press Ltd., 1959). As examples of authors who have come recently to insist that utility theory is not necessarily inconsistent with Marxian economics see the following: A.A. Konyus, 'The labour theory of value and econometrics' in *On Political Economy and Econometrics: Essays in Honour of Oskar Lange* (Polish Scientific Publishers, Warsaw, 1965); Leif Johansen, 'Labour theory of value and marginal utilities', *Economies of Planning*, 3 (1963); M Morishima, *Marx's Economics: A Dual Theory of Value and Growth* (Cambridge Univeristy Press, 1973).

18[+] From the Meiji Revolution onwards Japan achieved rapid economic development as a capitalist state. However, it must not be forgotten that the pre-conditions for this development were in preparation for a long time during the Edo era. That is, the Edo period was a feudal one, but because political power was concentrated in the hands of the Bakufu and travel between the capital Edo and the regions was frequent, goods had already begun to circulate on a national scale. Moreover, a money economy had quickly been formed, a section of agriculture commercialised, and merchant capital had already materialised. The level of education was also quite high. For these reasons, when the Meiji government stimulated and promoted trends already present in the Edo period, doing away with the feudal system of status, abolishing limitations on freedom of movement of labour and goods and freedom of occupation, reforming the land-holding system, and establishing a uniform currency system, etc., it fully established the conditions necessary for the development of modern capitalism. As a result Japan converted itself into a modern capitalist state in a short space of time. However, I shall deal with this development in more detail later.

19 H. Poincaré: *The Value of Science*, p. 79 (Dover, 1958).

20 For example, see P.A. Samuelson, *Economics*, 9th edn. pp. 95—7 (McGraw-Hill, 1973).

21[+] 'Expel the barbarians' and 'Revere the Emperor' were not the real aims of the lower order samurai. They were no more than the password which symbolised their real object — the building of a modern state. As proof of this, when it came to actual policy making, they swung between 'expelling the barbarian' and 'opening the ports'. Again, it was because so many people remembered that Japan had had a national unity, centring on the Emperor, before the coming of feudal government, that 'Revere the Emperor' was able to become a strong slogan in the founding of a modern nation state. Because they adopted 'Revere the Emperor' as their slogan, the lower order samurai secured at least the passive sympathy and support of each class, although it cannot be said to have been strong in all cases.

22[+] Although the system of compulsory education was supported by the nation it was many years before it was completed. However, the attendance rate for primary schools, which had reached 28% in 1874, was 50% in 1883, 67% in 1898 and 98% by 1912. These figures show an astonishing rate of diffusion of compulsory education, and they indicate how powerfully the people supported the government in its setting up of a modern nation-state.

23[+] It is not surprising that the universities of Japan, which were established under these historical circumstances, thereafter provided the training grounds for government officers and company personnel. When they are compared with the various European universities whose origins preceded the founding of the modern state, it can even be said that it is natural that Japanese universities, even now, are extremely submissive to the government.

24[+] These are: Mitsui, Iwasaki (Mitsubishi), Sumitomo, Furukawa, etc. On the other hand, Kōnoike, Hirooka (Kajima), etc., who were large merchants in the Tokugawa period, were unable to grow into industrial capitalists because they were unable to purchase government enterprises.

25[+] *Translator's Note:* The Rokumeikan, sometimes translated the Deer-cry Pavilion, was the name of the Western style building which housed an international club. The club was the idea of the then Foreign Minister, Inoue Kaoru. At the club the new aristocracy and high government officials, with their wives and daughters, attended garden parties, balls and bazaars, and generally mixed with Westerners. One of the purposes of the club was undoubtedly to strengthen the Japanese position in the protracted negotiations for the revision of the unequal treaties, by demonstrating to the West the 'civilised' nature of Japanese society. The club came under heavy criticism from certain sectors of opinion, and its life was not a long one; its function changed in 1890.

26⁺ One of the objects which the Meiji government pursued most vigorously in the early part of the period was the abolition of the feudal economic and social system, and the removal of the status system. To say that, seen from some points of view, the way of going about it was imperfect, and, seen with today's eyes less than thorough, is not to say that the Meiji government was a semi-feudalist, absolutist one. It did struggle vigorously against the status system; but on the other hand its attitude towards the emergence of democracy was very conservative. The Meiji revolutionaries did not value equality for itself; it was simply because the status system was inimical to the reproduction of the intelligentsia that they abolished it. They sought to supply the intelligentsia from every class of society, but they were not in the least prepared to relinquish the sovereignty of the intelligentsia.

27⁺ In an island country (a closed society) like Japan, a consensus within society is a much more important virtue than the recognition of the individuality of each person. Consequently, Article One of the seventeen articles which formed Japan's first constitution, promulgated by Shotoku Taishi in A.D. 604, emphasised the importance of harmony (*wa*). However, since it was important not because of its intrinsic value, but simply as a means of maintaining peace within society, the harmony that had to be protected was, as Shotoku Taishi correctly pointed out, harmony with the rulers, harmony with the majority. Consequently, people who disturbed this harmony, or whose opinions differed from those in authority, were exiled abroad or banished to an island. Thus, Japan from ancient time has always placed society first, and even in the postwar period where democratisation and individualisation are believed to have prevailed, its basic character has barely changed. I think that this type of 'harmony' is the essence of the spirit of Japan (Yamato Damashi).

28⁺ In the same big firm, the managers belong to 'modern Japan', while workers belong to 'premodern Japan'. In textile factories and mines one of these two Japans was severely exploited by the other.

29⁺ Even now, after the war, the citizens of 'premodern Japan' are proud of the products of 'modern Japan'. What the Japanese want to be valued for by foreigners is not Hōryū Temple, Himeji Castle or Kabuki; it is the zero fighter, the bullet train, electronic computers and mammoth tankers.

30⁺ Of course, as I have already indicated, the intelligentsia passed through several periods of danger; for example, the time when they came close to government based on clan cliques. Also, needless to say, the child born of a poor family had to overcome greater disadvantages than the child born of rich parents. However, compared with other countries, and compared with other aspects of Japanese life, it would be hard to deny that the distribution of membership of the 'modern state' and the 'premodern state' was fair and competitive.

31 For example, see O. Lange, *On the Economic Theory of Socialism,* ed. B.E. Lippincott (The University of Minnesota Press, 1952).

1. Techniques of production

1 Adam Smith, *The* Wealth *of Nations,* p. 110 (Penguin Books, 1970).

2 The first modern economist to draw attention to the genealogy of production was probably Leontief: W.W. Leontief, 'Introduction to a theory of the internal structure of functional relationships', *Econometrica,* 15 (1947), 361—73.

3 Hereafter in this book, in order to show machine capacity, the volume of labour and raw materials, etc., I shall use K_1 K_2, . . . , L and M. However, I shall also use these symbols to stand for the varieties of machinery, labour and raw materials themselves. The meaning intended by the symbols will be clear from the context.

4 Limitational production functions have been discussed by Georgescu-Roegen, Kaldor and others. N. Georgescu-Roegen, 'Fixed coefficients of production and marginal productivity theory', *Review of Economic Studies,* 3 (1935—6), 40—9. N. Kaldor, 'Limitational factors and the elasticity of substitution', *Review of Economic Studies,* 4 (1936—7), 162—5.

5 On the procedure for deriving the production function from a collection of processes, see: R. Solow, 'The production function and the theory of capital', *Review of Economic Studies,* 23 (1955—6); and P.A. Samuelson, 'Parable and realism in capital theory: the surrogate production function', *Review of Economic Studies,* 4 (1936—7), 162—5.

6 Smith (ch. 1 n1), p. 116.

7 Doubts about the national production function were first raised by Klein and Joan Robinson. L.R. Klein 'Macroeconomics and the theory of rational behaviour', *Econometrica,* 14 (1946). Joan Robinson, 'The production function and the theory of capital', *Review of Economic Studies,* 21 (1953—4).

8+ In order to produce the aggregate production function there has to be aggregation with respect to goods, in the form of lumping together a large number of goods into a small number, and there has to be aggregation with respect to producers, by lumping together a large number of producers into one producer. The fact that, if prices move proportionately, a group of goods can be summed and lumped together as one good (that is, no error arises through aggregation with respect to goods as long as prices change proportionately) was made clear by Hicks. (See *Value and Capital,* 2nd edn, part 1. Oxford University Press, 1946.) In the general case where prices do not always move proportionately, in order for correct results to be yielded by analysis based on an aggregate production function composed of appropriately defined indices, each production process (or each individual production function) has to fulfil certain special conditions. For an indication of how special these conditons are in fact, see for example F.M. Fisher 'The existence of aggregate production functions', *Econometrica,* 37 (1969) 553—77.

9+ As is well known, the conversion by Marxist economists of heterogeneous labour into 'abstract human labour' has been much criticised by non-Marxist economists of the modern school. However, neoclassical economists have defended the lumping together of individual capital goods into aggregate capital. If, on the one hand, they demand the kind of theoretical rigour which would forbid this kind of Marxist conversion, they ought, on the other, to put up with the disallowing of aggregate capital and hence, the aggregate production function, for reasons of this same theoretical rigour.

10 See P. A. Samuelson, 'Indeterminacy of development in a heterogeneous Capital model with constant saving propensity' in *Essays on the Theory of .Optimal Economic Growth*, ed. K. Shell, p. 223 (MIT Press, 1967).

2. The choice of techniques

1 Note that the output coefficients in B_i are given by positive values, the input coefficients by negative values.

2[+] In socialist states like the modern Soviet Union, where there are roughly 200,000 manufacturing enterprises and 20,000,000 or so different commodities, it is impossible for the central planning authorities to construct a consistent production plan for all enterprises. It is inevitable that enterprises should be made independent and that planning be conducted in decentralised fashion. For the circumstances in the Soviet Union and its experience in relation to this point, see A. Nove (Introduction n6), pp. 219—40.

3[+] Nove (Introduction n6), pp. 172—3. The bargaining between heads of enterprises and supervising ministries can be regarded as the most interesting problem in game theory to be found in socialist economies. At all events, the sociology of heads of enterprises is a most interesting topic.

4 On technical innovations in the Soviet Union, see Nove (Introduction n6), pp. 171—81.

5[+] Efficiency defined in this way is more general than the same notion defined when deriving the production function earlier. It can be regarded as an extension of that concept. There, an efficient production plan was the one which maximised the quantity of output, from amongst all those which used quantities of machinery, raw materials and labour that did not exceed the quantities of machines, raw materials and labour given as data. That is, efficiency was recognised as lying in the direction of increasing the quantity of output; it was not recognised as lying in the direction of economising on producer goods. However, efficiency is a concept which is related to productivity, and for that reason it has to be admitted that it is found in economising on producer goods and not just in increasing output.

6 A summary of the reform agreed upon by the September 1965 plenary session of the Central Committee of the Communist Party can be found in Nove, *The Soviet Economy*, 2nd edn. (Allen & Unwin, 1967). For more detail see E.G. Liberman, 'The plan, profits and bonuses'; A.N. Kosygin, 'On improving industrial management'; A. Nove, 'Economic reforms in the USSR and Hungary, a study in contrasts'; all in A. Nove and D.M. Nuti (eds). *Socialist Economics* (Penguin Modern Economic Readings, 1972). Liberman was the first Soviet scholar to advocate the profits method.

7 If we add to enterprise profits, defined in this way, the net income on capital goods (the total of $p_i z_i$ for all capital goods, minus costs for the maintenance of capital-depreciation plus insurance charges), we can derive profits on capital.

8 Here Q is the price vector of the processes $q_1, q_2, \ldots$, etc. which are recorded on a horizontal tape.

9[+] We assume that this sort of Z^0 exists.

10 I shall discuss in detail in chapter 4 how the point of maximum profits changes with changes in prices.

11 For example, A. Nove (Introduction n6), pp. 171—81.

3. The distribution of profits

1 Besides this, how successful the enterprise had been in reducing costs, and how far productivity had been raised were also considered when the size of bonuses was fixed. However, these were never more than secondary yard-sticks.

2 For the essentials of the reform see A.N. Kosygin, 'On improving industrial management', in A. Nove and D. M. Nuti (eds) (ch. 2 n6), pp. 319—34. It is probably not possible to regard the profits method as operating in a perfect form in the Soviet economy. However, I shall not take up that point here.

3[+] Where expenditure for the repair and maintenance of a machine is necessary, such expenditure per unit of service the machine renders is entered in P as the price of the services of owned machines.

4[+] Outputs enter Z as plus items, but for the time being I shall omit output items from the following analysis. I shall explain them later.

5[+] Since in (7) the existing quantities of factors $\bar{z}_j$ are measured with a negative value, and the input coefficients b_{ji} are also measured with a negative value, the fact that (7) is established signifies that there is an excess supply.

6[+] Unless the official price of the product is revised or its shadow price is set correctly, it is impossible to distribute all the profits to factors of produc-tion at their shadow prices. This is because to do so would require a sum greater than profits. That is, if we remember that in $-\bar{Z}$ factors of prod-uction are measured with positive values and the product with a negative value, then $-V^*\bar{Z}$ is the same as a valuation of producer goods at shadow prices minus a valuation of the product at shadow price; and so from $-V^*\bar{Z} = QX^*$, a valuation of producer goods at shadow prices = profits + a valuation of the product at shadow price; and if we consider that the final term is positive, then we can see that a valuation of producer goods at shadow prices (the sum which is necessary, when no shadow price is set for the products, for distributing profits to producer goods at shadow prices) exceeds profits.

7 This equality is evident from the definition of B_1.

8[+] Note that the right-hand side of (13) is $-V^{**}B_2X^*$ and not $-V^{**}\bar{Z}_2$.

9 Processes described by (16) are eliminated by assumption, and processes described by (17) by condition (2), which says that total profits produced are the same as total profits received.

10 See OECD, *Workers' Negotiated Savings Plans for Capital Formation* (Paris, 1970).

11[+] However, this does not mean that the Soviet Union is approaching capital-ism by stealth, or that it has recognised the free economy system. The fact that enterprises have to pay 'use charges' for capital goods does not presage a revival of the system of private ownership of the means of production in the Soviet Union. For further information on the trends in modern Soviet economics and economic thought, see for example, A. Zauberman, *Aspects of Planometrics* (The Athlone Press, 1967).

Moreover, we can measure the distortion resulting from ideology or the exploitation by ideology, by ascertaining to what degree actual 'ideological' distributions of profits differ from a rational distribution. Many authors have rejected Marx's exploitation theory as being unnecessary or mistaken, but there is probably no-one who would deny that 'ideological' distribution must be scrutinised critically through its relationship to rational distribution. On Marx's exploitation theory, see M. Morishima, (Introduction n17).

4. Changes in plan

1+ The prime attached to a vector shows its transposition. Consequently $(\bar{z}_1, \ldots \bar{z}_m)'$ is a column vector.

2 We have already considered in detail in chapter 3, how the rational distribution of profits can be prescribed as a minimisation problem in linear programming.

3 P. A. Samuelson, 'Comparative statics in the logic of economic maximising', *Review of Economic Studies*, 14 (1946–7), 41–3; M. J. Beckmann, 'Comparative statics in linear programming and the Giffen paradox', *Review of Economic Studies*, 23 (1955–6), 232–5; M. J. Bailey, 'A generalised comparative statics in linear programming', *Review of Economic Studies*, 23 (1955–6), 236–40.

4+ In the case where the groups of free goods and non-free goods are unchanged before and after the change in the profits vector, we can regard multiple processes as a single process. Where this is not so, the following situation may arise. Suppose now that there are two processes with different technical coefficients for some free goods and identical ones for non-free goods. Then if, after the change, these free goods do not remain free goods, these processes are multiple before the change but become distinct processes after it.

5 Here too, note that 'dependent' and 'independent' are defined in terms of a goods space which excludes free goods.

6 When $m_1 = \bar{m}_1$ (that is where all profitable processes are independent), this proviso is unnecessary.

7 In this case, note that quasi-free goods are classified as being in the same group as free goods, and quasi-unprofitable processes in the same group as profitable processes.

8 Where $n_2 = \bar{n}_2$ (that is to say, where the input–output relationships of all non-free goods are independent), this proviso is unnecessary.

9 The discussion below in the main follows Bailey (ch. 4 n3).

10 When outputs are restricted, the restriction will not be complied with if x_i falls, and so other x_i must increase.

11 Where quasi-free goods change into free goods (or the opposite occurs), we can deal with (v) and (vi) with basically the same method of analysis as on 98–106.

12+ Where quasi-free goods existed before the change in Q, we can derive the weak Samuelson inequality, $\Sigma \Delta q_i \Delta x_i \geq 0$.

13 We assume that before the change in $-\bar{Z}$, processes were either profitable or unprofitable, so that quasi-unprofitable processes do not exist. Where this assumption is not satisfied, we can do no more than derive the weak Samuelson inequality $-\Sigma \Delta \bar{z}_j \Delta v_j \leq 0$.

14 W. F. Stolper and P. A. Samuelson, 'Production and real wages', *Review of Economic Studies*, 9 (1941), 58–74.

15 For example, Chipman, Uekawa, Inada, Kemp, etc. For the whereabouts of these articles, see for example, K. Inada, 'The production coefficient matrix and the Stolper–Samuelson condition', *Econometrica*, 39 (1971), 219–40.

16+ Where there are two factors and two processes, this definition is reduced to the original definition of factor intensity (9). In this smallest of models there is no distinction between our later 'proper' intensity and 'broad' or 'general' intensity. By this definition we compare process 1 with the remaining process $2, \ldots, n$ in its use of factor 1. Where it uses factor 1 more intensively not merely than the remaining processes taken together, but than any subset of the remaining processes, with which it is compared under the assumption that the change in x_1 only influences that subset of $x_2, \ldots, x_n$, we say that process 1 uses factor 1 in 'perfectly intensive' fashion. This last definition is parallel to Hicks' famous definition of perfect stability (see J. R. Hicks (ch. 1 n8)).

In the case of perfect intensiveness, matrix C is the so-called P-matrix (a matrix whose principal minor determinants are all positive), and in the case of Hicks' perfect stability, C is an N-matrix (a matrix whose principal minor determinants are alternatively negative and positive). Hicks developed the comparative statics of the N-matrix, but the Stolper—Samuelson theorem is, in the 'perfect intensive' case, more related to the P-matrix.

17 By the Cramer formula the solution to (14) can be written in the form of (17), and that of (16) in the form of (17').

18 In fact Chipman, Uekawa, Inada *et al.* arrived at the negative conclusion that the Stolper—Samuelson theorem was only valid under extremely strict conditions because they understood it to mean that when q_1 increased, all other prices would fall.

19 T. N. Rybczynski, 'Factor endowment and relative commodity price', *Economica, n.s.* 22 (1955), 336—41.

20 That is, the elasticity of v_j in respect of q_j is greater than that of v_j in respect of another q_i.

5. The behaviour of the household

1 Max Weber (Introduction n7), pp. 226—41.

2 Translators note : $\bar{O}takamochibyakush\bar{o}$ (large farmers) received an area of land from the feudal landowner on payment of a fixed annual tribute. They were subject to feudal restriction — for example on the sale of the land. *Fudai Genin* (hereditary servants) belonged hereditarily to the $\bar{o}takamochibyakush\bar{o}$. *Shichimono hōkōnin* (indentured servants) were generally the offspring of impoverished farmers who were indentured to the $\bar{o}takamochibyakush\bar{o}$ for a fixed period for a sum of money. The period referred to begins in the early seventeenth century.

3 Consequently, it may be imagined that the households of farmers and owners of private businesses will have a larger propensity to save than will other households. This has been confirmed quantitatively for the economy of the USA. See L. R. Klein and A. S. Goldberger, *An Econometric Model of the United States. 1929—52*, pp. 6 and 51 (North Holland Publishing Company, 1955).

4 We assume in this discussion that only the head of the household has an income, and that the other members of the household have none.

5 M. Friedman, *A Theory of the Consumption Function*, National Bureau of Economic Research, no. 63, General Series, p. 26 (Princeton Univeristy Press, 1957).

6 Duesenberry derived the 'relative income hypothesis' from the 'demonstration effect'. J.S. Duesenberry, *Income, Saving and the Theory of Consumer Behaviour* (Harvard University Press, 1949).

7 For example, see P. A. Samuelson, *Foundations of Economic Analysis* (Harvard University Press, Cambridge, Mass., 1947).

8 See chapter 9 by Allingham and Morishima in M. Morishima *et al.*, *Theory*

of Demand: Real and Monetary (Oxford University Press, 1973).

9+ We can obtain real income by dividing income by a price index. If we use, as a price index, the Laspeyre index which takes x^0 as its basis, the price index is given by $P = px^0/p^0x^0$ and real income is M/P. We can see immediately from (1), (2) and (3) that $M^0/P^0 = M^2/P^1 > M^1/P^1$.

10 See M. Morishima *et al.* (ch. 5 n8).

11+ Try to think of drawing strictly L-shaped indifference curves for perfectly complementary goods.

12+ E. E. Slutsky, 'On the theory of the budget of the consumer', *Readings in Price Theory.* (Irwin, 1952). The Slutsky equation assumes that the change in prices is very small, and is normally written

$$\frac{\partial x_j}{\partial p_i} = X_{ji} - x_i \frac{\partial x_j}{\partial M},$$

where X_{ji} shows the substitution effect of the price of good i on good j. See J. R. Hicks (ch. 1 n8). On the general, non-differential form of the Slutsky equation (12), refer to T. Yokoyama, 'A Logical Foundation of the Theory of Consumer's Demand', *Readings in Mathematical Economics*, ed. P. Newman (The John Hopkins University Press, 1968).

13+ Hicks (ch. 1 n8) defined good j and good i as substitutes or complements according to whether the first term of the differential Slutsky equation is positive or negative. In the differential equation it can be proved that $X_{ji} = X_{ij}$ and therefore the substitutability and the complementarity are symmetrical. That is, if good j is a substitute for (or a complement with) good i, good i is a substitute for (or a complement with) good j. However, in the case of the non-differential equation (12), the symmetry of substitutability and complementarity cannot be necessarily true. Even where good j is a substitute for good i when the price of i changes, good i may be complementary with good j when the price of j changes.

14+ Hicks took the substitution effect as a marginal effect and wrote (20'), (20) and (19) respectively as

$$X_{kk} < 0, \sum_{j=1}^{n} X_{jk}p_j = 0, \sum_{j=1}^{n-1} \sum_{i=1}^{n-1} X_{ji}dp_idp_j < 0.$$

Note that

$$X_{ji} = \lim_{p_i^1 \to p_i^0} \left[\frac{x_j^{(i)} - x_j^{(i-1)}}{p_i^1 - p_i^0} \right]$$

Hicks' definitions of substitutes and complements only hold when it is possible to differentiate the utility function twice. Therefore, they do not apply to the case of L-shaped indifference curves.

15 Some of these problems are dealt with in M. Morishima *et al.* (ch. 5 n8).

16 If a consumer is indifferent between two series, each is given the same index number.

17+ The idea and the theorems of 'separability' are due to Sono and Leontief. For details, see M. Morishima *et al.* (ch. 5 n8), chapter 3. In this model, which ignores consumer durables, it would be permissible to assume that the scale of preferences for present goods is independent of future goods, and vice versa.

18 Compare this equation with the utility function in my article 'Consumer's behaviour and liquidity preference', *Econometrica*, 20 (1952), 223–46

(included in Morishima *et al.* (ch. 5 n8)). It can easily be seen that the latter is an extension of the former.

19 Because it is possible to apply the traditional theory to all individuals and organisations in this way, no limit can be set on the velocity of circulation of money in a given period.

20 R. W. Clower, 'A reconsideration of the microfoundations of monetary theory', *Western Economic Journal*, 1 (1967), 1–8.

21 It can be proved that u is an increaseing function of ϕ and f respectively.

22 D. Patinkin, *Money, Interest and Prices*, 2nd edn. (Harper & Row, 1964).

23 Analysis of the want-pattern effect has lagged far behind that of the substitution and income effects. For a few results of this analysis, see M. Morishima *et al*, (ch. 5 n8), chapter 9.

24 Translator's note. By the Major Industries Control Law of 1931, the government was permitted to 'rationalise' industry, eliminate 'wasteful' competition and sponsor mergers. As a result of the passing of the National General Mobilisation Law of 1938, this process of government intervention in the economy was accelerated. The government, by-passing the Diet, began to enact a series of extraordinary measures designed to control the national economy, such as the enforcement of price controls, rationing, and the allocating of labour and materials. It is the whole gamut of these controls that is referred to as the 'readjustment of enterprises.'

25[+] The boundary between functional and organisational controls is not clear. For example, if the allocation of producer goods to a particular enterprise is extremely small, conditions occur which are more or less the same as if that enterprise had been ordered to dissolve itself. During the war the Japanese government created such conditions in order to bring about a situation where 'enterprise readjustment' would receive general assent.

26[+] Later I shall sometimes refer to M as money income and N as points income for the sake of simplicity.

27 p, q represent row vectors, x a column vector.

28[+] The reason for this is obvious: where one of them is satisfied as a strict inequality, (i) or (i') occurs, and (iii) and (iii') do not come about simultaneously.

29[+] However, we assume that households have utility functions which are more or less the same. If households with very large money incomes prefer combinations of goods which are very economical as far as points are concerned, and households with small money incomes prefer combinations which require a lot of points, even rich households may have an excess of points and even poor households an insufficiency. Where the points rationing system is not a general one, but applies chiefly to inferior goods, such exceptional circumstances will arise.

30[+] (44) can be obtained at once if we substitute $p_i + rq_i$ for p_i in the usual income effect equation

$$\Sigma p_i \frac{\partial x_i}{\partial M} = 1.$$

(45) is (44) rewritten to take account of the first equation of (43).

31[+] If we put z_i for $p_i^1 - p_i^0$ in (19) we obtain (47). But in (19) we take good n as the standard of value so that $p_n^1 - p_n^0 = 0$; hence the sum in respect of i and j is confined within the range 1 to $n-1$. Even where this is not the case — even where we take the sum to n — (19) still holds, unless $p_j^1 - p_j^0$ are proportional to p_j^1. Where they are proportional (19) is 0 by (18). (Note that we assume the change in prices to be infinitesimal.) In the case of (47), since $p_j + rq_j$ corresponds to p_j^1, it is a condition that z is not proportional to $p + rq$.

32[+] Points prices q and the number of points issued N are decided by the state or the central planning authority. M is a datum. Since the prices of producer goods are also data, (52) and (53) are a part of a rather large system, and will give no more than a partial equilibrium. Thus, the numéraire problem, which I shall go into in detail in chapter 6, does not arise here.

33[+] When no points rationing system is introduced,

$$M = \Sigma p_i^0 X_i(p^0, M) = \Sigma p_i^0 S_i(p^0).$$

Assuming the minimum value of $\beta_1, \ldots, \beta_n$ to be β, then $\beta > \alpha$ by assumption. Since $q_i = \beta_i p_i^0$ by definition,

$$N = \alpha M < \beta M < \Sigma \beta_i p_i^0 X_i(p^0, M) = \Sigma q_i X_i(p^0, M);$$

that is, when the black-market value of points is 0, an excess demand arises for them.

6. The flexprice economy

1 J. R. Hicks, *Capital and Growth*, pp. 76—83 (Oxford University Press, 1965).

2 The best analysis of the recent inflation in Japan is contained in Takasuka Yoshihiro, *Gendai Nihon No Bukkā Mondai* (*The Problem of Price Inflation in Contemporary Japan*) (Shin Hyoronsha, 1972). Small and medium scale enterprises belong to the flexprice sector, while large enterprises belong to the fixprice sector. Following Takasuka, we can call the process described above 'productivity-differential inflation'.

3[+] The theory of 'competitive socialsim' has made it clear that we can run some sort of socialist economy according to the rule of competitive pricing. We shall return to this point in chapter 8 below.

4[+] As examples of those who have analysed negotiated prices, see T. Negishi, 'On the formation of prices' *International Economic Review*, 2(1961), 122—6; F. Hahn, 'On the statility of a pure exchange equilibrium', *Internation Economic Review*, 2(1962), 206—13. However, they lay down a rather unnatural rule relating to the change in the distribution of goods during the negotiated price process. As a result, price changes are no longer uncertain.

5 We assume here that the time variable does not vary continuously, but at discrete intervals.

6 $x_1', \ldots, x_n'$ is not necessarily the same as his planned holdings $x_1, \ldots, x_n$. Where he is unable to find a suitable partner in the market with whom to trade, $x_i' \neq x_i$.

7[+] In fact we obtain

$$\bar{x}_n - x_n = \frac{\Delta M}{\Delta p_n} + p_1 \frac{\Delta x_1}{\Delta p_n} + \ldots + p_n \frac{\Delta x_n}{\Delta p_n} + \Delta x_n$$

from (1) and (2). We may disregard Δx_n, and therefore we obtain the equation (3) in the text.

8[+] In my work in Japanese, I asserted for this reason that Samuelson's dynamic stability analysis can be used to explain price movements in a competitive market, but that it cannot be used to explain the process of change under a system of negotiated transactions (M. Morishima, *Dogakuteki Keizei Riron* (Dynamic Economics), pp. 5—11. Koyoto: Kobundo, 1950). The same can be said of the dynamic systems of Arrow and Hurwicz, which are developed forms of Samuelson's theory. Among the works aimed at explaining the principles of the negotiated transactions process, there is the theory of Negishi and Hahn (ch. 6 n4); but as I have already said, it seems to me that their work cannot yet be regarded as complete. For the work of Samuelson and Arrow and Hurwicz, see for example, P. A. Samuelson (ch. 5 n7); K. J. Arrow and L. Hurwicz, 'On the stability of competitive equilibrium, I', *Econometrica*, 26(1958), 522—52.

9[+] I shall discuss the problems of taxation and deficit financing separately in chapter 9.

10 O. Lange, *Price Flexibility and Employment*. (The Principia Press, Bloomington, Indiana, 1944).

11[+] Formula (9) tacitly assumes that it is possible to abandon or dispose of goods costlessly. If this is not the case, suppliers will attempt to pay a price to buyers when there is an excess supply; therefore prices may easily become negative.

12[+] The denominator will only become 0 when $p_1 + aE_1 \leqq 0$, and $p_2 + aE_2 \leqq 0$. If we multiply these inequalities respectively by p_1, p_2 and add them, we obtain

$$p_1^2 + p_2^2 + p_1 E_1 + p_2 E_2 \leqq 0.$$

Thus, if we take Walras' law into consideration, $p_1^2 + p_2^2 \leqq 0$. This is only possible when $p_1 = p_2 = 0$. However, since on the other hand we must have $p_1 + p_2 = 1$, this is contradictory. Therefore the denominator cannot become zero.

13 For example, where the curve (P, Q) rises along the 45° line over a certain interval, all points within this interval are fixed or equilibrium points.

14 It is possible for us to generalise our analysis; that is, both to conduct a global analysis of the process of price changes rather than a local one, and to consider the possibility of free goods. Analysis of the process of competitive trading has been conducted by many scholars under the name of 'stability analysis' (Arrow, Hurwicz, Hahn, Negishi, Uzawa, etc.). Of these treatments, what follows below is closest to Nikaido (H. Nikaido, 'Stability of equilibrium by the Brown-von Neumann differential equation', *Econometrica*, 27 (1959), 654—71. His analysis is global, but strictly speaking his price adjustment functions are somewhat different from ours. However, they may be regarded as belonging to the same family.

15 For example, see J. R. Hicks (ch. 1 n8), pp. 310—11.

16 At the equilibrium point the differential coefficient of the Liapounoff function with respect to time is 0.

17[+] When we are not restricted to $p_i + aE_i > 0$, instead of (14') we obtain

$$p_i(t+h) = \frac{\max[p_i(t) + ahE_i(P(t)), 0]}{\Sigma \max[p_j(t) + ahE_j(P(t)), 0]}. \tag{14''}$$

Thus, if we take into consideration

and

$$\max[p_i(t) + ahE_i(P(t)), 0] = p_i(t) + \max[ahE_i(P(t)), -p_i]$$

$$\frac{dp_i}{dt} = \lim_{h \to 0} \frac{p_i(t+h) - p_i(t)}{h},$$

we obtain

where

$$\frac{dp_i}{dt} = aH_i(t) - p_i(t)a\Sigma H_j(t), \qquad i = 1, \ldots, n,$$

$$H_i(t) = \begin{cases} E_i(P(t)), & \text{when } p_i(t) > 0, \\ \max(E_i(P(t), 0), & \text{when } p_i(t) = 0. \end{cases}$$

Next define the Liapounoff function as

$$V = \Sigma[H_i(t)]^2.$$

We may then use the conventional technique hereafter. For an analysis of global stability which takes into consideration the non-negativity of prices, see, for example, Morishima, *Equilibrium, Stability and Growth*, pp. 38—43 (Oxford University Press, 1964).

7. The Fixprice economy

1 J. M. Keynes, *The General Theory of Employment, Interest and Money* (Macmillan, 1936).
2 E. Glustoff, 'On the existence of a Keynesian equilibrium', *Review of Economic Studies*, July 1968, pp. 327—34. My criticisms appear to apply also to Arrow and Hahn, who followed Glustoff's ideas very closely, though I fear I may have misunderstood their difficult argument. K. J. Arrow and F. Hahn, *General Competitive Analysis*, pp. 347—69 (Oliver and Boyd, 1972).
3⁺ At the detailed level, my presentation and Glustoff's own analysis differ in the following two respects. First, he considers the existence of an under-employment equilibrium in a general equilibrium system which includes money; I disregard the existence of money and consider the same problem within the framework of a pure barter economy. Since it is indeed true that Keynes was opposed to thinking in terms of an abstract economy where money does not exist, we cannot restore Keynesian theory completely as long as we ignore money. But even though we disregard money, we consider no damage to have been done to the essence of Glustoff's arguments, and even in a barter economy with no money, Keynes-type involuntary unemployment may occur. Secondly, Glustoff says that he assumes rigidity of money wages; but what he calls money wages are wages standardised so that the sum of all prices (including wages) and the scalar of the existing quantity of money (his λ) becomes 1. Therefore they are a kind of real wages and certainly not money wages. (Using his symbols, w/λ is money wages, whilst w is not money wages.)
4 J. R. Hicks (ch. 6 n1).
5⁺ Glustoff regards each good i of the second kind as having its own fixed

minimum demand price $\bar{p}_i$, and its price is adjusted only when it exceeds $\bar{p}_i$. That is, his price adjustment function for a good of the second kind is

$$p_i(t + 1) = \max[p_i(t) + aE_i(t), \bar{p}_i], \quad i = m + 1, \dots, n.$$

Of course, strictly speaking, this differs from (2). However, it is not an essential difference.

6+ In recent years the attitude of trade unions has changed drastically from what Keynes assumed. Now they are very conscious of the real value of wages and demand compensatory wage rises.

7+ As you will observe, in actual capitalist economies, it rarely happens that capitalists directly own capital goods and hire them to enterprises. They invest what they have accumulated in enterprises, and with this finance capital enterprises purchase capital goods. Enterprises then distribute the profits which ought to be imputed to capital goods to capitalists in proportion to the size of their investments. When the quantities of the various capital goods held by an enterprise are fixed, and the proportion in which each capitalist invests in that enterprise is fixed, we can regard each capitalist as owning a fixed proportion of the total holdings of capital goods of the enterprise, this proportion corresponding to the proportion which his original investment represents of the total sum invested in the enterprise.

8 Here we are assuming the 'ideological' distribution of profits of a private enterprise society, and not the rational distribution of chapter 3. For details see chapter 3.

9 For simplicity, we ignore the question of raw materials.

10+ The case of the neoclassical system, where there are no effective limitations on the supervisory capacities of entrepreneurs, and hence constant returns to scale, will be discussed in the next chapter.

11+ Even equilibrium prices obtained in this manner are not perfect in the long-run. First, not only must entrepreneurial profits be at a maximum for each firm, but a balance has to be maintained between enterprises. If this were not the case, inferior firms would go to the wall and more profitable new firms would be established. Secondly, existing capital stocks change with the passage of time. That is, if we add to K_i^k the equilibrium gross investment H_i^k, and subtract the part which is consumed, we then obtain the quantity of capital good i owned by capitalist k at the beginning of the next period. Where the quantity of each capital good owned by each capitalist in the next period is equal to the corresponding quantity owned by him in this period (that is, where the savings of each capitalist are 0), prices will be unchanged through a long sequence of periods. But where this is not so, prices can change from period to period. That is, even if we assume that equilibrium prices which will satisfy (12) are established in the current period, these are not necessarily equilibrium prices in the next period. The equilibrium which we have obtianed here is a short-period one, given the quantity of existing capital. The problem of long-period equilibrium where the stocks of capital goods are also variables is outside our scope here.

12+ The idea of the formulation of a dual consumption plan for the case where the worker is unemployed and the case where he is not is famous as Clower's dual decision hypothesis (R. W. Clower, 'The Keynesian counterrevolution: a theoretical approach', in *The Theory of Interest Rates*, ed. Hahn and Brechling. St. Martin's Press, 1965). In fact, Glustoff, too, derives the amended version of Walras' law (14) using this hypothesis. However, independently of Clower, I demonstrated the possibility of involuntary unemployment in a Keynesian system, using exactly the same assumption as Clower, in my book *Shihonshugi Keizai no Hendō Riron* (*Dynamic Theroy of a Capitalist Economy*) (Sōbunsha, 1955). I apologise for the length of the following quotation from the relevant passage (pp. 24–6).

'We shall introduce the concept of "that quantity of labour which workers wish to supply on the presumption that there will be someone to employ them". Let us express this function by $h(w/p)$. But here there are two possibilities. The first is where the quantity of labour which workers put on offer on the above presupposition is less than the demand for labour; the second is where it exceeds the demand for labour. In the former case the condition is satisfied (that is, all labour can find an employer), so that the decisions concerning the supply of labour which are made on this presupposition will be effective, and the actual labour supply function is $h(w/p)$. However, in the latter case the presupposition is not satisfied, so that the decisions on the amount of labour to supply which were made on that supposition become inoperative; workers have to revise their decisions in accordance with conditions where the demand for labour is deficient. In this case, it is impossible that $h(w/p)$ is the actual function for the supply of labour. But where there is deficiency of demand for labour, workers will probably wish to guarantee that the volume of employment is as large as possible, and therefore they are likely to want to supply the whole of the labour demanded. Therefore, in this case, workers will decide to supply labour in just the quantity demanded, and the labour supply function will be N^D. Thus the combined labour supply function for the two cases is

$$N^S \equiv h(w/p), \text{ when } h(w/p) \leqq N^D,$$

$$N^S \equiv N^D, \text{ when } h(w/p) > N^D.$$

In the latter case, $h(w/p) - N^S$ is the quantity of labour which workers will offer as long as there is someone who will employ them, minus the quantity of labour which workers decide upon when there is a shortage of those willing to employ them. Therefore, it is the quantity of labour supplied which is given up by workers because of a deficiency in the demand for labour. We shall call this involuntary unemployment. Where demand is insufficient, that is, where $h(w/p) > N^D$, the supply of labour always equals the demand for it, and therefore the labour market must be in equilibrium. That is, there appears an equilibrium which is accompanied by involuntary unemployment. In contrast to this, where there is an excess demand for labour, i.e. where $h(w/p) < N^D$, the money wage rate will be increased until demand and supply are equal. Thus money wages will be raised when there is an excess demand for labour, but will be unchanged when there is a deficiency in the demand for labour. That is, when no external forces operate, and when the money wage rate is entrusted to the market mechanism alone, this rate is flexible in an upward direction but inflexible downwards.' Consumption is not a function of full-employment income, but of actual income (that is, the total of wages and profits corresponding to actual employment). Therefore, between the wages earned from the labour which workers would supply if there was someone to employ them and the consumption of workers, an inequality such as (13) will be valid.

13+ Suppose that $D = 0$. Then we must have $p_i + aE_i \leqq 0, i = 1, \ldots, m$;

$p_j = 0$, $E_j \leqq 0$, $j = m + 1 \ldots , n$. Thus we obtain $\sum\limits_{i=1}^{n} (p_i^2) \leqq - a \sum\limits_{i=1}^{n} p_i E_i$.

However, since in this case all wages are zero, it is not the extended Walras' law (14) which must be satisfied, but equation (24), as I shall explain. Therefore $\sum\limits_{i=1}^{n} (p_i^2) \leqq 0$. This means that all p_i are 0, which contradicts $\sum\limits_{i=1}^{n} p_i = 1$. Therefore D must be positive.

14 If we were to reflect once more on how we obtained the extended Walras' law, we should at once see that equality (24) instead of inequality (14) must hold in this case.

15[+] Glustoff applies Blauer's fixed point theorem. However, strictly speaking the price adjustment functions (4) and (5) do not satisfy the conditons of this theorem. Where worker a is unemployed and worker b employed, and where worker b is unemployed and worker a employed, the excess demand functions of the society are not the same, even though prices are the same, as long as the preferences of a and b are different. Therefore it does not necessarily follow that a single Q corresponds to a given P, so that we cannot apply Brouwer's theorem. This being so, a more general theorem is necessary; for example in Kakutani's theorem the set of Q corresponding to a single P has to be a convex set. In order to guarantee this an additional assumption is necessary. It must be possible to employ 0·6 parts of worker a and 0·4 parts of worker b, and so on.

16[+] Since we arbitrarily divided workers into two groups in the above example, as many underemployment equilibria can exist as there are ways of making this division. As a criterion for choosing one of these, Glustoff adopts a particular level of money wage (in fact a relative wage measured in terms of the composite good). That is to say, he considers that of the many underemployment equilibria which are obtained, an underemployment equilibrium which will give a particular externally determined level of money wage is established in the market.

17 Since the formula 'product prices = unit costs + profits' is an identity, it does not have the power to determine anything. The profits of this formula include not only payments for the services of capital and the rewards of entrepreneurs for their decision making activities in the running of enterprises, but also windfall profits (or losses). Normal profits are, of course, profits where windfall gains are zero; not only that, in many cases normal profits are regarded only as payments for the services of capital goods. This means that it is assumed that there is a sufficient supply of entrepreneurial ability and that this latter is a free good (therefore entrepreneurial profits are zero). We, too, who regard the volume of output as an independent variable, must recognise the fact that entrepreneurial ability does not become a limitation on output. Therefore, in our system, that part of profits over and above payments for the capital services is zero in normal circumstances. Where profits are thus defined, the above formula is no longer and idenity but an equation.

18[+] For Marx, unemployment occurred because of a shortage of capital goods. For Keynes, unemployment occurs while there is an abundance of capital goods. More correctly speaking, because there are plenty of capital goods gross investment is small, and therefore the volume of output is small by the principle of effective demand, so that unemployment occurs. For a detailed analysis, see for example, M. Morishima, *Theory of Economic Growth*, pp. 59—66 (Oxford University Press, 1969).

8. Decentralised economic planning

1[+] A state of affairs is said to be a Pareto optimum if no one can be made better off than he is in that state without making someone else worse off. Unless capital goods and labour are correctly allocated to enterprises by means of transactions or planning, a Pareto optimum will not materialise. On Pareto optima, see for example the first essay in T.C. Koopmans, *Three Essays on the State of Economic Science* (McGraw-Hill, 1957).

2 For example F.M. Taylor, 'The guidance of production in a socialist state', *American Economic Review*, 19(1929), 1-8; O. Lange, 'On the economic theory of socialism', *Review of Economic Studies*, 4(1936-7), 53-71 (both of these are reproduced in B.E. Lippincot (ed), *On the Economic Theory of Socialism* (University of Minnesota Press, 1938); J.A. Schumpeter (Introduction n4); J. Kornai and T. Liptak, 'Two level planning', *Econometrica*, 33(1963), 141-69; E. Malinvaud, 'Decentralized procedures for planning', in *Activity Analysis in the Theory of Growth and Planning*, ed. E. Malinvaud and M.O.L. Bacharach (Macmillan, 1967); G.M. Heal, 'Planning without prices', *Review of Economic Studies*, 36(1969), 347-62; M. Aoki, *Soshiki to Keikaku no Keizai Riron* (*Economic theory of organisation and planning*) (Iwanami, 1971).

3[+] Bergson's welfare function

$$U = F(u_1, u_2, \ldots, u_v)$$

which gives society's index of preferences u as a function of the preference indices u_i of the v individuals comprising the society is often given as an example of a democratic welfare function. However, a plan formulated using this welfare function will be more or less 'undemocratic'. The reason is that, in any society in which the problem occurs, v is an extremely large number, and therefore to be able to handle the problem we in fact have to classify its citizens into a number of groups, and assume that the people within each group have the same utility function $u_i(x^i)$. Whether the division into groups is done democratically, or bureaucratically by the central planning authority, the forcing of subtly different individual preferences into a few moulds means that freedom in comsumption is constrained. In the same way as we ought not to centralise the planning of production, it is equally, if not more, important that we do not plan consumption in a centralised fashion.

4[+] In what follows capital goods and labour are measured as positive values. Thus $\overline{Z} \geqq 0$. Again for the sake of simplicity, we think of $\overline{Z}$ as being fixed, but this assumption is not necessary to the analysis. We may hold that the supply of capital goods and labour generally depends on prices; and even if we replace $\overline{Z}$ with $S(p)$, the analysis below will need no amendment as long as $p_I D(p) = p_{II} S(p)$ holds in place of Walras' law (6) below.

5 J.A. Schumpeter (Introduction n4), p. 169.

6 We assume below that the state's demand for capital goods is a continuous function of prices. In the D of the left-hand side of (6), $\overline{Z}$ is not shown specifically as an argument of the demand functions of consumer goods, because it is consistently treated as a constant in what follows.

7 Since at a few points the excess demand functions are not single-valued functions of prices p_{II}, a somewhat delicate mathematical operation is required when prices are adjusted at such points. Moreover, equilibrium

prices can be obtained by other methods. For example, see H. Scarf, 'On the computation of equilibrium prices', in W. Fellner *et al.*, *Ten Economic Studies in the Tradition of Irving Fisher* (Wiley, 1967). For the sake of simplicity, we assume that there is only one set of equilibrium prices.

8 I shall explain the meaning of the productiveness of the matrix of input coefficients in more detail later.

9 L. Walras, *Elements of Pure Economics*, translated by W. Jaffé, p. 225 (Irwin, 1954).

10[+] Note that

$$\Delta p_i = p_i - p_i^0, \qquad \Delta X_i = X_i - X_i^0,$$

$$\Delta D_i = D_i(p_1, \ldots, p_n) - D_i(p_1^0, \ldots, p_n^0),$$

$$\Delta S_i = S_i(p_1, \ldots, p_n) - S_i(p_1^0, \ldots, p_n^0).$$

11 See equation (10) of chapter 5.

12 J.R. Hicks (ch. 1 n8), pp. 62-77.

13 This assumption is not indispensable for the discussion which follows.

14 For purposes of convenience in explanation we show the adjustment process in terms of difference equations, but we could obtain the same results if we were to show it in terms of differential equations.

15 For a discussion of the Leontief-Keynes system, see M. Morishima *et al.* (Introduction n2), pp. 76-115.

16 P and w are both vectors.

17 c_i, d_i probably depend upon P.* The reason why we specify the demand function as a linear equation with respect to income is simply for ease of explanation not for any reason of economic theory. However, the discussion which follows also holds true for the more general case where demands are non-linear functions of income, if appropriate amendments are made. For detail, see D. Gale, 'On equilibrium for a multi-sector model of income propagation', *International Economic Review*, 5, (1964), 185-200.

18 Since P* is the stationary solution of (18'), we have $P*(I - A) = w$. Since w is a vector of values added, it is positive.

19 w is a positive vector and A is a non-negative matrix, hence it can be proved immediately from (21) that P* > 0.

20 Note that $\sum_{l+1}^{n-1} \Delta p_i a_{ir.} = \Delta \bar{w}_r$, where w_r is the rth component of w.

21[+] Note that H_i is held fixed. Furthermore, we are assuming in this long-period analysis that the stock of capital goods K_i is fixed. This means that H_i has to have a special fixed value. The capital stock is consumed each year; when H_i is greater than the worn out part of K_i, then the latter increases, and when it is smaller K_i decreases. Therefore in order that K_i be unchanged, H_i must be set at a value which equals the wear and tear of K_i. The economy can be in a stationary state only in this special case. On the general process of economic change where this condition is not met, see M. Morishima (ch. 7 n17), especially the first five chapters.

22[+] However I should like to draw attention to the fact that, in the above analysis, gross investment H_i is fixed so as to be equal to replacement investment (that is the depreciation part of K_i). When we remove this assumption, then needless to say the enterprise as the executor of H_i reappears as the major actor in stability theory (or dynamic theory). Furthermore, it is noted that A must be productive in order for the product prices determined by (18*) to be non-negative.

23   Analysis showing how such a process will certainly lead to equilibrium prices $p_{\mathrm{I}}^{s}(t)$ corresponding to a given $p_{\mathrm{II}}(t)$ is to be found in M. Morishima, 'Some properties of a dynamic Leontief system with a spectrum of techniques', *Econometria*, 27(1959), 626-37, and also in M. Morishima (ch. 6 n17), chapter 4. Analysis of the same process is also contained in Malinvaud's paper in E. Malinvaud and M.O.L. Bacharach (ch.8 n1).

24+ In solving (34), we must note that when prices change, the techniques employed (and consequently technical coefficients $B(t)$), will sometimes change discontinuously. Although the change in the product $p_{\mathrm{II}}(t)B(t)$ is continuous, such singular points should be treated carefully.

25   See M. Morishima (ch.6 n17) chapters 4 and 5.

26   We assume below that the stability conditions derived in the previous section are satisfied.

27+ It was shown in chapter 5 that the sum of the products of the substitution effects and the changes in prices is non-posivite only with respect to the demands for goods. However, if we consider supply as negative demand, an identical inequality will also hold including supplies. In addition it is known that the sum of the products is 0 only where proportional price changes occur. However, $\Delta p_1 = 0$ for the numéraire and $\Delta p_k \neq 0$ for other prices; moreover the price of the numéraire is not 0, and hence all Δp_i cannot be proportional to p_i. Thus, we obtain (49).

28+ This can be proved as follows. Since $\Delta X_h = \Delta D_h + \delta D_h$ we have

$$\Delta X_h = \left[\left(\frac{\Delta D_h}{D_h} \bigg/ \frac{\Delta p_h}{p_h} \right) \cdot \left(\frac{\Delta p_h}{p_h} \bigg/ \frac{\delta D_h}{D_h} \right) + 1 \right] \delta D_h$$

$$= (-\epsilon\eta + 1)\, \delta D_h$$

Here ϵ is the elasticity of demand, and η is price flexibility. If $\epsilon\eta \leq 1$ then $\Delta X_h \geq 0$.

29   For example, see M. Morishima (ch.6 n17), chapter 2.

30   On the problem of converting heterogeneous labour, see M. Morishima, (Introduction n17), pp. 179-95.

9. Finance and full employment

1+   We here make W_j the income from employment of worker j, and a_j his allowance against employment income taxation. Assuming proportional taxation, his income tax T_j is

$$T_j = \begin{cases} t_W(W_j - a_j) & \text{if } W_j > a_j, \\ 0 & \text{if } W_j \leq a_j. \end{cases}$$

If we assume that the income of workers is at least the same as or greater than allowances a_j, total income taxation is

$$T_W = \sum_j T_j = t_W \sum_{s=m+1}^{n} p_s N_s - A.$$

That is, it is a linear function of employment income. (Note that $A = t_W \sum_j a_j$.) Workers' demand depends on prices and disposable incomes, but if we assume that each worker has the same propensity to consume, the demand of all workers together becomes a function of prices of consumer goods and aggregate disposable employment income,

$$\sum_{s=m+1}^{n} p_s N_s - t_W \sum_{s=m+1}^{n} p_s N_s + A.$$

Therefore we obtain the demand function (2). But since A is a constant, it is not shown explicitly in (2). We can obtain the demand function of capitalists (3) in the same way.

2+ Note that we are neglecting raw materials and depreciation of capital goods, so that $a_{1r}, \ldots, a_{lr}$ are zero for all $r = 1, \ldots, l$.

3 Of course prices and wages are stationary also in the case where (8) and (9) holds as equalities on the basis of a given prices—wages system. However, in this chapter, where our subject is the analysis of the employment creating effect of government expenditure, we assume that, before an increase in government expenditure, we have a state of affairs where some part of all factors of production lies idle: that is, a state of affairs where (8) and (9) hold with strict inequality, and there is 'poverty in the midst of plenty'.

4 A.C. Pigou, *A Study in Public Finance*, 3rd edn (Macmillan, 1947). The problem of how to determine public expenditure so as to maximise social welfare has also been considered by Samuelson. P.A. Samuelson, 'The pure theory of public expenditure', *Review of Economics and Statistics*, 46 (1954), 387-9.

5+ In the system of equations (1)—(10) we assume that all the Leontief input coefficients are zero, and ignore the inter-industrial repercussion effects which were the object of his input—output analysis. However, even if we were to take account of input—output relationships between industries, our conclusions would not alter. As long as the propensities to consume of workers and capitalists and their tax rates (marginal tax rates) are the same, we can properly and correctly undertake a macroeconomic analysis of the multiplier effects of investment on consumption and income, no matter what the input coefficients may be.

6+ By (35) the part of the first equation in brackets is associated with ΔX_i being zero, if it is negative. This part of the equation is zero if associated with a ΔX_i which is positive. The second equation is obvious because, by (36), the part inside the brackets is zero for all i.

7+ The reason for this is that if (35') were true as an inequality for all i, (35) would also hold as an inequality for all i. Thus we would have $\Delta X_i = 0$ for all goods, and consequently $\Delta F_i = 0$. Therefore (29) would have to hold as an inequality, and thus $\lambda = 0$. This is contradictory.

8 We assume that the constraints (5'), (6) and (40) satisfy the constraint qualification condition of the Kuhn—Tucker theorem. See, for example, M. · D. Intriligator, *Mathematical Optimization and Economic Theory*, pp. 56-60 (Prentice-Hall, 1971).

9+ For example, when we rewrite (21) as a complete system of equations including capital goods, the government expenditure multiplier originating from good 1 is

$$
\begin{bmatrix} \dfrac{\partial X_1}{\partial F_1} \\[1ex] \vdots \\[1ex] \\[1ex] \dfrac{\partial X_l}{\partial F_1} \end{bmatrix}
=
\begin{bmatrix} m_{11} \cdots m_{1l} \\ \vdots \quad\ \vdots \\ m_{h1} \cdots m_{hl} \\ 0 \ \cdots\ 0 \\ \vdots \quad\ \vdots \\ 0 \ \cdots\ 0 \end{bmatrix}
\begin{bmatrix} \dfrac{\partial X_1}{\partial F_1} \\[1ex] \vdots \\[1ex] \\[1ex] \dfrac{\partial X_l}{\partial F_1} \end{bmatrix}
+
\begin{bmatrix} 1 \\ 0 \\ \vdots \\ 0 \end{bmatrix}.
\tag{21'}
$$

That is,

$$
\frac{\partial X}{\partial F_1} = M \frac{\partial X}{\partial F_1} + \binom{1}{0}.
$$

Since $\Delta Y = p \dfrac{\partial X}{\partial F_1} \Delta F_1$, then

$$
\Delta Y = p[1 - M]^{-1} \binom{1}{0}
$$

when $\Delta F_1 = 1$. By dividing this by $\Delta G = p_1$ we obtain the multiplier originating from good 1.

10 It can be proved in the same way as it was for efficient marginal expenditure that λ is the multiplier effect of government expenditure at the maximum point.

11 For an empirical quantitative analysis of public expenditure multiplier effects, see M. Morishima and T. Nosse, 'Input-output analysis of effectiveness of fiscal policies for the United Kingdom, 1954', in Morishima. *et al.* (Introduction n2).

12[+] As stated in note 1 in this chapter, we are assuming the taxation function

$$
T_W = t_W W - A
$$

with respect to employment income. Here we have $A = t_W \sum_j a_j$ (where a_j shows the total allowances against taxation for the income from employment of worker j). An increase in t_W not only implies an increase in the coefficient relating to W, it also means an increase in A. However, in what follows I shall be concerned with an increase in taxation whereby allowances against taxation a_j are reduced as t_W increases, so that as a result A is kept unchanged. A similar assumption is made in the case of a decrease in t_W. Later I shall consider the case where t_{Π} has increased, and again there I shall assume, as above, that when t_{Π} increases there is an offsetting parallel decrease made in the allowances against taxation from profits income.

13 In this calculation we assume that, in the average which adopts the weights $p_1(\partial X_1 / \partial t_W), \ldots, p_h(\partial X_h / \partial t_W)$ and the average which adopts the weights $p_1(\partial X_1 / \partial t_{\Pi}), \ldots, p_h(\partial X_h / \partial t_{\Pi})$, 75% of price is distributed as wages and the remaining 25% as profits.

14 R.A. Musgrave and M.H. Miller, 'Built-in flexibility', *American Economic Review*, 1940, reprinted in *Readings in Fiscal Policy*, ed. A. Smithies and J.K. Butters, pp. 379-86 (Irwin, 1955).

15[+] For an econometric confirmation of the relationship whereby the public expenditure multiplier is large in a slump and small in periods of prosperity, see M. Morishima and M. Saito, 'A dynamic Analysis of the American Economy, 1902-1952', in Morishima *et al.* (Introduction n2).

16 T. Haavelmo, 'Multiplier effects of a balanced budget,' *Econometrica*, October 1945; reprinted in *Readings in Fiscal Policy* (Ch.9 n14) pp. 335-43.

17 In (18) the differentials with respect to G are all expressed as total differentials. This was because, at that stage of the argument, both t_W and t_Π were thought of as perfect constants. Now that we are treating them as variables, the differential quotients which we obtained putting them as fixed values should be shown using partial differential signs.

18 From the fact that $0 < c_W < 1$, $0 < t_W < 1$ and $0 < c_\Pi < 1$, $0 < t_\Pi < 1$.

19 See chapter 9, note 1.

20 Note that $\omega = \omega'$ implies $\pi = \pi'$.

21[+] When only a reduction in taxation is undertaken, a decrease by the dt_W (which is negative) determined by

$$\overline{dR} = (\partial R/\partial t_W)\, dt_W$$

is the only possibility which will keep the increase in the deficit to $\overline{dR}$. When this is done the increase in the gross national product is

$$dY = \frac{-c_W W}{1 - m'}\, \frac{\overline{dR}}{\partial R/\partial t_W}$$

On the other hand it is

$$\overline{dY} = \frac{1}{1 - \overline{m}}\, \frac{\overline{dR}}{\partial R/\partial G}$$

in the case where the same increased deficit is the result of an increase in public expenditure. If the increase in public expenditure is distributed among goods so as to produce $\omega = \omega'$ and $\pi = \pi'$, then $\overline{m} = m'$. If we also take (53) and (55) into account here, we obtain $\overline{dY} > dY$.

22 Haavelmo (Ch. 9 n16).

23[+] When prices and incomes change proportionately, we say that the volume of demand is a homogeneous function of degree zero of prices and income if that demand remains unchanged. This characteristic of the demand function was a conclusion of Slutsky's theory, as we saw in chapter 5.

10. Unemployment and the dual structure of the economy

1 The most important conditions for being chosen as a worker or employee in the modern sector were intellectual capacity and the ability to work in harmony with colleagues and superiors. Of course, the status and pedigree of the family and nepotism were powerful factors; but incomparably more important was graduation from what was thought to be a 'good' school. This was not only by reason of the fact that the individual's intellectual attainment was judged according to the fame of the school from which he came, but because, in a country subjected to the dictatorship of the intelligentsia, inordinate love for the 'old school' and for fellow pupils of that school predominated. Investment in their sons' education was, for parents,

the most profitable form of investment, and the fact that the zeal for education among the people in general was out of all proportion to their incomes was a way of striking back at the ruling class.

Thus despite the fact that workers and employees of the 'modern' sector were selected according to the criterion 'capacity', it is a fact that many people whose capacities were in a real sense equal to these were confined to the 'pre-modern' sector, and it is clear that differences in wages observed cannot be entirely explained by differences in the capacities of workers.

2 M. Morishima *et al.* (Introduction n2), p.250.

3[+] When we compare wage rates by industry calculated from the industrial input—output tables for Japan, and those for the United Kingdom in 1960 taken from the *Annual Abstract of Statistics* (Central Statistical Office, 1964), we find that a straightforward average of the wage rates in the 5 lowest-ranking industries formed the following proportions of a straightforward average of wage rates in the 5 highest-ranking industries: in Japan 36% in 1951, 43% in 1955, 45% in 1960 and 51% in 1965; in the United Kingdom, on the other hand, the figure was 72%. Even though inter-industry wage differences are narrowing, they are still large. See also M. Morishima *et al.* (Introduction n2), pp. 253—5.

4[+] We say that *A* and *B* have the same capacities where each would probably receive the income that the other is at present receiving were they simply to change places. The 6,700,000 people in disguised unemployment in Japan referred to earlier were not estimated strictly according to this definition.

5 Joan Robinson, *Essays in the Theory of Employment*, p. 84 (Macmillan, 1937).

6[+] What is meant here by the net product of each industry is what remains of an industry's output after subtracting what is consumed within the industry. Consequently, by the net output of agriculture, for example, we mean the net output after subtracting the consumption of agricultural products by farmers.

7 Among these assumptions there is the further tacit assumption that capitalists do not consume (the Cambridge savings function).

8 We assume in what follows that all applicants for employment are of equal capacity and ability.

9[+] We assume that there is sufficient land available to absorb the 'normal' quantity of agricultural labour.

10 Keynes' theory assumes a single sector model and therefore it cannot in principle analyse disguised unemployment.

11 We refer to this condition as the stability condition for equilibrium.

12[+] In type I economies the expansion of industry will not be accompanied by a decrease in the size of agriculture, but in type II economies the expansion of industry will inevitably be accompanied by a reduction in the size of agriculture.

13[+] In contrast to this, in countries where the ratio of agricultural to industrial wages exceeded 0.6 the proportion was at least 40%. See Morishima *et al.* (Introduction n2), p. 250.

14[+] However, in countries such as Peru and the Philippines, where the manufacturing sector is extremely backward, there is very little difference between industry and agriculture in the proportion of the engaged population made up of employed workers. Therefore our model is not appropriate for countries such as these.

Index